D1552877

THE FETISH
REVISITED

J. LORAND MATORY

THE FETISH
REVISITED

Marx, Freud, and the Gods
Black People Make

Duke University Press | Durham and London | 2018

© 2018 Duke University Press
All rights reserved

Printed and bound by CPI Group (UK) Ltd, Croydon, CR0 4YY
on acid-free paper ∞
Designed by Julienne Alexander
Typeset in Whitman by Westchester Publishing Services

Library of Congress Cataloging-in-Publication Data
Names: Matory, James Lorand, author.
Title: The fetish revisited : Marx, Freud, and the gods Black
people make / J. Lorand Matory.
Description: Durham : Duke University Press, 2018. |
Includes bibliographical references and index.
Identifiers: LCCN 2018010546 (print)
LCCN 2018017703 (ebook)
ISBN 9781478002437 (ebook)
ISBN 9781478000754 (hardcover : alk. paper)
ISBN 9781478001058 (pbk. : alk. paper)
Subjects: LCSH: Fetishism. | Africa—Religion. |
Marx, Karl, 1818–1883. | Freud, Sigmund, 1856–1939.
Classification: LCC GN472 (ebook) | LCC GN472 .M38 2018 (print) |
DDC 306.77/7—dc23
LC record available at https://lccn.loc.gov/2018010546

Cover art: Kota reliquary statue (SABA Collection E012).
More information on this image and others from the Sacred
Arts of the Black Atlantic Collection at Duke University is
available at https://sacredart.caaar.duke.edu/.

DEDICATED TO

OLUBUNMI FATOYE-MATORY

ỌMỌ ÒṢUN

ỌMỌ ALÁYÒ

ỌMỌ ALÁÙRÍN

AÙRIN ÀYÀN ELÙ

AÙRIN ÀYÁNKÓRO

MÀMÁ AYỌ̀

ÌYÁ ADÚMÁRADỌ̀N

OLÓLÙFẸ́ MI

ÒDÒDÓ MI

IYÙN MI

CONTENTS

A NOTE ON ORTHOGRAPHY

Throughout this text, I write the names of Nigerian Yorùbá gods in Yorùbá orthography, of Santería/Regla de Ocha gods in Spanish orthography, of Candomblé gods in Portuguese orthography, and of Haitian gods in Kweyòl orthography. While it is the premise of most worshippers that the Nigerian Yorùbá god of thunder and lightning, Ṣàngó, the Cuban god Changó, and the Brazilian god Xangô are the same being in different places, these cognate names are pronounced somewhat differently, and each national population tends to attribute different characteristics, emblematic numbers and colors, and social relationships to the worshipped entity. For example, Brazilian worshippers tend to regard Xangô as a pleasure-loving "mulatto" (*mulato*). And, as one archetype of masculinity, he is contrasted with the dark-skinned (*negro*), humorless, and hard-working Oggún. No such understanding of racial diversity and personal character shapes Nigerian and Beninese Yorùbá worshippers' understanding of Ṣàngó and Ògún.

Of course, a long-running dialogue (Matory 2005) among priests and scholars of diverse nationalities has created new variations within and overlaps among these national orthographies. For example, in the literature on Santería/Ocha, the name of the goddess of prosperity is equally likely to appear as "Ayé" (hybrid Spanish-Yorùbá orthography) and "Allé" (Spanish orthography). And, in recent times, the name of the Cuban spirit of the drums (Añá) has been Nigerianized as "Àyàn" (in unwitting contrast to the more modern Nigerian Yorùbá form, "Àyòn"). In recognition of the fact that the mythologies and ritual standards of these four related religions have diverged considerably and have yet to reconverge fully, I tend to favor the more locale-specific orthography. Two exceptions are "Abakuá" for the Cuban men's mutual aid society and "elekes" for the sacred bead necklaces of Cuban Santería/Ocha, as I do not recall ever having seen these words spelled without the k.

However, in quotes from written texts, I defer to the orthographic choice of the quoted author. When referring to the conceptual unit defined by the unity of a West African god, a Brazilian god, a Cuban god, and a Haitian god as cognates of the same antecedent being, I employ the English-language orthography. For example, I use the term "orishas" for the conceptual unit that unites the Cuban *orichas*, the Brazilian *orixás*, the West African Yorùbá *òrìṣà*, and the African American "orishas."

As in my last book, *Stigma and Culture: Last-Place Anxiety in Black America* (2015b), I use the lowercase term "black" to describe the phenotype of people whom third parties or I regard as visually similar to most sub-Saharan Africans. By contrast, I use the capitalized term "Black" as an ethnic self-identity, which may include some very light-skinned people who believe that their primary social identity is defined by the African part of their ancestry or the Africanness of their primary religious commitments. Hence, the Black people referred to in my title and the Black Atlantic generally include millions of nonblack people.

Finally, the alphanumeric code in parentheses beside the figure and plate numbers is the catalog number of the illustrated item on the Sacred Arts of the Black Atlantic website at Duke University (henceforth SABA), where virtually all of the images can be seen in color. Occasionally, I refer to an item for comparative purposes without including the photo in the text. In either case, you can use that code to search for that item on the website, where you typically can see several photos of and further details about each of these spirited things.

In May 2015, a group of scholars at the Ohio State University interested in Marx, Freud, and race invited me to speak about an earlier draft of this book. Like me, most of them were from humanities or social science disciplines where the citation of Marx and Freud signals healthy skepticism about social inequality and conservative values. So I expected some ambivalence—and indeed felt it myself—over my argument that these heroes of social theory had made some very unprogressive rhetorical uses of Black gods and Black people. The discourse of the "fetish" lassoes us into the role of a progressive Europe's regressive Other, a role into which gentiles had lassoed Jews, as well. And it is perhaps for that reason that Marx and Freud themselves appear ambivalent. I visit the long-running Western conversation about the "fetish" from as far away from the university as I initially could have imagined—not from as close as the very long tradition of Jewish and Black criticism of the West as a whole, not from as nearby as the long but somewhat more special- ized tradition of critical Black Marxism, and not even from the edge of the academic galaxy, where the occasional Black scholar takes the time to criti- cize psychoanalysis (e.g., Tate 1998)—but perhaps from as close to the very source of the term as I could get. I revisit the "fetishes" of Marx and Freud because for nearly four decades, more than two-thirds of my earthly life, African gods have danced in my head, not only shaping my every thought but also both internationalizing and transmogrifying my network of family and friends. Indeed, from their pots, packets, packed statuettes, and staffs, they have watched me writing large parts of this book and have regularly caused me to cast my eye one way rather than another. This book endeavors to articulate the overlooked lessons of these gods—the original, maligned referents of the term "fetish"—for European social theory.

But a number of unexpected and very material lessons still awaited me just off campus. There is hardly a day that I do not think about what Queen Ale- theia taught me in the hours before my OSU seminar. Here in the midwestern heartland, I was confronted anew by the central role of highly charged mate- rial things in religion, economics, governance, and intimate relationships— not the least of these being the erotic relationships of some average white Americans. This epiphany may strike some readers as politically incorrect, as many epiphanies are. It seems to resurrect the long history whereby Europeans and Euro-Americans have at times reduced Black people to our sexuality and regarded their engagements with us as a proverbial "walk on the wild side." However, what I have discovered so far in this world is not vulgar racism but a coincidence of deep spirituality and an almost predictable denial of the central Afro-Atlantic references of these identity-defining relationships, or, rather, the seemingly unconscious embedding of those references in emotionally super-charged black things.

A few hours before the talk, my wife, Bunmi, and I took a walk down the main commercial strip neighboring the campus—past a series of pizza and burger joints, bars, a Doc Martens shoe store, a Starbucks coffee shop, a Barnes and Noble bookstore, an Urban Outfitters clothing store, and other commercial establishments typical of US American college towns. Somewhere between what one white male undergraduate called the "sketchy" (read "poor and Black") part of North High Street and the new Short North Arts District, we came to a crossroads where the academic and the religious "problem of the fetish" intersected extravagantly—as if at the volcanic tip of three fiery subterranean streams—with the hidden sexual and racial desires of middle America. The Chamber, according to its business card, is "Ohio's Largest Fetish Store."

Behind its blackened windows were several rooms of glass cases, shelves, and racks of black leather clothing, masks, whips, leashes, collars, and studded bracelets; metal vaginal or anal hooks for use in leading the hooked person around or to tie them up and suspend them from the ceiling; plastic wands intended to cause painful and highly visible welts; electrical appliances for pleasure and pain; lubricants; suction devices intended to heighten nipple sensitivity, even to the point of pain; schoolgirl dresses; and padlocked male chastity devices (this is the item that most caught Bunmi's attention). These, I would discover, are the props of the "Scene"—that is, a range of settings where largely white-collar white Americans gather for serious and often explicitly spiritual play. Middle-class white American bondage, discipline, and sadomasochism (BDSM) and Master/slave (M/s) erotic relationships overlap in their logic, practice, and personnel with similar phenomena in the Netherlands, Germany, and the UK. In their simultaneous function to induce pleasure and pain, they well illustrate Freud's lessons about the ambivalent nature of the fetish and darkly illuminate the role of material things in the continual renegotiation of human social relationships.

The white shopkeeper—Queen Aletheia—was friendly, but she insisted that we leave our bags at the door, underlining the high price and the forbidden desirability of her wares. When I asked Queen Aletheia what a "fetish" is, the centrality of the *material things* she sold was too obvious for her to mention. She simply defined a fetish as "an obsession" and "anything that makes you happy." However, in her spontaneous narration and description of her wares, she emphasized the pairing of master and slave and the infliction of pain as sources of unparalleled ecstasy—particularly for the slave. Partly because of this vocabulary, it is difficult for me to understand the semiotics of this thing-mediated play outside the context of Europe and sub-Saharan Africa's mutual transformation over the past half millennium.

Indeed, a derogatory word for African hair is an alternative term for fetish play—"kink." Queen Aletheia distinguished kink from the world of "leather," which is specifically gay, but skin-tight black leather and latex are no less central to kink. The attire of both worlds is almost entirely black, and the ordinary forms of sexuality with which kink and leather contrast is called "vanilla," a common reference to the blandness of white middle-class life. Combined with the centrality of master-slave role play, this color coding and the common use of whips to inflict pain invite interpretation as a subliminal reenactment of circum-Atlantic racial history. The similarity of this phenomenon to blackface minstrelsy struck me immediately but, I later discovered, is overlooked in most, if not all, existing studies of BDSM (in discussing the racial dimensions of BDSM at all, Noyes [1997] is a rare exception). As in the blackface minstrelsy of the late nineteenth and early twentieth centuries, so it is in present-day BDSM that white people blacken themselves in order to express their deepest emotions about their intimate relationships. As in white American youth's consumption of Black music, there is in these other dramas a measure of ridicule and a good measure of identification with the Black and subordinated person. The irony is that the Enlightenment and subsequent generations of bourgeois democracy and socialism have employed their own images of the Black person and the slave as the defining opposites, or antitypes, of what the white citizen should be. Whereas the Enlightenment demonstrated the white bourgeoisie's worthiness of freedom by contrasting that class with slaves and Africans in general, Marx vocalized the same hope for the white working class by contrasting them with the "negro slave." Perversely, by this standard, BDSM sees in the slave a nocturnal antidote to bourgeois white people's exhausting diurnal pretense of self-sufficiency, all-competency, and good conscience.

Queen Aletheia observed that people who, in daily life, are normally in charge—such as judges, lawyers, and doctors—usually prefer to be slaves, also known as "subs" or "bottoms," during their fetish play. Conversely, Queen Aletheia thinks of herself as fully able to lead and take charge in daily life, but she has not had the opportunity to show her ability there. In her professional life and her quotidian social interactions, she is too eager to please. Consequently, in her fetish play she is always a master. She even showed us a picture of one of her slaves, a white Dutchman whom she met online but has never met in person. In his photo, he wore a collar and carried a sign saying, "It's nice to be a slave." "His thing is blackmail," explained Queen Aletheia, using a term I have always construed as an instance of linguistic racism and, more to the point, semantically connected to the web of color-coded honor and dishonor among the feudal societies of Europe, the plantations of Europe's diaspora, and the equally slaveholding societies of the Middle East.

Yet, in many of the twenty-first-century "dungeons" where BDSM is performed, there seems to be something unexciting, odd, or even abhorrent about conspicuous Black subordination to whites. For example, in a BDSM slave auction observed by Margot Weiss, most of the people sold were apparently white, and the highest bid went for "one well-known heterosexual white top from the South Bay [who] was being sold as a bottom for 'one night only'!" (2011: 3). "About an hour later," Weiss adds,

> a young African American woman with a round face and closely cropped hair was led up to the stage by a tall, severe-looking white man who held the leash attached to her collar. She was the only person to appear on the stage with someone else, so the man explained that he needed to tell us, the audience, a few things about his slave. As she stood there, back straight, staring straight ahead, her master, addressing us in a tight, steely voice, said that she was fit. As he spoke, he yanked up her dress to display her shaved genitals, and he then turned her around. Still holding her dress above her waist, he smacked her ass so hard she pitched forward; the leash attached to the collar around her neck stopped her fall. Turning her back around, he said she is very submissive and guaranteed to make us happy. . . . The audience was quiet throughout this display. When the bidding started, it was reserved; she did not sell for a lot of money. (Weiss 2011: 3–4)

In sum, the audience was the most excited about the submission of a "well-known heterosexual white" man and the least excited—and perhaps the most repulsed—by the submission of a black female. The novelty of bottoming by this *particular* straight white man may account for some or all of the high bid. But the patent disinterest in a Black woman's enslavement is consistent with Queen Aletheia's and others' reports to me in Ohio, West Virginia, and Durham, North Carolina (see also Brame, Brame, and Jacobs 1993). While much of the concern about BDSM among white feminists during the 1970s concerned female submissives', or slaves', ostensible betrayal of feminism, my preliminary, twenty-first-century research suggests that for many white American participants in BDSM, the greatest thrill derives not from the recapitulation but from the dramatic *inversion* of and relief from normative race, gender, and class hierarchies.

Noyes (1997: 4–5, 109–10) cites late nineteenth- and early twentieth-century German studies of sadomasochism regarding the range of the hierarchical social arrangements rehearsed and parodied in sadomasochistic role play and cites Fanon's ([1952] 2008) explanation of the frequency with which white men adopted the subordinate role in their sadomasochistic fantasies about and relationships with Black men during the era of European overseas imperialism. Fanon observed that, in the context of European overseas imperialism, race thinking denies half of the humanity of white people, projecting it onto Black people, and denies half of the humanity of Black people, projecting it onto white people. This process creates in each racialized party a longing to recover the repressed half of its humanity. Noyes's further, and more emphatic hypothesis, is that white male masochism accelerated at the height of imperialism as an expression of liberal guilt and in a reaction to the impending fear that the oppressed would turn the tables on their oppressors. Indeed, during the same epoch, Freud was anticipating a "race war."

In this world organized around the defiance of conventional taboos, sadistic scenes that too closely recapitulate the actual racial structure of sexual oppression and degradation at the foundation of the Atlantic political economy are the greatest taboo.[1] US American practitioners of kinky play and of the related practice of 24/7 Master/slave or Owner/property relationships often model their relationships explicitly on historical scenarios—including Greco-Roman and Hebrew slavery, medieval fealty, Victorian and Edwardian servitude (after the fashion of the British television drama *Upstairs, Downstairs*), Guru/chela, and military hierarchies—but studiously avoid and expressly deny the likeness of their relationships to the most immediate eponym of master-slave relationships in the United States (for a rich range of insider accounts of erotic M/s relationships, see Kaldera 2014). There may be multiple reasons for this denial. Perhaps one is that the greatest thrills in these sexual traditions come from transgression, and the confession that one is recapitulating a relatively recent and nearby social convention is a turn-off. However, particularly in the wake of the Civil Rights movement, white Master/Black slave relationships are indeed highly transgressive. It may also be the case that consistent revulsion, aversion, denial, inversion, and guilt expressed in regard to white male Master/Black female slave relationships flow from the repression of a socially unacceptable but widespread and powerful desire that, if indulged, might unleash latent or closeted racism and detonate all of the protections of human equality before the law that we have built brick-by-brick since Guinea-Coast Africans and western Europeans started talking in the sixteenth century. Some commentators on this practice explain their discomfort in precisely this way. I will pursue these themes further in my next book.

This book, however, concerns the lopsidedly ambivalent responses of middling populations—not-quite-white Europeans and Black traders in intercultural merchandise—to the Afro-European encounter of the past five-hundred-odd years. The nighttime mimesis of mastery by daytime subordinates may also offer some valuable hints about the cases at hand. The defining quality of a successful BDSM master is not his or her unfettered domination of the slave but his or her subtle and capacious knowledge of the diurnal master and nocturnal slave's psychology, which enables the nocturnal master to push the nocturnal slave to the edge of his or her tolerance for danger, pain, and humiliation and thus to the peak of his or her pleasure.

That the term "fetish" is used to describe these pleasurable but stigmatized activities is no accident. Nor is the fact that race appears to be such a cardinal, albeit subliminal, metaphor in the social roles and paraphernalia that Marx, Freud, and BDSM participants mobilize as they resist the rival role expectations of other parties. Today's concept of the fetish originated on the West African coast, where African and European traders disagreed about the value and agency of people and things. Heirs to this legacy of disagreement, Hegel, Marx, and Freud invoked materially embodied African gods—so-called "fetishes"—as the universal counterexample of proper reasoning, commerce, governance, and sexuality. Other Westerners, such as twenty-first-century practitioners of BDSM—and the selfsame Freud at certain moments—have embraced this term in reimagining and refashioning their intimate relationships. In common, all of these Western actors were engaged in the ritual and symbolic management of the slave within themselves—that is, both the simultaneous threat and promise of dependency on and subordination to people like them. BDSM masters illustrate the anxieties of the social shapeshifter, the parvenu, and the cultural and racial intermediary, as well as the exceptional insights and cruelty that their ambiguity and longing for personal dignity can sometimes inspire.

The present volume argues that the priests of Yorùbá and Kongo "traditional" religions, Cuban Santería/Regla de Ocha (henceforth Santería/Ocha), Brazilian Candomblé, and Haitian Vodou are not the bearers of some primordial, history-less tradition but heirs to the same sixteenth- and seventeenth-century legacy of semantic and moral conflict on the "Guinea Coast" that inspired the Enlightenment and post-Enlightenment discourse of the fetish in Europe. The sequel to this volume—tentatively titled *Zombies and Black Leather*—will focus on the intercultural dialogue between Haiti and the US about hierarchy, animated things, and disanimated people. These two volumes and the interactive audiovisual materials on the Sacred Arts of the Black Atlantic website[2] reveal the history shared by European social theory, white American fetishism, and the Afro-Atlantic religions, as well as the diverse social positionalities that generated these diverse responses.

BDSM dungeons are as far removed from the spirit possession ceremonies of the Guinea Coast and its diaspora as they are from Marx's nineteenth-century efforts to influence the European labor movement and from Freud's fin-de-siècle psychiatric clinic. Yet I argue that each of these phenomena embodies a thing-mediated, problem-solving struggle over who we humans are in our essence and how we are connected to other human beings. These struggles are not only social but also deeply emotional. At issue are the worth of dependency and hierarchy among people and the related question of the relationship between people and things. The foundation of this project is the insight that the so-called fetishes of the Afro-Atlantic religions have counter-parts in historical materialism, psychoanalysis, and white American BDSM, that each of these systems invests assertions about proper social order in certain physical props, and that these intellectual and material assertions about social order cannot be understood outside the context of their com-mon roots in a half millennium of Atlantic slavery and colonialism.

Contrary to the pretense of colonial-era social evolutionisms like Marx's and Freud's, Afro-Atlantic priests are their contemporaries, as well as impor-tant thinkers, actors, and leaders in the circum-Atlantic world. Like the most influential Afro-Atlantic priests, Marx and Freud were intermediaries between ethnoracial groups and between ranks in a hierarchical circum-Atlantic field. They are coeval and responsive to each other in real historical time, but the practice, the logic, and, concomitantly, the material props of their leadership differ in ways related to their different roles in a circum-Atlantic field of power. Each of the systems they founded endeavors to re-solve problems arising from the fact that other thinkers, actors, and leaders have imposed expectations about the distribution of value and agency that disadvantage people like Marx, Freud, and the Afro-Atlantic priests (see also Matory 2005, chapter 1).

Thus, the present volume argues against the assumption embedded in conventional notions of "fetishism" that, in contrast to African gods, Euro-pean social theory is a disembodied and socially neutral articulation of truths about all times and all places. Rather, it is as historical and as socially posi-tioned and materially embedded as any of the social phenomena to which it is applied. For example, the most influential insights of Marx and Freud were shaped by these men's ambiguous class, gender, and race amid Europe's integration into a global politics increasingly defined by the disadvantages of being black or insufficiently different from black people. So, for example,

Marx's *Capital* represented enslaved Africans not as the most abused of workers or, as in the case of the Haitian Revolution, the vanguard of revolutionary resistance to exploitation but, instead, as mute exemplars of how European wage workers like Marx should *not* be treated. Marx made his point through a reassessment of not only the value of commodities and factories but also, concomitantly, the relative agency of the white wage worker and the "negro slave." That reassessment combined a most radical appeal for the agency and worth of white workers with the most reactionary rhetoric of southern US slaveholders about the incompetency of Black workers. This elevation of the European wage worker at the expense of the "negro slave" follows the logic of what I described in my last book as "ethnological Schadenfreude" (Matory 2015b).

If Marx was motivated by the need to distinguish himself and his fellow European wage workers from Black people, the greatest advantage for sixteenth- and seventeenth-century African merchant-monarchs and priests, whose innovations shaped all of the Yorùbá-Atlantic religions today, lay in establishing their own efficacy as the conduits of foreign resources and mediators of local contact with foreign people. Their technology of integrating foreign personages into their own relational selves was usefully adapted to the needs of manumitted black people and their descendants, who needed to mobilize and manipulate clientelistic relationships in order to thrive under the adversarial and hierarchical conditions of the American republics (see, e.g., Matory 2005). That technology has also been useful to African and diasporic actors anxious to affirm family solidarity and mutual obligation despite international migration and conversion to other religions (Richman 2005). I argue that the commemoration, fortification, and regulation of challenged interclass or long-distance relationships remains a defining feature of ritual, priestly testimony, and the contents of Santería/Ocha, Candomblé, and Vodou altars.

In this dialogical analysis, the post-sixteenth-century ideas embodied in Afro-Atlantic altars are taken to illuminate their European counterparts as much as the reverse. By heuristically describing both European social theories and African altars as "fetishes," *The Fetish Revisited* highlights the fact that each is the articulation and materialization of a contested proposal about how such social relationships should work. Each of these "fetishes" nominates into socially recognized being a typology of actors, their powers and goals, and a set of norms governing those actors' interaction, norms prioritizing the interests of some of those actors over others'. Therefore, European social theories and African altars are to be judged not for their truth or falsehood but for their relative efficacy at rearranging people's social priorities in a context where there is more than one choice regarding how people should organize themselves and how the rewards of their coopera-tion should be distributed. So it matters that, whereas Marx failed in his own efforts to organize and elevate the working class through his re-valuation of commodities and factories, the Afro-Atlantic priests who mentor me have successfully organized diverse populations around their own re-valuation of material things. And they have done so in competition with the Abrahamic religions and with the post-Enlightenment ideas—including Marxism—that dominate contemporary nation-states.

Freud knew as well as Marx and the Afro-Atlantic priests that things and the value attributed to them powerfully mediate human relationships. So *The Fetish Revisited* also analyzes the ambivalent social relationships that Freud reorganized through the medium of couches, armchairs, cigars, alcohol, intaglio rings, pilgrimages to the Acropolis and Rome, his antiquities collec-tion, his father's fur hat, and his texts about the "savage." I argue that this reorganization was concerned as much with the enfranchisement of assimi-lated Jewish men as with curing neurosis.

The Fetish Revisited culminates in a detailed ontological, psychoanalytic, and class analysis of the spirited things that embody social relationships in the Afro-Atlantic religions.[3] Contrary to Marx's demeaning metaphor and his assumption that the so-called fetishist is blind to the source of the fetish's value, Afro-Atlantic priests typically know that it is people who make gods. These religions reconfigure interfamilial, interclass, interethnic, interracial, and intergender relationships through the liturgical assembly, re-valuation, and care of material things, many of which have been imported from Europe or by Europeans—such as Venetian and Bohemian beads, Scottish gin, Dutch schnapps and beer, French perfumes and champagne, Maldivean cowries, mirrors, satin, sequins, and soup tureens. Bohemia, incidentally, is not far from Freud's Moravian birthplace.

The spirited things of Europeans, Africans, and their descendants have not been produced in isolation from each other. They result from an exchange of gazes, ideas, and commodities among three continents. Moreover, they have come to be called "fetishes" precisely because Africans, Europeans, and their descendants have looked at them and intensely disagreed about the value and agency that can legitimately be attributed to them and their makers. And therein, perhaps, lies the intensity of the fetish's affecting power. Hence, this book rests on a heuristic definition of the fetish as a material thing animated by the contrary models of society and the contrary personal expectations of the people who—as Europeans and Africans, buyers and sellers, priests and worshippers, oath-givers and -takers, husbands and wives, masters and slaves, bosses and employers, teachers and students, and so forth—have rival relationships with that material thing. A thing is most likely to be called a fetish when it mediates the relationship between parties with very different or even opposite perspectives on their social relationship, perspectives that are also expressed in opposite perspectives on the thing itself.

Yet fetishes exercise the greatest and most enduring power over any given person insofar as he or she has internalized and can feel the opposing perspectives that constitute the fetish. Like the fetishes of Freud's patients and the paraphernalia of the gods in most religions, the most powerful spirited things of the Afro-Atlantic religions are deeply ambivalent—embodying simultaneously and sometimes in equal measure both faith and the anticipation of doubt, dissent, and disapproval; the adulation of the master's unbridled power and empathy for the suffering of the enslaved and the subordinated; the hope of protection and the anticipation of punishment for even the pettiest of infractions; the encouragement of pride and the potential for humiliation; the hope of supernumerary rewards and the impending threat of devastating loss. The more polarized the promise and the threat, the more exciting and enduring the fetish.

INTRODUCTION

Èṣù Láàròyé
Exu Larôiê
Èṣù, Lord of the Crossroads, who hears my pleas

Alaroyé Agó
Hearer of My Pleas, open the way

Papa Legba, ouvri bayè pou mwèn
Oh, Mighty Lord of Passages, open the gate for me

I salute the lord of the crossroads and of communication, whose main distinction is that he can turn order into disorder, communication into miscommunication, and vice versa.

Variants of the following story are told in virtually every locale where the gods known as the òrìṣà, the orixás, the orichas, and the orishas are worshipped.

Two dear old friends stood talking in the marketplace when Eshu strolled right between them.

"Did you see how that rude red-hatted man walked right between us?" exclaimed the friend on the right.

"What do you mean?" asked the friend on the left. "His hat was black!"

"Are you blind?" said the first friend, accusingly. "It was red!"

"No! You're crazy! It was black!"

The debate accelerated, and the insults grew less and less forgivable, until the hat-wearing man came back and again strolled between the friends, whereupon they realized that one side of the rude man's hat was red and the other black.

Red and black is the foremost sacred color combination of the god known in Nigeria as Èṣù or Elégbára, in Brazil as Exu or Leba, in Cuba as Elegguá, and in Haiti as Legba, but he can also be invoked by the juxtaposition of the similarly opposite black and white. In English, any of these avatars of the god may all be called "Eshu." He is the lord of the crossroads, communication, confusion, and virility. But he is not everywhere the same. In Cuba he is a small child, in Haiti a bent but wily old man. In Nigeria he is both. But everywhere his hallmarks are unpredictability, heterogeneity, irony, and contrasts of interpretation (see also Gates 1988).

In the Yorùbá-Atlantic world, *an* Eshu—that is, a human-assembled being made of laterite or cement and imbued by its contents and its ritual treatment with the life force and personality of this god—ideally sits at the entrance of every marketplace, entry gate of a compound, and exterior door of a shop or a residence. In the Yorùbá- and the Fòn-Atlantic traditions, he sports a huge penis or an emblem on his head that may be a hat but is more often a blade or phallic extension (ògo; see figures 1.1 and 1.2). In his most elaborate representations, a curved phallic structure on his head ends in a face looking to the rear. This emblem highlights his power to penetrate boundaries, to see and be seen by opposite worlds.

Eshu is most famously described as a trickster. He is that. However, he is also a Janus, simultaneously discerning the past and the future, the outside and the inside, this world and the Other. He is the male principle of penetration that complements the female principle of containment, which is the heart of the spirit-possession religions discussed in this book. Equally important to the argument of this book is the power that an Eshu—like other so-called fetishes—derives from being seen from contrasting but contemporaneous worlds. This is a defining feature of those materialized gods dubbed "fetishes" by European critics since the sixteenth century and especially since the Enlightenment. They stand at the crossroads of African and European worlds and are, in many ways, among the creations and the creators of those worlds. Through the juxtaposition of mirror-opposite geometrical shapes in opposite colors, the shrine house for Elegguá in plate 2 dramatizes this theme of communication between opposite worlds and opposite perspectives. It is striking, in a manner that will be explored below, that this juxtaposition between opposite colors and shapes is mediated by money—the cowrie-shell money of the Guinea Coast slave trade. Unless Eshu, with his spirit of unpredictability and love of contention, is saluted at the beginning of each meal, visit, ritual, or other project, he is likely to disrupt every human-made plan for that occasion. So I salute him here. Whereas Marx and Freud represent the fetish as a pathology, I argue, with an appeal for Eshu's supportive intercession, that fetishes are fulcrums of all social organization and self making, including historical materialism and psychoanalysis themselves. Like Eshu's hat, fetishes are things that both animate contrary social roles and are animated by contrary value codes. In ritual and social use, they both clarify subjectivities and facilitate their interpenetration.

FIGURE I.1 Shrine sculpture of the Yorùbá god Èṣù, probably from Nigeria. Note the phallic extension from the head, known as the *ògo* (SABA COLLECTION D125).

FIGURE I.2 Rear shot of Èṣù's *ògo*. Suggesting his ambivalence, the appealing face, with its stately expression, is matched by an animalistic, carnivorous face at the rear. The horse calls attention not only to the god's dignity but also to the god's deft movement between worlds, just as his two faces dramatize his ability to see both of them.

The Gods Dance on Hegel's Doorstep

On a cold and foggy February morning in Berlin, my wife, Bunmi, woke from a dream about scores of silver fish swimming the clear waters of the normally cloudy river that flows through Ìgèdè-Èkìtì, her Nigerian hometown and the origin of the Yorùbá river goddess, Ọ̀ṣun. Just as dreams were for Freud the "royal road to the unconscious," they are, for the priests of many Afro-Atlantic religions, windows on the Other world, which is also the inner world and, often, a revelation of the future. While the Enlightenment strove to establish a clear *distinction* between the subject and the object and between the European self and the African Other, the Afro-Atlantic religions simultaneously strove to clarify the *mutually constituting relationship* between the person and the universe, between the inner world and the outer, and between local populations and distant ones.

An heir to both *òrìṣà* religion and the Southern Baptist mission, Bunmi opened this window to me as we made our way, two days after the dream, to the Ilê Obá Silekê Temple in the Kreuzberg neighborhood of Berlin, a house of worship founded and led by Babá Murah Soares, a Candomblé priest originally from the coastal Brazilian state of Bahia (figure I.3). Yet, like other Candomblé priests, he identifies Bunmi's West African homeland as the origin of his gods.

Candomblé is an Afro-Brazilian religion of divination, sacrifice, healing, music, dance, and spirit possession. The only rival to its beauty is its complexity. Though this religion is headquartered in the coastal Brazilian state of Bahia, it has counterparts and offshoots all over urban Brazil. This religion also has historically connected counterparts not only in Nigeria and the Republic of Benin but also in Cuba, Trinidad, Haiti, Argentina, and the Cuban diaspora throughout the Americas, where converts of every ethnoracial background have joined in. In Brazil, believers attribute miraculous powers and exemplary flaws to gods known variously as *orixás*, *voduns*, *inquices*, and *caboclos*, depending on the Candomblé denomination.

Babá Murah's temple is consecrated to the *orixás* and the *caboclos*. The adventures, personalities, and kinship relations of these superhuman and transhuman beings are described in an extensive mythology and body of oracular wisdom, which also serves to explain the personalities and to model the options of their human worshippers, as well as the worldly relations among those worshippers and their neighbors. Through blood sacrifice and lavish ceremonies of music, dance, and spirit possession—and occasional visits to the Roman Catholic Church, whose saints are correlated with them—the gods are asked to intervene beneficently in the lives of worshippers and to keep their foes at bay.

FIGURE I.3 Exterior of Ilê Obá Silekê, a temple of the Brazilian Candomblé religion in Berlin.

Orisha-worship first came to Germany in the 1970s with Cuban students and young workers on contract in the socialist and officially atheist Democratic Republic of Germany, then commonly known as East Germany. Since then, mixed marriages, tourism to Cuba, and a growing interest in Cuban music attracted a number of Germans to the Afro-Cuban Santería/Ocha religion (Bahia 2012: 229; also Matory 2015a). Candomblé, its Brazilian counterpart, has attracted Germans through similar mechanisms (Bahia 2013: 9). One of the earliest *orixá* priests in Germany was Mãe Dalva, who arrived in 1979. Born in Bahia, she married in Berlin and worked as a street cleaner and housekeeper until the year the Berlin Wall fell, in 1989. Today, she has many online imitators (Bahia 2013: 8). Yet it was Babá Murah who founded the first Candomblé temple in Germany. The temple was initially operated out of Babá Murah's basement apartment in Berlin's Neukölln neighborhood, but in 2008 he and his German partner, Martin, rented and beautifully renovated their current headquarters, which is consecrated to an avatar (*qualidade*) of the god of thunder and lightning, Xangô. The temple's name, Ilê Obá Silekê, means "House of the King Xangô Aganju," who is identified with the "center of the volcano" and is closely linked to the sea goddess Iemanjá (Bahia 2012: 232–33).

An Enlightenment-influenced researcher and a relationship-influenced devotee of the *òrìṣà*, I immediately identified Bunmi's dream as a message from Ọ̀sun, for whom Bunmi now keeps two altars in our home in Durham, North Carolina—one assembled by Ìyá Ọ̀sun Òsogbo (aka Adedoyin Talabi Faniyi), high priestess of Ọ̀sun in the Nigerian town of Òsogbo, and the other by Doté Amilton Sacramento Costa, a high priest of the Candomblé religion, from the Brazilian state of Bahia.

Both Ìyá Ọ̀sun Òsogbo and Doté Amilton are frequent visitors to our home and have been part of Bunmi's transformation in recent years from a Baptist to a proud advocate of her ancestral Yorùbá religious traditions. As a young person, she would hasten her steps when she had to pass in front of a palace, a site she associated with the possibility of forcible marriage to the monarch, and she heard Christian-inspired tales that the god Ṣàngó, when appearing on earth in the body of his possession priest, could make a barren woman fertile, but her offspring would be born idiots. The world of the Yorùbá gods was, for her, fraught with gendered threats and anxiety, particularly those anxieties related to polygamy and husbands' domination of their wives. In fact, Yorùbá wives tend to earn outside the home and exercise a high degree of self-determination. However, the forms of gender asymmetry that Bunmi witnessed in her own birth home led her to admire the likes of Mary Wollstonecraft. Ultimately, it was my own African American devotion to Africa and the disempowering images of African women that she encountered upon immigrating to the United States that made Bunmi answer the call of the goddess.

Only recently—following that discussion of the manuscript at the Ohio State University—did Bunmi reveal to me that she had been dreaming about the òrìsà gods and their priesthood since she was a small child. In the recesses of sleep, she saw herself painted white with kaolin (efun). Such dreams, she offered, seemed to foretell a calling to resume her writing and her activism as a spokesperson of an Africa now maligned not only by Westerners but also by the fast-growing population of Pentecostals in her homeland. In that writing and activism, she now has a circum-Atlantic network of priestly and publishing allies, their devotion shaped both by a collaborative affirmation of orisha values and relationships and by these allies' simultaneous participation in social arrangements grounded in Muslims', Christians', and Western secularists' shared denunciation of those relationships and values.

That day in Berlin was the occasion of Bunmi's first visit to Germany's only Candomblé temple and the day of Babá Murah's annual festival for the sea goddess Iemanjá, a cognate of the Cuban Ocha goddess of the sea, Yemayá, and to the Nigerian Yorùbá river goddess, Yemoja. These goddesses might be regarded as the tutelary spirits of the maritime exchange that gave birth to the Afro-Atlantic world. Even in Nigeria, her river flows straight to the sea rather than meandering; even in the distant hinterland, her altars are rich in old marine shells, and her most intimate emblems include a mermaid figure resembling its counterparts on the prows of European ships. Indeed, in my scholarly pursuit of what is African within me, it was the mammoth New Year's festivals of Iemanjá on the beaches of Rio de Janeiro that led me ultimately to Yorubaland in search of the goddess's African sources.

Iemanjá, Yemayá, and Yemoja are among the most famous of the score of orishas worshipped around the Atlantic perimeter. Each of these gods personifies a network of natural forces, places, technologies, social conventions, human personality types, animals, herbs, possession priests, and consecrated things. Like many priests, Ìyá Òṣun Òṣogbo regards these gods as ancient ancestors, but not necessarily in the sense of biological forebears. She compares the worshipper's relationship with the god to my relationship with James B. Duke, the ostensible founder of a community to which I belong, Duke University. Similarly, when she was alive, the artist and òrìṣà priestess Susanne Wenger was no less a reincarnation of the goddess Òṣun and no less a mother to the current Ìyá Òṣun Òṣogbo for being Austrian-born. Yet the gods are ancestors in a further sense. They are models of human response to the dilemmas we face in any given sociocultural setting. In worshipping them, we contemplate the motives behind and the potential consequences of the good and bad choices that a person of a given archetypal personality or in a given archetypal situation might be tempted to make. Such reflective choices are a transformative and, indeed, creative dimension of ancestor-worship and of orisha-devotion alike. As a function of the social relationships that we create, transform, and are created and transformed by, these gods remain present in altars and in the bodies of living people. Each generation of altars and possession priests extends and transforms a god, just as a child extends and transforms its forebears' and role models' legacies.

The gods also vividly instantiate what is perhaps the most fundamental principle of Yorùbá cosmology—that the world is seldom merely what it seems. Another world lies behind this visible one, constantly influencing and being influenced by it. It is a world of unseen relationships made, unmade, remade, and transformed over time by the efforts of people in this world. We all possess certain powers of discernment that penetrate the veil of appearances. We sometimes come to recognize that the beings around us who appear to be ordinary people are actually animals, spirit malefactors or benefactors, visitors from the Other world, physical embodiments of fate brought from that world, or dead people who have remained too long in this world. We can also discern the signs of guidance sent back from the Other world by our ancestors. Sometimes geographical features, meteorological events, natural disasters, plants, animals, and even stones are the veils behind which the denizens of the Other world—and the signals they send—appear before us. However, with the benefit of divinatory tools and intuition, priests are experts at detecting the Other-worldly connections that underlie the apparent shape of things.

Much of the ritual in the Afro-Atlantic religions consists of efforts to monitor and regulate the cross-border movements of gods, unborn or deceased human beings, and other spirits who normally dwell in that invisible world that parallels our own. Events in that parallel world affect events in our world, and periodically the denizens of that Other world make dramatic appearances in our world, sometimes on their own mysterious volition and sometimes by the invitation and under the regulation of living human beings, sometimes as ghostly presences and sometimes as flesh-and-blood bodies. Like dreams, the Afro-Atlantic Other world mashes up what Westerners might call the past, the future, inner sentiment, and exogenous forces that affect the conditions of life. Yet what all of these Other-worldly apparitions have in common is that they remind us about interrupted, forgotten, or neglected relationships and that they demand a collective response—typically the hierarchical invocation of protection and guidance by a god, through a priest, and of a supplicant.

Moreover, it is not only a phenomenological reality but also a truism embedded in much Yorùbá-Atlantic parlance that the gods are made by people. The Other world is within us and among us, not only irrelevant to human life until we engage it through ritual but also dependent on our ritual action for its realization. It is in this way that Iemanjá came to Kreuzberg.

The occasion of Bunmi's and my visit on February 8, 2014, was the annual festival of this goddess of the sea. Along with similar Yorùbá-, Fòn-, and Kongo-Atlantic divinities in Trinidad, Haiti, Cuba, Brazil, Nigeria, Benin, and the US, Yemoja/Iemanjá/Yemayá and Oshun/Òsun/Oxum/Ochún preside over a circum-Atlantic religion that has now taken root in the European Union, more in Portugal and Spain than elsewhere, but at the center of old Protestant Prussia, as well. Nowadays the Candomblé religion creates, monitors, and regulates relationships not only between this world and the Other but also between central Europe and the great powers of the Black Atlantic.

We arrived at the Iemanjá festival late, but just in time to witness Babá Murah demonstratively expelling a group of German supplicants who had shown up in khaki, despite the long-standing and internet-publicized requirement that everyone in attendance wear only white. Babá Murah says that if he were not so strict, everyone would show up in black, which he describes as "Berlin's national color" and as a taboo in the Bahian homeland of his religion. Because other commonsense forms of devotion, rapport, and redistributive ethics from Brazil are not common sense in Germany, Babá Murah also instructs visitors to bring flowers or candles to the festival, to pay for the coffee they drink, and to contribute money for the sacred meal that follows the festival. However, he says that what Germans find most difficult to get used to is Candomblé's hierarchy. For example, one Enlightenment-inspired German journalist reportedly penned a complaint about the absurdity of a man sitting there in his chair—that is, Babá Murah—while others bow down before him and put their heads on the ground. But Babá Murah explains, "they are not bowing down for me, Samuel [his secular name]; they're bowing down for the *pai-de-santo* [the father-in-saint]"—then correcting himself—"for the *babalorixá* [the priest]."

Being Black and Brazilian, Babá Murah insists, he will never be German. However, he admits that on his not-infrequent trips to Brazil, his countrymen note that his Portuguese has a German accent. Moreover, he is now so Germanized that he delivers instructional lectures about his religion during festivals, and he answers direct questions about practice and belief (mostly without sarcasm). In Bahian Candomblé, people normally learn through discreet observation and performance, not explanation. Like all Afro-Atlantic priests Babá Murah is an exemplary mediator between worlds.

Fortunately, Bunmi and I, though imperfectly dressed, were spared the humiliating lecture. We were among the small handful of black or *mulato* people in the crowd of 80–100 people in the room, and besides Babá Murah we were the only people who could have passed for sub-Saharan; everyone else was caramel or wintry pale. Similarly, under such circumstances in Brazil, Bunmi and I have always been treated as special. Indeed, one early morning on a São Paulo street corner, a man spontaneously knelt and performed a salaam at Bunmi's feet. He certainly saw Bunmi's coffee complexion and radiantly white Nigerian attire, but he may have discerned in her some invisible power, as well. That day at the Berlin temple, the doorman simply handed Bunmi some white work pants to cover her blue jeans and signaled for me to remove my black socks, whereupon the three Brazilian drummers resumed their performance and the singer resumed his alternation between time-honored songs—some recognizable and others unrecognizable to a modern Yorùbá speaker—and prayers in the perfectly recognizable modern Yorùbá that one of the drummers had studied academically.

Before long, the gods began to appear alongside us. One minute, a thirty-ish white alternative healthcare practitioner (*Heilpraktiker*) from the German city of Duisberg was chatting with me amiably and expressing surprise at the connection between Candomblé and a West African people called the "Yorùbá." The next minute, his eyes shuttered, his body rocked gently, and his breath became a gentle snore. Like me, he was still standing up, but a god had quietly taken his head.

The first goddess to take the dance floor was the Cuban goddess who rules bodies of fresh water. Ochún mounted the body of Joaquín la Habana, a graham-colored male priest of Cuban Santería/Ocha, friend of the house, and commander of his own domestic temple (*casa-templo*) elsewhere in Berlin. This goddess's dramatic movement and laughter distinguish her from most apparitions of her Brazilian counterpart, the freshwater goddess Oxum (see, for example, SABA Collection C073). However, both Ochún and Oxum are associated with the wealth of gold, the coolness of fresh water and fans, the vanity of women's gazing in the mirror, the number five, and fish in abundance. Both share a great kinship and much iconography with the Nigerian goddess Òṣun, who is identified with a specific river, favors brass rather than gold, and does not openly laugh like Ochún. That Saturday night, after descending into the body of her Cuban son, Ochún not only laughed but also twirled, sparkled, and undulated like water, like a coquette, like joy itself. She clearly enjoyed herself.

On the way to the festival, for which our 5:15 P.M. arrival was very late, Bunmi had repeatedly reminded me—no, commanded—that we were going to leave the festival in time for a 6 P.M. Black History Month lecture at the *Werkstatt der Kulturen* (the "Atelier of Cultures"), a state-subsidized multicultural center in the same fashionable Kreuzberg neighborhood. The name of the center derives from a non-Hegelian and anti-Enlightenment strand of German thought—that is, the "Romanticism" of Johann Gottfried von Herder, Gustav Klemm, and Franz Boas—that, originally in the defense of German "cultural"/"spiritual" equality with the dominant French, posited the moral equality of all peoples' collective lifeways, or "cultures" (*Geister/ Kulturen*), including non-European ones. Even beyond the German-speaking lands, the tension between German Romanticism and the Enlightenment remains a lived reality at the heart of "fetish" talk.

Bunmi's previously insistent demands were soon forgotten as the river goddess Ochún ceded the floor to Babá Murah's Iansã (warrior goddess of wind and storm, and the Brazilian counterpart to the Nigerian Ọya, goddess of River Niger) and a young white German's Iemanjá twirled amid diaphanous waves of blue and white cloth. Though lacking the grace of the Ochún, the Iemanjá called to mind Marlene Dietrich's character in "The Blue Angel," a Weimar cabaret siren who lured the *spiessig* (or "square") schoolteacher Immanuel Rath to his moral and social downfall. Without knowing much about the young man whom Iemanjá had possessed, I intuited that his love of the goddess was well reciprocated and that his trance was not a downfall but an embrace and celebration of the young German's and of Germany's collectively heterogeneous self. Africa's siren call to Germany had also produced the celebrated work of Leo Frobenius and Felix von Luschan, founding fathers of African art history. The same country produced the founder of cultural anthropology, Franz Boas, the liberalism of the Weimar Republic, and, partly under the tutelage of the United States, the most vicious forms of Enlightenment-influenced scientific and legal racism. Yet from an Afro-Atlantic perspective, opposite reactions to the same object and the presence of multiple personalities in the same individual or nation are no surprise.

Spirit possession is the most dramatic public demonstration of the vessel-based Yorùbá-Atlantic model of the person. It is a public and visible transaction between opposite beings and between this and the Other world. In these moments, as when Ochún, Iansã, and Iemanjá came to Babá Murah's sacred party in Kreuzberg, everyone sees that these created gods are real, literally alive and powerful—indeed, powerful enough to make you abandon your previous plans. Yet, contrary to the tragicomic moral of *The Blue Angel*, that the encounter with the opposite world yields contradiction and destruction, Yorùbá-Atlantic priests see in opposite beings the opportunity for a constructive and reciprocal relationship. Indeed, the copresence of such beings within the self is normal.

These are not the only Afro-Atlantic gods I have met face to face. There are also the Fòn-Atlantic snake god, Damballah, the goddess of motherhood, Èzili Dantò, and the Gede, the playful spirits of death, whom I meet at similar festivals hosted by friends in Haiti and the United States (Matory in preparation). But I am also friends with Siete Rayo, the Cuban-Kongo spirit of thunder and lightning. I do not normally like cigars, but I have enjoyed smoking them with the Cuban slave spirits called *congos* and *muertos*, or "dead people," and I have partied with dead Brazilian Indians and Gypsies, too. In the Afro-Latin American religions, when the dead possess people, they not only give comfort and good advice but also sing, dance, drink, joke, and tell good stories, easing many a stressful life condition. Dead people can be fun. For his part, Pena Grande ("Big Feather"), the *caboclo* Indian spirit of my best friend in Brazil, has vowed that he will come whenever I call for help.

Babá Murah's temple sits in a carriage house at the back of a courtyard, known as a *Hinterhof*, surrounded by apartment buildings. It is soundproofed to prevent his German neighbors' complaints about the drumming. At the front of the court stands one tall building whose basement houses a dozen of Babá Murah's Exus, guardians of the front door and the passageway into the courtyard. One Exu—the slave of Babá Murah's Omolu, the lord of pestilence—stands beside and guards the door of the carriage house itself. These anthropomorphic beings are made of cement, with cowrie-shell eyes and mouths.

Like other Yorùbá-Atlantic gods, these are instances of a generic god called by a proper noun. Generically, Exu is the lord of doorways and crossroads, of sexuality and particularly virility, and of communication. Once placated, he keeps the house, the event, or the mission free from the disorder, the heat, and the inappropriate sexuality of the street (see plate 1). Uniquely in Brazil, he also has female avatars, known variously as Exuas, Pombagiras, and Maria Padilhas. Each altar embodying this being is also described as *an* Exu, as is the aspect of that generic god that manifests itself in particular priests and temples. And, according to common parlance, each of these instances of the god is "made" by the priest.

All around the *Hinterhof* courtyard are planters for the sacred herbs on which the practice of Candomblé, like other Afro-Atlantic religions, depends for healing and for the making of each materialized instance of the god, in an altar or in a priest. A floor above the festival space is Babá Murah's consultation room, where—on Mondays, Tuesdays, and Thursdays—he sits before a circle of beads and a glass of water and casts sixteen cowrie shells in order to divine the problems of people seeking his help. He then prescribes solutions through herbs and the invocation of the *orixás*.

The walls around Babá Murah's consultation room feature curtained storage for the imported powders, seeds, and vessels used in his sacred craft, as well as a half-dozen visible statues of Roman Catholic saints and other Caucasian-looking figures that, following Afro–Latin America's most famous form of "syncretism," represent and once camouflaged these African gods. Babá Murah's grandmother, he says, was baptized Catholic upon her arrival from Africa, so she passed these traditions down to her children and grandchildren, but she gave them the choice to be baptized or not. Unlike many Brazilian Candomblé, Cuban Ocha, and Haitian Vodou priests, Babá Murah declares forcefully that he is not Catholic but purely of the Candomblé religion. Cocoa-brown himself, Babá Murah says that these Caucasian-looking statues have nothing to do with the *orixás*, who are all Nigerian or Beninese and therefore black.

To him, the Roman Catholic statues are merely lifeless and inert leftovers from the superseded past, when his forebears saw some connection between the Catholic saints and the Afro-Brazilian gods. Like the black Saint Benedict above the stove in the kitchen, with his vase of parsley, his candle, and his cup of coffee, these white saints merely commemorate and give a visible presence to the love of the dead black relative who once owned them. Babá Murah says that they also offer white Germans an easier way to identify with the gods. The color of the priests and the worshippers, he hastens to add, does not matter in the least. In addition, two statues of the Hindu gods Shiva and Parvati also adorn the walls of Babá Murah's consultation room. But he said these were just gifts from Germans and have nothing to do with his religion. I recognize in these gifts the same strand of German Romanticism and spiritual cosmopolitanism that, as a teen, I encountered and loved in the Swiss-German writer Herman Hesse's 1922 novel about the life of the Buddha, *Siddhartha*. For Westerners in search of alternatives to the evils of

European warfare and racism, all non-Western religions seem to offer similar relief. Alongside these various statues sit the delicate staffs, helmets, crowns, and jewelry that various gods under Babá Murah's guidance will carry or wear when they possess their priests on festival days.

Sitting at the door of this second-floor consultation room is the trickster spirit Zé Pelintra—half Exu, half spirit of the dead, and protector of both the trickster spirits and the human tricksters of the street. Babá Murah's *caboclo*, or Brazilian Indian spirit, Seu Ventania, sits in the corner farthest from the front door, near the entryway to the sacred room of the *orixá* altars. During private divination sessions restricted to members of the temple community, Seu Ventania mounts Babá Murah. Although each of these beings includes an anthropomorphic image, his true power resides in a bowl of sacred substances underneath it.

Like his brothers- and sisters-in-the-saint (*irmãos-de-santo*), Babá Murah pays careful but not always fully obedient attention to the dictates of his own *mãe-de-santo*, or chief priestess, Mãe Beata of Iemanjá. For example, Babá Murah told me that Mãe Beata forbids the worship of Zé Pelintra and of his female counterpart, Maria Padilha, or Pombagira, since these entities bring trouble. Many of his brothers- and sisters-in-the-saint also defy Mãe Beata, because these mischievous, Eshu-related beings bring wealth and fame, too. Beyond that, when they mount their priests, dance, prophecy, and bless their audiences, everyone has fun.

The central function of Candomblé is to maintain personal and social health by diminishing the presence of some forces and otherworldly beings in the body and the community and by making, installing, maintaining, and enhancing the presence of others. Among the entities that need to be diminished in the temple are the unknown dead and Exus who have been sent by one's enemies. Certain other entities facilitate independence from one's elders and, so, are more attractive to entrepreneurial priests. Others, at least in Brazil, are more conducive to the respectability and therefore to the public and bourgeois sponsorship of a temple. Such beings are more attractive to the Candomblé establishment, which has more to gain from sponsorship than from entrepreneurialism and lively, plebeian entertainment (Matory 2005). However, as the case of Babá Murah's Zé Pelintra suggests, the unwelcomeness of any given spirit or force is provisional, and the ethic of managing heterogeneity and tension tends to prevail over the ethic—or even possibility—of completely or permanently removing any force or spirit from the life of the person or the community.

Locked away from public view, also on the second floor but behind the farthest door, is the heart of the temple, known as the *peji*. In that room sit the bowls and soup tureens containing the substance and power of the *orixá* gods—the herb-bathed and blood-fed stones, beads, and seashells of Oxum; Iemanjá; Omolu; the god of thunder and lightning, Xangô; the god of wisdom and purity, Oxalá; the god of herbal healing, Ossaim; the god of the hunt, Oxóssi; and the god of war and iron, Ogum, who rules my head. In the holy of holies, behind the ultimate door within this most sacred room, sits the sacred vessel of the goddess of wind and storm, Iansã, the ruler of Babá Murah's head. Her feeding and her festival are the culmination of each annual cycle of sacred festivals and the peak of the community's effervescence.

Babá Murah's world of spirited things sits at the center of one of twenty-first-century Berlin's most fashionable neighborhoods, and the festivals that keep them alive draw not only Brazilian and Cuban immigrants but also white European seekers from all over Germany, as well as Scandinavia. Yet the temple and its clientele are not "the return of the repressed" but the culmination of a long circum-Atlantic dialectic of mutual construction and transformation between Africans and Europeans (with moments of South Asian involvement), between Protestants and Catholics, between royals and plebeians, and between the bourgeoisie and the proletariat over the value of things and the obligations those things imply among people. Babá Murah's *Hinterhof* is not a place of pure otherness in the heart—and much less on the ruins—of Hegel's rationalist, anti-African city. It is a crossroads where some of the most momentous intellectual trends on the Atlantic perimeter meet again and face each other with renewed awareness.

Two Revolutions in Dialogue on the Atlantic Perimeter

William Pietz (1985) argues that the concept of the fetish originated on the sixteenth- and seventeenth-century West African coast, where Europeans condemned Africans' manner of attributing value and agency to material things. I prefer to describe the origin of what he called the "problem of the fetish" as a bilateral *disagreement* over the proper value and agency of people and things, because the African parties in this contest of ideas and social practices had cogent opinions and practices of their own, hitherto neglected in current discussion of fetishism—ideas that were highly effective in ordering the societies of the Guinea Coast and in preserving African advantages over their European trading partners. And they remain highly effective in organizing African-diaspora communities.

Pietz usefully calls attention to European merchants' use of African consecrated things as metaphors in their critique of Roman Catholicism and of aristocratic governance in Europe. It might be argued, then, that the Guinea-Coast encounter catalyzed a bourgeois-led European social revolution, the Enlightenment. At the crux of this revolution were debates about not only the worth and agency of things but also the relative worth of Africans, Europeans, and different types of Europeans in the circum-Atlantic political economy. As articulated by Hegel, Marx, and Freud, the anti-African trope of the fetish was central to a sequence of European social revolutions intent on conferring upon the European bourgeoisie and proletariat rights once limited to the European aristocracy, and doing so at the symbolic and material expense of Africans.

However, this was a moment of crisis for the emerging merchant classes of both Europe *and* Africa. It might be argued that this same sixteenth- and seventeenth-century Afro-European trade catalyzed some major reforms in West African spirit-possession religion and governance, as well—reforms that distinguish Ọ̀yọ́-Yorùbá religion and politics, Brazilian Candomblé, and Cuban Santería/Ocha from the likely antecedents of Ọ̀yọ́ imperial religion, as well as from West African Ewe religion and Haitian Vodou. From the sixteenth century to the eighteenth, the expansion of the inland Ọ̀yọ́ kingdom and its push to the Atlantic coastal ports involved not only literal equestrianism, which is well-known, but also the unique amplification of political delegation through royal wives, as well as possession priests and other palace officials who were (and are) analogized to horses and wives (Matory [1994] 2005).

So the Guinea-Coast encounter of European merchants with African monarchs, merchants, and priests catalyzed *two* social revolutions—one Euro-Atlantic and the other Afro-Atlantic. On the one hand, the Euro-Atlantic social revolution advocated the inherent equality of all white men and their individual, rights-bearing autonomy from one another. This new social ideal was based on the model of a band of brothers, and the prime actor imagined in this vision of society and history is a white man. On the other, the simultaneous Yorùbá-Atlantic social revolution idealized the hand-in-glove, hierarchical connection between actors from different families, ethnic groups, and places—a hierarchical connection modeled on royal marriage and horsemanship. The prime historical actor imagined in this model of society and history is a black royal wife (Matory [1994] 2005).

In many ways, Babá Murah precedes me in my project, which is to put the heirs of these two social revolutions back into explicit dialogue with each other. He does so in the service of community and healing, while I do so in order to enhance our understanding of what each party separately takes for granted about the value and agency of people and things. This dialogue also has the benefit of showing us, first, that European social theories are as material and as materially interested as the phenomena that they describe as "fetishism" and, second, that African spirited things are as filled with thoughtful and socially positioned ideas as are European social theories. *The Fetish Revisited* places Marx's and Freud's influential theories of the fetish in dialogue with the human-assembled gods of the West African Yorùbá, Brazilian

Candomblé, Cuban Santería/Ocha, and Haitian Vodou—that is, the gods who are the implicit point of comparison, or "source" (Lakoff and Johnson 1980), in this long-standing European metaphor for misplaced value and agency. Through vivid color images and ethnographic analyses of these gods, I show that Marx's and Freud's conceptions of the fetish both illuminate and misrepresent Africa's human-made gods. I ask of historical materialism and psychoanalysis the same socially contextualizing questions that anthropologists, deeply influenced by Marx and Freud, have applied to the study of African and African-inspired religions. I also show that the Afro-Atlantic gods illuminate the culturally specific, materially conditioned, and materially embodied nature of Marx's and Freud's theories.

Ethnological Schadenfreude and Lopsided Ambivalence in Central Europe

Marx and Engels turned the Enlightenment idea of the fetish, long an explicit description of African spirited things, into a household word and a leading metaphor in the theorization of their fellow Europeans' foolishness. I argue that Marx's and Freud's political programs and rhetorical strategies were shaped by the nineteenth-century rise of capitalism, overseas imperialism, pseudoscientific racism, and Jim Crow, as well as these men's own class insecurity. They were also shaped by these men's desire as secular Jews to escape the stigma, exclusion, and murder suffered by religious Jews.

Moreover, Marx's and Freud's theories rested on material furniture that might itself be described as a range of fetishes. Historical materialism and psychoanalysis invest great affect and agency in certain material things whose conflicting meanings endorse rival social configurations. And the vigor and influence of both historical materialism and psychoanalysis owe much to their principal authors' simultaneous identification with Europe's African victim and anxiety to prove themselves worthy of access to the privileges of white Europeanness based upon their superiority to that victim. Inspired by both Freud's fetishism theory and the Afro-Atlantic religions, this analysis of ambiguous things and ambivalent theorists is intended as a new lesson to both Marxists and Freudians. The hypothesis that the most enduring fetishes are ambivalent, a point dear to Freud's own theory of the fetish, amplifies my earlier ethnography of what I call "ethnological Schadenfreude" (Matory 2015b)—that is, the strategy of middling status groups to seek membership in higher-status groups by assenting to, and indeed proclaiming, the inferiority of a third, more vulnerable party.

The Fetish Revisited is both an elaboration on my earlier work about the Afro-Atlantic religions (e.g., Matory 2005, [1994] 2005) and an application of my more recent work on ethnological Schadenfreude (2015b) among US Americans of African descent to the eighteenth- to twenty-first-century interactions between Africans and Europeans that have profoundly transformed the intellectual lives of both populations since then. Ethnological Schadenfreude is specifically a process of *ethnic* self-construction, or ethnogenesis, by which people of stigmatized populations endeavor to escape their stigma and its related social encumbrances by deflecting that stigma onto a population whom they endeavor to construct as lower. However, a similar process characterizes class and national identities, and many religious ones, as well. While the justice-minded might expect stigmatized populations to stand up and denounce the unfairness of racial, cultural, class, and gender chauvinism generally, I hypothesize that the ambitious members of stigmatized groups more often declare to their tormentors, in so many words, "It is not we who deserve stigmatization and oppression; it's those people over there. *We're* actually ideal versions of *you!*"

It is worth reminding the reader that even today's most respected nations and peoples remain haunted by stigmatization and feelings of inferiority. In the eighteenth and early nineteenth centuries, it was French language and culture that marked elite status in the politically divided lands of German-speaking Europe, and German was regarded as a peasant language. In the mid-nineteenth century, Marx ranked even the most powerful of the German states, Prussia, with Russia in its political backwardness compared to France, as well as its economic backwardness compared to Great Britain. The people Marx sought to lead were chiefly the diaspora of German workers who, as economic refugees, sought work and higher wages in other lands.

After the Frenchman Napoleon Bonaparte defeated the combined ethnically German armies of Prussia, Saxony, Bavaria, and Württemberg at Leipzig, middle-class German-speaking intellectuals like Herder, Fichte, and Hegel tended to become more German-nationalist and to fret that their nation was behind the curve of European progress with respect to national unity, industrialization, and the possession of extra-European colonies. And they were driven by a desire to prove their equality with France and Britain. In sum, the burghers suffered under the eighteenth-century premise of French cultural superiority, while their nineteenth-century successors endured the premise that the whole world was an evolutionary ladder with the Anglo-Saxons or the French at its apex, a premise also implicit in French and British anthropology of the time.[1]

The German anthropologist Claudia Rauhut argues that Bismarck organized the Berlin Conference of 1884, whose aim was to divide Africa up among the European imperial powers, precisely in order to assert a role for

Germany in a European expansionist project hitherto dominated by the British and French. Bismarck and other Germans' sense that their nation had been outpaced in this project, adds Rauhut, was the reason that Germany's late nineteenth-century effort to acquire overseas colonies was so efficient and brutal, as illustrated by the heartless effort to exterminate the Herero and Nama peoples of what would become Southwest Africa and, later, Namibia (personal communication, November 2015). In the 1930s, according to the German anthropologist Richard Kuba, this German feeling of national backwardness and inferiority extended to a sense of the inadequacy of their European landholdings (or *Lebensraum*), as well, adding a psychological motivation to the well-known material motivations behind German expansionism *within* Europe (personal communication, October 2014). In the twentieth century, Germany's cycle of compensatory self-assertion and ignominious defeat rests upon and amplifies a long history of shame and fear of inferiority.

More broadly, in nineteenth- and twentieth-century Europe, nationalist political discourses and the nationally diverse sciences of race, folklore, and ethnology all embodied the efforts of diverse European peoples and classes to articulate and promote their respective places in the emergent hierarchy of nations and empires. Through their contribution of diverse ethnological artifacts to national museums, royals, new industrial elites, and missionaries (who often came from peasant and other subaltern European social origins) were locating themselves as knowing subjects and respectable citizens of the emergent bourgeois nation-state, defined by a shared superiority to the Africans and other non-Europeans whose crafts and bodies were "scientifically" displayed.[2] Thus, the theories of social-evolutionary and racial difference that structured these national museum exhibitions and other posttheological narrations of human history—including Marx's social-evolutionist historical materialism and Freud's social-evolutionist history of the mind—were not just about the non-European Other. They were also about why the narrator of this history deserved to be regarded as superior to that Other and not inferior to a range of fellow European populations that had previously—on the grounds of caste, class, region, ethnicity, or religion—professed superiority to the narrator and his people.

German-speaking central Europe hosted a range of such compensatory, chauvinist responses to feelings of national inferiority.

In the twentieth century, German feelings of collective inferiority to other Europeans formed the root of Nazism. Comparisons between Nazism and Donald J. Trump's populist nationalism—greatly subsidized by working-class and downwardly mobile whites' sense of inferiority and defeat—are not hyperbolic. Hitler's *Mein Kampf* ([1925–26] 1941) begins not with a proclamation of Aryan superiority but with a lament about the social disorder of the

German worker's household and about his lack of pride in himself compared to the French worker. Today, Germans remain a deeply embarrassed nation, torn between gratitude and indebtedness—on the one hand, gratitude for US mercy and kindness after World War II and the economic prosperity that resulted and, on the other, the humiliation of not only having collectively committed a heinous crime against other Europeans but also being a loser dominated by a network of foreign powers.

Yet the stigmatized are equally capable of self-interested empathy with fellow sufferers, and ethnological Schadenfreude is seldom uninterrupted by or unalloyed with such empathy. Offering an alternative to the idea that German speakers were underdeveloped versions of an ideal embodied in France and Great Britain, nineteenth-century German ethnology advanced the idea that every people has its own culture-specific imagination and quality of feeling that makes that people different from—but not inferior or superior to—other peoples. Following the late eighteenth-century cultural pluralism of Johann von Gottfried Herder (who originated the concept of the *Volksgeist*), his nineteenth-century successors Alexander von Humboldt and Adolf Bastian and his twentieth-century successors Leo Frobenius and Felix von Luschan identified in Africa's dignity a metaphor and metonym of German national dignity. It was Gustav E. Klemm, a Saxon, who first employed the current anthropological usage of the term *Kultur* (culture), which presupposed the equality of all peoples rather than their placement on a racial or cultural scale of rank (Kroeber and Kluckhohn 1952: 10). Thus, if my argument is correct, it is to a German reaction against feelings of national inferiority that we owe the tremendous contributions of both German gentile Leo Frobenius and German Jewish Franz Boas to cultural anthropology, African studies, and African American studies, as well as to Francophone African and Afro-Caribbean literature.[3]

In principle, the stigmatized, whether individuals or nations, have the option to join with a broad swath of their fellow sufferers to oppose all stigma and oppression. However, their more common reaction—increasingly common as circumstances thrust them toward the bottom of a hierarchy—is to seek the approval of their oppressors by deflecting their stigma onto others.

Compared to their German-speaking contemporaries (not to mention Freud's world-famous and equally non-Aryan cubist and fauvist contemporaries in Paris), Marx and Freud stand out for having chosen to demean Africans, even if (and perhaps because) they partially identified with Africans.[4] Since Hegel's *Philosophy of History* ([1822] 1956), Marx and Freud arguably have done more than any other scholars to turn African religion into a commonsense, universal metaphor for all incorrect valuation of things. As assimilated Jews, they represented some of the most extreme instances of German speakers' collective desire to convince others of their normalcy within post-Enlightenment European definitions of humanity and national citizenship. The intensity of their compensatory degradation of Africa seems to be indebted to the fact that their race, their regional origins, and their class made them especially vulnerable to exclusion from the dominant camp of unmarked European bourgeois whiteness.

Hannah Arendt (1944) describes a range of personality types that emerge from what she calls the "pariah" status of European Jews since their emancipation, including the hapless *schlemihl*, the impudent little guy, the rebel, the social critic, and the art collector. But she highlights the folly of the assimilated Jewish "parvenu"—an "inner slave" who perfectly adopts gentile culture, cooperates in his own people's oppression, and, in the end, suffers the same fate as other Jews. Sander Gilman sees signs of the parvenu in Marx and, to a far greater degree, Freud (personal communication, April 27, 2017). I focus on Marx's and Freud's use of the term "fetish," however, not because they were the only central Europeans in their day to employ the term in a way that singled out Africans for opprobrium but because the extremeness of their social condition highlights the exemplary human motivation behind this put-down. The other reason that I focus on them is that their theories of the fetish have been particularly fruitful for me, and I ascribe this fruitfulness to Marx's and Freud's own special degree of social ambiguity and ambivalence about their place in the global—and especially circum-Atlantic—empire of white Christendom.

Marx suffered under a radical shift in his own class status and Freud under a radical shift in the political status of Jews in central Europe. Marx's and Freud's own social ambiguity inspired a double-consciousness richly implicit in their theories—an uncertainty over whether to disambiguate themselves from Africans and claim whiteness or to dignify and defend their fellow victims of racial oppression. This ambivalence about human equality is implicit in their rhetorical use—indeed, fetishization—of the African, the enslaved African American, and our gods. However, the outcome of their ambivalence was, in the end, lopsided.

Freud's theory of fetishism (1927) seems a thinly veiled metaphor for his own situation as an assimilated Jew in an increasingly antisemitic Europe. And, for him, ambivalence is central to the structure of the fetish. According to Freud, the fetish embodies both the fearful hostility of the boy to his father and the boy's desire, in the end, to assume the father's role as an aggressor. Likewise, I will argue, Freud's rhetorical use of Africans and our gods embodies both his fearful hostility toward the white gentile father and his desire to impress and, in the end, to become that father.

This analysis draws force from the Freudian premise that the most highly charged fetishes enable the subject both to identify with the potential victim and, in alternation, to mime the safety and the power of the victimizer. "A fetish . . . doubly derived from contrary ideas . . . is of course especially durable. In other instances the divided attitude shows itself in what the fetishist does with his fetish" (Freud 1927: 157). For example, Freud hypothesized that, on the one hand, a patient who fetishized braids and enjoyed cutting them off of a woman's head looked upon the braid as a sign that his mother had escaped castration, since, when he met the female owner of the phallus-shaped coiffure, she still appeared to have a phallus. This sight thus relieved him of the fear that he himself was under a threat of castration by the father. On the other hand, in cutting off the braid, the part of the male fetishist that identified strongly with his castrating father enacted the role of the castrator (ibid.). Hence, the adult son's fetishization of the braid both reassured him that he would not be castrated and mimed the threat of castration to sons like him who break the father's rules.

It is difficult for me to take seriously Freud's premise that every boy mistakes his mother's genitalia for a product of castration by the father and therefore as a threat of the boy's castration. However, many consecrated things and ritual actions do appear to dramatize opposite roles in similarly hierarchical relationships, and they appear to be used to enact both caretaking, or defensive, and punitive roles in those relationships. The affective power of all fetishes appears to draw on this semantic, or hermeneutical, duality. The fetish cuts both ways. However, diachronically, the ritual process tends to culminate in ethnological Schadenfreude and the triumph of the father.

One key factor that makes both European and African sacralized ideas and things "fetishes" by my heuristic definition is the context of political, economic, or military *inequality* among the parties debating the proper order of the universe. The term "fetish" indexes the speaker's condemnation of one human-posited and human-enforced socio-cosmological order in the service of affirming another. Calling something a fetish is, most obviously, an assertion of the speaker's difference from and superiority to the fetishist. By claiming the right to judge the health and humanity of the African or Africanized Other, the speaker—whether a gentile but nonroyal citizen of royalist and francophile Prussia or an assimilated Jew in an increasingly republican but antisemitic Europe—includes himself in the company of people exempted from inferiority.

Since accusations of fetishism are not usually reciprocated by their victims, they index a defensive middling position in a global status hierarchy. However, in this book I reciprocate the charge. *The Fetish Revisited* thus submits the mental images and worldly furniture of Marx's and Freud's theories to comparison with the African spirited things that these men—partly in an effort to exempt their own people and ideas from the impending threat of invalidation—have fetishized. As I compare the books held sacrosanct in Europe and the altars held sacrosanct in Africa and its diaspora, I leave it to the reader to assess the effects of my own ambiguous positionality—as both a child of Africa and a Western scholar.

Just as Black America is the locus classicus of ethnological Schadenfreude (Matory 2015b), assimilated European Jews in the nineteenth and early twentieth centuries may well be the locus classicus of ambivalence. Likewise, the great Afro-Atlantic capitals of western Cuba, Bahia, and the Guinea Coast are capitals of ambiguity, a most-famous example of which is syncretism. In the impoverished quarters of Brazil and Cuba, statues and lithographs of Roman Catholic saints may, to put it simply, represent Roman Catholic saints or African gods, depending upon the setting and the momentary disposition of the viewer. In these settings, the borders between self and other, masters and slaves, Black and White, foreigners and compatriots, gods and saints are as unclear as they are clear in the dominant and segregated Protestant North Atlantic. The joint lesson of these cases is that the most enduring fetishes of both assimilated central European Jews and the scions of the West African merchant-monarchs are fraught with ambivalence inspired by middling positions in a racially stratified Atlantic world. Strategic assimilation and disambiguation are perhaps the most compelling motives behind the rituals, jokes, and fetish making of these populations.

Hence, I will argue, apparently abstract European social theories are no more universal, eternal "truths" than African gods are. Moreover, both gods and social theories are conceptual and material constructions that speak most vividly and truthfully about the world when they acknowledge their own social origins. European social theories and Afro-Atlantic gods are equally born of their creators' social ambiguity and lopsided ambivalence.

Africa as Europe's X-Ray

But our measurements of the vast lands of the self are far too small or too narrow if we leave out the great kingdom of the unconscious, that true inner Africa.
—Jean Paul, *Selina oder über die Unsterblichkeit der Seele*

Both historical materialism and psychoanalysis follow a post-Enlightenment tradition of making black and brown people into exemplars of mental dispositions that Europeans, as "civilized" people, have overcome. These theories also follow another equally European and post-Enlightenment tradition—

that of looking more deeply into oneself and rediscovering a stereotypical Africa right there in one's own European soul. For Freud, this "inner Africa" was a raging sexual brute called the "id"—an entity cloaked in darkness by the veneer of Western civilization and uncovered through the study of Western neurotics, Western children, and, in its purest form, the brown or black "savage."[5] Europe's projection of its own "dark" heart onto Africa is, to my mind, the paradigm and pinnacle of all fetishism. Hegel and Marx endeavored to expel this darkness from Europe, while Freud vacillated between efforts to show, on the one hand, that assimilated Jews like him have repressed and risen above this darkness and, on the other, that this darkness inhabited civilized gentiles as much as civilized Jews. Thus, particularly in Freudian analyses of fetishism, Africans can play opposite rhetorical roles— sometimes as the antitype of civilized humanity and sometimes as the proto- types of a shared humanity. Yet both formulations are studiously ignorant of African self-understandings and aspirations, reducing Africans to rhetorical tropes rather than human beings.

The Berlin-based cultural and literary historian Hartmut Böhme ([2006] 2014) argues that fetishes are not new in European cultural history: they are both ancient and omnipresent. Ironically, his own critique of other Euro- peans embodies the very fetishism that he criticizes. Böhme defines a fetish as an emotionally charged symbol that replaces the real phenomenon it rep- resents, hides it, represses it, or makes it unidentifiable to the believer. For him, the fetish is a thing that appears to bear a power beyond human author- ship, a power that both threatens the author and believer with harm and embodies his or her hope of salvation from that harm.

I might offer the following example. Medieval European principalities fought wars to capture or to retain bone fragments, burial shrouds, and al- leged fragments of the Holy Cross, items that both commemorated the horrible deaths of the martyrs and promised mystical healing and even protection from horrible deaths. Among the demonstrably material powers of these relics was their ability to attract tens of thousands of pilgrims to the church that housed them and consumers to the nearby markets. Conversely, they also induced rival principalities to raid the relics' owners and, in order to reroute those profit-generating pilgrims, take the relics home.

Böhme adds that, in Europe, fetishism is not a thing of the past, even as many Europeans reassure themselves of their own evolved rationality and in- sightfulness by accusing others—non-European and European—of fetishism. For example, Böhme bids us to look at the monumental architecture built by Hitler and Stalin, which, in Böhme's view, differs little from so-called African fetishes in its power to conjure collective imaginations and relationships. In the same way, no more or less realistically than African worshippers, supposedly rational Europeans in capitalist society enact a form of fetishism by falsely imagining that the foods, fashion, and celluloid fantasies they consume will bring them love and respect.

Like William Pietz, Böhme claims no knowledge of African or African-inspired religions, but he does point out the ethnocentrism of Enlightenment and post-Enlightenment European thinkers' presumption that Europeans are categorically more rational and less fetishistic than Africans. He does so with some support from the French historian of religion and diplomat Charles de Brosses (1709–77), the originator of the term "fetishism" and the main touchstone of Marx's and other eighteenth- and nineteenth-century European philosophers' references to the concept. De Brosses argued that ancient Greek, ancient Egyptian, and contemporary West African religion shared a *common* belief in the magical powers of certain objects (Böhme 2014: 156–59, 245).

Nonetheless, like the majority of critics of fetishism, Böhme reserves the prototypically African-coded term "fetishism" for phenomena he regards as disproportionate, reality-distorting, injurious, and, in a word, monstrous— such as the causes of overeating and anorexia, excessive devotion to fashion, phallocentric sexism in film, the nail fetishes employed by German civilians during World War I to fortify the national army ([2006] 2014: 200), and authoritarian architecture. Despite his occasional circumspection, Böhme's refrain that these monstrous phenomena constitute "the Africa in us" actually amplifies the anti-African prejudice at the heart of the Enlightenment, historical materialism, and psychoanalysis, rather than second-guessing it (Böhme [2006] 2014: 272, also 7). The ambivalence at the heart of Böhme's twenty-first-century critique of the ethnocentrism of Marx's fetish concept actually echoes the deep ambivalence of Marx and Freud about Africa. In fact, Marx and Freud, like African priests, have themselves created Janus-like fetishes that mediate between the roles of oppressor and oppressed. But Böhme, like Pietz before him, details only the European side in the Afro-European dialogue about the relationship between the world's explicit realities and its hidden ones.

The Agency of Things

In both Marx's historical materialism and Freud's psychoanalysis, physical things are the classical referents of the term "fetish," with the implication that the thing is merely a mistaken vehicle for a social relationship that a reasonable or mentally healthy person understands is really immaterial. Similarly, the prestige of theory rests on the premise that it transcends particular peoples, historical moments, actions and things. Yet, as Böhme ([2006] 2014) points out, even the most supposedly abstract theoretical ideas are made up of mental images of things. In a similar abstraction, the practitioners of kink tend to focus their definitions of the fetish on idiosyncratic *practices*, despite the fact that those practices almost always rely on an elaborately symbolic and affectively charged array of paraphernalia. It is the foremost premise of the present argument that ideas, actions, and things all depend on each other in the conduct of social life. What are the implications of the thingliness, or materiality, of the fetish?

The networked nature of people, ideas, and things is the focus of a rich scholarly literature, but we must avoid the risk of exaggerating the agency of things, as things are never self-sufficient in their meaning. Like other things that matter to people, a fetish depends on an infrastructure, or network, of people, animals, plants, places, and other things, for its existence and its functioning. For example, a piano is made of metal and wood, is made by metal- and wood-workers, and needs a building to support its weight and protect it from moisture and rapid fluctuations of temperature. Moreover, its importance in people's social and emotional lives depends on people's continuing to tune it, play it, gather around it, listen to it, and interpret its sounds based upon familiarity with a tradition of other people's having engaged in similar conduct and, often, upon the recollection of specific performers, occasions, and sounds associated with and triggered by that particular piano. In sum, like other things, the fetish depends on and is of a piece with a network of people, animals, plants, idea-images, sacred words, conventions, rituals, and techniques that actively sustains it.

In this analysis of the role of things (such as Eshu's hat and his òg̣ọ) in the making of human plans, identities, relationships, and hierarchies, I am partly inspired by Bruno Latour and his actor-network theory (e.g., Latour 2010; also Hodder 2012). In scientific research as in worship, the very reality of the things we investigate or worship depends on a network of instruments, dreams, people, social relationships, and rules. The things we work with in science, worship, and other activities do not necessarily possess volition. However, Latour argues that their shape, materials, and need for maintenance and adjustment inextricably shape how their users see the world, as well as how they think and act.

Yorùbá-Atlantic conceptions of agency both contradict and amplify Latour's sense of what things do in the world. For example, one implication of Yorùbá-Atlantic practice for actor-network theory is that no single fetishized thing can be looked at in isolation (see also Hodder 2012). Specifically, the fetishization of a thing is always of a piece with a network of things from which or to which value has been shifted and with a set of rival populations competing to dictate the terms of value relations among those things. Hence, to refer to a single physical item as a fetish is also to refer to the network of other items, people, and relationships that constitutes its field of power. In this discussion, I will at times refer to the part of a fetish that stands for the whole and, at other times, to the whole that stands for the part.

A school of art history allied to actor-network theory (e.g., Freedberg 1989; Gell 1998; Morgan 2005; Belting 1994) also emphasizes the power of material things—namely, artistic images and configurations of images—to compel certain ways of thinking, seeing, and feeling, and it documents the long history of "premodern" Europeans' recognition of the intrinsic power of sacred paintings and statues to do so. Despite centuries of Protestant icono-clasm, Latour and most of these other scholars doubt that so-called modern Europeans have really overcome the compelling power of material images and things. Rather, the modern iconoclast's othering denunciation of Afri-cans and of other ostensible nonmoderns is but a self-deception concealing an alternative range of falsely empowered modern European fetishes, rang-ing from modern art and consumer goods to monumental architecture and laboratory equipment.

While these insights are fundamental to the following analysis, I stop short of the recently fashionable abandonment of the idea of the "symbol" and of the Saussurean premise that signs are—more often than not and in more ways than not—arbitrary. Of course, there are onomatopoeias, and words are shaped by a nonarbitrary etymology and by meaningfully struc-tured patterns of inflection. However, it is virtually impossible to locate the exact counterpart of a word and category from one language in another lan-guage. And a referent recognized in one language may not be recognized as a reality in another language. Such incommensurability between semiotic codes and between perspectives is the fundamental condition behind the phenomena that I call "fetishes." A single material thing can also sustain more than one meaning or use, just as two different material things can be subjected to the same meaning or use. Latour and Hodder are wise to remind us of the networked nature of agency, and Böhme correctly highlights the dependency of thought on references to material things. However, as imagi-native animals, people can project a virtually infinite array of ideas and orga-nize an extraordinary array of collective activities around any given material thing, The extraordinary affective power of the fetish—and of the theorizing conducted in its name—arises from the contrary meanings that participants in a single cultural dialogue attribute to the fetish and the contrary social projects that they use it to endorse.

Ultimately, I ask in this book, what kind of rhetorical sign is the so-called fetish? European theorists have long presupposed their own asymmetrical privilege to apply this term to other people's highly cathected things and their own invulnerability to the accusation of fetishism. Yet the greatest lessons of this rhetorical sign may lie in its potential to reveal the social conditions of the intercultural dialogue that produced the so-called fetish. In this intercultural dialogue, I highlight what those who are normally accused of fetishism have to say back to our accusers. This talking back is in the very nature of the fetish, and a close examination of the contrary projections of meaning, affect, and power onto material things illuminates the contrasting positionalities and the rival social projects advocated by the interlocutors. This is not to minimize the affecting power of things but to highlight—as the Afro-Atlantic priests tend to do—the dependency of that power on continual human effort, cooperation, and rivalry.

The Priests Talk Back to Marx and Freud

The post-fifteenth-century Atlantic perimeter is not just a trade system but a geographically and materially coded repertoire of the self (Roach 1996). Hegel, Marx, and Freud are not the only ones who looked to the far shores of the Atlantic and found touchstones for their own respective self-definitions. Post-Enlightenment Europeans might favor the idea of Africa as a distant ancestor to or antithesis of themselves, but a temple of the African-inspired Candomblé religion—a product of the Atlantic slave trade and of Brazil's ongoing interaction with the Guinea Coast—sits at the heart of the fashionable Kreuzberg neighborhood of Berlin, Germany's and Europe's reunified capital. And the chief priest of the Ilê Obá Silekê temple, Babá Murah, has as much to say about Germany as Hegel, Marx, and Freud had to say about Africa. But his knowledge of Germany is considerably more empirical.

Babá Murah likes Berlin, but he finds his work there exhausting. One hard part of returning from his rare vacations is facing the constancy of work—cleaning and maintaining the temple facility—and the difficulty of continually switching back and forth between the semipossessed state required to perform divination and the fully conscious state required to do business in Berlin and deal with life's quotidian problems there. The hardest aspect of living in Germany, though, is the spiritual environment, which he calls "heavy" (*pesado*). "So many people—innocents and people who did not even know how they died—have died here [during wars]," he says, adding, "The whole of Berlin was destroyed." He likes Berlin, but every time he moves into a new apartment or place of business, one has to "clean, clean, and clean, because so many bad spirits [*espíritus ruins*] are there." Until he removed it, there was even a swastika, the word for which Babá Murah did not know, on the wall of his current apartment. And you have to keep cleaning, he says, because those spirits come back. Babá Murah says that his mission here is to "light a candle, giving light to these spirits."

But even that is difficult because "here, [people] don't have time; they have appointments (aquí, eles não têm tempo; têm hora [lit., they have "hour"])." "People make an appointment for a three o'clock consultation—they're always making appointments—and they have to be gone by five." They do not have or make the time fully to absorb the message of the *orixás* and then perform the necessary rituals. The slow rhythm of healing and harmonization with the Other world is as quintessential to *orixá*-worship as quick reply, production, and turnover are to late capitalism in Germany. In quotidian Berlin, as Marx, too, understood, the hour is the unit of value production. By contrast, in the temple, the chief time units are the annual calendar and the passage from one generation to the next.

It is for this reason and others that Babá Murah says he is not German and never will be. However, when he returns to Brazil, he also feels like a foreigner there. Not only do Brazilians identify something German in his manner of acting and speaking, but he himself sees things that are happening in Brazil and must ask himself, "What is this?!" Babá Murah cannot deny that Germany has become part of his life and his temple a Berlin landmark. He has been transformed by his role as an intermediary among multiple worlds. But, in his discomfort, he reveals the competing values of those worlds and, thus, the structure and substance of the fetish. The real-world Brazilian, Cuban, Haitian, and Nigerian worshippers of the Afro-Atlantic gods are as complex and ambivalent as any European social theorist. The difference is that few of the priests will construct the foreign Other as the antithesis of their ideal selves. Rather, it is the interaction with the Other that, quite normatively, makes them who they are. Just as the Abrahamic religions profess the exclusion of other religions, the Enlightenment and its scions have professed a relationship of oppositeness and antagonism to the Afro-Atlantic religions. Yet, when we most fervently declare ourselves the opposite of something, that thing becomes firmly embedded in our essence and consciousness. This book is a prolonged reflection on the Afro-German conversation at the foundation of fetish theory, a conversation incomplete without the input of the long marginalized priests and gods of the Black Atlantic. Babá Murah has brought them directly to the capital of German politics, philosophy, and ambivalence about the German people's role in Europe and the world.

My aim is to extend this dialogue and refine our social hermeneutics by giving full voice to the African side of this dialogue. I will present actual Afro-Atlantic priestly voices, communal rituals, and spirited things about which

Marx and Freud so freely and loosely speculated, as well as my own com-parative observations of the half-dozen Afro-Atlantic religious traditions on which I have now conducted thirty-six years of participant observation. I specialize in the study of what Robert Farris Thompson calls the "Yoruba-Atlantic" religions—West African Yorùbá religion, Brazilian Candomblé Quêto-Nagô, and Cuban Santería/Ocha, and I also have considerable experi-ence among the Fòn-Atlantic traditions of Brazilian Candomblé Jeje, Haitian Vodou, and Beninese *vodun*-worship, as well as some experience in the Kongo-Atlantic tradition of Cuban Palo, the Congolese (formerly Zaïrean) veneration of the *nkisi* gods, and the Cross River–inspired tradition of Cuban Abakuá.

Within these traditions, most of my friends and mentors have been priests of spirit possession, who, at the height of ritual, lose consciousness and turn into gods, moved by a consciousness foreign to the medium's own. Other priests within the Yorùbá-Atlantic traditions, known as *babaláwo* in West Africa and *babalaos* in Cuba, both priests of the Ifá oracle, transact with the Other world exclusively through conscious divination—that is, the casting of palm nuts and other consecrated implements whose numerical permutations cor-respond to extensive and somewhat standardized information about the supplicant's problem and its solution. Within these traditions, I belong to a category of uninitiated guests who are normally denied access to the most sa-cred spaces and information. However, thirty-six years of friendship and my own gifts of sacred information and goods from distant Afro-Atlantic locales have afforded me a degree of access unusual for a noninitiate.

The priests I have befriended during these decades reside on multiple continents. Many of them are highly cosmopolitan, living and working at the intersection of Western and African populations and lifeways. For exam-ple, Babá Murah has lived in Berlin for decades. Ìyá Òṣun Òṣogbo, Adedoyin Talabi Faniyi, was reared by a white Austrian refugee from post–World War II Europe. Another of my mentors is Marie Maude Evans, a Manbo Asogwe—that is, a priestess of the highest possible rank in the Vodou religion of southern Haiti. Residing in both Boston and Jacmel, Haiti, Manmi Maude—*Manmi* being the title of respect that is her due—is not only a Haitian Vodou priestess but also a Western-trained mental-health care professional. The Haitian Revolution and lore about the role of African "fetishism" in it appear to have played a central role in Hegel's early nineteenth-century thinking about German politics and history (Buck-Morss 2000), and the US occupa-tion of Haiti (1914–32) began as an effort to end Germany's lively commercial interaction with that island nation (Jean-Daniel Lafontant, in Matory 2015d). Oggún Fumi, a Santería/Ocha priestess from Santiago de Cuba, is knowledge-able about Marxism-Leninism. Thus, like the theories of Hegel, Marx, and Freud, the Afro-Atlantic gods are themselves indebted in surprising ways to

an old Afro-Germanic dialogue. In the orbit of other very current political ideologies, two of my main *santero* mentors in the United States—Babá Esteban
"Steve" Quintana and the *oriaté* diviner I call Joe Alarcón—are both proud Re-
publicans. And David Font-Navarrete is not only a Santería/Ocha priest but also
an ethnomusicologist and writing instructor at Duke University. His priestly
networks bridge Miami, New York, Havana, Mexico City, and Durham.

Hence, these priests and friends do not represent a frozen, homogeneous
"ethnographic present." While they share certain habits of speech and ritual
action that suggest some consistency in their thinking across space and over
time, I do not suppose that all of these priests agree about everything or that
what any given priest tells me is what he or she believes in every situation,
has always believed, or will always believe. Rather, at any given moment, a
priestly interlocutor is engaging his or her situation—including my questions and challenges—with a subset of the available precedents and variants
on a subset of the principles previously articulated or heard in his or her
sacred community. One must suppose that these engagements are partly
strategic, which is also what I suppose about the writings of Hegel, Marx,
Freud, and other European social theorists. Far from invalidating the ideas of
either African priests or European social theorists, an awareness of the situational and strategic nature of their statements helps us to understand those
statements better and to apply them more thoughtfully to the comparative
project.

What I record here is an ever-unfolding debate about value and ontology,
a debate shaped by cross-cultural intercourse, interreligious rivalry, competing material interests, and social hierarchy. The lives and the sacred traditions
of these priests fortify the case that understanding the idea of the fetish demands particular attention to the lived realities of not only West African but
also central European history and society, as well as the overlaps between
them. In this account, I have done my best to represent the opinions of my
friends faithfully. I am, of course, the ultimate editor of the years-long dialogues
that are condensed and paraphrased here, and I can claim no objectivity for
my selections. However, Manmi Maude has read all of the passages concerning her or her temple, and I have carefully revised these passages according
to her wishes. And a representative of Babá Murah has read all of the passages
about him, translated them to him, and communicated his revisions through
that representative. And I have incorporated them all, as well as David Font-
Navarette's revision of his own contributions. However, I am responsible for
any misunderstanding or misinterpretation appearing between these covers.

Each of the manifest gods and spirited things I have known in the Afro-
Atlantic religions might usefully be analyzed as fetishes. Of course, I refer to
these beings as "fetishes" not in the sense intended by Hegel, Marx, Freud,

and Böhme—as objects onto which people have *falsely* projected value, agency, or authenticity that *truly* belongs *elsewhere*. Rather, by "fetish," I mean to say that they are beings constructed and materially activated by humans, as all gods and spirited things are, that their value and agency result from a displacement of value and agency from other things or people, and that their legitimacy as concentrated repositories of value and agency is contested by the partisans of rival fetishes. In this sense, Afro-Atlantic gods and spirited things resemble multinational corporations, universities, nation-states, homelands, homes, and social theories. All of these institutions are networks of material things, plants, animals, and people animated by ideas asserted in the context of rival ideas about the value of and relationships among beings and things.

For example, consider the five US Supreme Court judges who, in *Citizens United v. Federal Election Commission* (2010), decided that corporations have the right to "freedom of speech," as if they were people. No less than people who believe that a river is an *orixá* and that a possession priest or cowrie-filled pot can become one, these judges experience the world through the sort of sign that I call a "fetish." In 2017 the parliament of New Zealand and, under its inspiration, a state high court in India conferred personhood upon certain rivers, making harms done to them punishable under the same terms as harm to people.[6] That such matters need to be addressed by legislatures and courts of law illustrates what is for me a defining feature of the fetish. What makes a fetish a fetish is not its falsity but the context of intercultural, interclass, intergender, or interpersonal controversy and contestation that leads some people to call the thing a fetish (in Hegel's, Marx's, or Freud's sense), while other people call it a true god, a true spirit, a true repository of value or agency, or an authentic metonym of some real force that matters.

Every fetish requires its participants to accept an order of reality and a shared conception of the desiderata made possible by it, as well as the legitimate means to pursue those desiderata, the problems that may result from ignoring this order of reality, and the possible means of resolving those problems. These collective convictions about the fetishized thing also entail a hierarchy of people competent to manage the social and material phenomena emanating from the spirited thing or network. Inattention to this hierarchy can forestall success or actively cause problems. Hence, a fetish is neither an idyll nor an inherent evil. The desiderata recognized and recommended by the fetish may or may not be fulfilled, and the fetish makes real a set of problems that may or may not be resolved. The fetish embodies and gives force to its makers' desires and goals at a specific time, place, and intersection of class interests, and it assembles communities not only around the pursuit of these desiderata and goals but also around opposition to their pursuit. There-

fore, the most reliable dividend of the fetish is not happiness but community and rivalry between communities. Such communities are therefore
always tension-filled.

I explore the hypothesis that, like the material things that psychoanalysts
call fetishes, both African gods and European social theories embody the
revolutionary's, the patient's, or the worshipper's ambivalence—his or her
simultaneous pursuit of relief from victimhood and identification with the
victimizer. Concealed within Marx's and Freud's resistance to the oppression
of people like them is also a subliminal desire to become the oppressor. It
is always difficult for the long-term oppressed *not* to identify with their oppressors, *not* to wish for what the oppressor has, and, as Fanon ([1963] 1971)
points out, *not* imitate and collaborate with the former oppressor. It is also
difficult for the oppressor *not* to identify with the oppressed, *not* to wonder
how the oppressed feel, *not* to wonder if the oppressed will turn the tables on
the oppressor, and, under controlled circumstances, *not* to don the persona
of the oppressed. In the context of an analysis of zombies and BDSM, this
phenomenon will be a major theme of *Zombies and Black Leather* (Matory in
preparation).

The only difference between the realness of Afro-Atlantic gods and that
of US American corporations (or, for that matter, universities, nation-states,
homelands, homes, and social theories) is that one can actually touch these
gods. And I have done so on many occasions. I have talked to them at festivals
and spiritual masses. And when they are nearby I sometimes feel a shiver or
a lump in my throat. These physical sensations might well have other plausible explanations, but there is, in the end, no neutral, objective explanation
of human experience that supersedes the perceiver's supraempirical biases
or her culturally and historically specific assumptions about what is valuable, about what or who is in charge of our lives, and about who owes what
to whom.

The gods of whom I speak are assembled, constructed, constituted, empowered, deposited, and interpreted in their worshippers and in their altars
by groups of social and ritual experts. These gods then become the guarantors
of communities and switching stations of the mutual obligations that people
arrange among themselves and between themselves and the universe. Thus,
the gods become powerful sources of orientation and control over the world
as people experience it. To observe that corporations do the same (through
papers of incorporation, contracts, logos, and theme songs) and that nation-
states do the same (through constitutions, treaties, flags, and anthems) is not,
for me, a criticism of corporations or nation-states. It is merely an ontological observation. But an element of their ontology as fetishes is that some
people deny their validity.

My deconstruction of Marx's historical materialism and of Freud's psychoanalysis may look like such a denial. In fact, my deconstruction is a case of dramatic irony and of ambivalence. I internalize their hermeneutics even as I remove Marx and Freud from the pedestals on which exponents of theory typically place them. This removal is necessary because those pedestals are the "negro," the "savage," and our religions, which are forced to sit in the mud beneath Marx and Freud in order to make historical materialism and psychoanalysis look as though they have grown out of purely intellectual air.

In the end, though, the worshippers of the Afro-Atlantic gods are no more right or wrong than other people are about their equally useful but human-made reifications, such as the mind, charisma, conscience, or abstractly quantifiable time (that is, the kind that "waits for no man"). They are no more right or wrong than the people who believe in individuality, corporations, races, cultures, society, revolution, discourse, or habitus. And they are obviously nor more wrong than believers in Marx's labor theory of value or in the inevitability of "class struggle" as the engine of history. I will also argue that they are no more wrong than those who would follow Freud in fetishizing the white penis as an embodiment of citizenship or follow Marx in constructing a "negro slave" as a volitionless antitype of the rights-bearing white worker. Those who successfully build communities through the enactment of these central European constructions and those who successfully build communities through the worship of Afro-Atlantic gods simply create and experience the world through different fetishes. Sometimes, central Europeans and the worshippers of Afro-Atlantic gods fetishize the same material things—such as black bodies—from different social positions, making our bodies the most enduring and powerful of fetishes.

Though Hegel and his scions Marx and Freud anchored the likes of Babá Murah and his gods at the starting line of human consciousness and history, the *orixás* and the *orichas* now dance on Hegel's doorstep, in the Berlin temple of Babá Murah. I will argue that they bring full circle a circum-Atlantic historical and intellectual dialectic no less evident in Afro-Latin American altars and gods than in Hegel's master-slave dialectic.

Please note that I have chosen not to follow the usual English orthographic convention of capitalizing terms like "Labor Theory of Value" and "Master-Slave Dialectic" and have eschewed the usual hyphen in terms like "use-value," as such conventions imply the scriptural nature of Hegel's and Marx's writings and, much like the capitalization of "God," the uniqueness, preeminence, and personification of the forces that these terms reify. And my aim is to illuminate, rather than reproduce or even dismiss, these instances of fetishization.

On the Material Conditions of Theory

As a child of the European Enlightenment, I am both heir and victim to the premise that European "thinkers" create abstract, disembodied, and historically transcendent ideas, in contrast to Africans' ostensibly illogical gestures and bedazzled enthrallment to things. Since the Enlightenment, self-described white people have relied on the disparagement of Africans' sacred material things as proof of their own European dignity and as a fulcrum for the valorization of their own material things, ideas, and priorities. Yet, as a child of Africa, I am aware that African consecrated things embody ideas to the same degree that European social theories do. From this point of view, I can also see that European theories endorse contestable social priorities and dwell in things as much as African gods do. Hence, this book is as much about the entanglement of European ideas in material things and social relationships as it is about the entanglement of African sacred objects and social relationships in ideas.

For example, the "visual culture" (Morgan 2005) and the physical things in the environments of European theorists are no less important to understanding their cognition than anyone else's. Marx wrote about factories in the abstract. However, for him, the factory managed by his friend and benefactor, Friedrich Engels, was no mere abstraction. It was an assemblage of physical things entangled in a network of rules, schedules, supply chains, cash flows, commutes by workers and capitalists, buyers, and distributors. Marx's distillation of what mattered in the actor-network (Latour 2005) of industrial capitalism was part of a debate in which Marx could surely appreciate why the labor theory of value is not the only nondelusional way to explain capitalist exchange. Both Marx's millennial dream of prosperous self-employment for the white worker and the rented piano in his living room spoke volumes about his own bourgeois aspirations, especially when considered against the backdrop of his own chronic poverty. Marx's network of ideas, things, and conditions suggests as great a commitment to enjoying the material comforts of the bourgeoisie as to overthrowing bourgeois rule.

Until the day he died of cancer, it may not have dawned upon Freud that his twenty to thirty cigars a day were smoking him (see also Latour 2010: 55), but his biographers and the curators of his homes-turned-museums reveal an actor-network empire rich not only in ideas and books but also in intaglio rings, portable anthropomorphic antiquities, a rug-laden couch, an upright chair from which Freud invisibly listened to his supine patients, scores of photographic portraits from which (apparently by design) the cigar is seldom missing, and a trove of clubhouse rules for the day-to-day management of the psychoanalytical brotherhood. The artifactories of Marx's and Freud's ideas and social relationships beg for an analysis, for which I offer some initial hypotheses here.

I will apply to European social theory the same questions that we Western scholars have long been accustomed to asking of African and other non-Western ways of thinking: How do the biographies, material interests, and material possessions of Marx and Freud help us to understand how they cognized and created their worlds? How do the perspectives of these influential central European social theorists correspond to their social positions and serve to enhance their social rank? I am no advocate of the vulgar Marxist position that people's social conditions inexorably determine their modes of thought. Rather, I hypothesize that, within any given cultural, social, and historical setting, any given symbolic or rhetorical representation of the world has the potential to honor and enrich some classes of people over others and that the representational choices that people make have an elective affinity (Weber [1904–5] 1958) with their social status in that setting. Bourdieu ([1984] 1988) calls this phenomenon the "struggle for classification."

It may be clear to many North American scholars that Marx and Freud help us to understand people and society better, but how might a recognition of these authors' unique social positionality amplify the lessons of historical materialism and psychoanalysis? Conversely, what blind spots do Marx's and Freud's latter-day followers perpetuate when they misrepresent the understandings and assertions of such European social theorists as transcendent, omniscient, panoramic, and socially neutral distillations of the truth about all societies, all social statuses, and all historical periods? My aim is to connect this central European biographical and historical archaeology of the "problem of the fetish" (Pietz 1985, 1987, 1988) with a comparative ethnography of the ongoing production, animation, and use of African- and African-diaspora spirited things—especially human-made gods—of the sort to which the term "fetish" has been applied since the run-up to the Enlightenment.

What Marx and Freud called "fetishism" is the displacement of agency and value from the site of its supposedly *real* production or existence onto something else. The direction attributed to this ostensibly wrongful displacement is a stipulation about which human relationships are more important than others and about where the attribution of agency and value should have stayed, with implications for what constitutes the proper conduct of human relationships, both of which are matters of opinion. Therefore, far from proving the users of the term right, the use of the term "fetish" reveals a social struggle over which relationships matter and how they should be conducted. Circum-Atlantic society in the nineteenth and twentieth centuries, when Marx and Freud were propounding their theories, was indeed a setting of debate among diverse parties with different stakes in the complex set of relationships fueled by capitalism, empire, and racism. Much of that debate occurred through the production, exchange, and use of things. Among the foremost topics of this circum-Atlantic debate were the relative rights of European industrial workers and enslaved Africans, men and women, gentiles and Jews in the nation-state. Strange as it may seem, Africans and our animated things became major foci of European debates about the value of things and the agency of people in Europe. This book offers an Africanist, materialist, and psychoanalytical perspective on this European strangeness.

In the spirit of Dipesh Chakrabarty's project to "provincialize Europe" (2000), we would do well to remind ourselves that the European writings that we read after the fact as abstract theory emerged not from pure intellectual air or timeless truth but from cultural conventions, material conditions, biographical circumstances, and political rivalries. The democratizing ideological and military battles in which Europeans have long engaged over the internal constitution of their nation-states are often treated as though they took place in isolation from the enslavement, extermination, and displacement of Native Americans and Africans. Actions of the sort taken for granted in extra-European venues—such as the British Empire's torture and murder of Kikuyu people in the gulags of colonial Kenya and the German Empire's attempted extermination of the Hereros—tend to be described as uniquely shocking when they take place within Europe. Moreover, some of the discourses at the foundations of white men's democratizing aspirations have taken black, brown, and female subordination as a fait accompli, implicit in such tropes as "hysteria," which constructs women as the locus classicus of insanity, and George H. W. Bush's much-repeated phrase "voodoo economics," which casts Black people as exemplars of magical and demonstrably wrong thinking and acting. Rather than privileging Europe's social critics as the fount of definitive values and objective knowledge, I cast an Afro-Atlantic eye on Europe that recognizes our shared humanity and our shared experience of marginalization and oppression.

Yet, provincializing Europe also requires me to provincialize myself. Born in the US during the 1960s and the son of a psychologist, I am also a native to the intellectual traditions of psychoanalysis. As a PhD student during the 1980s, I could not but absorb the Marxian "hermeneutics of suspicion" (Ricoeur 1973) that dominated US American critical theory during that era and continues to have a powerful impact on scholarly thought in the humanities and the humanistic social sciences. Yet, until 2014, when I spent my year in Berlin, my knowledge of the geography, architecture, economy, languages, ethnic identities, and conceptions of social inequality in Germanic Europe had been relatively abstract and heavily distorted by white American propaganda about western European "civilization" as the homeland of monolithic, superhuman perfection, rather than a crossroads of a very human diversity, complexity, and perplexity.

I had previously traveled in Western Europe, including Austria, but on this occasion I rediscovered Germany, the Netherlands, and Sweden specifically through a network of scholars interested in Africa and Latin America and with the intent to understand the roots of much influential European social theory in the taken-for-granted dialogue between Europe and the Black Atlantic. So my perspective on European social theory and its people is admittedly—and, I hope, profitably—Yorùbá-, Fòn-, and Kongo-centered.

Conclusion

I am not under the illusion that this book will easily move the true believers of historical materialism or psychoanalysis; in fact, it will surely rile them (or *you*, as the case may be). My aim here is not to provide a comprehensive account of the philosophical influences on Marx and Freud or to document the full and internally contradictory breadth of the movements that grew out of their work. Each of these traditions comprises a thicket of debates about what the founding father really meant, and there is no summary of anything they said that will not elicit a heated rejoinder about how much more subtle or complicated the truth of the scripture is. There is no reducing Marx or Freud to a single summary, much less a single explanation. Indeed, the highly cathected nature of debate among Marxists and Freudians about what the master *really* meant—and the attachment of these debates to divergent opinions about the right way to conduct our lives—are impeccable illustrations of fetishism. The best I can hope is that the reader will not allow debates over minutiae—however dear they may be to the partisan of one interpretive tradition or another—to obscure the main argument of parts I and II of the book or the foundation of the intercultural anthropology that follows: Marx and Freud were human beings exemplifying the same political or psychological impulses that they so insightfully identified in others; that those same impulses blinded them to some truths about themselves and others; and that the people they stigmatized similarly furnish useful insights into the impulses of Marx and Freud.

The multisited historical ethnography that I present and the numerous spirited things, or fetishes, that it descriptively and photographically documents suggest that the makers of these embodied spirits would return the criticism that European theory has thrown at them. With reference to a set of manufactured things and human-constructed gods from Nigeria, Benin, the Democratic Republic of Congo, Brazil, Cuba, Haiti, and the United States, I illustrate an Afro-Atlantic logic of the relationship among the cosmos, human beings, goods, and gods that belies the stereotypes propagated by the usual European suppositions about the African fetish and denaturalizes the ostensible truths that European social theorists have constructed as true in contrast to it. I also offer some thoughts about the theory-articulating role of things—such as factories, coats, pianos, cigars, rings, Greco-Roman statues, upright chairs, and couches—in the praxis of Marx and Freud. Here I turn the tables on European theory and highlight what is peculiar, material, biographical, perspectival, and religiously mist-enveloped in these ostensibly crystalline and universalist social theories.

At the same time, I offer evidence for the hypothesis that the altars of the Afro-Atlantic religions—and the numerous commodities they contain—reflect the genesis of these religions, as well, in the intercultural commercial zone of the Guinea Coast, where Portuguese and Dutch merchants inaugurated the concept of the fetish as we know it today. Guinea-Coast religions and their diasporic counterparts embody and transform the interests of sixteenth- and seventeenth-century Guinea Coast merchant-monarchs and priests, offering a social and commercial response to Atlantic capitalism just as historically specific, class specific, and materially interested as the social theories of Marx and Freud. Marx, Freud, and the gods Black people make not only illuminate each other's conceptual premises but also share rhizomatic roots in the Atlantic exchange.

Part Summaries

Part I argues that Marx's labor theory of value is no more empirically demonstrable than the theories that it critiques and that it is just as socially positioned in the perspective it articulates. By comparison with the ostensible incompetence of the "negro slave" and the supposedly minimal worth of his or her product, Marx affirms the collective agency of all European wage workers, the value of their product, and, by proxy, Marx's own worthiness of enfranchisement despite his ethnicity and downward class mobility.

Part II describes how Freud's insecurities about his race and his sexual orientation shaped psychoanalysis and inspired divinations about the human personality that uncannily resemble underdeveloped versions of the Afro-Atlantic religions. This argument employs the shared insights of psychoanalysis and the Afro-Atlantic religions to highlight the ambivalent nature of the empowered things at the core of the social organizations constituted by both psychoanalysis and the Afro-Atlantic religions.

Part III discusses the conceptions of value and agency embodied in the human-made gods of the Afro-Atlantic religions and the class interests they encode—interests very different from but no less contextually reasonable than those advocated by Hegel, Marx, and Freud.

In the end, what makes the conversation among Marx, Freud, and the Afro-Atlantic priests so interesting is that each invests value and agency in material things—indeed, often the same things—and that their investment of contrasting degrees of value and contrasting types of agency in these things is precisely what makes those things powerful, enduring, and electric in their effects on the communities for which they are touchstones.

The argument of *The Fetish Revisited* might be summarized in four main points.

First, theory is not a disembodied, universal truth but a creature dialectically related to the social environment, material surroundings, and material interests of the theorists.

Second, the term "fetishism" is a useful way to show the competitive and strategic nature of meaning making in the construction of European social theories, Afro-Atlantic gods, and numerous other socially effective stipulations about where value lies and who owes what to whom.

Third, like the most powerful and spectacular of African "fetishes," the most powerful and spectacular European social theories embody not only the social ambiguity but also the political and emotional ambivalence of their creators. Clearly *subordinate* parties find in the fetish a reminder of their humiliation and a promise of power through identification with the dominant. Surprisingly, some clearly *dominant* parties find in the fetish both a reminder of their power and the desirable promise of relief from responsibility for that power (Matory in preparation). It is my hypothesis that socially ambiguous people—such as parvenus, middle classes, racially ambiguous people, ambitious or high-status members of subordinated races, and subordinated members of high-status races—have the greatest stake in contemplating and resolving the structural oppositions and conflicting values embedded in the fetish. Off-white whites like Marx and Freud and coastal African merchant-monarchs are prime exemplars of this phenomenon. These cases also help to explain the irony that one country—Germany—is the source of both cultural relativism and Europe's most radically chauvinist nationalism.

Fourth, in the making of theories and of gods, the assignment of value and agency to one party regularly entails the devaluation and the zombification of (that is, the denial of agency to) other parties. For this reason, populations that are vulnerable to oppression are often highly articulate in trumpeting the even-greater inferiority of populations that they can conceivably place below themselves in the social hierarchy.

THE FACTORY, THE COAT, THE PIANO, AND THE "NEGRO SLAVE"

On the Afro-Atlantic
Sources of Marx's Fetish

For Germany the *criticism of religion* has been largely completed;
and criticism of religion is the premise of all criticism.

—Marx, "A Contribution to the Critique
of Hegel's *Philosophy of Right*"

Like much of the Enlightenment, nineteenth-century German philosophy focused on the critique of religion (Karatani 203: 4). Although Marx declared the criticism of religion complete, he also demonstrates the irresistibility of its pull. Marx's *German Ideology* extended the critique of religion to the state and capital, while *Capital* reimagined capitalism as one great religion ([1867] 1990: 164–65). While most scholars interpret the religious language of Marx's own critique of capitalism as ironic, it is equally obvious to me that Marx remains in thrall of both biblical millennialism and a theologically coded struggle for personal worth and opportunity that pitted Protestants against Catholics and both against Jews. What united them all was their agreement to place African "fetishists" at the bottom of the scale of human worth.

Ever since the eighteenth century, enslaved Africans have been the *éminence noire* behind white protagonists' pursuit of theological progress, social reform, and political freedom in the Atlantic world. The enslaved African has been represented as the opposite of the normal historical agent—whether as the instrument or the antitype of that agent—in his dogged pursuit of personal integrity and freedom. Yet, because I am a descendant of enslaved Africans, what looks like background to these self-appointed European protagonists of world history looks to me like foreground.

There are many ways in which to imagine the protagonists of history and the desiderata to which they are entitled. While scholars like Hegel, Marx, and Freud are nowadays treated as "theorists" of society, they were also socially positioned actors striving to reposition themselves on the scale of human worth and to advance themselves in the pursuit of their own culture-specific goals. Although they possessed little knowledge of or intrinsic interest in Africa and its diaspora, their hopes for themselves in a changing European field of power emerged against the backdrop of European global imperialism, the increasingly unequal terms of Europe's commerce with Africa, and the paradigmatically awful fate imposed on Africans by the Atlantic slave trade. Hence, my own archaeology of the fetish concept focuses on the trope of Africa, or Guinea, in two of the most influential European theories about the nature of value, agency, and who owes what to whom—that is to say, therefore, about the proper order of society. Indeed, as a metonym of "modern" Europe's African antitype, the term "fetish" is diagnostic of a long-term collective dialogue between Europe and Africa about proper social order, making this archaeology a study in the intersubjective self making of European theorists and African priests.

The current study, like most sociocultural anthropology, is devoted to placing diverse worlds into dialogue and, through comparison, generating common, "etic" terms and principles that explain cross-cultural variation.

Those principles typically concern the patterns of covariation among diverse economic, political, religious, kinship, ecological, and technological practices. In sum, we endeavor to create the common terms of value-neutral comparison and of a mutually respectful and reciprocally enlightening conversation among the inhabitants of culturally divergent worlds.

By contrast, Marx and Freud amplified an ethnocentric tradition of nineteenth-century evolutionary ethnology that compares the West to the rest, making the rest into a metaphor for what the West has overcome through the achievement of "civilization," what it still needs to overcome, or, very occasionally, what it has regrettably lost and needs to recover in a greatly modified form. According to this evolutionist model, the rest is to the West as the past is to the present and future, as the child is to the adult, and even as the mentally ill person is to her or his mentally healthy counterpart.

Rather, my argument emphasizes the contemporaneity of the West and the rest, examines the material influence of these imagined worlds on each other, and endeavors to illuminate the previously obfuscated subjectivity of cultural Others. This study refuses the evolutionary ethnologists' relegation of Africa and Africans to the past, instead inviting the silenced to speak back. Yet, far more than the vast majority of my university colleagues, I refuse the ethnocentrism that places theory and theorists themselves beyond the scope of ethnographic analysis.

The Afro-Atlantic Context
of Historical Materialism

Marx was a mid-nineteenth-century lawyer who, as a second choice, pursued a career as a journalist and labor activist. In neither profession did he manage to earn enough to sustain his family or to fulfill the bourgeois aspirations to which his upbringing had accustomed him. It did not help that he lacked an academic appointment and yet spent much of his time writing on political economy. His greatest influence was posthumous, shaped by the uses that others could make of his millenarian language and model of history. He generated his most influential language and reasoning while he was, for political reasons, exiled in England—a land he had long admired from afar as a model of the sort of economic development and prosperity that was then yet to evolve fully in the German-speaking land of his birth.

Marx argued that capitalism structures people's actions, dispositions, and worldviews much as a religion does. His description of capitalism and narration of its dynamic history focuses on the tension between who is doing the work of industrial production and who is receiving the rewards of it, as well as the tension between how people see their collective activities and what is really, in Marx's view, happening underneath. In the context of his own financial discontent, he formulated a general argument about the historical sources of and reasons for the general discontent of the population he collectively reified as "the workers" and "the proletariat": a system of social compulsions in which the fundamental operators were no longer people but social constructions that he called "commodities" (objects manufactured expressly for the purpose of exchange) and "capital" (profits mobilized for the purpose of generating more profits).

Under capitalism, for Marx, the paradigmatic form of labor is the industrial labor of free, wage-earning factory workers. For Marx, the primary problem with this system is that the manner in which commodities are imagined justifies a maldistribution of the proceeds of labor, a maldistribution that favors the owners of capital, or the capitalist class, over the workers. Marx's intended contribution to early nineteenth-century political economy was a razor-sharp focus on the unfairness of reigning patterns in the distribution of profits from manufacture and on the history-making rivalry between wage workers (that is, the "proletariat") and wage payers (capitalists). For Marx, it is labor that generates all profit and is the foundation of all social organization. Therefore it is the laborers who deserve to reap all of its benefits.

Marx's binary classification of the actors under capitalism—capitalists and proletariat—appears to reflect his personal social experience, his hopes, and his fears. He minimized and even actively denied the contemporaneous existence, labor, subjectivity, and importance of a third class: the tens of millions of mainly African or African-descended enslaved people whose labor was integral to the process through which European and Euro-American capitalists, according to Marx himself, falsely imagined that their money was, by itself, giving birth to more money. Marx also imagined out of existence a range of other actors in this system, including the Native Americans whose land was appropriated for the founding of Marx's much-idealized United States of America, which he described as "virgin soil colonized by free immigrants" (Marx [1867] 1990: 931fn1), as well as the coastal African merchant-monarchs who, through trade and the ritual transformation of social relationships, also seem to have seen themselves as making cowrie-shell money give birth to more cowrie-shell money. (More on that subject in part III.)

The Afro-Atlantic priestly heirs to these sacred traditions have long been more successful at making and mobilizing the collective subjectivities that they prescribe than Marx was at creating or mobilizing a unified proletariat through his own preferred fiction—that is, that labor alone produces value and does so in proportion to its duration. Indeed, as the reader will see, Afro-Atlantic priests ritually make and install such collective subjectivities in people's heads, resulting in dramatic performances that the patients of these rituals typically swear are completely involuntary on their part.

Because they live in a world physically and socially connected to but imaginatively different from that of Marx, Afro-Atlantic priests do not typically cognize the social roles in production or profit making as "proletariat" versus "capitalists." Yet Afro-Atlantic priests far more effectively cognize a phenomenon common to the imagined worlds of both Europeans and Africans. Marx and most Marxists tend to explain *away* the ritual processes of collective value and subjectivity making that create, for example, races, nations, ethnic groups, and cults, even though these social units are much more consciously real to their participants than are the proletariat and the capitalist class. Typically, for classical Marxists, races, nations, ethnic groups, and cults are "superstructural" fictions concealing the *real* agents and operators of history. Yet the Marxist faith in unseen and often ineffective collective agents—proverbial "classes-in-themselves"—hardly seems more empirical than the subjectivities conjured by capitalists and African priests. Indeed, the Marxist prediction that the "working class" will ultimately recognize itself as a collective entity is of a piece with the equally false prediction that all religion is on the way to disappearing.

Like all prophecies, Marx's was less an uncanny premonition or scientific extrapolation than a recommendation about the ways people should act toward each other in the here and now. The limited efficacy of Marx's class ontology has always lain in the *hope* that it inspired, not in its descriptive or predictive accuracy. Marx's historical materialist prophecy was a quasi-religious element of Lenin's success in building the Soviet Union. In ritualized and forcible ways—and not as the historical inevitability predicted by Marx—Lenin and others successfully induced new forms of collective subjectivity in large swaths of Eastern Europe, China, and Southeast Asia for a period of about sixty years. Like all prescribed subjectivities, those forged by Lenin and Mao had their adversaries and contained much internal resistance. As Benedict Anderson ([1983] 1991) observed, the proletariat of socialist Europe and Southeast Asia always identified *more* with the ritually manufactured nation-state than with the international proletariat (see also Postone 1993: 13).

The socialist nation-states tended to eschew the highly effective capitalist-nationalist strategy of cementing racial solidarity between white capitalists and the white workers in the same nation-state through collective violence against a racial Other—domestically and in the nation's overseas colonies. However, the authoritarian governments in the Soviet bloc failed to erase xenophobia and racism, a fact made evident by the waves of racist and xenophobic violence unleashed after the fall of the Soviet Union. Since the late 1980s, many in the proletariat of the former East Germany and Eastern Europe have made sport of assaulting nonwhite visitors to their countries, and, under former KGB agent Vladimir Putin, Russia has become the global epicenter of white Christian nationalism. Though less violent, anti-African racism is popular and profound in postsocialist China, as well. The greatest evidence of the weakness of Marx's socialist ontology, though, is that the socialist actor-networks of which proletariat subjectivity was a linchpin have collapsed since 1989, while the actor-networks of the Afro-Atlantic religions continue to grow. The state-planned industrial economies that Marx imagined would reappropriate capitalist technology and liberate everyone by fairly distributing surplus production did not ultimately work. However, my main point is not that Marx was wrong but that the pretense that he was more right or more scientific than the people he calls fetishists lacks any empirical basis.

Marx wrote his history and critique of capitalism in the midst of a circum-Atlantic war over the fate of the enslaved African, whom he turned into a metaphor for the fate of the "wage slave." Of course, Marx was sympathetic to the "negro slave," but the first volume of *Capital* expressly employs the enslaved African American not as a human victim of capitalism or protagonist in its overthrow but as a "pedestal" ([1867] 1990: 925) for the display of *European* workers' suffering. That enslaved person could hardly take comfort in being the lens, rather than the target, of Marx's concern.

Moreover, against this backdrop, Marx's appropriation of African gods as the paradigmatic metaphor of the European foolishness at the root of European workers' suffering is difficult for me to regard as natural or innocent. Marx was critical of religion generally, but he embraced and amplified a gentile European tradition of singling African religion out for special contempt. I see an element of ethnological Schadenfreude in this tandem marginalization of the "negro slave" and singular put-down of African gods, since Marx was himself vulnerable to the sort of marginalization and contempt that he passed on to Africans. Not only Jewish, he was also downwardly mobile in class terms. He stood to gain by advances in the rights of other white workers, and, like the white settler colonists he celebrated, he stood to gain psychologically from the symbolic put-down of Black workers and economically from the marginalization of their agency and interests. Not-so-white whites like Marx and Freud had a special stake in putting Africans down: it clarified their own standing as whites entitled to the full benefits of European citizenship.

In anticipation of my argument's being misread, this is not to say that historical materialism is merely an automatic reflex of Marx's cultural, structural, and biographical background (nor is psychoanalysis of Freud's). It is to say that Marx's vocabulary is soaked in culture-specific assumptions indigenous to certain social positions within the nineteenth-century circum-Atlantic political economy. His use of Black people and our gods as the paradigmatic antitypes of human aspiration reflects one such social position and foreshadows a similar strategy adopted by Freud. Marx's, and later Freud's, amplification of white gentile tropes that had also been used to put down Jews cannot be taken for granted. It appears to be a strategic, even if possibly unconscious, choice.

William Pietz's "Problem of the Fetish"

In the 1980s, a then–graduate student in the humanities named William Pietz published three articles exploring the pre-Enlightenment roots of the fetish concept in post-Enlightenment Europe. Pietz ultimately traced the "problem of the fetish" back to the sixteenth- and seventeenth-century encounter between African and European traders on the Guinea Coast of western Africa. These traders, notably Portuguese Catholics (whose word *fetisso* is the root of "fetish") and Dutch Protestants, expressed the view that Africans were capricious in ascribing godly power to material things. Further, they mocked the Africans for attributing great value to objects that these Portuguese and Dutch critics represented as relatively worthless, such as beads and seashells.

Their readers' ignorance about Africa had its strategic uses. Over the course of the seventeenth century, Dutch Protestant merchants in particular—from Pieter de Marees to Willem Bosman—encrusted the term "fetish" with their own radical opposition to almost all material embodiments of the divine and with the premise that fetishism was the root cause of not only bad business dealings but also political despotism. In the writings of these merchants and of the social critics who later quoted them, the African fetish was thoroughly flexible in the forms of crime and foolishness that it was fit to exemplify. In a potentially infinite array of disagreements, it could be used by one European to cudgel another and, in equal measure, to legitimize the speaker and blacken, as it were, his rivals' reputation and rank. Protestants used it to cudgel Roman Catholics, and the merchant class used it to condemn aristocratic encumbrances on their upward mobility, such as tariffs and trade barriers. In this intra-European struggle, Africa became both hostage and proxy.

Frustration at defeat or disappointment in trade negotiations must have been a further phenomenological element of the "problem of the fetish." The social order articulated by African gods prevented European merchants from getting their way in competitive transactions with their African hosts. For example, the Europeans could not travel wherever they wanted in the African interior (Pietz 1988: 115n19), preventing them from taking over the West African hinterland (1988: 108). They could not buy whatever they wanted (1988: 110–11, 115) or trade with whom they wanted (1988: 115–16n21). African merchants reportedly kept "fetish"-backed promises to each other to the detriment of their commitments to their European trading partners (1988: 115n20). The Europeans rarely spoke African languages and, in their ignorance, behaved like children, calling their African counterparts every bad name they could think of—stupid, arbitrary, irrational, capricious, and ignorant of natural causation—when those trading partners socially engineered their own domination of the terms of trade in the markets of the sixteenth- and seventeenth-century coast (consider also Thornton 1992). Despite the apparently greater technological efficiency and causal efficacy of European weapons, African "fetishes" conferred market advantages upon the African merchants and monarchs such that, for centuries, they held European merchants and would-be colonialists in check.

For all of their faith in the rationality of their own market mechanisms, European mercantilists have never hesitated to hamstring their competitors through arbitrary regulations and monopolies, or to destroy their own productive resources and the entire environment in the pursuit of short-term profit. Nor has the great "rationality" of Calvinist-inspired capitalism prevented the devastating effects of boom-and-bust cycles and continual downward pressure on the wages and well-being of productive workers. Hence the "problem of the fetish" is not an ethnographic observation about Afro-Atlantic gods but a concept in contrast to which European merchant-adventurers—along with the Christian priests who accompanied them—projected European foolishness onto Africans and articulated the socially positioned frustrations of a specific class of Europeans with their savvy African trading partners and with their European rulers and rivals.

The Dutch merchant Willem Bosman wrote his own influential account of Guinea's "fetish problem" after thirteen years on the coast. He was called home in 1701, when his supervisor was dismissed for malfeasance. Bosman's 1702 report was first published in Dutch in 1703 and then translated into French and English in 1705, as well as German in 1706. In its day, it was the most influential among the dozens of published European accounts about the Guinea Coast, and it was frequently plagiarized. His account of the "fetish problem" was read by Linnaeus, Adam Smith, David Hume, E. B. Tylor, Voltaire, Charles de Brosses, Isaac Newton, John Locke, Pierre Bayle, and Edward Gibbon. In this way the culturally biased and class-interested ideas of frustrated Protestant merchants who did not speak the languages of their African trading partners offered up a major rhetorical foundation of the Enlightenment—that is, the African and his "fetishes" as the antitypes of Europe's proper future—and ultimately influenced Marx himself.

I will argue that the idea-bearing material forms of the West African and West African–inspired orishas and voduns arose from the same coastal West African mercantile encounter as the Enlightenment "problem of the fetish" and have been shaped deeply by the interests of sixteenth- and seventeenth-century West African merchants and merchant-monarchs, who created empowering, noncausal social relationships using objects that European merchants and writers—in their own ignorance and ethnological Schadenfreude—dismissed as trivial. Perhaps the most obvious sign of the conjoint genesis of the European "problem of the fetish" and the Yorùbá-

Atlantic religions is the preoccupation in both with beads. The Dutch and Portuguese merchant-adventurers on the Guinea Coast were as obsessed with claims of their triviality (e.g., Pietz 1987: 39, 1988: 112n12) as Afro-Atlantic priests were and are with their divinity-inducing "flash" (Thompson 1983; Drewal and Mason 1998) and their long-distance relationship-demonstrating diversity.

It should noted that the seventeenth-century Dutch merchant critique of Guinea Coast society and its subsequent plagiarism by European critics of European political and economic arrangements was class specific. At the same time that members of the Dutch merchant class were mocking West African government and trade practices, Low Country aristocrats were engaged in an elaborate and willing alliance-building exchange of gifts with the Christian rulers of the West-Central African Kongo kingdom, which not only supplied seventeenth-century Europe and the Americas with boatloads of slaves but also dispatched numerous polyglot, literate, and elegantly dressed ambassadors to European royal courts and to the capital of Dutch-occupied northeastern Brazil. In 1636, the governor of Dutch Brazil, Johan Maurits, Prince of Nassau-Siegen, took court portraitist Albert Eckhout to Recife, where, around 1642, the painter vividly captured the luxurious Afro-European regalia of several noble emissaries sent from the Kongo kingdom of Soyo. On the basis of these visual encounters, he created a dignified and detailed image of African royalty that would circulate widely in aristocratic Europe. Between 1687 and 1740, the French company Manufacture Gobelins crafted, for sale to the elite, luxurious tapestries based on a painting by Eckhout that Maurits gifted to Louis XIV—*The King Carried by Two Moors* (Fromont 2014: 115–23, 153–54, 166 plate 29). These tapestries were sold and exchanged in Europe for decades and perhaps centuries. The image of black Africa as royal and a potential Christian ally to the West correlates with the European royalist and aristocratic values that were under threat by a rising mercantile bourgeoisie and, like European royalism itself, have endured amid the spread of the bourgeois values and anti-African disposition of the Enlightenment (see plate 3).

Moreover, Portuguese and Dutch traders' expressions of contempt for beads may have expressed a measure of nation-specific sour grapes. Having acquired glass-making technology from Syria, the Venetians in the late thirteenth century produced exceptionally high-quality glass beads that imitated gemstones and acquired a similar value. From the fourteenth century on, highly trained and licensed craftspeople from the Venetian island of Murano employed secret techniques for the production of beads that were sought after by elites across the globe. This creativity was directly driven by African tastes and African demand (*Venice-Murano* 2015). Not until the late eighteenth century did the Bohemians begin to rival the quality and desirability of Venetian bead production. Try as they might, craftspeople in the Netherlands, France, Germany, and Portugal were never able to compete (Francis 1999: 65). The Portuguese and the Dutch clearly envied the Venetians' and the Bohemians' skill at satisfying this profitable demand, and they had every reason to resent their own long-running dependency on Venice as the source of the most sought-after beads.

Enlightenment Ambivalence and Hegel's Change of Heart

In the eighteenth century, slavery was a root metaphor for what bourgeois European and Euro-American social critics wanted to transcend as they sought to recover the "natural" rights denied them by European royalty. The Enlightenment philosophers Hobbes and Locke, for example, were highly conscious of slavery, beginning with the assumption that people start out naturally free, only later to become enslaved by despotism. Oliver Cromwell and the antiroyalists resisted their "enslavement" to English royalty, just as many Europeans and Euro-Americans resented their "enslavement" to the tyrants who taxed them, limited their smuggling, and otherwise limited their participation in governance. Yet this objection to "enslavement" functioned alongside the plaintiffs' heartless enslavement of Africans.

Indeed, the lofty, abstract, and theoretical language of eighteenth-century European Enlightenment discourse about "freedom" might be read a symptom of its advocates' cognitive dissonance, perhaps also explaining why many latter-day analysts of eighteenth- and early nineteenth-century European political "theory" overlook copious evidence that sixteenth- to eighteenth-century Europeans and Euro-Americans knew a great deal about the enslavement of Africans in their day and that the source of their metaphorical references to slavery was literal, contemporaneous slavery, rather than to biblical, Greco-Roman, or imaginative models of slavery (Buck-Morss 2000). And they were perhaps embarrassed but also highly aware of the coincidence of their own figurative flight from slavery while they and their nations literally enslaved others. Hence, the tendency to read Hegel's, Marx's, and Freud's writings as pure, abstract theory with no intentional reference to the real-time context of the African slave trade and racist oppression, as pointed out by Buck-Morss (2000), requires a degree of obstinacy. Slaveowners' lofty aspiration to their own freedom is no irony or mere coincidence; slaveownership is the paradigmatic condition of the aspiration to "freedom" and of the lofty but vague terms in which they chose to express it (Patterson 1982). Their language represses the bloody reality and economic centrality of African slavery in eighteenth- and nineteenth-century European life.

For example, Adam Smith's canonical argument for freedom from excessive taxation, regulation, and royal monopolies, *The Wealth of Nations* (1776), says little about Africa but, in the tradition of his Dutch merchant sources, his few mentions of that continent are uninformed caricatures mainly intent on making a point about Europe. The author was aware of the African slave trade as a contemporaneous historical reality, repeatedly blaming that trade for Africa's poverty. However, Smith gives no sign of caring much about the enslaved; the focus of his allegory is not on the slave's lack of freedom but on the exemplary failings of the African "despot," a stock character in the Enlightenment drama. Africa's purpose in this tale is to exemplify the deficiency of factors that Smith believed would guarantee Europe's prosperity—the division of labor, the presence of branching rivers to facilitate international commerce, and the minimization of the taxation, regulation, and trade monopolies that encumbered international commerce in Europe's then-few African colonies, but his references to African despotism are a cliché, immortalizing Bosman's allegorical critique of excessive taxation, regulation, and monopolies by European despots.

This is not to say that Smith advocated the enslavement of Africans or was an anti-Black racist. Indeed, he observed that Africans had managed to resist the conquest that had befallen Native Americans due to Africans' superior level of economic development. More subtly, what he did was obscure the literal suffering of the enslaved African and, in a move typical of the Enlightenment and the writing of Marx as well, cast the often-slave-trading and -slaveholding European bourgeoisie as the real and most justly aggrieved slaves—a rhetorical move more fetishistic than any displacement of value and agency that I have seen in the Afro-Atlantic religions. Yet Marx would far exceed him in the boldness of his rhetorical gesture.

The exponents of the Enlightenment and their bourgeois contemporaries were certainly collectively divided and sometimes individually vacillating or ambivalent about the banalization of Black slavery and the denaturalization of white servitude. The Dutch lamented their own "enslavement" not only to the Spanish Crown but also to the "luxury" and "greed" that flowed from their newfound and partly slavery-based wealth. Some Enlightenment thinkers' most intimate relationships were structured around slavery, such as Thomas Jefferson's sexual relationship with Sally Hemings. And, as far back as the sixteenth century, some bourgeois Englishmen found sexual arousal in being bound and whipped like slaves (Noyes 1997), foreshadowing present-day white American kink and M/s relationships, which treat social equality and freedom as anathema to intimacy and, like many religions, associate rapture with surrender.[1] What unites such white seekers of freedom and intimacy—whether they treat slavery as the antitype or as the model of their fulfillment—is a strange evasion of the centrality of Black slavery in the spiritual self making and the social transformation of Europe since the eighteenth century. Their road to fulfillment sits on the unsettled and still-haunting graves of many a silenced Black slave. Both Smith and Hegel, touchstones in Marx's appropriation of Enlightenment rhetoric, vacillated between two rhetorical alternatives: (1) the embrace of the African as the exemplary fighter for freedom and (2) the more psychologically and materially profitable conclusion that Black people are a counterexample proving that all men who are *not* Black deserve to be free. Hegel's change of heart exemplifies both ethnological Schadenfreude and the bottom line that, from the early nineteenth century on, a great many of Europe's and even East Asia's leading programs in the pursuit of "freedom" have relied on a rhetorical and logical appeal to exempt the speaker's own nation, class, ethnic group, or religion from the fate suffered by Africans (on East Asia, see, for example, Dikötter 1997). This rhetoric has been a tool of bourgeois and proletarian aspirations, has accelerated with the rise of the nation-state, and has particularly characterized non-Black populations whose race, religion, ethnicity, or nationality made them ambiguous candidates for the promise of "freedom" for non-Blacks.

Hegel's 1822 *Philosophy of History* was a landmark in constructing Africans as the paradigm case of absurd reasoning and justifiable exclusion from the benefits of democratization. However, Hegel had not *always* spoken ill of the African. Unlike *The Philosophy of History*, his earlier text, *Phenomenology of Spirit* (1805–6), actually seems most sympathetic to the contemporaneous victims of real slavery. For example, reversing the "natural rights"–based historical model of Hobbes and Locke, Hegel argued that servitude is the precondition to freedom. In that earlier text, Hegel's famous master-slave dialectic—also known as the "dialectic of lordship and bondage"—actually declares the subjectivity of the servant superior to that of the master, and, in its real-time context, Hegel's advocacy of freedom seems to imply its author's abolitionist sentiments.

For Hegel, the master-slave dialectic is a stage in the evolution of a person's consciousness. People evolve from being merely conscious of sensations to being conscious of categories, ideals, empirical reality, and their need to conform to a set of communal ethics. Through the master-slave dialectic, they also develop a sense of God and an ethically oriented and altruistic communal spirit that they can pass on to others. According to Hegel, the master-slave dialectic occurs in one's early encounter with another person, in which one naturally wishes to dominate the other as if he or she were non-human, but such domination deprives one of the human interlocutor whose recognition is a precondition to one's own self-recognition as human. As the fixed point from which he or she judges and regulates others, the master is uncreative and unfulfilled until he or she recognizes his or her total dependence upon the slave. The slave, by contrast, is taught that he or she is a thing intended solely for the service of the other. The need to serve compels the slave to be inventive and creative, and the experience of abjection compels reflection. Hence, it is ultimately the slave who realizes him- or herself through creativity and productivity, and he or she does so before the master does. By rebelling against enslavement, the slave achieves the ultimate and ideal form of personhood. Indeed, this rebellion is a crucial moment in the achievement of freedom and real humanity.

The model of slavery, or servitude, that Hegel employed as a metaphor in his study of the evolution of human consciousness is usually assumed to derive from ancient Greece and Rome or from some pure idea of slavery in Hegel's mind. Blind to the contemporaneous reality of slavery and of the Haitian Revolution, historians of European philosophy tend to assume that Hegel derived his metaphor and his ideas about slavery from Fichte, Plato, Aristotle, or his own imagination (Buck-Morss 2000: 843).

However, Buck-Morss points out that Hegel was writing during and after the Haitian Revolution of 1791–1804, a series of events about which the European reading public of his day knew a great deal. Hegel appears to have read about it in, for example, the journal *Minerva* and the *Edinburgh Review*. Buck-Morss argues that Hegel's master-slave dialectic was also indebted to the author's readings of contemporary newspaper articles and to his communication with his Freemason brothers in Haiti. Thus, Hegel derived his metaphor from a literal consciousness of the Haitian Revolution, and, in *Phenomenology of Spirit*, he seems to have celebrated as inevitable the spread of the idea of freedom that the Haitian Revolution itself represented to the world. In Buck-Morss's argument, it was the Haitian Revolution that inspired Hegel's innovation of previous European ideas about the origin of freedom. Whereas Hobbes and Locke had located freedom in primordial nature, Hegel located it in the dialectic of oppression and rebellion, an idea that appears again in Frantz Fanon's 1961 book (translated into English in 1963) *The Wretched of the Earth*.

In marked contrast, Hegel's *Philosophy of History* ([1822] 1956), written two decades *after* the Haitian Revolution, condemned Africans in general as barbarous, childlike, and wildly prehistoric due to the deficiencies of the African "spirit"—which he had come to regard as governed by impulse and incapable of abstract and generalizing thought. Yet the abstraction of Hegel's own thinking about the human spirit and its progress—like that of generations of his interpreters—can be read as a denial of real-world African suffering and as proof of opportunism in his shedding of the African from his aspiration to collective human progress. Apparently in response to the decline in Haiti's economic productivity and to Haitian King Henri Christophe's despotism (about which he also read in the *Edinburgh Review* during 1817–19), Hegel chose to infer that this initial experiment in freedom and self-realization failed not because all such experiments are risky but because this one was "African."[2] He thus sidestepped the more logical implication that the political freedoms he advocated were a risky proposition in Europe, as well, where German speakers like Hegel suffered under the suspicion of their own natural inferiority to their French-speaking and Francophile rulers. Obviously, by that time, Hegel himself was guilty of *excessively* and *interestedly* generalizing thought.

Hegel had also committed the worst possible mistake for a historian—the failure to consider the interests and biases of his sources. The most widely published contemporaneous commentators on the Haitian Revolution were Europeans who had financial reasons to regret that revolution, as a result of which they had lost invaluable human and landed property. So they were unlikely to have laid much blame for the new Haitian nation's financial troubles and its undemocratic political responses on the devastating reparations payments that France exacted from the new nation, effects similar to those that Germany itself would experience after World War I. Nor did Hegel possess the foresight or breadth of wisdom to note that very few democratic revolutions—least of all the French Revolution, the US War of Independence, and Germany's infamously rocky road toward liberal democracy—have quick or tidily democratic results (Berman 2017 and 2013; Taylor 2016).

Hegel's use of African and Haitian religions as Enlightenment-inspired paradigms of the absurd remains alive and well in George H. W. Bush's now-proverbial 1980 characterization of Ronald Reagan's trickle-down economic theory as "voodoo economics" and *New York Times* columnist David Brooks's infamous blaming of Vodou for the ill effects of the 2010 earthquake in Haiti (Brooks 2010). Neither were they the first, nor have they been the last Western opinion makers to cast Haitian and, more broadly, African-inspired religions as the paradigm case of *un*enlightenment.

Its logical and empirical gaps notwithstanding, Marx (and later Freud) took Hegel's arguably Schadenfreude-laced version of human history for granted, reducing the Black agent to a starting block for lower-status Europeans anxious to catch up with their European social superiors. As members of a European religious and racial category even more vulnerable than Hegel's to the same disqualification to enter the race, Marx and Freud amplified this narrative at least partly in order to rescue themselves from the rock-bottom fate that had befallen Africans and African Americans.

FIGURE 1.1 Karl Marx (1818–83).

FIGURE 1.2 Frederick Douglass (1818–95).

FIGURE 1.3 Sigmund Freud (1856–39).

The intellectual archaeology that I have undertaken asks about the biographical reasons, in real European lives, for which these two progressive and iconoclastic men chose to exploit and amplify the puerile and, at the time of their writing, also widely contested cliché that Africans are foolish and that our religions are the locus classicus of mistaken attributions of agency and value. Both Marx and Freud generally eschewed the biologically determinist racial science of their day, but they also stocked their social evolutionism with a vocabulary and logic that contemptuously highlighted these men's difference from and superiority to Africans. This archaeology will further show that Marx's and Freud's claims about the true indexes of value and repositories of agency are hardly more objective, real, or convincing than the ones proposed by priests of African-inspired religions. For Marx, the commodity is the elemental fetish of capitalism, in that the people confused by capitalist exchange falsely credit the commodity with a value beyond the timed amount of labor that the workers have invested in it. Yet I argue that Marx's labor theory of value itself defined the source of the commodity's value tendentiously and advocated a moral order with despotic implications for African slaves and other Black workers. I submit that the elemental but unwitting fetish of historical materialism and of psychoanalysis is the Black man.

Contrary to the current uses made of his work in the humanities and some social sciences, Marx was not an abstract, disembodied theory machine mechanistically graphing a purely evidence-based diagram of economic history for all times and places. Rather, he was a mid-nineteenth-century human being born in central Europe with culture-specific aspirations and historically specific social and material problems of his own. Sperber (2013) highlights Marx's financial problems, but a further major fact unspoken in the usual twentieth- and twenty-first-century reception of Marx—unspoken even in Sperber's own account—is the influence of Marx's own racially ambiguous character and the insecurities that it inspired in the context of nineteenth-century European antisemitism. I maintain that the rhetoric of Marx's claims about value and history reveals precisely that insecurity. Moreover, Stallybrass (1998) argues that specific material things of exchange in Marx's life—namely, his pawned overcoats—gave rise to Marx's theory of commodity fetishism. I will explore how Marx animated these and other highly cathected material things—black bodies, the factory, and the piano—with his ambition, his disappointment, and, in a word, his ambivalence about his own race and class.

The "Negro Slave" in Marx's Labor Theory of Value

Marx is usually described as a mid-nineteenth-century "thinker," and he is credited foremost with challenging, but also building upon, Hegel's idea that history is the dialectical progress of ideas. Marx's alternative, anti-idealist theory of historical materialism—which we inevitably read partly through the priorities of his friend Friedrich Engels' posthumous editing of Marx's opus—is described as Marx's chief contribution to scholarly theory. Historical materialism is normally and, in my view, erroneously taken for a theory explaining human history in all times and places. This social evolutionary theory posits that every society changes according to a similar series of historical stages, which are driven by the efforts of the dominant class to exploit the workers and by the revolt of the workers when, at the end of each stage, they have been too impoverished by the current system of exploitation to bear any more suffering. The next historical stage begins with newly invented labor-saving machines that temporarily raise the working and living conditions of the workers but also begin a new cycle of increasing exploitation and then rebellion. In sum, history is propelled by class struggle. In fact, though, Marx's ostensibly transhistorical and universalist argument and selection of evidence were designed in the context of an effort to improve the lives of one specific class of people—nineteenth-century European wage workers. Marx's fetishization of the "negro slave" manifests the lopsided ambivalence that flows from ethnological Schadenfreude. He wished the best for the European workers without expressing any hope for the amelioration of desperate African American lives. Worse—and this is an instance of what I am calling "fetishism"—he shifted credit for the value production of the enslaved and sympathy for his or her suffering away from the enslaved and to European workers like himself.

The complications of an observer's real life do not invalidate his or her observation; they contextualize and potentially enrich that observation. So let me be blunt. Marx did not observe the world from a throne on a culturally neutral and socially transcendent version of a heavenly cloud. As Jonathan Sperber observes, Marx was an exiled, impoverished journalist crusading for the interests of industrial workers, especially the interests of similarly exiled German-speaking workers who had spread out all over Europe in search of a livelihood that the underdeveloped mid-nineteenth-century economy of German-speaking central Europe could not provide. Marx was also crusading, against great racial and class odds, for his *own* dignified place in society and history. I argue that in his crusade, the exiled German-speaking proletariat was an attractive ally and proxy for his own aspirations. Marx's historical materialism most certainly illuminates the exploitation of white workers and its structure, but a reading of historical materialism in its social, cultural, and biographical context also helps us to understand what Marx failed to acknowledge or understand—why the European proletariat has so often remained loyal to its bourgeois and aristocratic countrymen and why white low-status and not-so-white whites have often been so hostile toward the rights of Black people.

Marx's "Negro Slave": The Antithesis of Value and Agency

One of the most astonishing aspects of Marx's critique of capitalist exploitation is its marginalization of slavery and the enslaved from the story of capitalism and that critique's erasure of the Haitian Revolution from the history of the workers' resistance to capitalism. Though Marx wrote extensively about the early part of the US Civil War—a war centrally concerned with the problem of slavery in his time—and sided with the abolitionist Union forces, his description of the structure of capitalism strangely relegated the massive and contemporaneous institution of Black slavery and its commodity products to the wispy realms of metaphor and prehistory. By a peculiar rhetorical sleight of hand, Marx turned the real enslavement of Africans into a "pedestal" for the display of the ostensibly focal problem of capitalism, the undeserved suffering and disfranchisement of European workers.

This displacement of pathos and agency from literal slaves onto metaphorical ones was every bit as fetishistic as what Marx condemned as "the fetishism of commodities." Marx managed to convince himself that literal, contemporary slavery and real contemporary slaves did not merit his attention in the critique of capitalism, because they were ostensibly something of the past (consider Fabian 1983). Marx added the contradictory allegation that the enslavement of Africans in the Americas had been gentle until the rise of nineteenth-century industrial capitalism. Yet he was conveniently blind to the fact that the massive seventeenth- and eighteenth-century sugar industry in the Americas was as capitalist and as industrial as anything in nineteenth-century Europe and that it was far more exploitative and more often fatal to its workers. Like Hegel's late writings, Marx silenced the Haitian Revolution in his account of the workers' potential responses to capitalism.

Marx intoned the same metaphorical plea for the emancipation of the European wage worker that the Enlightenment issued on behalf of the bourgeoisie. In an ingenious rhetorical move, Marx dramatized his theory about the unfairness of the European proletariat's condition and about the overall course of history by calling European industrial workers "wage slaves," with the implication that enslavement is inappropriate for European workers and that they should be included in the dispensation that had, almost a century earlier, promised the European bourgeoisie the same essential rights previously monopolized by the European aristocracy.

What makes this a case of ethnological Schadenfreude is that, despite the centrality of the "wage slave" metaphor, Marx then does everything in his formidable rhetorical power to relegate the "negro slave" to the *prehistory* of capitalism. Marx argued, "The Negro labour in the southern states of the American Union preserved a moderately patriarchal character as long as production was chiefly directed to the satisfaction of immediate local requirements" ([1867] 1990: 345, also 377, 925). He thus characterized slavery in the US South as essentially "patriarchal," relatively kind, and oriented toward local production and nonalienating exchange until some ostensibly latter-day, exogenous, and atypical subjection of that system to the demands of the export economy, when, suddenly, a slave trade ensued in order to supply capitalist agricultural production.

Marx's argument that "negro slavery" was normatively more benign than "wage slavery" strikingly parallels arguments mobilized by *defenders* of slavery in the Confederate states. Quoting T. R. Edmonds with approval, Marx wrote, "The motive that drives a free man to work is *much more violent* than what drives the slave: a free man has to choose between hard labour and *starvation* . . . , a slave between [hard labor] . . . and a good whipping" (Marx [1867] 1990: 1027–28fn26, emphasis mine)—as though the corporal punishment suffered by the enslaved were little more that the occasional spanking Marx gave to his daughters. Marx's quotation of Edmonds continues, "the master of the slave understands too well his own interest to weaken his slaves by stinting them in their food; but the master of a free man gives him as little food as possible" (ibid., Marx's emphasis; see also 925).

"Conditions of economy . . . under a natural system," Marx observed in summation, "afford some security for human treatment by identifying the master's interest with the slave's preservation" (377), adding, "the slave-owner buys his worker in the same way as he buys his horse. If he loses his slave, he loses his capital, which he must replace by fresh expenditure on the slave-market" (ibid.).

Marx attributed the strategy of working the enslaved until they died fast but profitable deaths to (1) some ostensibly latter-day period "once trading in slaves is practised" (377). The other two ostensibly exceptional conditions that Marx represented as disrupting normative slavery were (2) when slavery came to satisfy something other than "immediate local requirements" (345), and (3) the ostensibly exceptional setting of "tropical" or "swampy" areas (377).

Contrary to Marx's strategic and selective account, the international commercial trade in enslaved people was the founding condition of all African slavery in North America and in the Americas generally. African slavery in the Americas, including the US South, had always been primarily oriented toward exportation—of forest products, rice, cotton, tobacco, sugar, rum, and minerals. Working the enslaved for maximum profit, even unto their early deaths, characterized slavery everyplace in the Americas *except* where and when the abolition of the Atlantic slave trade limited the supply of enslaved workers. An illegal international slave trade and a legal domestic one remained its lifeblood long after the importation of enslaved Africans into the US was outlawed in the late eighteenth century and into Brazil in the mid-nineteenth. In the nineteenth century in both Brazil and the US, a massive domestic slave trade resulted in the widespread and traumatic dismemberment of enslaved families.

The corporal and capital punishment of the enslaved were often gruesome. Everywhere in the slaveholding Americas, masters feared disobedience, flight, rebellion, poisoning, and mystical violence by the enslaved, inspiring anticipatory violence and quick punishment, including whipping, burning, branding, and live incineration; the amputation of ears, noses, and feet; the severing of Achilles' tendons; castration; execution; and nightmarish forms of posthumous dismemberment and display. And the North American regime of slavery that Marx implied somehow preceded export-oriented slavery was no exception (e.g., Higginbotham 1978). In the conduct of chattel slavery, physical degradation and the loss of some human "capital" served to guarantee the compliance and productivity of the rest, and the long-term honor of the slaveholder in these highly honor-conscious societies was worth more than the cash value of any given enslaved person. Moreover, slave-owners often left the day-to-day administration of the system to commercial whipping houses and propertyless overseers, whose resentment of the master and class Schadenfreude toward the enslaved generated its own considerable level of unsupervised cruelty and violence.

It seems that a man as literate as Marx would have seen lithographs of the hot-iron brands on the breasts and ghastly networks of scars on the backs of whipped slaves, as well as some of the grotesque instruments of torture and, indeed, starvation used to punish runaways and other recalcitrants. Among the enslaved, even the most brutal forms of rape went unpunished. In fact, they were incentivized by their outcome—an exorbitant increase in the master's capital. Yet the physical and financial motives for white men to rape Black women also inspired the jealous violence of white women, from which there was no reliable refuge. Runaways were legally subject to castration, facial brands, the removal of ears and toes, and other forms of mutilation (Ball [1998] 2014: 100). The mid-nineteenth-century abolitionists widely circulated visual images of the slaves so victimized, as well as detailed slave narratives that further substantiated them. Among those abolitionists were fugitive slaves who told their own life stories before audiences of hundreds, in the United States and Europe. Marx also presents himself as unaware of the constant threat of permanent separation from one's children, parents, spouses, and friends because the selective culling and sale of human beings, like that of any other investment vehicle, was highly profitable. The well-published vocabulary of the South's rampant internal slave trade cognized these human beings as livestock, and they were subjected to the same treatment as livestock whenever necessary for the financial well-being of their owners (e.g., Dew 2016: 87–166).

In Marx's day, Harriet Beecher Stowe's best-selling 1852 novel, *Uncle Tom's Cabin*, spread knowledge of these phenomena throughout the Western world. Moreover, as a journalist specializing in the coverage of the US American Civil War, Marx could not have been unaware of these facts. And nothing about the widely known history of the Atlantic slave trade could have led him to believe that these forms of cruelty were extrinsic to early American slavery or unique to its late or, in Marx's view, only *recently* capitalist phase of African American enslavement. No, ignorance cannot explain Marx's rhetorical choices and blindspots. Perhaps he disbelieved the abolitionists. In either case, his euphemization of the slave's suffering was clearly a means to an end that he regarded as higher than abolition or the honest evaluation of the agency and value of the enslaved.

In sum, when Marx directly described US slavery, he treated its cruelty as nonessential and, under normal circumstances, nullified by the economic interest of the planter in the well-being and longevity of his human property, an interest unmatched, according to Marx, by the unmitigated cruelty of the capitalist toward the wage laborer. Thus we are led to believe that "wage slavery" is *even worse* than real slavery! A man as intelligent and well-read as Marx could surely have—and probably did—think this matter out more clearly and empirically. But empiricism was neither the method nor the aim of this theory. The tale that slavery in the US South started out as and normatively remained "patriarchal," rather than profit oriented, was a myth invented by slaveholding planters precisely to resist abolitionism. That Marx embraced that myth rather than applying his usually incisive skepticism to the ideology of the ruling class is peculiar indeed. One is tempted to view it as an opportunistic sacrifice of the real African slave for the benefit of her wage-earning European counterpart.

But the slave was not alone on this pyre. The effects of slavery in the Americas were not only cruel but also long-term and intergenerational. Every descendant of North American slaves still lives with others' pervasive doubt about our humanity and with the widespread denial that the system has harmed us at all, as well as the outsized but economically irrational hostility of working-class whites. Such doubt and hostility are built into the US social order. That is why, unlike most white Marxists, I cannot dismiss Marx's narrative treatment of the "negro slave" as an innocent and incidental backdrop to his story, any more than I can excuse Donald Trump's degrading words about women, minorities, and people with disabilities as incidental to his ostensible defense of the "little guy" or as nonessential to his appeal to the white American working class. The "moderately patriarchal character" that Marx attributed to colonial North American and US slavery was not an empirical assessment of any documented period of North American slavery but a linchpin of Marx's protest on behalf of the European wage laborer. In so narrating the history of real African slavery in the US, Marx found common cause with the southern slaveholders. Indeed, like the fable that gods created men, Marx's own narrative inverted the truth. Just as nineteenth-century capitalism alienated the labor value of the wage worker, Marx displaced the pathos of African American enslavement onto European wage workers.

Even worse by the standards of his own apparent ethics, Marx also alienated the labor value of the enslaved African. To the point of contradiction, Marx offered every rationale he could think of to highlight the efficiency of the European wage worker in contrast to the ostensibly precapitalist inefficiency of the "negro slave." On the one hand, Marx argued that, because the enslaved worker could count on being fed no matter how little he or she produced, the enslaved worked inefficiently and could not be trusted with the delicate tools that would have made his or her production more efficient (e.g., Marx [1867] 1990: 303fn18). On the other hand, he argued that, because the enslaved do not identify with the products of their labor, only direct cruelty could make the enslaved do his or her job, contradicting his assertion elsewhere that US slavery had been "more or less patriarchal" (925). Emphasizing the evolutionary inferiority of the enslaved and their noncontemporaneity, Marx compared them to feudal workers in their alleged inflexibility and inability to shift to new skilled endeavors (1014, 1034).

Contradicting himself again, he added that slavery lent itself only to monoculture, and not to some ostensibly more capitalist and efficient type of agricultural production (1014). Did feudal workers typically practice monoculture? Despite Marx's insinuation, nowhere in the history of capitalism is it self-evident that monoculture is noncapitalist, precapitalist, or less efficient than its alternatives in generating profit. Indeed, monoculture is *the* characteristic form of capitalist agriculture, not evidence of slavery's inefficient, precapitalist nature. Moreover, the Latin American processing of sugar by the enslaved was an innovative industrial process requiring a high level of skill. The North American cultivation and processing of rice (e.g., Carney 2001) were also highly skilled trades established, propagated, and processed largely by Black artisans adapting African technology to North American geography.

Again, like much social evolutionist reasoning, Marx's rhetoric is less a conscientiously empirical and logical account of the past or of the cultural Other than an allegorical argument about the proper value priorities of the target audience. Marx was advocating for the enfranchisement of the white proletariat by constructing it as uniquely modern, productive, and efficient.

However, if slavery-based production was so inefficient, why were naval blockades and laws required to end the overseas slave trade? Why were the Civil War and the hard-fought legislative and judicial battle for abolition necessary to end it in the US, Brazil, and the extant European colonies in the Americas? Why did American slavery not die under the weight of its own unprofitability?

Radically contrary to Marx's argument, the enslavement of Africans in the Americas was, according to the Gilder Lehrman Institute of American History, central to eighteenth- and nineteenth-century global capitalism: "Slave labor did produce the major consumer goods that were the basis of world trade during the eighteenth and early nineteenth centuries: coffee, cotton, rum, sugar, and tobacco" (Gilder Lehrman Institute 2014). Moreover,

> in the pre–Civil War United States, slavery played a critical role in economic development. One crop, slave-grown cotton, provided over half of all U.S. export earnings. By 1840, the South grew 60 percent of the world's cotton and provided some 70 percent of the cotton consumed by the British textile industry. Thus slavery paid for a substantial share of the capital, iron, and manufactured goods that laid the basis for American economic growth. In addition, precisely because the South specialized in cotton production, the North developed a variety of businesses that

provided services for the slave South, including textile factories, a meat processing industry, insurance companies, shippers, and cotton brokers. (Gilder Lehrman Institute 2014)

Slavery remained profitable to the end, and it fired the textile mills of British and northern US capitalism with cotton that lacked any more efficient or supposedly more capitalist source. There is little doubt that slavery was highly profitable to its individual investors. Fogel and Engerman ([1974] 1995) argue that investments in US slavery were more profitable than even the highest-yielding investments in manufacturing (see also Conrad and Meyer 1958; Stampp 1956; Genovese 1974; Baptist 2014; Schermerhorn 2015; as well as an overview of this literature in *Economist* 2013). In 1860, just before the US Civil War, the estimated value of the human beings owned in the South was half again greater than the combined value of the railroads and manufacturing combined, and, far from declining, the price of an enslaved African American in New Orleans, the prime market in the lower South, had tripled since 1800 (Dew 2016: 139). Foundational to this scholarly work is Eric Williams's *Capitalism and Slavery* ([1944] 1980), which argued that the African slave trade and slavery in the Americas indispensably financed the industrial revolution in England.

It should also be noted that nineteenth-century slavery was not limited to agriculture, much less to low-skill production. Enslaved Black people—many of them highly skilled—were a major proportion of the workers in the mines, railroads, and steel mills of the Confederacy. Even after the official abolition of slavery, hundreds of thousands of African Americans were dragooned into lifelong, unpaid labor after conviction on the trumped-up charge of "vagrancy." Some of the largest and most successful capitalist companies in the twentieth century, such as US Steel, profitably enslaved Black industrial workers at a time when unenslaved white wage labor was also easily available. And they did so not out of paternalism but because it was more efficient and profitable than hiring white wage labor to do the same job (Blackmon 2008). Multiple recent studies document the inventiveness, technical superiority, and superior profitability of US African American slave workers relative to their free white counterparts (e.g., Vlach [1978] 1990; Carney 2001; Risen 2016). These qualities were well known to the slaveholders, and they are the subject of an enduring but normally whispered lore among the white beneficiaries of this alienated Black legacy. However, the tradition of displacing the credit for slave productivity onto the masters, and the often-violent determination of postbellum working-class whites to monopolize the skilled trades, have created a very different public transcript (see also Klein 2013). Thus, many Anglophone US advocates and critics of slavery join Marx in falsely positing that slaves were inefficient producers. Whomever Marx's rhetoric was intended to benefit, its minimization of the genius, labor, and suffering of the "negro slave" is either smugly ignorant or cavalierly cruel.

Marx's rhetorical premise and the common sense of most twentieth- and twenty-first-century US Americans that direct cruelty to workers is an inefficient motor of high-quality production is far from universal. Present-day Spanish and Portuguese speakers say of hard workers who achieve commendable results that they have *trabajado como negros* (worked like blacks, i.e., slaves).[1] Among the Latin American nations where this expression is common are Cuba and Brazil, which enslaved millions more people than the United States, and did so for decades longer. They would know.

Moreover, the Latin American priests I know systematically contradict Marx's assumption that physical cruelty was the only motivation for the enslaved to do a good job. And the archives confirm their view. Despite the inevitable cruelty of slavery, the enslaved often identified closely with their masters, sought their favor, and took pride in the success of their estates. Indeed, the economic failure of the estate could result in the selling off of the enslaved and the emotionally devastating separation of their families. Moreover, in Brazil, Cuba and parts of the US South, many of the enslaved were entitled to keep a proportion of the proceeds of their labor. These proceeds could sometimes be used to buy their freedom. The incentives for efficient production on the part of the enslaved were numerous.

Compared with much of the scholarship of his time, Marx's work has proven friendly to many antiracist projects. However, Marx himself concluded the first volume of *Capital*, the only volume of his magnum opus on the laws of capitalism fully written and edited by him, with the following words: *"We are not concerned here with the conditions of the colonies*. The only thing that interests us is the secret discovered in the New World by the political economy of the Old World, and loudly proclaimed by it: that the capitalist mode of production and accumulation, and therefore capitalist private property as well, have for their fundamental condition the annihilation of that private property which rests on the labour of the individual himself; in other words the *expropriation of the worker*" ([1867] 1990: 940, emphasis mine).

The "worker" whose interests "concerned" Marx was clearly not the slave in the colonies but the "German working class" ([1867] 1990: 95). In *Capital*, volume 1, which Marx's friend Engels called "the Bible of the working class,"[2] Marx sought to persuade German wage workers of the injustice of their condition and the wisdom of his solution, which was based on the labor theory of value. And he did so by comparing their ostensible mistreatment to the more obvious and taken-for-granted mistreatment of the slaves in Europe's colonies, which Marx is "not concerned with," except as a source of rousing rhetorical tropes. He quotes Horace's *Satires*: "The name is changed, but the tale is told of *you*" ([1867] 1990: 378, emphasis mine). Of whom? The German wage worker, not the enslaved Africans themselves. In sum, Marx's historical materialism was not a socially unpositioned theory equally "concerned with" all times, places, or types of people. It was an exhortation to a specific class, in which colonial slavery was less a reality to be investigated evenhandedly or redressed humanely than a rhetorical trope useful in establishing the racial inappropriateness of white workers' mistreatment in Europe. Indeed, that seems to have been slavery's greatest historical and emotional value to Marx. Colonial slavery was not his concern, he did not identify with the enslaved, and he was not addressing them.

Some readers might excuse Marx on the grounds that most of the enslaved in the Americas could not read his book. Yet Marx was a contemporary of hundreds of highly literate white abolitionists and many Black ones, as well, such as the highly literate Frederick Douglass and David Walker, not to mention their Afro-Brazilian counterparts Luiz Gama, André Rebouças, and José do Patrocínio. Marx simply chose not to recognize them as coeval subjects in the history of capitalism or as allies and leaders in the struggle for workers' rights.

The premise behind Marx's vivid comparison of wage labor to slavery was that no person naturally wants to work for another and that capitalism—the relentless pursuit of profit—depends on the violation of the worker's natural desire. When one person works for another, the employer can sell the proceeds of the worker's labor, hand over to the worker a reduced proportion of the proceeds, and keep the rest of the proceeds for himself. Marx argued that people with access to land of their own will, instead, naturally produce just enough for themselves and will avoid working for others (for one of many equally "natural" counterexamples, see Malinowski [1922] 1984: 60–62). Therefore, in order to generate capitalist profits in the colonies, capitalists did boldly what they sometimes had to do more subtly but, according to Marx, more ruthlessly in their metropolitan homelands. They forcibly displaced people from their land and imposed upon them taxes in cash or labor that would force them to work for the capitalists ([1867] 1990: 48, 932, 1028, e.g.).

Yet, in the service of points that he really wanted to make about Europe and of what he hoped would be a better future for the German wage workers, Marx sometimes distorted or truncated the realities of colonial life. Metaphors tend to suck the life out of their sources. Marx's scattered and bloodless references to the "slave mode of production" generally concerned ancient times. He also repeatedly spoke of slavery in the Dutch East Indies, in the making of the fortunes of capitalist Liverpool, in the tropical Americas, and, above all, in the southern United States. He did so with profound disapproval, but he described these instances of slavery *not* as central to the structure of nineteenth-century capitalism but, instead, as evidence of capitalism's past, founding moments and, therefore, of the inner essence of wage work. These ostensibly pre- and protocapitalist phenomena were thereby treated as mere *harbingers*—and not contemporary or central instances—of the principle that, for capitalists, profit is all that matters. Wage labor is like slavery in the sense that it results from the displacement of the workers from land on which they could have produced enough to support themselves, so that working for the capitalist, at ever decreasing wages, is their only alternative to starvation ([1867] 1990: 378, 685, 937).

However, despite the incidental sympathy for the "negro slave" that is apparent in the "wage slave" metaphor, the "negro slave" is clearly nowhere among the protagonists or the intended beneficiaries of Marx's tale about the suffering of wage workers under capitalism, about the sources of profit under capitalism, and about the workers' heroic and ostensibly future role in creating alternative social relations of production. For example, where are Haitian slavery and the Haitian workers' successful revolution in his account of capitalism and the workers' resistance to it?

Marx's Enlightenment forebears used the Guinea-Coast African as an allegory for their complaints about European monarchs and priests and as a foil to the aspirations of the bourgeoisie. Similarly, Marx used the "negro slave" as an allegory for his complaints about the European capitalist and as a foil to the aspirations of the European proletariat. His contrasting portraits of the benignly treated, incompetent "negro slave" and the cruelly treated but efficient wage worker defied facts and casually invalidated the interests of the enslaved and their descendants. The hardship of the enslaved was invoked chiefly for the convenience of the white proletariat. Slavery was represented as cruel when that cruelty could be used to indict the capitalist and kind when that ostensible kindness could be used to do the same. And by denying the profitability of slavery, Marx bolstered the argument that the European wage worker is the lone creator of European wealth, the most intensely exploited victim of the system, and the noblest potential leader of its overthrow. Moreover, by denying the central and ongoing role of colonial slavery in generating materials and profits for British and Anglo-American capitalists, Marx also obscured the fact that slavery subsidized the livelihood not only of white royals and burghers but also of white wage workers, as well.

Marx's encomium to the European worker rests on the claim that that worker's unique efficiency and singular impoverishment by capitalists are the sole profit mechanism of capitalism, which Marx has defined as though the contemporaneous phenomenon of colonial slavery were but an early, superseded part or nonessential aspect of sixteenth- to nineteenth-century capitalism ([1867] 1990: 918, e.g.). This definition is a miracle of theoretical abstraction from the real context and structure of the economic practices that Marx intends to criticize. This evacuation of the "negro slave's" suffering and labor power, along with the wholesale displacement of that suffering and labor power onto the white worker, is little different from the phenomena that Marx describes as "fetishism." Like Haitian zombification, which I will discuss more thoroughly in *Zombies and Black Leather* (in preparation), Marx's move has multiplied one person's agency by evacuating another's. My ultimate point, though, is not that Marx's theory of fetishism is wrong-headed. Much less is it a consequence of confusion. Instead, historical materialism is an interested and, to many, inspiring allegory for Marx's own convictions about proper social order and the proper distribution of its rewards. The Afro-Atlantic perspective from which I read historical materialism removes Marx and his theory from the Black "pedestal" on which Marx and the advocates of disembodied theory have placed them and relocates Marx and Marxism in the historical mud from which they so fruitfully grew.

In his metaphorical effort to persuade European wage workers of the justice of their cause, Marx's greatest feat of theoretical abstraction and distortion lies in the one positive colonial phenomenon he documents. Marx celebrates—as counterexamples of the metaphorical "enslavement" of the free (white) worker and as examples of his proper condition—those parts of the US and Australian settler colonies where almost all of the (white) workers have land of their own, where they can thereby resist the capitalist's coercive demand for their labor, and where they therefore enjoy a high standard of living and culture (e.g., [1867] 1990: 934–36). Astonishingly, Marx makes it clear that his audience of German wage workers is intended to identify with these white American workers at the expense of the Australian Aborigines and Native Americans who had been displaced, infected, or murdered in order for the white workers to obtain this land. When we fail to look squarely at the black and brown "pedestals" upon which historical materialism rests, Marx's theory appears to float in thin air.

At moments, Marx does lament the fact that similar land in another settler colony, South Africa, was stolen from its indigenous African inhabitants ([1867] 1990: 48), or he laments the fact that white wage workers in the US could not effectively organize against the capitalists as long as the (white) wage workers had to compete with "negro slaves" (whose alleged inefficiency suddenly disappears from Marx's reasoning; [1867] 1990: 414). However, writing on behalf of the international class of free white workers, he sees no fundamental reason to object to the continuous upward flow of Black people's surplus labor to whites of all classes in the US or to white people's racial monopoly on the guarantee of full citizenship. In slave and free states in the US, throughout Marx's lifetime, free Black workers suffered discrimination and murderous violence at the hands of white workers anxious to protect their privileged access to land and to the best-paying jobs. In slave states, nonslaveholding whites profitably served as overseers, drivers, police, hunters, and lawful murderers of the enslaved when they fled.

It is not absolutely clear to me whether Marx's failure to consider these facts resulted from ignorance or from strategic omission in the service of his social priorities. However, every historical ontology—that is, every conception of what counts as a social actor, of the role categories that explain these actors' patterns of action, and of what defines the needs, interests, and desiderata of each such category—rests on culture-specific conceptions of possibility, and it prioritizes the interests of one set of actors over others. The respective historical ontologies of historical materialism, psychoanalysis, and the Afro-Atlantic religions are no exceptions.

Marx may not have been fully able to anticipate the degree to which presumptively white "wage slaves" would, in the twentieth century, endeavor to guard their racial privileges by excluding Black "wage slaves" (a category Marx fails even to acknowledge) from the labor unions, but he surely knew about the Draft Riots of 1863, in which free, aspirationally white, largely Irish, and in many cases immigrant workers in New York—who were initially reacting to class inequalities in the drafting of soldiers for the Union Army—quickly displaced their aggression onto their free Black neighbors, burning down Black-owned businesses and homes, an orphanage for Black children, and the homes of abolitionists. They randomly attacked Black people in the streets and ultimately murdered eleven of us. Marx's portrait of the European worker's nobility and fitness for future leadership panders to a very specific intended audience, one that seems to include the author's own aspirational self.

Marx's vision of a worker's idyll on the cleared lands of the US and Australia was clearly not intended to represent the experiences of the colonized and the enslaved with accuracy or with an eye toward their agency or the value of their products. It was intended to show European wage workers that, without being fully aware of it, they were being reduced by capitalists to a status explicitly inappropriate to their formally free state and implicitly inappropriate to their race. Marx's failure to name the relationship between race and freedom in the settler colonies also enabled him to overlook the relationship between whiteness and the self-perceived interests of European workers.

The Labor Theory of Value

The key to Marx's assessment of capitalist exploitation is an idea—the labor theory of value (LTV)—that is critical of but also indebted to a series of pro-capitalist British political economists, such as Adam Smith (1723–90) and David Ricardo (1772–1823). In sum, Marx contrasted the ghostly value that he thought the dupes of capitalism attributed to commodities with what he regarded as the real determinant of their value—the amount of time that the wage worker had invested in their production relative to the amount invested in the production of the other commodities for which it would be exchanged. And to prove the foolishness of those dupes, Marx implicitly compared them to Africans. In truth, Marx's calculation of the value of a commodity is no more empirical than the conceptions of value and agency implicit in the Afro-Atlantic religions. To the same degree that Marx viewed *production* as the preeminent determinant of a commodity's value, Afro-Atlantic priests assume that *exchange* is preeminent in the social process because it is what creates people in the first place. Each of these conceptions is culturally and historically grounded, racially positioned, interested, and ambivalent.

For Marx, following Smith, Ricardo, and possibly Hegel, the real value of a commodity was not determined by its use value—that is, by the specific practical use of the commodity or by the degree of its usefulness. Water, for example, is infinitely useful but is not commercially valuable to the same degree. The fact that we can exchange a commodity with one use (say, fifty bottles of rum) for one with a totally different use (say, ten bolts of linen) further demonstrates that the real value of a commodity differs from its use value. One cannot use rum in the same ways that one can use linen.

For Marx, real value is not equal to exchange value, either. Under capitalism, we regularly exchange x quantity of one commodity with one use (or its cash equivalent) for y quantity of another commodity with another use, producing the illusion that this cash stands for some self-existent but invisible substance that is shared by both sets of commodities. For example, the fact that one could exchange fifty bottles of rum for ten bolts of linen suggests to the naive that there is some invisible and inherent value inside of rum that is qualitatively identical to the invisible and inherent value inside of linen, and that five times as much of that ghostly substance of value exists in one bolt of linen as in one bottle of rum. Marx called the popular belief in such a mythologically inherent substance of value "fetishism." For Marx, as for the classical British political economists, the real value of a commodity is not such an invisible, ghostly substance.

It was David Ricardo who first observed that mechanization tends to deprive workers of jobs and reduce the wages of the remaining employees, both of which observations suggested that labor is the main source of a commodity's value and profit. And Marx agreed. Because competition among manufacturers continually drives down profits, Ricardo reasoned, the only ways to maintain profitability are to (1) find new markets, (2) ask consumers to pay only for the cost of maintaining and, when necessary, replacing the machinery, forgoing any profits from mechanization itself, (3) mechanize the factory further, enabling one to fire workers, and (4) reduce the compensation of the remaining workers. Once (1) all of the new markets are exhausted, (2) market competition has reduced consumer prices to the minimum cost of repairing and replacing the machinery, and the profits from mechanization have been reduced to zero, (3) and mechanization has enabled the employer to minimize the workforce—all of which conditions Ricardo regarded as inevitable—the chief remaining determinant of capitalist profits is the degree to which the capitalist can (4) force the worker to produce more commodities for less compensation. Moreover, it follows from conditions (1) to (3) that once all of the workers have been fired, it is no longer possible to produce profits. This chain of inevitabilities is what suggested to Ricardo that the labor time of the workers is the *primary* constituent of the value of the commodities they produce. Thus, Ricardo provided the foundation of Marx's critique of capitalist exploitation.

However, according to Levine (2008: 93), the Left Ricardian Thomas Hodgskin was "one of the first to draw the *absolute* equivalence between value and labor" (emphasis mine), thus shoring up Marx's moral absolutism. According to Marx's LTV, not just *most* but the *entire* value of a commodity is produced by the labor of the worker, measured by the collective labor time needed to produce that commodity (or its cash equivalent) relative to the collective labor time needed to produce the commodities for which it might be exchanged. Marx observed that the sum paid to the wage worker gravitates toward the minimum cost of keeping the worker fed, clothed, housed, and entertained according to the conventions of the time. However, because the wage worker has no way of making a living other than by selling his labor power, the capitalist can compel him to produce a quantitative value of goods beyond the value of the wages needed for the worker's sustenance. Marx called the gap between (1) the wages paid to the worker in exchange for the time he has spent manufacturing the commodity and (2) the price the capitalist fetches for the commodity "surplus value," and he classified the capitalist's expropriation of this surplus value as an act of theft, tolerated by the worker only because the worker and the capitalist have been taken in by the "fetishism of commodities." Marx's pejorative metaphor for this ostensible disorder of European thought and society is clearly indebted to the later Hegel's ignorant and opportunistic parody of African religion.

While the labor theory of value seems intuitively right, the empirical reality of pricing—or the quantity of one commodity that any given person is willing to sacrifice in order to obtain a given quantity of another commodity—is an entirely different matter. Marx's definition of real value is more a moral prescription than an observation about the nature of exchange in any known system (or empirical instance) of production and exchange.

For example, all sorts of things were made at enormous costs in labor time (and large fractions of the collective's labor time) but will never be bought at a price commensurate with Marx's measure of value. Such items can be either worthless, like the first blanket my Aunt Hilda knitted, or priceless, like this book. Some will consider these temporally mispriced items gifts (i.e., items theoretically not subject to an even-Steven exchange of labor time) rather than commodities. However, like commodities proper, these, too, were made expressly in anticipation of exchange. Moreover, as a buyer, I hardly ever know how long the worker took to make an object. That unknown factor therefore has no bearing on the price I am willing to pay for it. And this price is unlikely to correspond to the commodity's labor time content in any accidental way or at a long-term, average, and aggregate level, either. The LTV rests on numerous obfuscations.

I am aware of arguments (which I find unconvincing; see, e.g., Marx [1867] 1990: 133, 152, 170–73) that Marx intended for his LTV to apply primarily to a purely capitalist society amid pure commodity exchange (e.g., Harvey 1982: 60). Even if that were Marx's intention, capitalism as Marx defined it does not even exist in the most capitalist of capitalist countries. In *Capital*, volume 1, Marx himself argued forcefully that the value of any given good or service is defined by the proportional relationship between the number of worker-hours needed to produce it and the number of worker-hours needed to produce the totality of other exchangeable goods and services in that society. Insofar as *any* categories of labor are not rewarded in proportion to the time invested in their production, then *not even the purest commodity produced in that society* can possibly be valued exactly according to the proportion of the society's overall labor time that is invested in its production. The giving of any gifts in that society and, by extension, the unremunerated commodity production of the nineteenth-century "negro slave" automatically disrupt the labor-time and ratio-based logic of Marx's LTV. That is, insofar as people in capitalist societies also employ slaves or give gifts that are not reciprocated by gifts of equal LTV-based value, *no* object of exchange in that society is actually exchanged according to Marx's model. For example, my possession of a useful object that I have received as a gift diminishes my need to buy a similar object on the open market, thus affecting the price that similar objects will be able to fetch on the open market. Moreover, contrary to Marx's premise, societies are not isolated from each other. No capitalist society in real historical time has been sufficiently isolated from slaveholding or noncapitalist societies for the labor-time and ratio-based determination of commodity prices *within* the capitalist society not to be distorted by exchange with societies lacking wage labor.

My second, related objection to the labor theory of value is that supply and demand matter. Insofar as he considers the effect of supply on the real value of a commodity, Marx repairs his model by positing that scarcity is solely a function of the elevated quantity of labor time required to locate or extract that commodity from its place of origin (Marx [1867] 1990: 130). He fails to recognize the diversity and the agency of suppliers, who may collude to limit the supply and thereby raise the price of a commodity to consumers—as, for example, African trade societies on the early-modern Guinea Coast did and other cartels do—independently of the amount of labor time it takes them to locate or extract that commodity. Moreover, the prices of gold and oil go up and down pretty independently of how many hours it takes for someone to remove a unit thereof from the ground. In these cases, demand affects price more than labor time does. Prices will also go up even if, while demand and labor time remain steady, supplies decrease.

And, above all, culture matters. Apparently sane, well-educated people pay what are, to my mind, nonsensical amounts of money for diamonds and gold. Diamonds and gold do not acquire more value than beads for their "natural" use value or for the labor time needed to produce them. At the height of European overseas commerce, European merchants encountered numerous African and Native American peoples who had significant access to gold and silver and did not employ those substances as money. Such European merchants sensibly recognized the preference of many peoples for cowrie shells, beads, and enslaved people as the generalized media of exchange and measures of value. The divergent cultural values of the buyer and the seller, and of their other anticipated trading partners, are always powerful determinants of a commodity's value and provocations to talk of "fetishism." Yet the accusation is no more objective coming from the pot than from the kettle.

"Supply and demand" is perhaps most economists' and political economists' best effort at recognizing culture. And the independence of this variable is far greater than Marx was willing to acknowledge. A person's willingness to engage in any given type of labor is a function of far more than the host society's level of economic development. Within the same capitalist service economy that hosts her Christian or secularist coworker, a Muslim flight attendant may not be willing to serve alcohol and a Muslim cashier may not be willing to handle a customer's package of bacon. Similarly, a population's unwillingness to buy bacon and alcohol or to sponsor industries that fund apartheid and Zionism, promote global warming, or deny healthcare benefits to their workers can have as powerful an effect on "the economy" as can the seemingly inexorable impulse of capitalists to produce for the sake of profits. Cultural differences, class differences, gender differences, religious differences, and differences of life stage all increase the likelihood that even the seller and the potential buyer of a fatty piece of pork or of a diamond wedding ring will attribute different types and degrees of value to the same commodity.

Marx's theory, like other European social theories, is not a map of ultimate realities in every time and place. He overlooked or effaced important elements of capitalist social conditions and practice during his own time, and his oversights, some of them strategic, reflected his gendered, ethnic, and racial relationship to the emergent European nation-state. Much like the Dutch Protestants' accusation that Roman Catholicism is "fetishism," Marx's deployment of this term not only dramatizes the wrongness of European capitalism by comparing it to African religion but also insinuates that Marx embodies the anti-African aspirational ideal of the European Enlightenment even more thoroughly than the gentile bourgeoisie does. To me, the labor theory of value is no less shaped by the competitive pursuit of profits within Atlantic capitalism, no less religious, and no less fetishistic than the positions Marx was criticizing.[3] Perhaps what makes the Afro-European crossroads the locus classicus of "fetishism" is precisely the anxiety of threatened classes and races of Europeans to deflect stigma from themselves and onto Africans, appealing for the fate of Africans not to befall them.

CHAPTER THREE

Marx's Fetishization of People and Things

Marx well illustrates Böhme's contention that even the most supposedly abstract theoretical ideas are made up of mental images of things. Marx's references to the "negro slave" are descended from Hegel's references to the slave and the African fetish in the history of human spiritual progress. Marx claims to restore the material basis of reality to Hegel's spiritual dialectics. However, Marx is guilty of his own form of airy abstraction.

Among the commodities great and small that Marx juggles algebraically in order to work out his historical materialist theory of value and historical progress—diamonds, wheat, boot polish, silk, silver, gold, corn, cattle, yarn, linen, paper, clothing, coats, iron, teas, coffee, and sugar—the most valuable commodity of all is conspicuously vaporized: enslaved Black people ([1867] 1990: 125–77). Marx recognized them neither as living, breathing, suffering, and productive people nor as commodities. Nor, as he struggled to end the conversion of the industrial worker into a thing, did he treat the enslaved African as a person wrongly converted into a commodity. Rather, he expressly and unselfconsciously turned the "negro slave" into a stone "pedestal"—a rhetorical chit wagered in the recalibration of the value of the European wage worker. Like Hegel before him and, after him, the contemporary practitioners of BDSM and M/s, Marx is strangely evasive about the centrality of Black slavery in the spiritual self making and the social transformation of Europe in the eighteenth and nineteenth centuries. Marx calculated the value of any given commodity as the ratio of the duration of collective labor time needed to produce it relative to the duration of collective labor time needed to produce every other available commodity, Black labor time disappeared into a cloud of unknowing and mysteriously re-appeared, its origins unrecognizable, in the enhanced and socially autonomous competence of white labor. Marx worked this fetish magic by establishing a priori the polar opposition and absolute inequality between two types of worker, denying the value of slave labor in order to amplify the value of white wage labor relative to that of white capitalist management. By evacuating the "negro slave" of his or her of productivity, Marx himself turned the once-thingified white worker into a historical super-hero and the "negro slave" into a thing with no more agency than a pedestal. The "negro slave" has been eviscerated and discarded like Popeye's can of spinach.

So why did Marx wish the best for the European proletariat and so willingly sacrifice the "negro slave"? I hypothesize that Marx's own ambiguous class and racial identities, and the social encumbrances they imposed, explain a great deal about the Black fetish he made: Marx himself was a downwardly mobile petit bourgeois and an off-white European who, like the wage worker, suffered under the need to sell his labor power but, even more than most European wage workers, was bypassed by the full benefits of colonialism and slavery. Marx hitched his wagon to that of the ambitious European and Euro-American working classes because Europeans' collective domination of the black and the brown had already extended the privileges of aristocracy from the hereditary lords to the propertied bourgeoisie, and the best hope of an impoverished Jewish man was to be included in the next echelon of whites in line for inclusion—non–property holders. A step ahead of Arendt's fixed typology, Marx was a rebel pariah bent on becoming a parvenu.

Neither under Napoleonic nor under Prussian rule had the newly emancipated Jews received automatic admission to the game. European overseas imperialism, settler colonialism, and the enslavement of Africans had subsidized the expansion of the circle of comfort and honor beyond the European aristocracy to include the European bourgeoisie. The rhetoric of Marx's plea for the inclusion of the proletariat in that same circle was also a plea for his own inclusion, obscuring his own racial and class ambiguity. Marx constructed the European proletariat as the main agent of history and the class most deserving of rescue. Propertyless but neither brown nor black, Marx told a tale of the proletariat that also appears intended to be a tale of himself.

It is perhaps for these reasons that Marx's "negro slave"–thing bears such a resemblance to the Haitian *zonbi* (Matory 2015d). On the one hand, Marx's "negro slave"–thing is quite unlike the usual slave in the religions of the West African Ewe (Rosenthal 1998) and the African diaspora. For most African American populations, the slave is the relative or the ancestor whose ingenuity and forbearance under difficult circumstances represents the best in us.

In the Anglo-Afro-American political tradition, as in early Hegel, the slave is the paradigmatic aspirant to freedom. In the Afro-Atlantic religions, the slave is the paradigm of tirelessness, materially and immediately effective labor, amoral service to those who feed him, and apocalyptic vengeance against social superiors who fail to live up to their end of the bargain (Matory 2007).

On the other hand, the Haitian walking dead, or *zonbi kò kadav*, work hard but without consciousness or volition and are frightening not because they threaten to harm other people but because they are what virtually every Haitian fears being turned into—a person socially dead, bereft of family and friends. The "negro slave" is an object of pity, but merely an object. Breathing but mindless, he is merely the alarm clock that wakes the European "wage slave" to his proper place in the world. The "negro slave" is less a person than a thing—a living, breathing antitype of the fulfilled human being that Marx sees as the deserved status of the European industrial worker. In effect, as a Haitian priest might put it, Marx has "zombified" the enslaved African, transferring the victim's agency and potential for value production to the white proletariat.

Marx's representation of the enslaved African is not inevitable. His "negro slave"–thing is quite unlike the Afro-Atlantic sacred slave, who is tireless, competent, and potentially vengeful. He is equally unlike the slave in Hegel's *Phenomenology of Spirit*, whose servitude makes him the paradigm of self-awareness and social consciousness. Marx has chosen to render the "negro slave" more like the African in Hegel's later *Philosophy of History*—the antihuman who proves real (i.e., white) people's worthiness to rule themselves democratically. The Black man is the precious sacrifice demanded by Marx's fetish.

Indeed, Marx's rhetorical abracadabra draws on 300 years of Protestant common sense in the era of the slave trade. Drawing attention away from a slew of debatable premises, Marx poetically declares, in effect, you must be as *confused as an African* if you don't believe his definition of the real nature of value. Under the threat of looking as stupid as an African, Marx's readership is embarrassed into accepting *two* premises of Marx's proletarian advocacy. After the labor theory of value itself, the second premise is that people as foolish as Africans do not realize that it is people who make gods.

Yet Marx himself is scarcely aware of the degree to which he and his "theory" defer to the power arising from things. Historical materialism itself inhered in animated, physical things—not only the Black "pedestal" but also the factory, the overcoat, and the piano—that moved and shaped Marx and the other denizens of his world in ways beyond their consciousness and volition. These material things gave form and focus to Marx's hopes and fears. Marx attributed an inexorable historical agency to industrial capitalism, his ideas were funded and shaped by his overcoats, and his piano appears to have been a siren of his unsustainable bourgeois aspirations. More-over, Marx sacrificed the soul of the "negro slave" in the mystical hope of fulfilling those aspirations. Marx's historical materialism was itself a fetish. But he seemed not to know it.

Indeed, Marx's "negro slave" alerts us to the fact that his theorization of fetishism—that is, the displacement of agency from people to things—has an obverse side: the selective stripping of agency and value from some people and their displacement onto other people and things. Through the rhetorical mechanism of the LTV, Marx displaced the agency of the "negro slave" and the value of his products onto the white proletariat and, through the proxy of the white wage worker, established Marx's own whiteness.

A fetish is a social allegory entailing a network of objects, stories, rela-tionships, and rules of exchange, but it becomes a fetish chiefly within the ecology of the competition for rank, loyalty, or profit. The fetish dramatizes and is an instrument of opposite conceivable courses of collective action. It normally includes in its body and its rituals both a commemoration and a denial of rival value codes and the positions of rival actors. This definition is heuristic—intended less to generate a science separating real fetishes from nonfetishes than to call attention to the shared ecology of Western theory and African religions, which are all too often treated as separate and as indepen-dent of the historically specific problems and aspirations of real and coeval human actors. Let us consider not only the previously unrecognized disani-mation of the "negro slave" but also some hitherto-underexamined animae in Marx's coat, his piano, and the factory in whose shadow he lived.

The Overcoat and the Factory

As telling as the absence of enslaved Africans from Marx's kitchen-sink lists of commodities is the superfluity of Marx's mentions of "coats" in his algebra of commodity value and the centrality of the factory. Stallybrass (1998) finds it significant that, in *Capital*, Marx mentions coats over and over again as examples of the commodity. During his exile in London, poverty had repeat-edly forced Marx to pawn his own overcoats, his family's clothing, and his wife's family heirlooms, which, at the pawnshop, became mere commodities, stripped of the social history and emotionally charged memory of their pro-duction, acquisition, and use. Marx briefly noted the interdependency and the reciprocally accelerating dynamic of exploitation in the English cotton mills and on the cotton plantations of the US South ([1867] 1990: 571). One might explain the vastly greater vividness of Marx's account of the mecha-nized cotton mill in terms of its centrality to the Industrial Revolution in England and to Marx's greater access to statistics about it. However, I would add that there was something deeply personal—and lopsidedly ambivalent—about Marx's connection to the factory and to the coat. And this ambivalence is structured by Marx's own ambiguous class and race.

Stallybrass offers a poignant biographical backdrop to Marx's analysis of factory-made commodities in general, which Marx argued are, during the process of capitalist exchange, similarly stripped of the history of personal life and labor that have made them (see, e.g., Marx [1867] 1990: 132, 133, 134, 136, 140, 141, 142, 144, 145, 147, 160, 167, 169). Stallybrass argues that by generalizing his personal experience with highly cathected but alienable things, Marx inferred that the erasure of the commodity's personal history was the general mechanism by which the European proletariat was deprived of the proceeds of its hard work and suffering. *Capital* resurrects the human history of the commodity's production, in a manner analogous to Marx's own repeated efforts to recover his sentimentally important overcoats from the pawnshop.

But it is also fair to ask why the "negro slave" did not deserve a similar resurrection of his or her humanity—that is, a similar recognition of his or her role in the unremunerated production of the cotton that helped Marx himself to avoid starving and helped him to recover his overcoat long enough to enable his wintertime visits to the British Museum, where he conducted the research upon which *Capital* was based. As Stallybrass (1998: 190) points out, "to the extent that the Marxes survived on Engels' generosity, they lived on the profits of the cotton industry." Marx's benefactor, Engels, earned his living in a Manchester cotton mill supplied by slave-grown cotton. The "negro slaves" who planted, weeded, and plucked that cotton in the hot sun, whose fingers were lacerated by the bolls, and whose backs carried the bales to market were, for all of their efforts, deprived of their freedom; mutilated physically and psychologically; separated from their husbands, wives, and children; and subjected to the total intergenerational theft of the surplus value they produced. By rights, my children and I should have inherited some of the capital that they produced. Instead, the proceeds of their labor power were shifted to a chain of European American settler colonists and metropolitan Europeans, some of which ended up as Engels's cash handouts to Marx himself. Marx's magnum opus, *Capital*, was not the product of his labor alone. It was and is a fetish that conceals many hours of "negro slave" labor that subsidized its research, formulation, and material production.

To be clear, I don't think that Marx favored actual "negro slavery." What I am saying is that he romanticized it, falsely declared it a relic of the past, opportunistically denied its essential cruelty and profitability, and used it as a vivid allegory for white wage workers' ostensibly incomparable suffering under capitalism. The real, contemporaneous condition of the "negro slave" was of no interest in Marx's forensics. Therefore, in his model of capitalism and the worker's potential resistance to it, Marx erased the actual history, the productive power, the skills, and the revolutionary agency of the "negro slave." The problem with this German worker–centered model of capitalism and its overthrow is not that it endorses the enslavement of Africans (or of Southeast Asians) or merely that it is racist but that (1) Marx's theory of capitalism is not the universal and culturally neutral history of capitalism that many latter-day scholars take it to be and that (2) it actively diminishes the economic contributions of Africans to capitalism, a contribution that benefited Marx and other German workers in a way that, if recognized, would also help us to understand the German workers' disinterest in following Marx's plan for an exclusively working-class political party.

Unlike Marx, most other nineteenth-century German-speaking workers could see the substantial material benefits of their alliance with the bourgeoisie and the royalty of the German-speaking states. By the mid-nineteenth century, all of these European classes were reaping the material and psychological benefits of their cross-cultural and collectively white dominance over the colonized and the enslaved. Each of these classes—European aristocrats, burghers, and wage workers—was in a position to decide whether its greatest hope and psychological advantage lay in identifying with the most oppressed Africans or with the most oppressive Europeans. Marx made a highly ambiguous decision, one that is no more fair or rational than the decisions of the Guinea Coast "fetishists." Like other fetishes, as Freud would later observe, Marx's "negro slave" was a vehicle of ambivalence: Marx both pitied him and castrated him. Marx was a Prussian-trained lawyer in London whose his skills were far less transferable than those of Prussia's manual labor diaspora, and whose political exile was even more impoverishing to him than their economic exile was to them. Hence, the white proletariat's alliance with white capitalists was working out better for them than for Marx, perhaps further illuminating Marx's own Janus-faced approach to the cruelty of slavery.

However, contrary to his overall argument that these exchanges at the pawnshop stripped each overcoat of its personal history, Stallybrass also shows that, even as Marx and the pawnbroker exploited the commercial exchange value of the coat, Marx never forgot where and when he acquired any given overcoat. He animated any given overcoat with sentiments that compelled him to recover it whenever possible. Beyond Stallybrass's point, it seems obvious that the pawnbroker never fully denied the social origin of the commoditized coat, either. Pawnshops normally keep a record of who pawned an item and withhold that item from resale for a certain period, thereby giving the original owner the first opportunity to buy back this socially spirited thing. Hence, Stallybrass's view that the stripping of the coat's human history might have inspired Marx's theory of commodity fetishism requires a caveat. Perhaps what made the coat such a repeated fulcrum of Marx's forceful re-valuation of the commodity is that fact, that, like the most enduring and powerful of fetishes, it embodied his own ambivalence. For Marx, as for the pawnbroker, the coat both affirmed and denied the social history of the coat.

In his essay Stallybrass argues poignantly that Marx developed a special empathy for the proletariat because he himself had fallen from the station of a middle-class lawyer with aristocratic connections in Prussia to that of a proletarian or subproletarian in London. Jonathan Sperber's 2013 biography further clarifies the personal backdrop of Marx's intriguing but often supraempirical claims about value, agency, and history. This backdrop creates a strong impression of Marx's ambivalence toward the working class and toward his own race and class.

Under the early nineteenth-century empire of Napoleon Bonaparte and under Prussia, Marx's birth family was surrounded by antisemitic violence, even as assimilated Jews were promised equal rights. Facing career discrimination as an aspiring notary and lawyer, Marx's father, Heinrich, embraced Enlightenment rationalism, converted to Protestantism, and made a respectable living. However, Karl could not sustain his family's upward social mobility (Sperber 2013: 9–22). He identified himself as a member of the "economic plebs" (Levine 2008: 93). As a freelance journalist, he was not precisely a wage worker, but he depended for his livelihood on the sale of his labor power, a condition by which Marx defined the exploitation of the wage worker, as well. We cannot say for sure whether Marx felt ashamed of his poverty, stigmatized by his Jewish ancestry, or both. However, neither his continual pursuit of loans nor his frequent pawning of personal clothing and family heirlooms could have been comfortable.

Among the factors that made Marx's pursuit of respect difficult was that he was a philandering husband who could not pay his bills. He continually had to beg his mother and his rich friend, the industrialist Friedrich Engels, for money. Amplifying his sense of desperation, Marx appears to have been enthralled with the very conventional bourgeois values and ambitions of the prosperous class to which he had been born and from which he had fallen.

In his personal life, he endeavored to be a patriarchal, virile male breadwinner, obedient to the bourgeois expectations of his day. Despite constant debt, he tried to keep his two legitimate children in music and art lessons. He supported one and sometimes two domestic servants, one of whom he secretly impregnated. Marx must have felt deeply ashamed that he could not take care of his family without Engels' constant charity. Marx's sense of capitalism's injustice may have been rooted partly in the tension between his bourgeois aspirations and his poverty.

The role of the commodity and of the factory in Marx's allegory of proper social relations is already well-known. For Marx, each embodies the surplus value unfairly skimmed off the proceeds from the sale of the workers' labor. While the building and the machinery of the factory look like an autonomous agent of production and like an autonomous source of productivity owned by the capitalist, they were, to Marx, nothing but the reified form of the stolen labor of past generations of laborers. By centering his theory on the factory, Marx demonstrated the exploitative character of then-current relations of production. However, he also vividly drew attention away from all of the other sites where value was being negotiated, such as the homes, plantations, royal courts, shops, and temples where people also had to choose whether to dispense limited resources in exchange for one desideratum or another. Marx also equated management and sales with exploitation, thereby vaporizing the labor of people like his factory-managing benefactor, Engels—people whose labor consists of intelligently coordinating other workers or distributing goods in accordance with the uneven demand for them, both of which can be difficult, costly, and risky tasks.

In Marx's life and livelihood, the factory was no more an abstraction than were his overcoats. It was the abstracted spirit of, among other factories, the specific cotton mill where Engels skimmed off the surplus labor that kept the underemployed Marx and his family fed and sheltered. It was both a site of managerial labor (which might indeed have been exploitative) and a source of life-sustaining charity. The Schadenfreude-laden diminution of the "negro slave" in Marx's historical materialism is striking and, I have argued, motivated by Marx's ambiguous racial and class status. Equally striking is the contrast between, on the one hand, Marx's denial of the material benefits he drew from the agrarian enslavement of African Americans and, on the other, his intense criticism of the industrial factory. Particularly in light of Engels's management of a cotton mill, the absence of cotton from Marx's extensive opening discussion of commodity fetishism in *Capital*, volume 1, in contrast to the repetitive mention of linen, reads like an evasion of Marx's own immediate connection to the exploitation of the "negro slave." It is difficult not to recognize in this lopsided critique of capitalism a double-edged ego defense—one that exaggerated his sense of unjust suffering relative to the "negro slave" and also resentfully denied Engels's credit for the charity upon which Marx shamefully depended for his livelihood. Middling populations tend to resent their inferiors and their superiors equally, but their survival depends on the careful sublimation of the latter resentment. Marx seems to have displaced his resentment of Engels onto the abstract "factory."

Deus ex Machina: The Piano and the Millennium

Against the backdrop of his poverty and his ambivalent dependency on cotton- and factory-generated largesse, the piano in Marx's living room acquires special significance. It appears to embody a class disappointment and hope at the root of Marx's millenarian dream. Marx could neither sustain the bourgeois lifestyle he desired nor mobilize a purely working-class party to abolish the intra-European hierarchy that kept that lifestyle just beyond his reach.

Even as poverty forced him to beg for alms from Engels, Marx kept his daughters in piano lessons, recalling the historically specific and culture-specific aspirations of an emergent nineteenth-century middle class to mimic the airs of the European aristocracy. Around the LTV, and undoubtedly to the discordant tune of his daughters' piano practice, Marx constructed a whole model of history and of its proper subjects based upon the notion that the now-penniless European workers would one day, through historical materialist inevitability, achieve the lifestyle of the piano-playing petit bourgeoisie, a lifestyle that he himself had been accustomed to in childhood and was constantly in danger of losing.

The labor theory of value was clearly insufficient to inspire other propertyless workers to follow Marx onto the field of battle against capitalism and the rule of the bourgeoisie. At least after 1850, as Marx's proposals for an all-proletarian political party failed and the workers chose other leaders over him, he amended the labor theory of value with the idea of an inexorable teleological history that would inevitably bring his aspirations to fruition. Marx made the millenarian prediction that improvements in manufacturing technology would make it possible one day for people to work so little that they could practice art and scholarship all day.

This prediction could not reasonably be construed as a mere extrapolation from the known course of history to date. Indeed, it sounds like Marx's bourgeois daydream about the life that he would have liked for himself and his family. As Sperber suggests, Marx may have projected his own exilic, millenarian dream—a dream frustrated by his failure as a bourgeois breadwinner—onto the European working class as a whole. It would also be fair to say that Marx fetishized history itself—that is, he turned the contradiction-driven and ostensibly inevitable flow of events into an autonomous, willful agent—and prospectively credited it with the ultimate reversal of his own personal downward mobility, lack of agency, and leadership failures.

Marx's salvific historical prediction recapitulated a template found equally in the messianic tales of the Hebrews' various exiles. It served as Marx's trump card in his vituperative competition with more effective leaders, who were more willing to compromise with the bourgeoisie, were better liked by the workers, and, incidentally, displayed less contempt for the workers' own thinking about their own conditions and identity options. For example, Marx and Engels called the workers "knot-heads" (Sperber 2013: 502). Like much of the Hebrew Bible, historical materialism was a triumphal tale told by the defeated.

Marx's own imaginative but strategic conception of class history resulted in bizarre betrayals of principle and of the workers themselves. For example, he endorsed political deals that denied farmers and workers relief from desperately impoverishing and oppressive situations. And he did so because he felt that such short-term relief might delay the revolution. Sperber also shows that Marx manipulated and misrepresented his relationship to the Paris Commune (a short-lived, 1871 proletarian urban revolt against what Marx regarded as Napoleon III's counterrevolution), and he shut down the International Working Men's Association to prevent its democratic transformation, all because Marx wanted to preserve images that would give hope to future actors who might endeavor to carry out his programs (Sperber 2013: 502–60).

Despite their failure as empirical observations or even as empirically grounded extrapolations, some prophecies become inspirations for real people to act in certain ways or even to change the world. Yet prophecy-inspired social movements are seldom exactly the ones predicted, and they do not prove that history has a will of its own.

In the end, Marx's prophecies illustrate, rather than disprove, the power of fetishes in the hands and minds of the people who believe in them. After Marx's death, Engels's influential editing, compilation, and redaction of Marx's ideas focused on the post-1850s exilic and last-stand millenarian phase of Marx's thinking about history and political economy. In Russia, Lenin used Engels's selective redaction of Marx as an inspiration to revolution. Marx's fetish—man-made and Engels-amplified though it was—had power. It inspired the twentieth century's most influential revolution—the Russian Revolution. Engels's redaction of Marx's ideas was also taken by the outgunned socialists of western Europe as an assurance that they could hold fast to their hopes for revolution without throwing themselves suicidally into battle.

Race, Religion, and the Lopsided Ambivalence of Historical Materialism

What we regard in hindsight as theory should not be abstracted from the historical context, personal circumstances, or strategic goals of its articulation and use. Marx's redefinition of commodity value through the negative proxy of "negro slaves" and his own interactions with coats, factories, and a piano embodied a proposal for the revision of circum-Atlantic social relations that was as potentially liberating for Marx as it was oppressive to Black people.

Marx seemed generally opposed to slavery and racial discrimination, but his private correspondence reveals deep ambivalence. On the one hand, Marx condemned the racial chauvinism of Joseph Arthur de Gobineau. Marx also analogized the US oppression of African Americans to the English oppression of the Irish, and he condemned the racism of white workers in the US South as complicit in a divide-and-conquer strategy by the southern white elite. Sperber adds that Marx objected to his partly African-descended son-in-law not on the grounds of race but on the grounds of the son-in-law's lack of a steady income, an ironic lack of empathy that, in my view, may or may not have been related to race.

However, it is not just a matter of speculation that, in pursuit of a solution to their European social problem, Marx and Freud also constructed the African as the constituent Other. Marx's private condemnation of a Jewish rival for leadership of the workers revealed the ambivalence of the *assimilé* and the parvenu. Indeed, Marx could have been the poster child for Fanon's *Black Skin, White Masks* ([1952] 2008). In his private correspondence, he employed "a fantastic array of anti-Semitic invectives . . . and anti-Semitic stereotypes" (Sperber 2013: 342), suggesting an ego-defensive denial of his own vulnerability, a denial consistent with the equally deflective, anti-African rhetoric of fetishism. For example, Marx wrote of a rival Jewish labor leader, Ferdinand Lassalle, "It is now completely clear to me, that, as proven by the *shape of his head and the growth of his hair*, he [Lassalle] stems from the Negroes who joined the march of Moses out of Egypt (if his mother or grandmother on his father's side did not mate with a nigger). Now this combination of Jewry and Germanism with the negroid basic substance must bring forth a peculiar product. The *pushiness of this lad is nigger-like*" (Sperber 2013: 411, italics mine).

Of course, Marx himself was vulnerable to all of these charges and insinuations. Not only was he reputedly pushy, but also, on account of his swarthy complexion, his friends and family called him "The Moor" (e.g., Sperber 2013: 38; Stallybrass 1998: 198). Indeed, by the shape of his head and the growth of his hair, Marx bears an uncanny resemblance to the nineteenth-century African American abolitionist Frederick Douglass. And he was not alone. European gentiles who disfavored Jewish enfranchisement had long observed similarities of complexion, hair, and physiognomy shared by Jews and "mulattoes" like Douglass. Marx's Afro easily rivaled Douglass's (see figures 1.1 and 1.2).

In a judolike retort to the racism that opposed their enfranchisement in the democratizing states of Europe, Marx and Freud turned their eyes toward the biologically egalitarian, socially antiegalitarian, and globally oriented so-cial evolutionisms of nineteenth-century England and France. If the social evolutionist ethnologist E. B. Tylor and the exponents of the French Enlightenment were correct in the conviction that biology is not destiny, then the assimilated descendants of European Jews could claim to have evolved far enough toward civilization to deserve full citizenship and inclusion in the privileges of whiteness. This logic necessarily sacrificed the aspirations of unassimilated Jews and Africans to equal economic and political rights within the emergent global empire centered on Europe.

From the start, Marx's program for pan-European social equality rested on a radical denunciation of religion and of Judaism in particular, which he characterized as ego-centered, profiteering, and Jesuitical in its circumvention of the law in the service thereof. He argued that the investment of human beings' naturally collectivist nature—or "species being" (*Gattungswesen*)—in the state follows the same logic whereby religious people project their own collective agency into a heavenly being, leading the general populace to think of themselves as self-serving individuals naturally driven solely by competition and the pursuit of profits through commercial exchange. Marx characterized Judaism as the very spirit of this self-alienated ideology and slavish conduct in bourgeois society (Marx [1843] 1978). Though he had been born Jewish, Marx thus dramatized his difference from the "Sabbath Jew" and the "everyday Jew," or "huckster," while the first volume of *Capital* highlighted how different he and his kind were from the African "fetishist" and the "negro-slave."

Nazism and its premise of Aryan racial superiority would later stonewall this sort of *assimilé* appeal, rejecting the social evolutionist premise of human biological equality and the possibility of any non-Aryans' self-improvement through cultural assimilation. Ironically, Nazism—like late Hegelianism—shared with Marx and Freud's campaigns the motive to achieve full inclusion in the privileges of Europeanness for a population that had felt excluded from (or not yet fully included in) those privileges. In the case of Nazism, this population was the German people as a whole.

Marx's proletariat clearly has a skin color. And it is not mine, or that of most Afro-Atlantic priests. At his most miserable, Marx's proletarian looks like a European, and, at his most fortunate, he looks like a white settler colonialist. Similarly, Freud would flirt with Zionism. Marx's "negro slave"–thing—a neighbor or involuntary servant to many of those white settlers—is but a European fetish, haplessly proving, by his ostensibly opposite skin color, that the status of the slave is not natural to the European worker. Indeed, while Marx was writing and during the decades that followed his death, not-quite-white emigrants in flight from exploitation in Ireland, southern Europe, and eastern Europe homesteaded on Native American land and founded labor unions in the United States that made a policy of excluding African Americans from the collective identity of the proletariat and from the benefits of collective bargaining. The labor unionists had adopted the typical colonial- and imperial-era strategy of demanding their share of surplus value based not only upon the class that *distinguished* them from the capitalists but also upon the race that *united* them with the capitalists. Marx's millenarian cry on behalf of the white proletariat pantomimes his own fear that lower-class and not-so-white Europeans would be left out of the benefits of Europe's domination of the rest of the world. Marx's class-based model of exploitation focused on the wage workers' declining *percentage* of the surplus value that they ostensibly created, rather than the *gross* gains in surplus value that white workers also secured as white capitalists grew wealthier through the expropriation of resources and labor from the colonies.

Conclusion to Part I

Historical materialism embodies the ambivalence of a man between races, between religions, and between classes—one who, in all of these ways, struggled for earnings and honor amid the rise of the bourgeois nation-state and European overseas empire. Downwardly mobile in class and the son of a convert from Judaism to Protestantism, Marx employed nonracist British and French social evolutionism to articulate the hope of greater rights for the white working class and, by proxy, for himself. However, following the model set by the Enlightenment, and particularly the later writings of Hegel, he did so through a theory that defined Black people as the paradigm of illogicality and incompetence, by contrast to which Marx and the white proletariat are made to look particularly worthy of equality with—and even supremacy over—their white exploiters.

The parallel Afro-Atlantic social revolution prioritized the constructive *intersection* of contrary classes, races, religions, and genders, such that the ideal person is defined not by contrast to a stigmatized class or ethnoracial Other but by her virtue at introjecting the Other. Even in the context of Europe, Marx's strategic and rhetorical choices were not inevitable. They contrast with European aristocrats' dignified portraits of African royalty, as well as the choices of the early Hegel and of the German Romantics. Marx's own biography and the material furnishings of his intellectual life help us to understand the motives behind his particular intervention in a circum-Atlantic social revolution with ideological roots on the sixteenth- and seventeenth-century

Guinea Coast. The exponents of the European branch of this social revolution were typically lower-status Europeans seeking upward mobility by distinguishing themselves sharply from the enslaved African, the paradigmatic victim of the exclusion and abuse from which the scions of the Enlightenment wished to exempt themselves. The vulnerability of such lower-status Europeans to similar treatment persuaded some of them to defend and dignify Africans, while that vulnerability persuaded others to clarify why it was the Africans, and not they, who deserved such treatment.

Marx's lopsided ambivalence skewed toward the latter strategy. Marx's ambivalence animated his "negro slave," his coats, his piano, and Engels's cotton mill with intense, contradictory, and lopsided affect. By analyzing Marx's supercathected material things as "fetishes" in this way, I aim not to invalidate the program of social reform that they embody but to emphasize the materiality and real-world character of Marx's "theory," the circum-Atlantic and intercultural frisson at its roots, and the ambivalence that makes these material things such powerful switching stations of social relationships.[1] What makes the commodity a "fetish," in my terms, is not the self-evident wrongness of Marx or his adversaries but the fact that Marx consciously advocates a *rival* interpretation of the commodity's value—an interpretation that, I have argued, is more usefully defined by its social positionality and by the social reforms it advocates than by its objective or empirical correctness.

Each fetish encompasses a historically and culturally specific paradigm of recommended social relations conducted by a peculiar network of ostensible entities, relationships, rules, idea-images, and things through which reality is meant to be experienced. Every fetish also anticipates doubts about and rival alternatives to its construction of the world. In sum, it embodies a tension between rival ideas about what matters in the world and how it is classified and about what constitutes an actor. For example, any given fetish may simultaneously recognize and also anticipate doubts about the reality and the value-producing potential of "individuals," "spirits," "corporations," "economic classes," "nation-states," or any one of an infinite range of other possibilities, such as "wage slaves" and "negro slaves." Hence, each fetish also encompasses an idea—and its contrary—about which types of human effort and aspiration are possible and legitimate, as well as how people should cooperate and how the proceeds of cooperation should be distributed. Marx's fetish also encodes a prediction about the inevitable past, present, and future course of events. However, like the Bible, Marx's narrative started out as a wishful story told by a defeated narrator and often became the self-narration of people who victimized others under the pretense that, otherwise, they themselves would be victimized.

Marx's fetish proposes a logic of "advancement" for humanity that is appealing to me in many ways. For example, it denies the antecedent idea that the spirits governing our collective lives are independent of human action and imagination and of our material, biological, and social being. Historical materialism undermines the antecedent idea that kings and capitalists are the uniquely real agents and the true heroes of history. However, like any other fetish, the labor theory of value hides as much as it highlights and undoes as much as it does, precisely because even its most useful insights unselfconsciously embody the social position and the self-defensive interests of its author. And those interests haunt the theory more powerfully because they are covered by the white cloth of theoretical abstraction, algebraic x's and y's, and, in translation, mysterious capitalizations and hyphenations. Marx deserves considerable credit for applying Hegelian dialectics to early nineteenth-century political economy and for the originality of highlighting the inequalities in the distribution of surplus value that are encoded in the capitalist logic of commodity exchange.

Yet, like most sarcastic people, Marx represented his adversary in satirical terms that neither captured their thinking fairly nor fully justified or consistently explicated his own position. From my point of view, the just-so, as-if models of capitalism articulated in Marx's definition of the commodity and its value look no less religious than the ostensible misunderstandings of value and agency that he attributes to everyday workers, capitalists, and Africans. Marx's argument by analogy, that capitalism must be unfair because it resembles an African religion and political economy, acquires its power not only from the fact that this displacement of worthlessness from the European wage worker to the African and the "negro slave" sang a song familiar to the European Protestants of his day but also from the fact that this put-down of Africans was casual, comical, satirical, and implicit—a semiabstraction—rather than a careful description of African, Haitian, or Afro–Latin American religion and society that the reader was invited to examine for empirical gaps and biases. Marx's rhetoric does not invite us to inspect the real people or the real situation to which the alleged wrongs of capitalism are being compared. Instead, Marx treats the suffering of these people at the hands of European and settler colonialist capitalists and wage workers as a mere "pedestal" for the display of the superior suffering and nobility of white wage workers. Indeed, much as the late Hegel blames enslaved Black people for their own enslavement, Marx implicitly represents capitalism's greatest victim—in the guise of the African "fetishist"—as the culprit responsible for the whole unjust system.

When we abstract theory from the socially positioned and intercultural frisson experienced by European merchants and social theorists, it is easy to forget that the term "fetish" possesses an extant, real-world referent with its own socially positioned perspective on the same intercultural encounter. It should also be remembered that, for the past half millennium, both Europeans and West Africans have been towering participants in a shared circum-Atlantic symbolic and political economy. West African societies, like European societies, have long practiced a mix of market exchange with profit orientation, asymmetrical gift-giving, and relationship-building exchange. Indeed, these types of exchange have never been entirely discrete in West African or in European societies. In these ways, the European and African social revolutions that have negotiated and renegotiated the value and agency of people and things over the past five hundred years have done so and only partly in contrast to each other and, unambiguously, under materially linked social conditions and in dialogue with each other.

Amid this dialogue, Marx followed the Dutch Calvinist merchant-adventurers on the Guinea Coast and the protagonists of the Enlightenment in drawing a sharp contrast between, on the one hand, the agency and value-conferring capacity of people and, on the other, the non-agentive and "naturally" utilitarian value of things. In Marx's model, a corollary to this dichotomy is the sharp contrast between the ideally value-producing, independent, and totally agentive subject (i.e., the landholding white settler colonist) and the non–value producing, dependent, and totally non-agentive "negro slave."

Afro-Atlantic priests tend to imagine no such dichotomy. For them, each person or thing is a potential subject and a potential object, depending on the priest's engagement with him, her, or it through rituals of exchange. In fact, through ritual, each person and animated thing vacillates between states of subjectivity and objectivity, and this vacillation defines the normatively nonegalitarian social relationships typical of Afro-Atlantic society. Indeed, the copresence and reciprocal relationship between subject and object, between agent and patient, between producer and produced, and between the possessor and the possessed is precisely what constitutes every person and animates every sacred thing, or fetish.

Confronted with Marx's Enlightenment-inspired model of society as a unity among equal producers without enduring asymmetrical debts to each other, the average Afro-Atlantic priest is left wondering, "What, then, is the basis of social relationships?" African and Latin American newcomers to Protestant Europe or the US often value their increased freedom from the hierarchical relationships with and the asymmetrical material demands of relatives and neighbors in the homeland. But they also feel lonely, wondering how Protestant Westerners survive their anomie. They then seek solace in religions modeled on royalism, feudalism, slavery, marriage, and the pastoral herding of sheep, dramatizing the restoration of relationships of mutual dependency with supercathected crowns, scepters, croziers, whips, and chains. In these religions, worshippers eschew the egalitarian, even-Steven exchanges of cash and commodities that define the actor-networks of Western individualism.

Before we turn to the further complexities and insights of the Afro-Atlantic gods, let us examine the fetishes that operationalized the brotherhood of psychoanalysis. Like Marx's historical materialism, Freud's psychoanalysis not only critiqued religion but also deeply imbibed its language, in many ways reproducing the forms of fetishism—or displacements of value and agency from their proper human location—that it sought to cure. Also like Marx, Freud struggled to disambiguate himself amid the gentile suspicion that he, too, deserved the fate of the African. However, whereas Marx tried to deanimate things and project value-making agency solely onto the white industrial laborer, Freud and the Afro-Atlantic priests have both highlighted the internally heterogeneous nature of human subjectivity and the normality of rituals that give life to material things.

PART II

THE ACROPOLIS, THE COUCH, THE FUR HAT, AND THE "SAVAGE"

On Freud's Ambivalent Fetish

Psychoanalysis emerged at the height of European imperialism in Africa and amid the debate over whether Jews and women were more like Africans or more like European gentile men in their anatomy, health, intelligence, and lawfulness, and therefore in the rights they deserved within the emerging nation-states of central Europe. Moreover, Freud seems to have struggled with homosexual desires, desires that the gentile medical establishment had come to think of as a brand of "fetishism" threatening to the health of the nation-state, further diminishing Freud's hopes for acceptance as a full bearer of the rights to which a pale-skinned, heterosexually married, gentile European man was entitled.

Marx's and Freud's ambiguous racial identities provide an indispensable backdrop to this archaeology of the fetish problem. Marx and Freud were assimilated Jewish men facing sometimes fatal questions about their belonging and right to a livelihood in the emerging nation-states of central Europe. On the one hand, Marx's mother and many of his admiring colleagues called him "The Moor." Similarly, on account of his very dark eyes and hair, Freud's mother lovingly called him her "little blackamoor," suggesting a pattern of voluntary self-identification with Africans—albeit not without ambivalence—by this class of assimilated central European Jews. According to a similar vocabulary, they faced rejection by their gentile countrymen and women.

In the SABA Collection, item 1059 shows a *Sarotti-Mohr* (Sarotti Moor doll), the mascot of Berlin's Sarotti chocolate shop and an affectionate early twentieth-century representation of the sort of blackamoor to which Marx's and Freud's family and friends compared them. Although the original character was invented in 1918, this doll was probably made in the 1950s. This depiction of a black child is strikingly humane and dignified, particularly in contrast to its typically contemporaneous white North American counterparts.[1] More in line with the bourgeois logic of the Enlightenment, European antisemites employed a related racial vocabulary and imagery to demean Jews.

Even with European overseas imperialism at its height in the 1880s and 1890s, the metropolis was beset with inner conflicts. France was in demographic and military decline within Europe, the Austro-Hungarian Empire was coming apart, an economic depression hit in the 1890s, and liberal Europeans were torn between the pretension of Enlightenment "civilization" and the savage realities of colonial domination. It was against this backdrop that European sexologists came to name and diagnose a whole range of European sexual dysfunctions as "fetishism" (Nye 1993; Noyes 1997).

Yet, in the history of Europe, it is no surprise when Jews or Roma are scapegoated as the chief embodiment or even cause of this social and psychological crisis. Just as Hegel had characterized Africans as prime exemplars of foolishness, so had he characterized Jews as an atavism in European culture (Gilman 1993: 83). The rise of Darwinist biological evolutionism and scientific racism in the mid- to late nineteenth century amplified Hegel's eighteenth-century brand of antisemitism with claims that Jews were the disproportionate bearers of mental and physical disease, minions of rabid capitalism, quacks, drug addicts, effeminates, homosexuals, and people therefore unworthy of citizenship in the emerging nation-state. Even their way of speaking German—called "Mauscheln"—came to be regarded as a symptom of permanent hereditary inferiority and outsider status (Gilman 1993).

Like other assimilated central European Jews, Marx and Freud must have felt vulnerable to such antisemitic stereotypes. However, they did not tend to deny their truth. Instead, both Marx and Freud advertised their personal difference from the kind of Jews who, they appear to have agreed, *deserved* to be stereotyped—that is, unassimilated eastern Jews, merchant Jews, immigrant Jews, and so forth. As a scientist and a physician, Freud worked hard to prove the nonracial nature of these differences, which, in theory, would free a culturally assimilated Jewish man like himself from persecution.

Amid the rise of European overseas imperialism, the atrocities committed by the Belgians in Congo (1885–1912), the German effort to wipe out the Hereros in Southwest Africa (1904), racial segregation in the US (1890–2015), and the scientific racism that justified these phenomena, Marx and Freud were aware of the parallels between their own vulnerable position and the similarly perilous position of Africans and African Americans from the mid-nineteenth century to the early twentieth.

Awareness of these parallels was widespread in Europe. For example, during the 1890s, European minorities were called "the negroes of Europe," in a clear comparison of their oppression to that of African Americans. In the popular parlance and professional science of the era, central Europeans also frequently called Jews and other European minorities "blacks," "Africans," "primitives," and "Kaffirs" (an insulting term of Arabic origin that Freud joined the Boers in calling the Zulu people [Freud (1913) 1946: 18; Gilman 1993: 18–23]). Jews were described as "black and ugly" (see also Gilman 1993: 160), as well as "prognathous" like Africans (with the craniometric implication of simian unintelligence). In overall appearance, they were frequently compared to mulattoes, and Jewish religion was characterized as superstitious, illogical, and full of sophistry (Gilman 1993: 151). Neither the emancipation and assimilation of the Jews in early nineteenth-century Europe nor the brief emancipation and assimilation of US "negroes" during late nineteenth-century Reconstruction diminished the dominant caste's hunt for markers of underlying, permanent, and biological difference between the dominant and the subordinate. In fact, such emancipation and cultural assimilation *accelerated* the hunt for such markers, which, in a dialogue between the two continents, gave rise to a science of hidden, underlying biological difference.

The notion of ethnological Schadenfreude helps us to understand the anti-African (and antifemale) vocabulary of Freud's efforts to convince himself and others that he deserved membership in the elite of Europe's emerging global empire, exempt from the exclusion suffered by women and the heartless violence suffered foremost by Africans. Yet Freud's own racial and sexual ambiguity and, therefore, his vulnerability to the diagnosis of "fetishism" inspired in him some African-looking—but, by Afro-Atlantic standards, underdeveloped—insights into the centrality of ambivalence in the human character and into the role of things in the management of ambivalence. However, in his extensive analysis of others' fetishism, Freud failed to recognize the degree to which he himself, as the founder of psychoanalysis, was also creating a fetish. Like that of Marx, his drive to transcend religion produced a remarkably religious-looking worldview. Psychoanalysis was every bit as allegorical in its vocabulary, concrete and sacralizing in its iconography, ecclesiastical in its hierarchy, and invested with the anticipation of dissent as are the Yorùbá- and Fòn-Atlantic religions. And unlike Marx, Freud successfully mobilized a thriving community of devotees to his fetish during his own lifetime. The immediate and towering success of Freud's fetish may indeed be indebted to its likeness to the African fetishes that he implicitly belittled.

It is a further feature of Jews' "discreditable" status (Goffman 1963) that they are vulnerable to the ethnological Schadenfreude of the very groups that they endeavored to use for the same rhetorical purposes (also Matory 2015). For example, possessing no greater knowledge of Marx's and Freud's people than Marx and Freud possessed about them, Afro-Cuban *santeros* describe potentially consecrated but unconsecrated things as "Jewish" (*judíos*), denoting their powerlessness and unworthiness of respect. In the Cuban Palo tradition, a normative *prenda*, or cauldron dwelling of an *inquice* god, contains a crucifix, which embodies and denotes the god's willingness to act only in moral ways. By contrast, because it lacks a crucifix, a "Jewish" *prenda* is amoral. If such a *prenda* is paid to do so, he or she will commit even the most morally reprehensible acts on behalf of his or her master. Implicit in this vision of the cosmological hierarchy is the view that normative *santeros* and *paleros* share in the goodness and sacredness of European Christians to the degree that the Jew does not, and that joining in the denunciation of the Jew is proof of the normative Afro-Cuban initiate's Christianness, goodness, and innocence.

The contents of what English speakers call the human "mind" and "heart" are a mystery to others and, often, to the self. However, psychoanalysis and Afro-Atlantic religions are both sciences grounded in the most crucial life skills of subordinated populations, which include, as Hegel's master-slave dialectic suggests, the discernment and management of other people's unspoken feelings and motives through attention not only to their words but also to their deeds, gestures, silences, and slips of the mask. Part II applies the similar social expertise of a fin-de-siècle central European Jew and of Afro-Atlantic priests to the discernment of the ambivalent feelings and motives behind psychoanalysis itself. It should be noted that members of the early leadership of psychoanalysis regulated its tight-knit community and professional organization by formally and informally psychoanalyzing each other, the published results of which are the source of much of my evidence, as well.

The Fetishes That Assimilated
Jewish Men Make

Whereas Marx's fetish—that is, the actor-network of value-conflicted things, people, practices, and ideas making up historical materialism—explicitly addressed a European class problem, Freud's fetish explicitly addressed a gender problem and implicitly addressed a sexual orientation problem. Just as I have argued in connection with Marx, I will argue that Freud was also addressing a racial problem. Since the nineteenth century, relatively unmarked and dominant European populations had employed metaphors of Africanness to justify the oppression of Jews, Irish people, Mediterranean people, and other relatively marked European populations. For such marked Europeans, disambiguation—that is, the demonstration of their difference from and superiority to the likes of Africans—was difficult to resist as a response to intra-European discrimination and as a strategy of potential escape from oppression.

For example, recapitulating Marx's litotic rhetoric, Freud exploited the post-Enlightenment logic that his contrast to the definitively inferior "savage" or African qualified even a sexually closeted Jewish man for citizenship in the emergent national republics of Europe. In sum, I argue that the anti-African fetishes of Marx and Freud appealed for the citizenship of assimilated Jewish men by displacing the stigma they suffered onto not only Black people but also onto unassimilated Jews and, in Freud's case, onto women, as well.

As they endeavored to direct Europe's fire away from themselves and toward Africa, few of these stigmatized Europeans truly felt vulnerable to the large-scale enslavement and mass murder that were taking place in the personal fiefdom of Belgian King Leopold known as the Congo Free State (1885–1908), events coincident with Freud's invention of psychoanalysis. But, long before the Nazis began stoking their ovens in the 1930s and '40s, Freud must have felt an intuition of his naïveté about the threat to not-so-white Europeans. Psychoanalysis hedged its bets with an appeal for the gentile master's empathy to the European Jew and the "savage" alike. Freud both confirmed the imperialist's and the lynch mob's myth that black and brown men are sexual "savages" and, at the same time, told the gentile, "The name is changed, but the tale is told of *you*" (Marx [1867] 1990: 378). "The savage is within you, too." Such is the ambivalent, Janus-faced nature of psychoanalysis.

The ambitious gentile champions of the Enlightenment had long employed a similar strategy—and, in cases like Hegel's, had shown similar ambivalence. But I argue that the doubly ambiguous and doubly acute condition of assimilated Jewish men in the nineteenth century made their choices especially fraught and especially productive for our understanding of how fetishes work. Part II is a close thematic reading of Freud's most comprehensive biography, written by a fellow psychoanalyst and one of Freud's closest acolytes. This biography reveals much about Freud's life that Freud endeavored to hide from the public while he was alive. This close reading is paired with an analysis of Freud's own writings and supercathected material possessions, which ultimately shed light on Marx, the Afro-Atlantic religions, and Freud himself.

Though erotic fetishes like shoes, noses, and fur were the material foci of Freud's theorization of the fetish, I will argue that Freud's greatest fetish—or supercathected thing embedded with dueling value codes and premises about proper social order—was the penis itself. Yet Freud's talking cure and his pursuit of citizenship for assimilated Jewish men in the emergent nation-states of central Europe rested, sometimes literally, on a number of additional material things of profoundly conflicted significance—the couch and the upright chair, alcohol, cigars, fraternity rings, the Acropolis, Rome, and an extensive collection of antiquities. In part III, this same material-textual mode of analysis will be used to illuminate Afro-Atlantic animated things and the gods Black people make.

Freud was especially articulate about the forms of complementarity, hierarchy, ambivalence, and ambiguity embodied in the sexual fetish. Combined with an awareness of his own sexual and racial ambiguity, Freud's theory of fetishism is employed as an especially vivid model for the polysemy and ritual efficacy of the fetish. Freud called attention to the filial ambivalence embedded in the most compelling fetishes, but to me, Freud's own life and work reveal how the fetish also clarifies, inverts, and works out hierarchical dichotomies related to class, race, religion, sex, and sexual orientation with symbolic reference to each other. Inspired by Freud, Victor Turner (1967, e.g.) detected this sort of polysemy in African rituals. In turn, African rituals make it obvious to me that Freud's fetish is just as polysemic, ambivalent, hierarchical, and intent on wish fulfillment.

The aim of this part, then, is to clarify the personal race- and sexual orientation–related problems that Freud faced and tried to redress as he wrote publicly about gender identity and religion. Like other fetishes, I will argue, Freud's psychoanalysis is best understood not as an ethereal idea or disembodied philosophy but as a historically and culturally specific network of people, things, idea-images, conventions, and relationships that enhanced some people's forms of agency and value production at the expense of others'.

Psychoanalysis: A Theory, a Practice, and a Furniture of Ambivalence

Psychoanalysis is not only a form of therapy but also a theory of human nature in general, a social movement, and a set of material things. The dreams of Sigmund Freud (1856–1939) are the primary data upon which this theory was founded, a phenomenon with many parallels in African and African-diaspora religions, not to mention their Native American counterparts. Psychoanalysis was consciously Freud's attempt to understand the relationship between the "mind" and the body, as well as how man (I use this gendered noun advisedly) became a conscious animal. But it was also Freud's self-aware attempt to make a living based upon these ideas and to achieve respect as an assimilated Jewish man in an era of rising antisemitism. With this movement, he sought to immortalize himself through the spread and triumph of his theory throughout the West and its permanent institutionalization as a profession that enjoyed the esteem of gentiles.

Freud was subject to discrimination particularly in light of the rising racial science of his day. He was born on May 6, 1856, in Freiberg, Moravia, then part of the Austro-Hungarian Empire and now part of the Czech Republic. It was then a provincial and economically dying town where Czech nationalists scapegoated Jews. His family would move to Vienna when he was four, and that more cosmopolitan environment helped make him eligible for an ambiguous sort of redemption through the relatively nonracist theories being generated by the social evolutionist ethnology of his day. While Freud avoided publishing information about his personal life and, indeed, endeavored to destroy the most revealing correspondence about it, his intimate friend, acolyte, and biographer Ernest Jones divined many of the personal motives behind Freud's intellectual and social project, motives more than circumstantially related to the racially ambiguous ranking of Jews within the emerging nation-states and translocal empires of Freud's day. These motives were also related to Freud's personal struggle to achieve dignity as a bourgeois gentleman, despite his father's low financial and social standing, his own early difficulties in establishing a career sufficient to support his beloved fiancée, and, at the height of his exposition of psychoanalytic theory, his then–socially unacceptable homosexual feelings toward his colleague, the Austrian physician Wilhelm Fliess.

Jones ([1953] 1961) showed that from childhood on, Freud dreamt of and predicted his own grandeur, perhaps redressing the shame he felt about the apparent submission of his father, Jacob, in the face of antisemitism.[1] Jones wrote that

> his father never regained the place he had held in his esteem after the painful occasion when he told his twelve-year-old boy how a Gentile had knocked off his new fur cap into the mud and shouted at him: "Jew, get off the pavement." To the indignant boy's question "And what did you do?" he calmly replied: "I stepped into the gutter and picked up my cap." This lack of heroism on the part of his model man shocked the youngster[,] who at once contrasted it in his mind with the behavior of Hamilcar when he made his son Hannibal swear on the household altar to take vengeance on the Romans. Freud evidently identified himself with Hannibal, for he said that ever since then Hannibal had a place in his fantasies. (Jones [1953] 1961: 19)

Over the years, Freud vocally identified with not only Hannibal (after whom he modeled his own aspirations to conquer the West) but also Alexander, Napoleon Bonaparte's Jewish general André Masséna, Oliver Cromwell (after whom Freud named his second son), and, when he finally moved to the land of his dreams, England, William the Conqueror (Jones [1953] 1961: 19, 519). Freud's desire to claim and conquer a Europe that had repeatedly subjugated his people and slighted him personally was a continual theme in his storytelling and self-analysis. But his stories also exemplify the general ambivalence of the dominated toward their dominators, combining rebellious anger with adulation and emulation. It is perhaps for these reasons that Freud rhapsodized over his visits in adulthood to the Acropolis, regarding those visits as the fulfillment of a forbidden wish to outdo his father (Jones [1953] 1961: 323). Freud had also nursed a lifelong dream of visiting Rome (Freud [1899/1900] 1965; Jones [1953] 1961: 245). These sites are among the defining touchstones of a civilization that Freud was desperate to join and from which his people had, since the rise of Christianity, suffered perennial exclusion.

Freud worshipped the Europe represented by these sites, but, according to Jones, a deep-seated ambivalence kept him away from Rome for many years, despite the extensiveness of his travel in northern and central Italy through-out that time. Despite the powerful desire to "gain possession of Rome, the 'Mother of Cities,'" which desire he shared with fellow Semite Hannibal, he was repeatedly "thwarted by some nameless inhibition when he was on the point of success" (Jones [1953] 1961: 246). For years, Freud could force himself to go no closer to Rome than the town of Trasimeno, which he reached in 1897. It was the very place where Hannibal had halted his own march. According to Jones, it would take Freud four years of self-analysis to conquer his psycho-logical inhibition and "triumphantly" enter Rome (246).

Psychoanalysis is one of multiple theories of human nature that arose from the "power/knowledge" (Foucault 1980) of European men amid Eu-rope's intensifying exploitation of Africa, Asia, the Americas, and the Pa-cific and amid the simultaneous struggle over the distribution of its rewards among different European classes, genders, and races. Psychoanalysis is an exemplary and widely useful hermeneutics of people's ambivalence toward one another and of its expression through symbolism, projection, conden-sation, inversion, and, most relevant to my argument, displacement. Freud used his own dreams as a site illustrative of these semiotic processes, the intent of which he took to be the fantasy fulfillment of his daytime wishes (Freud [1899/1900] 1965). However, like Marx's labor theory of value and other social "theories," psychoanalysis was no merely abstract inference from a socially unpositioned or unmotivated view of the facts. Psychoanalysis was also a wishful answer to a specific, real-life social problem as seen from the viewpoint of its main authors—secular central European Jewish men con-fronted by their own ambiguous position in the racial science, changing sex-gender arrangements, and national-imperial political order of the late nineteenth and early twentieth centuries. Indeed, its richness as a theory may derive from the depth of its founders' practical need to discern their fellow citizens' dangerous ambivalence toward them and from these founders' in-trospective examination of their own ambivalence as stigmatized people. Psychoanalysis embodied a wish fulfillment—to vindicate the humiliation of Freud's father, to deny Jewish inferiority and alienness from the Western empire, and to produce an income sufficient for Freud to become a domestic patriarch. And psychoanalysis did so, in the manner of dramatic irony, with ambivalence, symbolism, projection, condensation, inversion, and displace-ment. As Freud articulated his theory, sought to establish its legitimacy, and worked toward its immortality, he never lost sight of the social problem that arose from his ethnic Jewishness.

As a secular hermeneutics, psychoanalysis also bridged the rival value codes of religion and post-Enlightenment science. Though Freud was radically atheist, psychoanalysis replaced sixteenth- and seventeenth-century theories of and therapies for demoniac possession, a subject about which Freud had read extensively (e.g., Jones [1953] 1961: 225–26). Psychoanalysis relied on many of the familial metaphors at the heart of African and Abrahamic religions alike, and it organized its own cult, or society of acolytes and healers, according to both demonological and familial metaphors. Also despite his atheism, Freud repeatedly cited Virgil's *Aeneid* in a manner suggesting that psychoanalysis was an alternative, subterranean religion parallel to the religions that appeal to the powers of heaven: "If I cannot bend the gods above, then I will move the infernal regions" (Freud [1899/1900] 1965: 647fn; see also Jones [1953] 1961: 234).

I sympathize with Freud's motives and his methods. Even if, at times, Freud preferred not to scrutinize his own motives, he did not in general seem to think himself and his acolytes immune to the insights of psychoanalysis (on the need to examine the psychological motives behind psychoanalytical theory, see Jones [1953] 1961: 207, 310–11, 423, 426, 427, 432, 451–52, 490). Indeed, the entirety of this book is a form of participant observation in the psychoanalytical project (not to mention the projects of historical materialism and the Afro-Atlantic religions). Moreover, due to Freud's influence on my mother (a child psychologist) and on the anthropologists Margaret Mead, Ruth Benedict, and, above all, Victor Turner, my discipline and my own opus might also be characterized as lay elements of this cult. Hence, my exploration of the ulterior social motives behind psychoanalysis is also an exploration of my own.

The Accident of Psychoanalysis, or Theory as a Search for a Livelihood

Freud's influential theoretical innovation emerged from a combination of personal disposition and accident. His boyhood dreams of becoming a general or minister of state ran into the wall of antisemitism, which largely confined Viennese Jews to careers in industry, business, law, and medicine. As a Jew, Freud did not enjoy the same degree of access to academic and research appointments as his gentile peers (e.g., Jones [1953] 1961: 141). He was ill-suited to business, but his philosophical and speculative nature was also ill-suited to laboratory science. Measurement, precision, and exactitude were not among his fortes. To his disadvantage, the late nineteenth-century discourse of science was replacing religion and philosophy as a source of answers to the deep questions of culture, history, and ontology. Freud pursued a medical degree partly to prove that he was not lazy, but, for him, the main virtue of his career choice was its promise of a relatively reliable income. Predictably, once he graduated, he did not enjoy the clinical practice of medicine.

Throughout the 1870s to the 1880s, Freud was driven by the martial impulse to prove his own and his ethnic group's worthiness and by the need for an income sufficient for him to marry. In the laboratory and the consultation room, he continually sought to make new and distinctive discoveries that would distinguish him from the pack and guarantee his fame and livelihood. His efforts typically ended in failure, as when he exaggerated the therapeutic efficacy of cocaine and underestimated its addictiveness. Nothing won him the recognition he sought until his fellowship with the Parisian neurologist Jean-Martin Charcot offered a rationale for his future "talking cure"—a distinctive and ultimately profitable form of clinical practice that sidestepped the aspects of clinical practice that he disliked. In an age when the foremost scientific and medical researchers in Europe were devoting themselves to reducing the mind to brain physiology and chemistry, Charcot's hypnosis of "hysterical" patients suggested that the physician's work on the supposedly immaterial mind could effectively heal the body (Jones [1953] 1961: 180, 192).

Charcot's discovery enabled Freud to *reinterpret* the "demons" of his European antecedents, but Freud was not ready to give them up. Contesting the biological or organic reductionism of the leading neurologists of his day, he ultimately interpreted dreams, slips of the tongue and pen, jokes, fainting, and free association—his own, his acolytes', and his patients'—in order to divine an other world that was otherwise immune to sensory investigation and empirical testing. Based on evidence from Charcot's hypnosis, Freud endowed the "mind" with the autonomous power to cause pathological physical symptoms when it was disordered. Thus, Charcot supplied the ostensibly scientific groundwork for Freud's distinctive brand of therapy, the quasi-priestly guild that formed around it, and the livelihood of Freud and his family.

It should be noted that not all cultures recognize the existence of a ghostly, nonphysical organ of the sort implied by the term "mind," or *Geist*; that not all cultures distinguish the "mental" from the "physical"; and that not all cultures even associate thought exclusively or even principally with the vicinity of the brain or the head. In Yorùbá, for example, thinking is typically called "stirring one's insides" (*ro inún*), and the "insides" referred to are typically located in the belly. The Ewe and Mina of West Africa use similar language (Judy Rosenthal, personal communication, December 21, 2015). In Yorùbá, the stirring of the head (*ro orí*) is associated only with the most superficial type of awareness—typically the knowledge of superficial manners and expected behavior. For example, a child who leaves a chair out of place may be chastised for failing to stir his head. By contrast, a child who pursues the short-term pleasure of bad company, rather than planning for the distant future, is guilty of the far greater failure to "stir [his or her] insides," an act that entails not only forethought but also reflection, analysis, and empathy with other people (Olubunmi Fatoye-Matory, personal communication, January 19, 2018).

Thus, Freud's defense of the autonomy of the "mind" was culture specific, contrary to the scientific fashion of the day, and economically strategic in its contrariness. It rescued him from disqualification as a physician despite his ineptitude in the laboratory. The grounding of "psychopathology" in social experience, rather than heredity, bore the additional benefit of excusing assimilated Jews from the emerging racial "science" that attributed their allegedly disproportionate afflictions to a permanent form of racial inferiority and suggested their collective unworthiness of citizenship.

At its most abstract level, where the usual analysis and citation of disembodied "theory" tend to dwell, psychoanalysis is a theory about human nature, as well as a means of helping any given person to achieve inner harmony—or at least social and emotional functionality and self-acceptance—by recognizing the universal elements of human thought that, often unconsciously, underlie his or her conduct. The assumed backdrop of these universals is each person's aggressive desire for sexual gratification and the ways in which the nuclear family—that is, what Freud presumed to be the universally central social relationship among father, mother, and child—constrains that gratification.

Freud regarded the individual process of maturation and the collective process of civilization as a progressive intensification of the constraints on sexual gratification and on aggression against rivals, of which sexual rivalry was the paradigm case. In the ontology of psychoanalysis, Western children (who have yet to internalize self-constraint), Western neurotics (who have failed to adjust to the constraints imposed by civilization), and "savages," or "the primitive races" (who allegedly lack self-constraint), all reveal relatively unvarnished human nature and thereby showcase the savage forces that underlie the buttoned-up behavior of even a normal, civilized person (Freud [1913] 1946). The premise that the "savages" resemble "civilized" neurotics and "our" Western children was the foundation of what Freud regarded, at least for a time, as his best book—*Totem and Taboo: Resemblances between the Psychic Lives of Savages and Neurotics* ([1913] 1946).[2]

It should be noted that Freud's insulting analogy was in no way original. Indeed, it had long been used to justify the enslavement of Africans. In a proslavery address to the Class of 1773 at Harvard College, a graduating senior asked, "who[,] I beseech you, ever thought the consent of a child, an ideot [sic], or a madman necessary to his subordination? Every whit as immaterial, is the consent of these miserable Africans, whose real character seems to be a compound of the three last mentioned" (Kennedy 1993: xix).

Freud observed that normal, civilized people tend to believe that their conduct and feelings follow a consistent, rational pattern of socially acceptable behavior. However, he also argued that the conscious persona, or "ego," is but a partially successful effort to tame the ultimately indomitable unconscious forces underneath, which include both the "id" (the personification of the aggressive infantile impulses seeking gratification) and the "superego" (the internalized personification of the constraints imposed by one's parents). According to Freud, these indomitable forces inevitably assert themselves—even in the most civilized and psychologically normal person—through dreams, slips of the tongue, jokes, and contradictory behavior, all of which can be interpreted as symbolically coded revelations of unconscious forces.

Psychoanalysis as a Neo-Religion

A religion is: (1) a system of symbols which acts to (2) establish powerful, pervasive, and long-lasting moods and motivations in men by (3) formulating conceptions of a general order of existence and (4) clothing these conceptions with such an aura of factuality that (5) the moods and motivations seem uniquely realistic.
—Clifford Geertz, "Religion as a Cultural System"

Early psychoanalysis strongly resembles other institutions that have been called religions, not only in Geertz's general sense of religions as symbolic systems but also in the sense that it borrowed from Greek mythology, Judaism, and the European pagan exorcism of demons. It also proselytized and enforced doctrines immune to empirical verification, and it tightly policed membership.

Every religion is a system of beliefs, idea-images, and material things, as well as an organization of conduct constructed with reference to them. The early history of psychoanalysis provides evidence of the same truth about self-described sciences. Jones vividly describes the interpersonal relationships and the social organization of the "psychoanalytical movement" (Jones [1953] 1961: 272), revealing the use of belief, ritual, and supercathected, relationship-affirming objects in its acolytes' discernment and regulation of their ambivalent cooperation. The comparison between psychoanalysis and the Afro-Atlantic religions illuminates what is peculiar—and not disembodied, abstractly theoretical, universally applicable, or transhistorically true—in the assumptions about human relations that early psychoanalysts held sacrosanct. But not only that. The socially contextualized analysis of each of these ritual systems (psychoanalysis and the Afro-Atlantic religions) helps us better to understand the other. Just as the comparison of the Afro-Atlantic religions to psychoanalysis highlights the ambivalent roots of the

Afro-Atlantic religions among the African middlemen in sixteenth- and seventeenth-century Afro-European capitalism, the comparison of psychoanalysis to the Afro-Atlantic religions highlights the role of material objects in the social organization of this European "theory." These two systems are almost equally equipped with insights about the fractal nature of the self and about the normalcy of conflict inside of each person.

Freud never "disowned" his Jewishness (Jones [1953] 1961: 460), but he took a great distance from Jewish religion and did virtually everything in his power to guarantee that he, his idea-monument, and his posterity would be remembered not as Jewish but as Western. Freud wanted to conquer the West, and, in order to do so, he was willing to sacrifice elements of his borderline-white identity—and the interests of his Jewish acolytes. Freud claimed to be "one of the most dangerous enemies of religion." Nonetheless, German and Austrian critics called psychoanalysis "mystical" and deemed it "witchcraft" (302, 388, 460). Psychoanalysis might be regarded as a neoreligious working out of bourgeois identity with reference to phenomena like hysteria, which had long been described in explicitly religious terms (225–26). Yet, against the dominant trend among his neurologist colleagues in Germany and Austria, Freud defended the prescientific conviction that the essence of a person and the locus of his agency are immaterial rather than physical. For psychoanalysis, that immaterial agent is the "mind."

Yet, contrary to the antecedent bourgeois Western vision of the healthy mind as integrated, Freud believed that neurotics and psychotics—like the people diagnosed in earlier periods as victims of demoniac possession—provided evidence that *every* person is made up of *multiple* invisible personified beings. So even in healthy, "civilized" society, he argued, a person is not really an integrated being. Enlightenment ideals notwithstanding, as Bruno Latour (1993) puts it aphoristically, "We [Westerners] were never modern." Perhaps Freud's denunciation of religion bore the marks of what psychoanalysts call a "reaction formation"—that is, speech or behavior that asserts the opposite of one true but repressed feeling or wish. Freud's protests *against* religion may actually be a measure of the *religiosity* of psychoanalysis and of Freud's awareness that his gentile fellow physicians and citizens stigmatized religion in general and Judaism in particular.

Like historical materialism, psychoanalysis semisecularly reinterpreted the biblical Edenic/messianic complex and other ancient mythology. According to Freud's "theory," a fundamental constituent of the mind is an aggressively sex-obsessed and gratification-oriented being (the id). Though repressed by social forces, it reveals itself through periodic disruptions in the persona of a "civilized" person and, because it has been repressed, appears in distorted form. Thus, for Freud, man is not a special animal but an instinctually wild animal under wraps, longing to return to his original condition (Jones [1953] 1961: 350, 422). Similarly, after the fall, Adam and Eve shamefully have had to clothe themselves but are still permanently defined by impulses for which they originally felt no shame. However, Freud more consciously identified the ancient Greek myth of Oedipus as the paradigm case of an ostensibly panhuman myth of social origin, leading him to search every available myth, text, and antiquity for the theme of the son indulging his ostensibly natural desire to kill his father in order to possess his mother as a tool of his own sensual self-gratification (Jones [1953] 1961: 474).

Psychoanalysis grew from these religious roots and is steeped in religious imagery, but Freud's vision of inherent human selfishness unites it with a specifically European ideological revolution dating from the Renaissance and the dawn of Western capitalism, one that similarly protests its nonreligiosity despite the high degree of faith and low degree of empiricism it rests upon. Sahlins (1996) charts the revolution in Western thinking as follows: Like Buddhism, pre-Renaissance Christianity assumed that the world is hell and that only death provides rest. But after the Renaissance and with the dawn of capitalism, Westerners tended to stop regarding renunciation as good and greed as bad. We Westerners came to think of ourselves as initially deprived and to think of the greedy pursuit of material wealth and comfort as a desirable motor for the perfecting of the world. Western social theorists and laypeople alike came to explain human social life as the product of individuals' avaricious pursuit of objective and fixed biological pleasures and needs, with the thought that our inherent selfishness also demanded, lest we destroy one another, the restraining functions of the state. Marx ([1843] 1978) expressly analogizes the projection of our collective spirit, or "species-being," onto the state to religion.

The talking cure posits that the social is antagonistic to the individual, rather than essential to the very genesis of the person. Social relationships are assumed to be not the source of happiness but the *limit* on a person's ability to achieve happiness. The individual is naturally selfish and aggressive, intent on owning another person, not even for reproductive purposes but for selfish pleasure.

This sort of thinking is culturally and historically specific (and indeed *religious* according to Geertz's definition and Marx's analogy) on the grounds that it is just as reasonable (and indeed far *more* reasonable to most non-Westerners and noncapitalists) to think of culture and society as *facilitators* of or *indispensable means* to a person's survival and pleasure. Far from being the ultimate, demonic driver of our culture, our biological pleasures and needs could be said to have coevolved with our culture. Without culture, we would not know how to survive individually or what is desirable to eat or own, much less what is delicious and pleasurable.

Psychoanalysis shares with the Afro-Atlantic religions the premise that multiple people live within the same body and that our connection to those people typically derives from family history. However, the Afro-Atlantic religions and psychoanalysis posit and produce very different sets of symbols, moods, motivations, appetites, human actors, and social collectives. For example, the family histories that populate the paradigmatic subject of the Afro-Atlantic religions are typically many generations longer than those of the nuclear family and many species wider. And the main aim of Afro-Atlantic religions is the creation and reinforcement of relationship through the idiom of parturition and marriage, rather than competitive self-satisfaction.

Peter Geschiere (2013) observes that psychoanalysis revolutionized existing Western bourgeois understandings of the socialized adult individual by recognizing the individual's rootedness in a conflict-ridden nuclear family. The explicit aim of the "talking cure" was to analyze the feelings that emerged from the history of one's birth into the ostensibly universal male-dominant nuclear family. The paradigmatic subject in psychoanalysis is a male intent on owning a woman, a woman whose purpose is to cater to the male's needs and wants, for no other purpose than consumer gratification—not even, as Engels had argued, to perpetuate a bounded hereditary dynasty of enduring wealth (Jones [1953] 1961: 377; Engels [1884] 1978), much less the Afro-Atlantic goal of creating relationships.

Like the subsidiary characters in his world, the paradigmatic subject in psychoanalysis contains within him multiple spirits that pull him in different directions. Two of these spirits (the ego and the superego) are generated by the emulation and fear of the father, and they have an antagonistic relationship to the Ur-self, or id, which, like a tyrannical "demon" (Jones [1953] 1961: 179, 224, 232, 494), torments the civilized person from within. Though internally fragmented, psychoanalytical man is remarkably individualistic. For Freud, even sociology is nothing but applied psychology (477). The ultimate explanation of human behavior is the individual's pursuit of individual bliss and the satisfaction of all desires, not the pleasure of connection to other people, animals, plants, meteorological phenomena, and things. Freud's theory modifies Enlightenment-era social contract theory regarding how Westerners evolved from the ostensible social Ur-state, in which individuals pursued their bliss and satisfaction without regard to the bliss and satisfaction of others. Yes, they founded civilization by agreeing to limit their individual pursuit of gratification for the net benefit of the group. Freud added, with a wish revealing both his historical epoch and his aspirations to imperial whiteness, that the result of this contract was that civilized men were able to conquer peoples who had not limited their individual pursuit of gratification—that is, those walking ids known as "savages" and the "primitive races" (475–76).

Though not consciously recognized by Freud, the wish fulfillment at the core of psychoanalysis is Freud's fantasy of identification with an imperialist white gentile father. Freud's comparisons of conquered "savagery" and conquering "civilization" projected the real-time conditions of nineteenth-century overseas empire onto the psychic life of Western man. The paradigmatic subject in psychoanalysis has internalized the nineteenth- and twentieth-century gentile empires in the governance of which he hoped to join. Embedded in this postreligious model of the universal nature of the human mind is the casual assumption that the civilized person needs to dominate the savage—both in the world and in the mind. Just as important, Freud was generalizing his own compensatory wishes to the psychology of all "civilized" men. Freud's welcome in their company was not assured, helping us to understand the ambivalence in his model of male personality development.

Freud was deeply ambivalent about the West—as threatened by its Christianity as he was worshipful of its Greco-Roman foundations. Identifying with the gentile conqueror and seeking to inherit his throne, Freud and his followers even described their movement to gain adherents and conquer the West in religious terms, as a "crusade" (Jones [1953] 1961). However, Freud's diagnostic vocabulary tended to favor the neopagan. He visualized the forces that moved him, his patients, and his acolytes not only as "demons" but also as "evil geniuses" (287) and "spirits" (325, 517). Jones repeatedly employs the term "divination" to describe the psychoanalytical detection of the battle among the beings in one's head that causes a person's feelings and conduct (232, 243, 303, 329). Psychoanalysis was a cult of psychological and political affliction, in which Freud recognized that he himself was in need of healing related to the rival "demons," "spirits," and "tyrants" that afflicted him (see Turner 1967 on cults of affliction). In therapy, the aim of psychoanalysis is not to purge these neopagan spirits but to become aware of them and to accept the eternal struggle between the individual and society that is the inner dynamic of the fractal self (Jones [1953] 1961: 330).

Freud analyzed his own life in numerological terms and predictions of the sort proposed by his father figure and intimate Wilhelm Fliess (Jones [1953] 1961: 287, 363, 365, 379, also 451–52). These predictions often related to Freud's own mortality, with which he was obsessed even before he contracted cancer. Fliess once predicted that Freud would die at fifty-one, contributing to Freud's obsession. When he outlived the predicted date in February 1918, Freud made the characteristically dry comment: "That shows what little trust one can place in the supernatural" (Jones [1953] 1961: 363).

However, another occasion seems to have suggested to Freud and his acolytes that he himself was clairvoyant:

> In 1906, on the occasion of his fiftieth birthday, the little group of adher-
> ents in Vienna presented him with a medallion, designed by a well-known
> sculptor, Karl Maria Schwerdtner, having on the obverse his side-portrait
> in bas-relief and on the reverse a Greek design of Oedipus answering the
> Sphinx. Around it is a line from Sophocles's *Oedipus Tyrannus*, . . . ("Who
> divined the famed riddle and was a man most mighty"). . . . .
>
> At the presentation of the medallion there was a curious incident.
> When Freud read the inscription he became pale and agitated and in a
> strangled voice demanded to know who had thought of it. He behaved
> as if he had encountered a *revenant*, and so he had. After Federn told
> him it was he who had chosen the inscription, Freud disclosed that as
> a young student at the University of Vienna he used to stroll around the
> great arcaded court inspecting the busts of former famous professors of
> the institution. He then had the phantasy not merely of seeing his own
> bust there in the future, which would not have been anything remarkable
> in an ambitious student, but of it actually being inscribed with the *identi-*
> *cal* words he now saw on the medallion. (Jones [1953] 1961: 243–44)

Psychoanalysis was a neopagan system of divination and healing that encoded a plea from a racially stigmatized faction of the bourgeoisie for the
modification of the recalcitrantly Christian and increasingly racist terms of
the nineteenth-century social charter. The European pagan elements of this
modification offset the Christian biases of that charter, while its binary and
markedly anti-African social evolutionism offset the elements of racial science that were especially deleterious to the hopes of assimilated European
Jews. As a form of therapy and an organization of therapists, psychoanalysis
managed the struggle—within the individual and within the psychoanalytical community—between the savage black and the civilized white potential
of the parvenu Jew through ritually approved ways of inspecting each other's
dreams, speech, conduct, and possessions. The backdrop of these inspec-
tions was an approved neoreligious history and theory of human nature with
roots in Europe's interethnic and imperial history.

The Fetish as an Architecture
of Solidarity and Conflict

Woven together, the scattered threads of Freud's writings and his autobiographical comments to his acolytes strongly suggest that his theory was a working out of his own demons. For example, Freud abstractly attributed intellectual curiosity in general to sexual curiosity and sibling rivalry in particular (Jones [1953] 1961: 380–81). And, in talking to his acolytes, Freud was explicit about how the birth of his sibling rival Julius provoked his own curiosity about the infantile perspective on family life. Moreover, during a critical phase in the formation of psychoanalysis, Freud's focus on sexuality in his ambivalence-based theory of the mind seems to have been motivated by his sexual curiosity about Wilhelm Fliess. Freud seems to have been equally conscious of this motivation and anxious to suppress that consciousness. Freud wrote the following to his acolyte Sandor Ferenczi: "You not only noticed, but also understood, that I *no longer* have any need to uncover my personality completely, and you correctly traced this back to the traumatic reason for it. Since Fliess's case, with the overcoming of which you recently saw me occupied, that need has been extinguished. A part of homosexual cathexis has been withdrawn and made use of to enlarge my own ego" (Freud qtd. in Jones [1953] 1961: 281).

Throughout his life, Freud did his best to cover up his powerfully homoerotic relationship with Fliess, a fellow Jewish physician and family man (Jones [1953] 1961: 281). Jones reports that, although Fliess was two years younger and intellectually mediocre, Freud idealized him and treated him as a father figure (188, 191). The height of Freud's intellectual productivity, in the 1890s, coincided with an intense friendship between Freud and Fliess that Freud later described as a "homosexual cathexis," or unhealthy homosexual obsession (281, also 207, 258). Freud wrote to Fliess, "I can write nothing if I have no public at all, but I am perfectly content to write only for you" (196). It was Fliess who supplied Freud with the later premise of psychoanalysis that people are born bisexual or "pansexual," and it was under Fliess's influence and at the height of Freud's intimacy with him that sexual impulses became the center of Freud's "ever widening explanation of both normal and pathological mental processes" (189, 192). Together, Freud and Fliess also explored the connection between sexual arousal and nasal inflammation, examining each other's noses for evidence (188, 200). In the middle of this relationship, in 1895, Freud reportedly ended for good his sexual relationship with his wife.[1]

This apparent homosexual affair seems to have been critical to the development of psychoanalysis. However, Freud seems to have regarded his own homosexual feelings and this possible sexual relationship as inconsistent with the monumental patriarchal image of himself that he wanted to survive him. He destroyed the letters that Fliess had written to him, endeavored to have his letters to Fliess destroyed, and, apparently for the same reason, forbade his close friend Arnold Zweig to write his biography (Jones [1953] 1961: 186, 507, 510, also 281, 371, 374, 377). Freud's efforts to hide the evidence of this affair, alongside his picture-perfect but sexless heterosexual nuclear-family life, seem designed at least partly to evade the nineteenth-century stereotype of Jewish men generally as effeminate and sexually perverted. His Viennese origins made him doubly vulnerable to such suspicions of perversion.

Like other *assimilés* from dominated populations and sexual minorities (Fanon [1952] 2008), Freud was internally divided and deeply ambivalent about himself and his people, which may help us to understand his great articulacy about a range of issues that the Yorùbá-Atlantic religions also address vividly. Like Yorùbá-Atlantic priests, Freud knew that his self was not unitary, and he was prepared to generalize this self-understanding to others. He inferred from personal experience something that most people would rather not confess, even to themselves—that the self is shaped by ambivalent motives. Freud's ideas are deeply illuminating, but they are not made more correct or universal by the habit of theory to ignore the cultural, political, and biographical circumstances of their genesis. In fact, a comparison between the circumstances that generated the similarities and differences between psychoanalytical and Afro-Atlantic thinking is likely to teach us a great deal more than these two types of fetish could teach us separately about the nature and management of ambivalence in social relations.

Freud sought gentile approval not only during his lifetime but also after his death. He wanted his ideas and the institutions that propagated them to survive him, and thoughts of this matter amplified his self-reported *Todes-angst* (fear of death). He wanted to leave behind something that would "jus-tify [his] existence" (Jones [1953] 1961: 226). In *Totem and Taboo* ([1913] 1946), Freud imagined the following primordial scenario at the roots of civi-lization: a band of brothers murders their father in order to take possession of the women he had monopolized, but then, in guilt, they reinstitute the father's repressive laws all the more forcefully (see also Jones [1953] 1961: 226, 291). Hence, like many religions, psychoanalysis and the brotherhood that Freud assembled around it explicitly addressed its founder's and fol-lowers' fear of death (Jones [1953] 1961: 272, 424, 458). Freud detected this mythic theme in—or projected it onto—myths the world over. Indeed, it provided a model for Freud and his followers as his death approached. Divin-ing parricidal rebellion all around, Freud gathered around him a subgroup of his "sons" who, in anticipation of reinstating the father's law, policed the boundaries of psychoanalysis even more doggedly than Freud. They com-peted for his approval and he for their loyalty, all of them applying the tech-niques of psychoanalysis to divine the depth of each other's loyalty and the unconscious motives behind each other's moments of seemingly parricidal dissent. In effect, psychoanalysis was not only the tool of their therapeutic trade but also the model and regulatory mechanism of the memorial com-munity they were determined to build for eternity.

Freud's pursuit of immortality through his psychoanalytical sons was fraught with anxiety about the ultimately suicidal character of his role in the mythic scenario.

The Psychoanalytical Band of Brothers

Psychoanalysis became the foundation of a professional brotherhood, or guild, and of many livelihoods. This foundation relied on a range of social ar-rangements that Freud and his acolytes worked hard to produce: the guild's agreement over correct practice, its monopoly over training, a network of referrals, a publishing house sustained by donations from guild members, and other forms of collective self-regulation, all intent on promoting the popular legitimacy of their field. Through organizational charters, meetings, tribunals, and correspondences, the brotherhood enforced Freud's law and punished deviations from standard belief and practice according to psycho-analytical modes of divination, correction, and official excommunication.

Livelihoods depended on the respectability and regulated supply of psy-choanalytical services. Members of the brotherhood referred patients to one another, thus subsidizing the income of newer acolytes, and a good deal of cash passed among Freud, his family, and his followers during times of need. Donations and dues from the fraternity funded the publication of the movement's sacred texts.

Freud and Jones wrote forthrightly about the inescapably racialized economics of psychoanalysis. Freud consciously sought to vindicate his professional marginalization as a Jewish person, as well as his father's humiliation for the same reason (e.g., Jones [1953] 1961: 246). He counted his legacy valid and his immortality assured only insofar as it garnered the recognition and esteem of gentiles. Indeed, he wanted to conquer the gentile West with his fetish. Yet the pursuit of posthumous dignity for Freud and for psychoanalysis was no mere matter of pride. Freud and his followers also depended on psychoanalysis for their daily bread. The legitimacy of Freud's "talking cure" and the longevity of the field depended on a "struggle . . . for recognition" (Jones [1953] 1961: 451) and on the autonomy of its standards and authorizing procedures from the antisemitic and physiologically reductionist medical establishment of central Europe.

Moreover, the survival of this new brotherhood depended on the principle of supply and demand. That is, the growth of this professional community depended on the growth of interest in the field, and the existing practitioners' livelihood depended on the limiting the number of licensed practitioners. New acolytes depended on old ones to pass down their surplus patients. Fluctuations in the political economy, such as the effects of Germany's reparations payments after World War I, also directly affected the growth of the brotherhood and the ability of Freud and his followers to make a living (e.g., Jones [1953] 1961: 386, 461, 488–89).

Some of Freud's apparently strategic choices fueled deep resentment among his European Jewish followers (e.g., Jones [1953] 1961: 273). Freud asked his fellow Jewish psychoanalysts to develop their "masochism" and tolerate his dogged efforts to cultivate Swiss Protestant psychoanalyst Carl Jung as the heir to the leadership of the psychoanalytic movement: Jung, "being a Christian and the son of a pastor, can only find his way to me against great inner resistances. His adherence is therefore all the more valuable. I was almost going to say it was only his emergence on the scene that has removed from psychoanalysis the danger of becoming a Jewish national affair" (Jones [1953] 1961: 261). However, in calling upon their "masochism," he acknowledged both the harm he was doing to them and his awareness that, as Jews, they would feel affronted by his non-merit-based favoritism toward a gentile.

Freud's concessions to North American gentile aspirants to the brotherhood fueled a further split among his followers. Freud welcomed US American gentiles despite the fact that many of them were nonphysicians. However, anxious to protect their status within the medical field, the physician-psychoanalysts in the US—who, like their European counterparts, were mostly Jewish—reviled Freud's laxity in admitting the nonphysicians. In the US physicians in general had then only recently secured their dominant and near-monopoly status in the delivery of legitimate health care, and among physicians, the professional acceptance of psychiatrists has remained the most tenuous (Jones [1953] 1961: 467–69). Many of Freud's followers resented the sense that the gentiles' more desirable religion offset the Jews' marginal but still slightly superior professional qualifications. Conversely, Freud saw his Jewish acolytes' resistance to being sidelined as a threat to the posthumous survival of the guild and to his own livelihood. Though acutely attentive to his own insecurity as a Jew, Freud dramatically dismissed theirs and, like many members of dominant echelons facing charges of discrimination, represented himself as the real victim: "My enemies would be willing to see me starve; they would tear my very coat off my back" (273).

Adherence to the brotherhood was measured primarily in terms of conformity to the views expressed and therapeutic techniques endorsed in Freud's publications and circular letters, as well as Freud's pronouncements at conferences about how those writings should be interpreted. A committee of Freud's most loyal acolytes was given the charge to establish and defend psychoanalytical orthodoxy (e.g., Jones [1953] 1961: 327, 423). Jones himself wrote the "Psycho-Analytical Charter," which "defined psychoanalysis as work employing Freud's technique, thus excluding all the other pretenders to the name" (475). However, psychoanalysis remained a fissiparous movement, in which the causes of conflict were continually divined and redressed—at times successfully and at times not—through psychoanalytical techniques (296, e.g.).

As in most religious movements, so too in the brotherhood of psychoanalysis, small differences of doctrinal interpretation and ritual practice occasioned angry and permanent ruptures. Freud frequently broke with close friends and colleagues on account of ostensibly intellectual and doctrinal disagreements, as when Alfred Adler reassessed the relative priority of sexuality and aggression in the determination of human behavior. A similar rupture occurred when Otto Rank and Sándor Ferenczi proposed a form of psychotherapy that emphasized birth trauma over the Oedipus complex as the root of adult neurosis, as well as a therapeutic process focused on the analysis of how patients act out in adulthood, rather than on the exhumation of repressed impulses from early childhood (Jones [1953] 1961: 281, 416, 423). A founding member and sometime leader of the committee, Jones described such instances of dissent in the religious language of "heresy" (429).

Jones's denial of Freud's widespread reputation for dogmatism actually gives additional evidence of it, and Jones himself gave many examples. Freud confessed, "I . . . find it hard to assimilate alien thoughts that do not quite lie in my path" (Jones [1953] 1961: 311, 417). And, whether Freud consciously demanded it or not, many of his followers, as Jones summarized the protestations of Ferenczi, "could never dream of departing by a hair's breadth from Freud's teaching" (417). Freud was highly conscious that truth is not spread by merely rational argument, because the deeper truth, for Freud, is that people's minds do not work rationally. Analogizing persuasion to seduction, Freud offered the following advice on the psychology of effective proselytization to the Viennese writer Stefan Zweig: "Psychoanalysis is like a woman who wants to be won but knows that she is little valued if she offers no resistance" (523). Jones himself praised "unwavering conviction to the truths of psychoanalysis" and a "friendly but uncompromising way of coping with opponents" as great services to the movement (451). The aim of such efforts was "to win new adherents" (451, also 449).

In its proselytization, formality of recruitment, official regulation of belief, resentment of apostasy, and, indeed, struggles over money and succession, psychoanalysis was much like an evangelical religious cult. Despite Freud's classification of psychoanalysis as a "science," his recommendations regarding the defense and dissemination of his ideas evaded the empirical standards usually set forth in the justification of Western empirical science. I, too, sense that as means of persuading most audiences, self-confidence and heartfelt anecdotes of one's personal experience work far better than principled or statistical argument, which usually only makes opponents dig in their heels. The unconventionality of psychoanalysis as a science does not invalidate it, any more than the trade pacts of sixteenth- and seventeenth-century West African merchants invalidated the gods who enforced those pacts. The validity of African gods and European social theories lies not in causation but in the efficacy of the cooperation that they structure.

Dissent and the Divination of Parricide

English speakers tend to reserve the word "tribe" for nonwhite or ancient white populations. "Witchcraft" tends to be reserved for phenomena in these same populations. However, much like the conventional referents of witchcraft, certain key forms of dissent and role usurpation within the early twentieth-century psychoanalytical community were treated as potential or attempted murder.

Following a premise worthy of application to every religion, movement, and science, Freud understood that within his movement, much of the dissent regarding doctrine and proper practice was a proxy for conflicts over unstated social rivalries and emotional conflicts. Freud and his followers systematically analyzed each other's feelings and conduct in terms of the relationships and tensions predicted by the Oedipal scenario. Freud employed the vocabulary of fatherhood in checking the independence of his "sons" and "heirs" (e.g., Jones [1953] 1961: 409). Freud seems to have regarded all of his followers as assets and to have lamented their departures from his doctrines, from his movement, or from any of its numerous organizations as filial losses and as potential threats to his authority (426, 427, e.g.). Being a gentile, Jung was the prize target of Freud's efforts to get and retain followers, to conquer the West, to secure his posthumous immortality, and perhaps even to complete his own assimilation. For these reasons, Freud called Jung his "son and heir" (253), his "Crown Prince" (319), the Joshua to his Moses (254). Freud's letter condemning Ferenczi's inappropriate "struggle for independence" addresses the latter as "Dear Son"—a form of address that Jones calls half jocular and half analytical—and ends with the coda "With fatherly greetings, your Freud" (330).

Perhaps in fear of Oedipal parricide, Freud reacted sharply against disciples who strayed from the monumental idea that he identified as his legacy. The early psychoanalytical movement depended on the official consensus that Freud himself—in his role of father and judge—was uniquely rational and that none of the conflicting demons in Freud's head compromised the truth, objectivity, or universality of his message. So any reference to Freud's own neuroses was an act of heresy and, in effect, apostasy. Hence, the final split between Freud and his heir-apparent followed Freud's attribution of Jung's intellectual dissent to an unconscious motive and then Jung's counter-accusation regarding Freud's own psychopathological motivation. Jones summarized the events that followed Freud and Jung's last attempt to make up:

> Freud pointed out to Jung that [Jung's] conception of the incest complex as something artificial bore a certain resemblance to [the now-estranged] Adler's view that it was "arranged" internally to cover other impulses of a different nature. Others had commented also on the resemblance, and Jung resented the implication of having any connection with Adler. He now wrote angrily to Freud saying that "not even Adler's companions think that I belong to your group," this being a slip of the pen for "their group." [Fn: This kind of slip is easy enough in German: one only has to write a capital letter instead of the small one with "*ihrer*."] Since [Jung] had been insisting that [Jung's] attitude to [Jung's] new ideas was purely objective, Freud could not resist incautiously inquiring of [Jung] whether [Jung] was objective enough to pass an opinion on [Jung's own] slip of the pen. It was asking for trouble with a man in Jung's sensitive mood and by return of post there came an explosive and very insolent reply on the subject of Freud's "neurosis." (Jones [1953] 1961: 323–24, fn in original)

In other words, Freud suspected Jung had become disloyal to Freud and his ideas, and Freud found divinatory evidence for this suspicion in Jung's slip of the pen: he had mistakenly written *ihrer* with a capital *I*. Once Freud so frontally challenged him, Jung's prior ambivalence and guilt gave way to open rebellion. In declaring that Freud could be diagnosed just as Freud had diagnosed others, Jung usurped Freud's statutory role as father and supreme judge.

Jung was not the first or the last of Freud's "sons" to rebel. Freud deeply disagreed with Ferenczi's modified theorization of the nuclear family scenario at the heart of psychoanalysis. Ferenczi argued that the therapist could counteract the unkindness that patients had suffered at the hands of their parents by enacting the role of a loving parent, kissing the patient and allowing the patient to analyze the therapist along the way. In his critical letter to Ferenczi, Freud accused him of enacting the role of the playful mother—rather than the psychoanalytically prescribed role of the stern father—in the analytical relationship. Freud warned that the playful mother role entails the risk of erotic involvement between the psychoanalyst and the patient. Freud then sarcastically called his acolyte "God the Father Ferenczi," highlighting the hubris of Ferenczi's deviation from standard psychoanalytical theory and practice and, concomitantly, from the proper behavior of a son, the cause of which Freud divined as Ferenczi's out-of-control unconscious desire for independence from Freud. Freud said that he was therefore obligated to put Ferenczi in his juvenile place. To this end, Freud wrote, "Since you like playing a tender mother role with others, then perhaps you may do so with yourself. And then you are to hear from the brutal fatherly side [i.e., from Freud himself] an admonition. That is why I spoke in my last letter of a new puberty . . . and now you have compelled me to be quite blunt" (Freud to Ferenczi, in Jones [1953] 1961: 487, see also 422).

Freud also divined that Ferenczi's "pathological" divergence from the orthodoxy had resulted from "psychical and intellectual decay" (492) and unconscious "personal animosity" (491) toward Freud. In the service of a "forcible cure" (490) for this pathology, Freud prescribed that Ferenczi become the next president of the International Psycho-Analytical Association. Noncompliant, Ferenczi dismissed Freud's prescription, declaring that "he couldn't credit Freud with any more insight than a small boy" (491). With these words, Ferenczi was accusing Freud of being the real child.

Despite Ferenczi's ostensible "psychical and intellectual decay" and unconscious animosity toward Freud, he showed the intelligence to read the 1933 Reichstag fire in Berlin as a sign of imminent danger to Freud in Vienna, and he offered the caring advice that Freud flee to England immediately (Jones [1953] 1961: 490–93). In psychoanalysis, such ambivalence—the simultaneous hatred and love of the father—was and is regarded as proof, rather than disproof, of the theory.

Within the divinatory framework of psychoanalysis, worries about parricide and fratricide were linked. For example, Jones explains as follows his conflicts with Otto Rank over the editing of the *International Journal of Psycho-Analysis* and thus illustrates the divinatory power of psychoanalysis to predict a person's future conflict with others:

> I had known that Rank had suffered much in childhood from a strongly repressed hostility to his brother, and that this usually covered a similar attitude toward a father. . . .
>
> For three years I lived with the fear lest Rank's "brother-hostility" regress to the deeper "father-hostility," and I hoped against hope that this would not happen in Freud's lifetime. My fear was unfortunately justified, since at the end of that time Rank openly expressed an ungovernable hostility against Freud. (Jones [1953] 1961: 411)

Freud and Jones worried constantly about the potential impact of a premature parricide and of fissiparous conflict among the brothers. And, during his lifetime, the death of organizations intent on perpetuating his legacy caused Freud deep distress (Jones [1953] 1961: 424).

In an examination of the likeness of self-proclaimed scientific theories to religions, psychoanalysis may seem like low-hanging fruit. But Latour (2010) convincingly applies this same comparison to the laboratory sciences, as well (consider also Kuhn 1962). Latour and Woolgar's study of laboratory life ([1979] 1986) shows the extensive use of trial and error, analogy, play, use of artificial proxy variables, machines that reify the variables that they simply appear to be measuring, jealousy, grandstanding, stray anecdotes, persuasion, public relations, funding efforts, political lobbying and support, competition for the pursuit of recognition, suspicion about subordinates' potential disloyalty, evaluations of other laboratories' reputation, judgment calls intent on distinguishing facts from artifacts, ex post facto reification of variables, and selection among diverse possible explanations or constructions of a causal process go into the creation and conventionalization of a fact, even in this seemingly objective world. Latour and Woolgar summarize:

> We shall specify the precise time and place in the process of fact construction when a statement became transformed into a fact and hence freed from the circumstances of its production.
>
> A fact only becomes such when it loses all temporal qualifications and becomes incorporated into a large body of knowledge drawn upon by others. ([1979] 1986: 105–6)

The authors thereby deny that even laboratory science is an objective observation of the world "out there," in contrast to the ostensibly fictional or interpretive observations embedded in literature, literary criticism, and religion. Laboratory science is a social and imaginative process of interaction with the world in which the establishment of authoritative facts, ideas, reasons, and theories relies on forgetfulness about the material conditions of their construction. Psychoanalysis and the Afro-Atlantic religions do not fare so poorly in this comparison. Each episteme is the contested assertion of a perspective or apperception embodied in things—be they couches and upright chairs, calabash altars, or laboratory equipment.

Psychoanalytic Theory as an Act of Compensation

Like Marx, Freud suffered a race, religion, and class problem as he struggled for gentile social acceptance and economic well-being in central Europe. At the height of European imperialism, Freud's gentile fellow scientists moved to formalize a global racial hierarchy, to correlate it with a Darwinian evolutionary logic, and to justify a socially Darwinist outcome that had already resulted in the enslavement, displacement, or near extermination of numerous darker peoples. And it took little effort for dominant European populations to cast fellow light-skinned Europeans—such as the Irish, the Sami, and the Jews—in the same undeserving hue. It was in this foreboding environment that Freud sought to secure for Jews—or, at least, for assimilated central European male Jews like himself—a place on the *white* side of history. In its vocabulary, empirical deficiencies, tendentious logic, and potential benefits for discreditable Europeans, Freud's rhetorical use of black and brown people recapitulates the rhetoric of the German burghers seeking equality with their Francophile rulers and that of Marx's pursuit of the white workers' and his own off-white equality with the white bourgeoisie and aristocracy. In addition, Freud consciously struggled with a gender and sexual orientation problem, through which psychoanalysis inflected his race, religion, and class problems.

Freud was the son of an unsuccessful wool merchant, and he grew up poor. Jones writes that Freud had been "brought up in a penurious environment with small opportunity for social intercourse and experience. In his early letters to his future wife he several times confessed to a sense of inferiority at not having acquired social graces" (Jones [1953] 1961: 372).

Despite his generosity and the social manners he later acquired, adds Jones, "one would hardly think of him as a man of the world" (Jones [1953] 1961: 372). Further revealing his class origins, he had a persistent "habit of hawking and spitting induced by his chronic catarrh and over-smoking." Jones continues, "Western patients unaccustomed to such behavior could be disturbed by it, whereupon Freud would chide them for their squeamishness" (372).

Sander Gilman (1993) argues that, in an era of rising antisemitism and increased opportunities for women in the sciences, psychoanalysis was Freud's competitive appeal for Jewish male citizenship in German-speaking society and in its gentile-dominant medical and scientific community. In response to the demeaning allegation of antisemites that Jewish males are physically and psychologically like women, Freud emphasized the value of the penis in establishing a person's value. Thus, Gilman observes pithily, Freud's psychoanalytic theory sought "to divide humankind into only two classes—male and female" (1993: 199), with the implication that the difference between having a penis and having none is much more important than the difference between a Jew's circumcised and a gentile's uncircumcised penis. Freud called the failure of antisemites to recognize the essential likeness of circumcised and uncircumcised penises a "narcissism of minor differences." Freud was insinuating that heterosexual Jewish men deserved inclusion because they are better than women of any religion or race.

Freud's theory of penis envy and castration anxiety flowed from the postulate that penises are naturally admirable (Freud 1927: 153), with the collateral implication that women are born with a deficiency (an idea that, as the reader will see, is quite strange to the Afro-Atlantic religions). For Freud, it was natural for a child to perceive his mother as a man with a part lopped off, such that a girl naturally experiences penis envy and a boy comes to fear that he, too, might one day be castrated for disobeying his father or for trying to usurp the father's ostensible female property.

Had Freud been more introspective and willing to acknowledge the racially marked nature of his aspirations, he might have explicitly identified the white penis as his own fetish. At times, Freud recognized his "homosexual cathexis," but it is equally predictable according to his theory that he appears to have repressed that threatening self-awareness. Psychoanalysis also predicts that the denial of such unconscious realities would give rise to an obsession with the realities so denied, which may explain why Freud's psychoanalysis is preoccupied with the penis and with men's fear of being surgically reclassified by a male authority figure as a woman. It is difficult for my priest friends, for me, and, for that matter, most contemporary Westerners *not* to view Freud's preoccupation with the penis and the threat of its removal as bizarre, so it begs for analysis in terms of Freud's own peculiar social setting and psychological makeup.

This theory-based struggle for European Jewish manhood also addressed the racial criteria for citizenship in the emerging nation-states and overseas empires of Europe. By calling the penis Freud's chief fetish, I do not mean that he *mistakenly* identified it as the chief repository of the rights proffered to the bourgeoisie by the Enlightenment; his gentile contemporaries did the same thing by attempting to limit those rights to people with an uncircumcised penis. In my argument, it is not error but displacement and disagreement that turned the penis into a fetish of Freud and his antagonists, who together placed the penis at center stage in the struggle over the boundaries of central European citizenship. In that struggle, Freud asserted, in effect, that the color of the penis—white or nonwhite—mattered more than whether it had a foreskin. Freud's argument of images dramatized the reality that a penis can be a staff of authority or a danger to its bearer. Within Europe, circumcision had justified one's exclusion or even murder. Within the broader context of Europe's international empires, Freud shifted the danger toward the black or brown penis, telling the same false tale about the sexual indiscipline of the "savage" that his gentile contemporaries had told about Jews in Europe but were increasingly telling as a justification of colonialism, segregation, and lynching. Freud's supercathexis of the penis bore and amplified the terrible energy of this circum-Atlantic debate. And Freud's suicidal relationship to the cigar may well have embodied his own terrible ambivalence.

The penis and the threat of its removal are emotionally supercharged by the opposite values projected onto circumcision by central European gentiles and Jews. While Jews had historically seen it as a positive sign of membership in the community of Jewish men, Freud believed that nineteenth-century central European gentiles saw it as a form of castration that delegitimized Jewish claims to citizenship in the nation-state. Freud explained antisemitism as insane gentile men's response to the sudden childhood awareness that Jewish boys are circumcised, which reminds gentile men of the allegedly primordial and universal fear of boy children that their fathers will castrate them. Moreover, it had not been missed—either by Jews or by antisemitic gentiles—that Jewish, African, and Australian Aborigine men had circumcision in common (Gilman 1993: e.g., 187–88).

It is much easier to understand why the paradigmatic subject in psychoanalysis fears castration when we consider the possibility that the main father in Freud's Oedipal scenario is not his natural genitor but his gentile pater and that the son in this scenario is specifically the Jewish male parvenu. Freud's literal father was hardly the castrator; even for Freud, his father was most memorably the castrated party. In Freud's self-analysis, his scaling of the Acropolis fulfilled a wish to outdo his father (Jones [1953] 1961: 323). However, Freud's juxtaposition of the Acropolis and his father implies that the father in Freud's Oedipal scenario was not simply the father of the nuclear family. He embodied the tension between Freud's natural father, or genitor, and the pater he wished to emulate and replace—the gentile law giver of the European host nation. And in the lopsided ambivalence of the parvenu, the natural, Jewish father takes the hindmost. By knocking off the hat of Freud's genitor, Freud's gentile pater castrated Freud's natural father, giving Freud's own fear of castration a referent far beyond the dynamics of the nuclear family. Freud's fear of castration by the father becomes an allegory of Freud's and, more broadly, Jewish men's emasculation and disenfranchisement by the West.

Whether a literal father or a literal son, the parvenu must fear that, despite his appeal for acceptance by the gentiles, he will suffer the fate that he has implicitly endorsed for the "negro slave," "savage," and even the unassimilated Jew, the genitor of the parvenu. Indeed, by scaling the Acropolis, Sigmund assumed the role of his pater by killing his genitor. Freud's dream of conquering the West was thus a lopsidedly ambivalent one. It came at the cost of his natural father's life and legacy. Freud's Jewish sons in the brotherhood of psychoanalysis seem to have intuited the implications of this aggressive wish for them.

Freud's 1927 article on fetishism cryptically alludes to the major and potentially genocidal consequences of the "narcissism of minor differences." "In later life a grown man may perhaps experience a similar panic," Freud wrote, "when the cry goes up that Throne and Altar are in danger, and similar illogical consequences will ensue" (1927: 153). He says nothing more, but, in the historical and political context—a year or two after the publication of *Mein Kampf* (1925–26)—Freud's intended meaning becomes clear: the Nazis were reacting to their castration anxiety in an infantile or insane manner. Puzzlingly, though, Freud long seemed to suppose that, by explaining it, he had escaped the threat posed by this childish insanity. In the run-up to the Nazi invasion of Austria, Freud long resisted his acolytes' efforts to convince him that the threat was grave, delaying his departure from Vienna for London.

Freud first discussed fetishism in 1905, in the context of an effort to classify and explain the psychology of a patient who, instead of desiring sexual relations with the socially normative sexual object—that is, in the case of a male patient, an adult woman's vagina—is aroused by a man, a sexually immature person, an animal, a particular type of clothing, a specific nonsexual part of the female body, or a particular color of hair (Freud [1905a] 1910: 18). In a manner indebted to the language of Portuguese and Dutch traders on the Guinea Coast about Africans' appreciation of beads and alleged sacralization of found objects, Freud attributed these attractions collectively to the "over-estimation" of nonsexual phenomena and to "cases in which for the normal sexual object is substituted another which is related to it but which is totally unfit for the normal sexual aim" (17). Of course, the Dutch and the Portuguese had not identified Africans' fetishism as primarily sexual. It was

Freud who mobilized the racial logic of Victorian colonialism and Jim Crow in order to construct black and brown men as walking ids.

According to Freud, the fetish object "is in demonstrable relation with" the ideally female object of the male patient's desire "and mostly with [her] sexuality" (18). In sum, to Freud, the fetish is an "unfit substitute . . . for the sexual object" (17). But *whose* judgment of the "normal" and the "fit" was being taken for granted here?

Even within Freud's world, sexual norms varied across time, space, religions, classes, and political movements. For example, the Nazis condemned the Weimar Republic (1919–33) as a phase of sexual libertinism, and much of the German-speaking world projected the same stereotype of libertinism onto Viennese people and Jews generally. Moreover, regarding "the normal sexual aim," Judaism seems to be much more flexible than Christianity with regard to the parts of the body fit for sexual use, at least within marriage. For example, Maimonides's *Mishneh Torah* declares that

> since a man's wife is permitted to him, he may act with her in any manner whatsoever. He may have intercourse with her whenever he so desires and kiss any organ of her body he wishes, and he may have intercourse with her naturally or unnaturally [traditionally, *unnaturally* is interpreted as referring to anal and oral sex], provided that he does not expend semen to no purpose. Nevertheless, it is an attribute of piety that a man should not act in this matter with levity and that he should sanctify himself at the time of intercourse. (Maimonides, *Mishneh Torah*, Hilkhot Issurei Bi'ah [laws concerning forbidden relations], 21:9)[2]

If Maimonides's twelfth-century legal opinion and late nineteenth- and early twentieth-century rumors among central European gentiles had any empirical counterparts in Freud's secular Jewish world, then Freud's references to "the normal sexual aim" bear the hallmark of his internalized worry about the gaze of *spiessig*, or "square," Christians toward Jews. In this context, Freud's accusation that non-Western "savages" are sexually undisciplined looks like a strategic deflection of the same accusation by *spiessig* Christians toward Jews and Viennese people and its displacement onto black and brown people.

Freud's references to fetishism were not merely a dead metaphor or metonym: they expressly appropriated the Enlightenment's degrading portrait of Guinea Coast religion. Freud wrote, "This substitution [i.e., European erotic fetishism] is not unjustly compared with the fetich [*sic*] in which the savage sees the embodiment of his god" (Freud [1905a] 1910: 18). Freud's analogy also leaves me wondering where, if not in material things, the gods of the "savages" are *suitably* or *normatively* embodied, and according to whose norm. Freud was, after all, an atheist, who would therefore have no opinion of his own about where a god should *properly* be embodied. So his analogy serves only to insinuate that Freud himself is, by virtue of his authority to diagnose the wrongness of the "savage," a European as "normal" and "civilized" as the audience to which he was pandering. Like the antithesis of the properly treated European worker that Marx identified in the "negro slave," Freud's "savage" was a pedestal lifting up racially and class ambiguous men like Marx and Freud at the undeserved expense of the ostensible "savage," especially the African.

That is not to say that Freud's observations, or the works of Marx and other nineteenth- and twentieth-century European social evolutionists, lack merit as descriptions of European social and personal pathologies. Indeed, the description of European pathologies is Marx's and Freud's principal stated aim. Yet their gratuitous and illogical put-down of non-Western peoples appears to serve supernumerary purposes that, because of their implicitness, have escaped most readers' skepticism and have, for the same reason, effectively dramatized the naturalness of Marx and Freud's own claim to a "civilized," white, and male citizenship that many of their central European contemporaries had denied them.

What Freud calls the fetish is a material thing that reminds a neurotic adult man symbolically of the mother's "missing" penis. And this fetish first comes into being at the shocking childhood moment when the child notices his mother's lack of a penis and infers that the father, the giver of law, has cut her penis off. A "civilized" and psychologically "normal" man has adapted to the idea that he must give up his infantile desire for his mother and concede that the mother belongs to the father. However, a person who has never adapted to the trauma of witnessing the ostensibly castrated state of the mother (and is therefore neurotic) fixates on a symbolic object that he associates with the mother's missing penis. That object is typically chosen on the grounds that it is or resembles the last thing seen before the shocking discovery, a moment now otherwise forgotten due to traumatic amnesia. Such material things—shoes, noses, braids, and fur are the chief examples highlighted by Freud—then become a fetish for the adult man, indispensable to his sexual arousal.

Like the preoccupation of psychoanalysis with castration and its fetishization of the penis, Freud's focus on noses, fur, and hair is most fruitfully read with reference to its cultural, historical, and biographical context. For example, traumatized by his father's emasculation, Sigmund remembered that the hat knocked off of his father's head had been a fur hat. Freud's identification of noses and hair as common targets of such hypercathexis inspires a similar reading, since central Europeans in Freud's day regarded both noses and hair as important markers of Jewish difference.

Noses hardly seem a fit candidate for Freud's hypothesis that fetishes are typically the last thing seen before the boy's eyes land upon the anatomical site of his mother's erstwhile castration. Freud's basic hypothesis about the selection of the fetish object seems inapplicable to noses. The nose is nowhere near the vulva. Moreover, my African nose in no way resembles a penis; because of its shape, I would have chosen the tongue—out of all of the possible organs at that height on the body—as a more likely candidate. However, with a stretch, I can vaguely imagine how European noses do. Biographically speaking, the demonstrable connection between noses and penises is that, in the midst of their rumored love affair and at the time that Freud first theorized castration anxiety, Freud and Fliess regularly examined each other's noses as they explored the theory that noses are erogenous zones neurologically connected to the penis. The resemblance of pubic hair to animal fur makes it an obvious candidate for Freud's hypothesis. But, as Marx's antisemitic and anti-African takedown of Ferdinand Lassalle suggests, central Europeans also used Jews' mulattolike hair color and texture in the justification of Jews' pariah status.

Conversely, people who loved Marx and Freud called them by pet names highlighting their quasi-African appearance. Though loved as a "little black-amoor," Freud also introjected the gentile patriarch's murderous attitude toward the African "savage." At the heart of Freud's concept of the fetish is just such ambivalence on the part of the fetishist, whereby the strongest fetishes and the ritual practices surrounding them mime the roles of both castrator and castrated—and, I might add, those of gentile and Jew, and of European and African.

Gilman is undoubtedly correct in observing that Freud endeavored "to divide humankind into only two classes—male and female." But the full citizenship of assimilated Jews in the emergent nation-states and overseas empires of Europe also depended on the successful division of the world into two further classes of humanity—the "civilized" and the "savage." Freud described this lower rank of humanity with other phrases, as well, such as "primitive man" (Freud [1913] 1946: 4), "primitive races" (30), and "savage and semi-savage races" (3), in which class he included the "Melanesian, Polynesian and Negro races of Africa" (17), "races in America, Africa (Madagascar), North and Central Asia" (26), Australian Aborigines, Fijians, Sumatrans, Maoris, and so forth. I must say that what Freud means by "races" is not perfectly clear to me. Like its German cognate, the term "race" was used to describe peoples long before the emergence of a socially stratifying science of hereditary racial differences among such peoples. Freud's social-contract theory implies that peoples change over time, and he cites the nonhereditarian social evolutionism of Lewis Henry Morgan, for whom "savages" are defined by their place on a ladder of technological advancement, rather than their color. However, the "races" that Freud singles out for their "savage"-ness are exclusively nonwhite. Freud's social evolutionism was not systematic but opportunistic. It seems intended to rescue some people more than others from the existential threat posed by nationalism, imperialism, and the pseudoscience they supported.

More akin to the reigning pseudoscientific racism of his day is Freud's postulate that these races of men "are more subject to temptations than we are, and hence require more extensive protection against it" (Freud [1913] 1946: 14). In the absence of extreme rules of avoidance—according to at least one Dutch missionary cited by Freud—such "savages" would even find it irresistible to have sex with their own daughters (16). Freud does not explain why so-called savages "are more subject to temptations than we are," but he relies on a large measure of psychoanalytical and, more generally, colonialist a priorisms in order to conclude that the races of men who he shows are the *most* restrained in their choice of partners and the *most* careful to avoid sexual impropriety (that is, the Melanesian, Polynesian, and African "savages") are also *actually* the most oversexed. Really, this is precisely what he argues.

From an Afro-Atlantic point of view, all of this sounds like the snow calling the ash white. The Martinican psychoanalyst Frantz Fanon ([1952] 2008) recognized clearly what Freud and his European successors had overlooked. First, the European imagery of the "savage," and particularly of black people, projects all that is "dark" within the European himself onto the other. And, instead of embracing Freud's evolutionary model of the difference between the "savage" and the "civilized" or the "black" and the "white," Fanon shows how the two social categories are the complementary ontological creations of colonialism. *Totem and Taboo* vividly illustrates Fanon's point.

Europeans have spent much of the past five centuries defining the enslaved and the colonized as lascivious, aggressive, and murderous in order to excuse rape, aggression and murder that Europeans have made a habit and a political institution of inflicting upon us. In turn, Freud's adoption of this European imperialist point of view and narrative persona strikes me as a wish-fulfilling denial that many of his fellow Europeans have already cast him in the same role as the colonized and the segregated. Much of the European scientific community even regarded psychoanalysis itself as proof of the stereotype that the Viennese and the Jews themselves are sensual and lacking in sexual self-control and that Jewish people—assimilated or not—are primitives. Freud offered the alternative view that it is not European Jews but the colonized alone who deserve to be so stereotyped. Perhaps it seemed to Freud that the most effective way to escape being bullied is to become a bully oneself. Freud's accusation toward black and brown men was comparable to the blood libel leveled against the Jews, who had been accused of sexual indiscipline, as well.

Yet Freud's invocation of the term "protection" contains lopsided measures of tenderness and hostility toward the "savage." On the one hand, Freud's invocation of the so-called savage's need for "extensive protection" is coterminous with the usually disingenuous vocabulary of colonial conquest, once euphemistically described as "the white man's burden." For example, between the 1880s and 1920, the British called the area that would become the settler colony of Kenya the East Africa Protectorate. Indeed, in *Totem and Taboo* ([1930] 1961), Freud writes of "the savage" with the patronizing sympathy of a Kipling. This parlance suggests that women actively tempt all of us men, and we men all need protection from them (in Freud's case, the tempter may have been a man). But, in what sounds like a rationalization of colonialism, Freud accused the "savages" of being particularly ineffective at controlling their drive toward aggression and murder, even less so than European neurotics. Ultimately, by asserting that people who repress their selfish pleasure seeking out of respect for their fellows come to dominate other groups, Freud seems to blame European overseas imperialism on Africans' and Pacific Islanders' ostensible lack of self-control, as well as Europeans' need to protect them from their own extreme disposition to sexual transgression and violent behavior (Freud [1930] 1961, [1913] 1946: 14; Jones [1953] 1961: 477–78).

Moreover, in the US American settler colony, the accusation that non-white men are oversexed by nature had infamously murderous consequences for thousands of African American men during Freud's lifetime. In the wake of African American emancipation, the closer a Black man got to a voting booth, the more white American men insisted we were sexual monsters unable to control our lust for white women unless we were violently kept in line by white men. Since emancipation, allegations of Black male savagery and hypersexuality—along with the official denial of white men's wholesale rape of Black women throughout the period of slavery and Jim Crow—have justified both the murder and the violent policing of Black men and the infantilizing "protection" of white women (Hall 1983). During Freud's lifetime, the Ku Klux Klan and the Knights of the White Camellia are the most dramatic examples of this phenomenon. Freud joined this terrorist bandwagon as he alleged that savages require "more extensive protection" against their own ostensible sexual indiscipline. It would be difficult to believe that Freud was unaware of lynching in the United States.

Freud's movement succeeded nowhere more impressively than in the United States, a place that intimidated Freud and whose sexual prudishness inspired his contempt (Jones [1953] 1961: 265–66, 269). Though it may appear otherwise, it is no irony to a Freudian that this sexually explicit movement achieved its greatest success in one of the West's most conservatively religious and sexually repressive nations. The United States found in Freud a way to deal with its own deep ambivalence about not only sexuality but also race. It is no mere coincidence that the ascendancy of psychoanalysis in the US during the early twentieth century coincided with the rise of segregation, the disfranchisement of Black voters, and the lynching of hundreds of African American men, which was generally justified in terms echoed in *Totem and Taboo*. Victorian colonialism, Jim Crow, and psychoanalysis shared similar premises about race, offering similar opportunities and posing similar dilemmas to assimilated Jews. The pseudoscience and popular discourse of Black male sexual savagery remained widespread and politically influential—as in the infamous Willy Horton ad run by presidential candidate George H. W. Bush and his campaign manager Lee Atwater—well into the late 1980s, convincing many white American men, rich and poor, that they had the need and the right to monopolize political and economic power in the country that we share (see also Hall 1983; Frankenberg 1993).

From the opening pages of *Totem and Taboo*, Freud establishes a dichotomy between two classes of humanity, which may be the subliminal, and therefore the most powerful, message of the book to his intended audience. While they may laugh at the cleverness or be distracted by the flimsiness of any particular evidence-based argument in the book, readers are rhetorically seduced into embracing the unargued postulate that brown and black people are like the ancestors, the children, and the mentally ill neighbors of "civilized," white people, in that they had failed to repress their rapacious libidos. Freud repeatedly offered explanations of the otherwise perplexing behaviors of "savages"—such as totemism and "an unusually high grade of incest dread" ([1913] 1946: 9)—in terms of such behaviors' alleged similarity to the behaviors of Freud's neurotic patients. Note that, like the sixteenth- and seventeenth-century Dutch Calvinist merchant-adventurers on the Guinea Coast, Freud was inclined to compare Roman Catholics—the majority of his patients—to primitives, insofar as Roman Catholics, too, prohibited cousin marriage, which Freud apparently did not regard as "real incest" ([1913] 1946: 10, 14)! The justification of social hierarchies always requires such mental gymnastics from those anticipating benefits from those hierarchies. Not to be taken for granted in Freud's time and place, the subliminal message of *Totem and Taboo* and therefore the most powerful one was that the assimilated Jewish male narrator belonged to an "us" that is defined by whiteness, civilization, and likeness to the German-speaking gentile audience.

Freud's durable stipulation that "savages," or "the primitive races," are like Western children and neurotics itself requires an anthropological, historical, and psychological analysis. As recently as 1982, I heard from a colleague in the art department of then-liberal Phillips Academy, Andover, that the excellence of African and Oceanic art lies in its likeness to the unselfconscious art of children. Freud's racialized dichotomy between the "savage" and the "civilized" corresponded, not accidentally, to the nineteenth- and twentieth-century classes of the colonized and the colonizer. A certain version of theory-producing Europe had produced a "natural history" classifying Jews and other European minorities alongside non-Europeans as objects of taxonomy and ranking. However, by explicitly citing the social evolutionists, Freud also implicitly renamed the knower and the subject of history.

Through the countless and authoritative references to "we," "us," and "our," the narrator of *Totem and Taboo* established his own membership in a class defined by its knowing posture and by its oppositeness to the "savage"— that is, "the society of the white races of Europe and America" (20) and the "civilized races" (9, 21), an exclusive club that is presumed to amalgamate Freud and his audience as one. This society is defined by the equivalence of its amalgamated and collective trinity of noble ancestors—the Romans, the Greeks, and the Hebrews (26).

This subliminal declaration of racial commonality and equality between Freud and his largely gentile audience must be read against the backdrop of many gentile Europeans' antecedent and contemporaneous denial of that Jews and gentiles are racially identical or equal. Like all ethnological Schadenfreude, Freud's "argument of images" rested on the trope of contrast as a source of meaning (Fernandez 1986; also Saussure [1912] 1983): because they are not "Melanesians, Polynesians, and the Negro races," assimilated Jews must be "white" and therefore "civilized" like the audience that Freud addresses in the first-person plural. Freud's movement of the boundary between "us" and "them" begged what was then an open question in Europe and drew its hypnotic power from its subliminality. By this veiled argument, a denial that European Jews are civilized or that "the Negro races" are uncivilized would be tantamount to denying the superiority and distinction of white gentiles, as well.

This subliminal argument of *Totem and Taboo* must be understood in the context of Freud's well-documented sense that his medical colleagues had excluded him from their guild on racial grounds and his enduring fear that his new science would be dismissed on the grounds of its Jewish origins. Freud's personal collection of artifacts embodies a similar subliminal message about Freud's place in the binary hierarchy of races. Though apparently intended to give a view onto the deep psychology shared by all of humanity, Freud did not include artifacts from the societies that *Totem and Taboo* said reveal human psychology at its most unvarnished. Rather, his proudly displayed collection excluded the artifacts of the same dark "races" that the narrator of *Totem and Taboo* excluded from his collective identity. Freud gathered around himself sculptural monuments of and a visual argument for the racial self that he wished to claim.

Psychoanalysis did, by the end of Freud's life, achieve a considerable following among gentiles, particularly in the English-speaking world, which, thanks to Freud's own image management and the general taboo on exploring the personal backdrop of theory, paid little attention to Freud's ambiguous racial and sexual identities. He established his whiteness and acceptably European bourgeois male sexuality partly by affirming and amplifying the imperialist vision that it is the "primitives" and the "savage races" who—like Western children and neurotics—lack sexual and social self-control. Through their stark contrast to people like Freud, the fetishists dramatize Freud's own membership in the class of humanity that he redefined as his own.

It should be noted that Freud resisted a number of contemporaneous intellectual trends that recognized the equality of whites and nonwhites. For example, Freud eschewed the liberal nineteenth-century German ethnological tradition exemplified by his German Jewish counterpart Franz Boas, the founder of US American cultural anthropology. And, even though he knew the Polish-British anthropologist Bronislaw Malinowski personally, Freud showed little interest in the incipient Anglophone ethnographic literature inspired by Malinowski, which prioritized the "native's point of view." Instead, Freud choose to prioritize the research of nineteenth-century and turn-of-the-century British and French armchair ethnologists—such as James Frazer, E. B. Tylor, Lewis Henry Morgan, John Ferguson McClellan, Robertson Smith, and Lucien Lévy-Bruhl (see also Jones [1953] 1961: 287, 290, 291, 502)—who largely opposed pseudoscientific racism but also stratified the world into populations made inferior or superior by virtue of the degree of technical, social, or intellectual progress assigned to them by the European author. In the ostensibly objective evolutionary ranking of the world adopted by Marx and Freud, the brown or black "native's point of view" was entirely irrelevant.

Thus, Freud spoke strategically to the dominant caste as if in their own voice, endorsing the premise that the dominant values of European gentile and bourgeois society were uniquely normal and given by nature, even as Freud knew that he himself fell short of this standard. Yet Freud also insinuated into his argument the perspective of the dominated. Freud urged toward the "savage" not hatred but pity—the thinly veiled sister of contempt—and what he called "protection," the thinly veiled sister of domination. To him, they were not simply "cannibals" but "*poor naked* cannibals" (Freud [1913] 1946: 4, emphasis mine). For underneath we are all driven by the selfish desire for sensual gratification and the willingness to engage in murderous aggression in order to achieve it. Yet in the service of social harmony, civilization, and the socialization of civilized children, normal "civilized" adults repress and disavow these desires, without actually extinguishing them. Freud thus reminded heterosexual European gentiles that the "savage" lurks within them, that even "normal" love contains a measure of fetishism, and, privately, that they should tolerate male homosexuals.[3] This is one of the many ways in which psychoanalysis manifests the same ambivalence that Freud attributed to the most enduring and powerful of fetishes. The mercy that he recommended for the "savage" might one day save the likes of Freud himself, but his ultimate aspiration was to join, seamlessly, the ranks of the dominant.

With charity to himself, his fellow Europeans, and (other) men who have sex with men, Freud reminded the heterosexual male European gentile that we are all imperfect. He added that civilization and proper sexual citizenship lie not in our unchanging ontology as civilized gentiles or not-quite-civilized Jews but in our ability to suppress our rapacious desires for the greater good of the European empire, at least when we are dealing with other Europeans. Underneath, he said, we are all fetishists, but not always in a bad way. Freud observed, "A certain degree of such fetishism therefore regularly belongs to the normal, especially during those stages of wooing when the normal sexual aim seems inaccessible or its realization deferred." In some cases, a normal man is attracted to a woman *on condition* that she possesses certain characteristics—such as a particular hair color, type of clothing, or even bodily defect (Freud [1905a] 1910: 18). The case becomes pathological," Freud added, "only when the striving for the fetich fixes itself beyond such determinations and takes the place of the normal sexual aim; or again, when the fetich disengages itself from the person concerned and itself becomes a sexual object" (18).

This encomium to romantic love among the "civilized" did not stop Freud from treating the "savage" as an incomplete person who, like the neurotic European fetishist, was presumed to treat his fellows as though they were not whole people contained fully within their bodies. The "savage" was spared no reduction, singling out, or distortion that would make him useful as a foil to the kind of European Freud wanted to be accepted as. For example, it is suspicious that Freud constructed "savages" and neurotics as the exemplary fetishists, with the implication that they are the typical people who, instead of recognizing the whole person they are dealing with, focus on that person's accoutrements and isolated anatomical features. However, such behavior is one of the defining features of human culture. It is difficult for me to imagine a society in which a person's clothing is *not* a focus of attention—to a degree and in a way fruitfully described as fetishistic—as others judge whether the wearer is attractive, not to mention marriageable, powerful, smart, deserving of employment, or worthy of citizenship. If any populations are the paradigm case of this phenomenon, it is Western consumer socie-

ties. Freud's mannered self-display through photographs—and theory—most
powerfully illustrates this likely human universal. To its vocabulary, central
Europeans added not only a cross-culturally widespread interest in people's
nose shapes but also a rarer concern about hair color as fetishistic markers of
otherness, with particularly intense implications for Jewish people in the era
of racial science. By attributing the ostensibly excessive fixation on specific
body parts and inattention to the whole person to "savages" and "neurotics," Freud seemed indirectly to criticize his gentile countrymen's antisemitic
preoccupation with Jewish noses and hair color.

Moreover, the nineteenth-century industrial mass production of clothing
and the decline of sumptuary laws in the "modern" West made clothing—
such as garters, shoes, and fur hats (like that of Freud's father)—an increasingly important means of asserting valued social statuses, particularly among
the stigmatized and the status anxious. Thus, the projection of relationships
such as attractiveness, marriageability, and respectability onto clothing was
likely a much *more* conscious and emotionally charged practice among emancipated Jews in the emerging consumer societies of central Europe (not to
mention twentieth-century African Americans, among whom the preoccupation with clothing and hairstyle is well documented) than among the people
Freud called "savages," "primitive races," and "poor naked cannibals."

Moreover, Freud's obsession with the penis and with the threat of its loss
crescendoed in parallel to the crescendo of European antisemitism and may
well have been an unconscious defense against it. Freud's last and most widely
cited essay on fetishism appeared in 1927, one year after the publication of the
second volume of *Mein Kampf*. In the interethnic family drama of the West,
psychoanalysis itself might be read as a counterwish—for the assimilated
Jewish man to restore his foreskin and don the crown of the gentile patriarch.
Indeed, Freud declined to have his sons circumcised (Gilman 1993: 86), and
he sought to adopt an uncircumcised gentile as his principal son and heir.

Of course, Freud was not entirely sanguine about "civilization." Like
Weber ([1922–23] 1946) and Durkheim ([1893] 1947), he conceded that
civilization reduces people's happiness—according to Freud, by constraining the fulfillment of their infantile wishes. However, Freud regarded such
repression as beneficial to social progress (Freud [1913] 1946, [1930] 1961).
Civilization came about, he said, through the "discovery that a number of
men who were placing limits on their own gratifications were stronger than
a single man, however strong, who had been accustomed to gratifying his impulses unconstrainedly" (Jones [1953] 1961: 477–78). This version of social-
contract theory counterfactually presupposes that id-repressing discipline,
peace, and justice are the norm among the civilized conquerors, just as selfish

indiscipline is the norm among children, prehistoric Westerners, and the contemporary "savage races" whom Europeans were, in Freud's day, actually displacing, colonizing, raping, enslaving, exterminating, and, in the Congo Free State, punishing with the removal of their limbs for their failure to meet production quotas.

The truth is that no population on the planet is responsible for more deaths and the destruction of more lives than gentile European men, but Freud felt moved to gain their acceptance and alliance. And I cannot pretend not to understand why. Freud also helped them to make peace with the moral burden of the history by projecting their collective crime onto others. In the United States and Europe, psychoanalysis coincided with and reciprocally influenced numerous movements intent on liberating "civilized" people from their repression, many of which exploited the psychoanalytical image of black people and other "savages" as walking, dancing, and talking ids. In the late nineteenth and early twentieth centuries, white Americans were learning to embrace their own emotional and putatively animalistic side, in cultural arenas as diverse as blackface minstrelsy, the boom in American football from the 1890s on, and the jazz craze of the 1920s to the 1950s. As in European cubism, so too in US popular culture, Black people became symbols in white people's efforts to discover and recover the elemental and primal aspects of their humanity that they had renounced since the Enlightenment. Our bodies have been seen as the dangerous and delectable, living and breathing form in which the demons long repressed in Westerners rematerialize. In the bodily form of black men, the so-called "inner Africa" attracts adulation and murder in almost equal measure. The sacralization of the jazzman in New York and Paris coincided with the quasi-religious bacchanal of lynchings in the US South, attended at times by hundreds of white men, women, and children who often took home body parts and preserved them as souvenirs.

Had they given it any thought, Freud and his acolytes would likely have attributed the heartless behavior of "civilized," white colonialists and lynch mobs to the aggression inherent and equally resistant to repression in the psyches of all human beings. To me, it is an equally worthy sociological hypothesis that the working-class Belgians who administered "justice" in the Congo Free State were passing on forms of aggression generated by mistreatment and feelings of inferiority in their home society, and then resolving their psychic distress by identifying with and miming the authoritarian behavior of their own oppressors. Violence is more intrinsic to the role of the conqueror than to that of the conquered. Hence, Freud's use of the "savage" as the prime exemplar of violence and vice is nothing short of colonialist fetishism.

I find useful and convincing Freud's analysis of the fetish as a material thing empowered simultaneously by the fetishist's fear and desire and by the opposite roles in the social relationships that the thing mediates, though I am more certain than Freud that these are normal and widespread phenomena, not confined to contexts of sexuality or psychopathology. And, I have no use for Freud's odd premise that every boy experiences a momentarily conscious and forevermore-unconscious fear of castration by his father, which will explain much of his antisocial or ambivalent behavior during adulthood. To me, Freud's overemphasis on castration is made meaningful not by its empirical accuracy with reference to males in every time and place—as the designation of psychoanalysis as "theory" implies—but by the significance of the penis in Freud's resolution of the emotional conflicts of an assimilated Jewish man in the new, gentile-dominated nation-states of central Europe. The penis, and particularly the white penis, was Freud's own principal fetish: he and many of the antisemites against whom he mounted his implicit argument for Jewish male enfranchisement projected onto the white penis the unique power to confer citizenship, a logical entailment of which was the devaluation of nonwhite penises and vulvas of any color. Freud's efforts to disambiguate himself racially and in gender terms from other stigmatized populations comes together in his famous dictum that a woman's sexuality is as inscrutable and deficient as "the dark Continent" (Freud [1926] 1959; Gilman 1992: 169).

However, his effort often took the form of humor at the expense of the "savage" and the "negro." In general, Freud recognized jokes as the fantasy fulfillment of wishes based on repressed sexual and aggressive impulses. His view of which sexual and aggressive impulses drive a man to tell another man a sexual joke about a woman is clear, but he does not explain what inborn wishes are fulfilled by such jokes about "negroes" and "savages." Freud did celebrate what he calls a "genuinely successful" joke about "a display by savages: 'in ceremonial undress'" (Freud [1905b] 1960: 211). Over the years, Freud also repeatedly told a joke comparing himself to the lion in an 1886 cartoon where a yawning lion says with disappointment and impatience, "Twelve o'clock and no negro."[4] Indeed, noon was the usual starting time for Freud's psychotherapy sessions. Freud is said to have told variants of this joke to his inner circle of colleagues over the course of several decades. Freud's identification with the lion in this joke is no matter of speculation. In his role as a therapist, Freud expressly compared himself to a lion fighting against his resistant patients, whom he called his "negroes," with the implication that the psychoanalyst's relationship to the patient is one of aggression and domination. Indeed, according to Freud's gentile acolyte and biographer, the Welshman Ernest Jones, Freud designated a specific American patient as "his negro." Against the backdrop of Europe's colonial relationship with its dark-skinned and recently pacified victims, Freud clearly delighted in imagining himself as the opposite of the "savage" and the "negro," and indeed as the predator who dramatizes his whiteness and his conquering power by devouring the "negro." This rhetorical gesture calls to mind Bismarck's effort to demonstrate a backward Germany's equality with France and England by calling the Berlin Conference of 1884 to divide up Africa and through the genocidal ruthlessness of his troops' conduct in Southwest Africa.

But such gestures may also contain an element of ambivalence.[5] Freud's own theory of "joke-work," by analogy to his concept of "dream-work" ([1899/1900] 1965), suggests that his joke fulfills the wish of the jokester and his audience to evade the fate suffered by the prey, suggesting that the jokester and his or her audience could, under other circumstances, have been the prey. Indeed, the Moorish-themed pet names that identified Marx and Freud with Africans were diminutive, suggesting a further, domestic back-drop to Marx's and Freud's triumphalism over Africans. Just as the models of and for political and religious communities are often drawn from family life, the models of and for family life are often drawn from the wider world of politics and religion. Marx and Freud were passing on the hot potato of not only anti-Jewish racism in the wider society of central Europe but also infantilization in the microsociety of family and friends. Both entailed an uncomfortable degree of vulnerability.

Although Freud failed to consider the hierarchical social context and the lopsided sympathies manifest in these psychological processes, he usefully highlighted their complexity, arguing in his article titled "Humour" (Freud 1928) that jokes like his own about "no negro at noon" shift the focus of attention away from the most tragic elements of a situation—that is, from the painful death of the devoured negro to the ironically industrial-era clock watching of the fictional lion—thereby unconsciously assuring the raconteur and his audience that their own situation is not so bad. This scenario thus presupposes that the teller sees him- or herself as potentially suffering the same situation as the butt of the joke—in this case, the "negro"—but at least situationally able to displace his or her own vulnerability onto that "negro."

It is also true that, in the 1905 book on jokes, Freud recounted many self-deprecating jokes by Jews about themselves. Yet this gallows humor presented the victims of bad situations laughing at their own situations with admirable equanimity and wit. But because of my own racial positionality, it is difficult for me not to notice that Freud's references to the "negro" and the "savage" never present those characters as speaking subjects capable of intellectual complexity or ego-defensive wit.

It is not that Freud was uncritical of white people. Indeed, World War I left him disappointed that the "white race" had not fully transcended its id and inner "savage" (Freud 1915), but Freud's disappointment rested on the ex-

pectation that the civilizational superiority of the "white race" should naturally have prevented the savagery of World War I. His expectation ignored the
centuries of atrocities that the supposedly civilized "white race" had committed against Africans and Native Americans and, by contrast, assumed the
obviousness of the expectation that the "negro" is nothing more than a walking id—a mute beast or, worse, unthinking meat, not even capable of the
minimal planning, observational skills, or knowledge of self-defense that a
normal human being would by then have mobilized if a lion had sat daily in
the same place at the same time picking off his neighbors.

Freud's joke theory suggests that, as the raconteur, Freud ambivalently
identified with both the lion and the negro. But if he did so, he learned nothing from the analogy. Sadly, the historical record reveals denial rather than
"reflection" (ìronún) on Freud's part. Had Freud "stirred his belly" (ro inún)
in the Yorùbá sense, he would have recognized his own and other European
Jews' imminent vulnerability to the fate of the feckless "negro"—that, however much they wished to identify with the imperial lion, they and the negro
ultimately shared the status of prey. It is clear that much of the ego-defensive
comfort that Freud derived from this joke lay in the fact that he had convinced
himself that he was not a "negro" and in the hope that his relatively light
skin and Western clothing—and not merely a difference of circumstances—
thoroughly distinguished him from the "negro." Freud's jokes seemed to fulfill the wish to join the gentile colonialist in destroying that "negro" and thus
further denying the part of Freud himself that is "negro."

Ironically, Freud's portrait of the feckless "negro" foretold his own bizarre
procrastination as others urged him to flee the imminent Anschluss—the
Nazi annexation of Austria in 1938—and many European Jews' later self-
accusation that they did not fight back soon or hard enough. If Freud's joke
was ambivalent, its ambivalence was too lopsided or he too childish to recognize how much of himself he was projecting onto that "negro."

In sum, Freud's semimetaphorical use of African religion as the paradigm of misplaced value and disordered subject-formation also seems to have
embodied an effort to disambiguate himself racially and to clarify his own belonging in the dominant global caste of the nineteenth- and early twentieth-
century imperial world. His related use of the African as a metaphor and
projection of Europeans' sexual aggression had murderous implications for
people like me and implications less palliative for assimilated Jews than
Freud seems to have hoped. In the run-up to the Shoah, his laughter at the
"negro" and self-distancing from the "savage" must have become painfully
awkward.

Whereas Althusser (1969) called psychoanalysis "the science of the unconscious," I would prefer to call it the science of ambivalence and its management

(consider also Freud [1913] 1946: chapter 2). People tend to have mixed feelings about themselves and about others. Moreover, the conflicting motives that drive people's behavior are often invisible to them. These are realities of which psychoanalysts and the worshippers of the Afro-Atlantic gods are equally aware. Psychoanalysis shares in common with the Yorùbá-Atlantic religions the idea that the forces shaping a person's thought and conduct are multiple, that the most important of those forces are invisible, and that each of those forces is like a being with a volition of its own.

In both the Afro-Atlantic and the psychoanalytic fetish, dreams are frequently used as means of divining the volition and action of these forces. Moreover, as Jones shows among the multiple organizations devoted to keeping Freud's ideas alive, the practitioners explained their own ambivalent behavior toward each other in terms of the compelling power of such invisible forces (e.g., Jones [1953] 1961: 426–27, 451–52). However, psychoanalysis and the African-inspired religions give different names to those forces and to the worlds where these forces reside. The systematic second-guessing of other people's explicit motives is not only good social science but also an artifact of the social precarity suffered paradigmatically by Africans under the threat of kidnapping during the slave trade and the divide-and-conquer strategies of colonialism, as well as by assimilated Jews in the emergent liberal nation-state. If this "hermeneutics of suspicion" (Ricoeur 1973) were unrealistic, one might be tempted to call the constant concern of these two populations about the masked ill will of others "paranoid." Assimilated central European Jews like Marx and Freud responded to this precarity with a mix of ethnological Schadenfreude—that is, through the denigration of Africans, unassimilated Jews, and women in order to highlight their own belonging in the master race and sex—and an identification with and revalorization of the downtrodden. Their fetishes often looked both ways and spoke with two voices—the castrator and the castrated. These men were ambivalent, though lopsidedly so. And I submit that this lopsidedness is both compensatory and strategic. It entails an aspiration to whiteness and a hedging of the theorist's bets.

Like the Yorùbá-Atlantic religions, psychoanalysis is a cult of affliction (Jones [1953] 1961: 330–31), in which the practitioners are qualified by their experience of affliction to cure others, and the members earn their living by applying the cure to other afflicted people. Indeed, it might be argued that all European social theory is a cult of affliction, and that psychoanalysis is the social theory least likely to deny it.

CHAPTER SIX

The Castrator and the Castrated
in the Fetishes of Psychoanalysis

Freud's analysis of the fetish noted in the most enduring and powerful fetishes the enduring ambivalence of the patient, who saw the fetish as the tool of both the father's threat to castrate the patient and the patient's identification with the father as castrator. Freud's interpretation of his patients' excitation and distress might fruitfully be read as a projection of his own ambivalence about the West and of the inner conflict that he suffered as a result of his own ambiguous status—as both a potential victim of castration by the gentile father and a potential team member in the perpetration of such violence—in the global social hierarchy created by Western Christian imperialism. Freud's racial and class ambiguity calls attention to the class and national ambiguity of the Enlightenment's advocates, as well.

The Dilemma, the Ambivalence, and the Choice
at the Heart of Nineteenth-Century Social Theory

Like Marx, Freud was ethnically Jewish and was probably aware that even Hegel—vulnerable as he was on the grounds of class and nationality—arrogated to himself the right to classify Jews as a primitive contamination within modern Europe. Freud utterly rejected Judaism as a religion but could not escape the antisemitism that identified him with religious Jews. He sought acceptance among his gentile colleagues and fellow Europeans, but, against the rising pseudoscientific racism of his day, he sought to redefine Jews not as a race separate from white, gentile Europeans but simply as a European people at a different but superable stage of social evolution. In effect, Freud had designed a secular neoreligion that prioritized the pre-Christian spirituality of the West, denied Jews' similarity to the circumcised Africans, and allowed assimilated Jews to escape the implications of their biological ancestry. This secular Jewish religion attempted to thread a needle at its sharp end. The "theory" that emerged was also a product of moral choices specific to, but not fully determined by, the cultural, political, and material conditions of Freud's life.

Like the Black *assimilés* sketched in the work of Frantz Fanon, Freud was deeply ambivalent about European "civilization." He at once worshipped it and resented feeling reviled by it. For most of his life, he dreamt of not only prospering but also of conquering the West with his ideas. Among his greatest fears was that psychoanalysis would be dismissed as a merely Jewish philosophy. So, even at the cost of offending his loyal majority of Jewish followers, he worked tirelessly to recruit gentile followers, Carl Jung foremost among them. Yet even Jung rejected him. Like that of the Black *assimilé*, the strategy of the Jewish parvenu was risky.

Not all European or German-speaking scholars have been as quick as Marx and Freud to classify the colonized as precursors to civilization and as the social opposite of assimilated Jews and other decent Europeans. Again, eighteenth, nineteenth, and pre–World War I German ethnology featured numerous publications and museum collections that dignified non-European cultures and African cultures in particular, such as the works of Johann Gottfried von Herder, Adolf Bastian, Leo Frobenius, Franz Boas, and Felix von Luschan. At risk of classification as laggards in the progress of capitalism, republicanism, democracy, and national unification, these German-speaking burghers articulated a vision of history in which all peoples could possess equal dignity or, at least, in which dignity could be found in non-European races as well. Neither the murderous racial chauvinism of the Nazis nor the British and French social evolutionist put-down of the colonized, which Freud adopted, was inevitable. Marx's and Freud's theories of the fetish were positioned and strategic choices among the symbolic options in their respective times and places.

Inspired by the writings and legacy of Herder (1744–1803), Bastian (1826–1905) and Luschan (1854–1924) asserted the dignity of Germans, Russians, and Africans in similarly egalitarian terms. For example, after the British "punitive expedition" of 1897, Luschan rushed to London to acquire for German museums as many as possible of the bronze busts and plaques and carved ivory tusks that British troops had stolen from the palace of the Oba of Benin and then auctioned off to pay for the expedition. Luschan is reputed to be the first European authority to argue that these West African sculptures were the product of an African impulse, rather than having been inspired by African contact with the Portuguese. By proxy, their acquisition by Germany demonstrated not only Germany's equality with other museum-keeping nations but also the validity of Germany's own independent cultural heritage.

Though eventually overwhelmed by the racist ideas that culminated in the rise of the Nazis, this liberal tradition in nineteenth-century German ethnology survived in the deeply influential work of Freud's contemporaries Boas (1858–1942) and Frobenius (1873–1938). Frobenius was the Protestant-born but eventually "neopagan" grandson of a zoo operator who sometimes hosted *Völkerschauen*, or quasi-zoological "people shows." Eventually, this autodidact explored Africa in a manner influenced by late nineteenth-century imperialist conventions, but he also deeply identified with and immersed himself in African culture, financing his repeated his visits to the continent by collecting and selling African art in Europe.

Frobenius saw Germans and Russians as royalist and in this way culturally similar to the spiritual "Aethiopians," in contrast to the French and the English, whom he saw as similar to the materialistic "Hamites." This German identification with the "Aethiopians" is especially remarkable in light of the "Hamitic hypothesis" that had emerged in nineteenth-century England and France. It posited that pastoral Caucasian Hamites were responsible for introducing whatever civilization might exist in among the Negroid or Khoisan populations of Africa. In a single rhetorical gesture, Frobenius stood up for the dignity of the Germans, the Russians, and the Aethiopians, representing them all as oppressed and unjustly maligned by their actual inferiors—the French, the British, and the Hamites. Frobenius believed that any given culture today is the product of decay from antecedent grandeur, and he regarded the African antiquities that his teams exhumed or copied with the support of wealthy Germans as evidence of a truly grand African past that deserved recognition as among the world's most important legacies. Moreover, he regarded his discoveries and collecting as an honor to Germany in its competition with England. Indeed, in their riposte, the British colonial government tried him for the theft of Nigerian antiquities.

Frobenius's reading and field research on Yorùbá religion produced some impressive art-historical results—impressive both in their scholarly quality and in their influence on subsequent Africanist art history and African studies. He might justly be called the founder of Africanist art history. Some of this success resulted from his skills in the social politics of his era. He captivated Kaiser Wilhelm II, a range of wealthy Germans, the German and American general public, and African and African-diaspora intellectuals. Even the Nazis seem to have respected him and his wealthy supporters too much to shut down his Frankfurt-based research institute until after he died in 1938, the year before Freud's death.

This legacy of Afro-German identification helps us to understand the apparent irony of the Nazi propagandist filmmaker Leni Riefenstahl's segueing from Romantic filmmaking about the snow-white elegance of the German warrior body to coffee-table photography of the obsidian-black elegance of the southern Sudanese warrior body. However, as in other cultural and historical settings, fear and hatred often coincide with attraction. Nazi propaganda included highly degrading images of the West African soldiers who fought on behalf of the French, but some family lore passed down from the generation of the Allies' occupation of Germany contains a powerful dose of desire. Since 1988, three Germans have separately told me what they say is the oft-repeated story in their families about the first time their forebears saw a Black person face to face. In each case, a parent or a grandparent, around two years old at the time, was reportedly sitting in the middle of the street as the US troops rolled into town. When a tank halted in order to avoid running over the child, an African American soldier descended from the top of the tank and walked toward the child. The family panicked in the fear that the Black man would eat the child, but, instead, he picked her up and gave her a chocolate bar.

At the most superficial level, this story conveys many Germans' recollection of the US occupiers' wealth and generosity, in contrast to the relative poverty of the English and the French and the vengeful cruelty of the Russian occupiers. Yet the story also resurrects the long-running European association of Black people with not only chocolate but also coffee and sensuous pleasure more generally. Since my first visit to Germany, I have perceived a far greater appreciation of Black beauty there than in the US. For example, in 1988, the toy department of Berlin's ritziest department store, KaDeWe, sold a half-dozen beautiful and naturalistic Black baby dolls, the likes and the number of which I had never seen in a US department store of any sort (see also SABA Collection 1059). And I am not the only dark African American I know who feels far more attractive to white Germans than to US Americans of any color. And yet, some white Germans have told me that they segued from mild curiosity about Black people to passion and even marriage because a parent had absolutely forbidden that curiosity. Even in 2014, German friends warned me not to enter certain neighborhoods in the former East Berlin, as my family and I were not unlikely to be assaulted there by racists.

In sum, there was nothing inherent in the bipolar *Zeitgeist* of the German-speaking world that required Freud's (or Marx's) particularly degrading posture toward Africans. That posture requires an explanation attentive to Marx's and Freud's personal experience.

It must be emphasized that the dilemmas of in-betweenness in a status hierarchy are not unique to German speakers or to Jews, and that scholars close to Marx and Freud also expressed a diverse range of solutions to these dilemmas in their work. For example, Malinowski—a foundational figure in our discipline—was close enough to Freud to visit him on his deathbed, but Malinowski's firsthand observation of social order in the Trobriand Islands (Jones [1953] 1961: 523; Malinowski [1922] 1984) does not seem to have made a dent in Freud's strategic fiction of the colonized. Malinowski was just as racially ambiguous as Freud, but Malinowski's ambivalent discursive strategy leaned more toward equality with his nonwhite mentors. Like Freud, he opened his foremost book-length account of the non-Western Other with repeated declarations that he is a "white man" (e.g., 1922: 4, 6–7), and he persistently called his mentors "savages." However, he also advertised his advantages as a Slav in understanding the "savage." In explaining the disposition and the advantages of ethnographic participant observation, he wrote,

> It is good for the Ethnographer sometimes to put aside camera, note book and pencil, and to join in himself in what is going on. He can take part in the natives' games, he can follow them on their visits and walks, sit down and listen and share in their conversations. I am not certain if this is equally easy for everyone—perhaps the Slavonic nature is more plastic and more naturally savage than that of Western Europeans—but though the degree of success varies, the attempt is possible for everyone. (Malinowski [1922] 1984: 21)

Yet even Malinowski was ambivalent, identifying the features of low-status Trobrianders as "prognatic, negroid faces, broad, thick-lipped mouths, narrow foreheads, and a course expression," as though the physical anthropology of the day explained their low status ([1922] 1984: 52).

Near the opposite extreme was another visitor to Freud's deathbed—the French Jewish ethnologist Lucien Lévy-Bruhl (Jones [1953] 1961: 502), whom Freud greatly admired. Lévy-Bruhl's resolution of the dilemma of the borderline white was closer to Freud's. Indeed, Freud's attribution of "childlike" analogical thinking (which also characterized civilized narcissists) to "savages" may have derived from his reading of Lévy-Bruhl's theory about the "prelogical" nature of non-Western thought (Lévy-Bruhl [1910] 1985). One wonders why Freud did not see in his own therapeutic uses of free association and the symbolic interpretation of dreams, jokes, and verbal "slips" a similarly "prelogical" detection of analogy and multiple planes of meaning in a single phenomenon. Why did he not see his use of such analogy-based divination in the management of social relations as similarly "childlike"? A common feature of ethnological Schadenfreude is the use of shared human characteristics, such as analogical thinking and postprandial torpor, as evidence of the unique inferiority of the ethnological Other.

It must also be said that there was nothing inherently liberal or egalitarian about nineteenth-century German ethnology's Afrophilia. For example, Frobenius was expressly opposed to republican democracy and to the demotion of the Prussian king. And while eighteenth-century Herder credited each people with its own distinctive, hereditary, and intrinsically valid national spirit (*Volksgeist*), he held a negative view of interaction between peoples of different cultures and religions, associating it primarily with foreign imperialism, colonial domination, and the "parasitism" of trade minorities (Herder [1784–91] 1968: 12–13, 28ff., 130, 142, 144, 160–61, 162, 163, 359, 382, e.g.). This conjunction of German nationalist ideas was in some ways egalitarian and cultural relativist. However, it also presented a major challenge to the Jewish aspiration to citizenship in the emergent nation-states of central Europe.

It is ironic that Herder's Romantic logic of universal equality among peoples also classified Jews as a foreign contaminant to the emergent German nation. This irony perhaps helps us to understand why Freud felt the need to ratify the Enlightenment's put-down of West Africa's embodied ideas, even as he appropriated them in a much-simplified form. Ultimately, Jews fared little better than Africans in the Enlightenment-inspired effort to stratify the "races" on a universal scale of worth or progress. Like Africans, Jews were regularly fetishized as embodiments of what a central European should not be. I have argued that Marx's and Freud's ambiguous racial position and Marx's ambiguous class position help to explain not only their displacement of stigma onto the African but also their exceptional insightfulness about the workings of fetishism itself.

Hence, my application of the term "fetish" to European social theories and Afro-Atlantic gods alike is comparative and heuristic, rather than derogatory, in its intent. I do not, however, recommend the use of the term to either European social theories or Afro-Atlantic gods alone outside of this context, as it is too likely to be construed in such an isolated context as derogatory. Here I employ the term heuristically to describe the foundation of a social relationship mediated by not only highly cathected material things but also vivid idea-images and a compelling history of precedents regarding who can make, sell, acquire, give, use, and interpret the cult objects; under what circumstances and according to what procedures these things can be exchanged, used, and interpreted; and with what transformative consequences in the life of the community.

Both historical materialism and psychoanalysis were material reimaginations of the social order in which the assimilated Jewish male spokesman of the new social order was assigned to a newly made collective identity better suited to his personal aspirations, and the black person became his antithesis, *uneasily* justifying the new role of the Jewish male, since each invocation of the Black fetish also kept alive *rival* fetishes, figurations of the proper social order had defined Jews as no different from blacks.

Like fetishism, ethnological Schadenfreude is essentially ambivalent, albeit lopsidedly so. The subject's delight in the downfall of others rests on the subliminal awareness that the subject him- or herself is vulnerable to the same sort of downfall. It is expressly sadistic and latently masochistic. Both ethnological Schadenfreude and fetishism entail the fetishist's simultaneous identification with the castrator and the castrated, with the oppressor and the oppressed.

The Spirited Things of the Post-Jewish White Brotherhood

Early psychoanalysis was not a mental idea or a therapeutic method alone. It was an actor-network assembled under specific historical conditions and in response to specific social problems.

The material things in which the early psychoanalytical movement invested intellectual work, emotional energy, and money included not only a vividly reimagined idea-image of the son in the nuclear family and a merging of the assimilated Jewish man into the idea-image of Western man but also physical monuments (such as the Acropolis, the multiple museum houses devoted to Freud's memory, a well-preserved collection of Freud's artifacts, and canonical books), furniture (such as the conjunction of the rug-strewn couch and the upright chair), intoxicants (such as alcohol, tobacco, and their delivery systems), and insignia of membership (such as intaglio rings). Though typically ignored in latter-day discussions of Freud's theory, such material things were pillars and projections of his community's vivid reimagination of the person and of the West generally. The spirited things of the early psychoanalytic movement continually invoked not only a mind irreducible to the brain but also a sovereign band of European brothers whose membership would be defined by the color of their penises rather than the intactness of the foreskins.

Freud gave many symbolically coded and relationship-infused gifts to his acolytes and received similarly iconic gifts from a far wider circle of admirers. Yet he was explicit about the ambivalence of the gift. Like the French sociologist Marcel Mauss ([1923–24] 2000), Freud identified in gift giving an unconscious aggression and a demand for gratification (Jones [1953] 1961: 482–83). Hence, he accepted some gifts and rejected others, depending upon his view of the sincerity of that relationship. Freud would also likely approve of the hypothesis that, in general, the power of the supercathected things in his actor-network lies in the ambivalence that they embody. I hypothesize that, like the most enduring and powerful fetishes generally, the spirited things of the early psychoanalytical brotherhood dramatize opposing roles and thereby clarify complementary subjectivities. They embody not only the antagonism between the castrating father and the potentially castrated son but also—through the proxy of maleness and femaleness, analyst and analysand, Europeanness and the Africanness—the opposition between the gentile pater and the Jewish genitor.

Ultimately, the rituals through which Freud's fetish was mobilized resemble what Weiss (2011) calls a "power exchange." Freud's theoretical clarification of these roles postulated the supremacy of the male, the analyst, the European, and the pater at the same time that he dreamt of his own imperial conquest of the West. By the same token, Freud's implicit endorsement of colonialist oppression also endowed Europeans' "inner Africa" with supreme force. The Shoah suggests the failure of this wish-fulfilling fetish, but, for another half century, psychoanalysis prevailed.

Intaglio Rings

In his efforts to construct a self-sustaining guild for the practice of the "talking cure" and to guarantee its solidarity in the elevation of Jewish dignity, Freud distributed rings among his followers. Like many of the antiquities in Freud's extensive collection, the intaglios in the rings he distributed were Roman and Greek, embodying Freud's worship of the West, particularly in a form stripped of the antisemitic cultural and political impulses that had, since the Middle Ages, characterized Jews' experience of the Christianized West. This phenomenon calls to mind the rings and other membership insignia in Freemasonry, of which Hegel was a member, as well as the conferral bands, buttons, and rings that denote membership in the *Burschenschaften* and other fraternities in German-speaking Europe—brotherhoods whose middle-class membership united to advocate a new nationalism in central Europe. They sought in national citizenship a new equality with the Francophile nobility of the German-speaking lands.

According to the Freud Museum London, Freud gave intaglio rings "to his closest colleagues beginning in 1912 with the formation of the Committee, an exclusive group of supporters who defended Freud and psychoanalysis in the wake of dissenters such as Carl Jung and from criticism from outside of

FIGURE 6.1 Ring with blue glass intaglio, first century B.C.E.–first century C.E.; silver setting, twentieth century. Gift of Sigmund Freud to the German psychoanalyst Ernst Simmel in 1928 (http://www.freud.org.uk/about/collections/detail/10158/).

the field. After the original Committee dissolved Freud continued to present rings to his closest friends and supporters."[1]

It was Freud's acolyte and biographer Jones who proposed the formation of the Committee, based upon the following boyish inspiration: "The whole idea of such a group had its prehistory in my mind: stories of Charlemagne's paladins from boyhood and many secret societies from literature" (Jones [1953] 1961: 327). However, it was Freud himself who came up with the idea of membership rings. Freud also seems to have compelled those who joined the brotherhood to drink alcohol, even when they had, prior to joining, avoided it (266, 275). And, according to Puner (1947), Freud found nonsmokers annoying, such that almost all of his followers ended up smoking, the very habit that would kill the father of psychoanalysis.

The passing nature of Jones's mentions of the role of alcohol, tobacco, and finger rings in Freud's recruitment of his heirs suggests not the unimportance of these material embodiments of his thinking but their taken-for-grantedness in the middle-class fraternities and freemasonries of Europe. Intense alcohol consumption remains a mechanism of social bonding in US American college fraternities today. The antique Roman and Greek intaglios in these rings (figure 6.1) embody Freud's longing for a version of Western brotherhood based not on Christendom but on a form of whiteness and of self-intoxication that did not exclude Jews.

The Couch and the Upright Chair

The most visible furniture of Freud's thinking and of his "talking cure" was the upright chair and the couch—really a chaise longue—sensuously covered with overlapping Middle Eastern pile rugs in dark geometrical patterns. Sitting at the head of the chaise longue, invisible to the supine patient, the upright chair seems to embody, even posthumously, Freud's theoretical posture and studious obfuscation of his own personal life.

Yet Freud's office furniture says something more about the materiality of that theoretical posture. Unlike the usual furniture of the medical examination room and the laboratory, the upright chair and the chaise longue are domestic furniture, drawn from the dining room and the living room, where Freud so self-consciously performed his "normal" heterosexual marriage and family life. In the light of Freud's personal sexual history and in contrast to the standard medical office furnishings of his day, the upright chair and the chaise longue must be read as a statement.

But a statement of what? On the one hand, this furniture reflects and informs Freud's model of psychological and psychiatric normalcy. First, it validates the power of the mind over the body and, therefore, the efficacy of touch- and sight-free communication between doctor and patient. Second, by recreating the bourgeois home environment in the consultation room, it endorses the normalcy of the bourgeois family—whether Jewish or gentile—as the defining social context of psychic life. And, third, it underlines and celebrates Freud's patriarchal mastery of this psychosocial configuration.

On the other hand, like the most powerful fetishes, the upright chair and the chaise longue look both ways. Sitting in the upright chair for an hour at a time for a half-dozen sessions per day must have been extremely uncomfortable for Freud, one of the many discomforts, emotional and physical, that he saw in civilization. This chair calls attention to the particular discomforts associated with the marble throne of the all-knowing patriarch in Western theory and theology. I have also often wondered why Freud's couch is covered with and surrounded by geometrically patterned Middle Eastern rugs. In the West, rugs are normally intended not to cover couches but to mark the borders between living spaces and to direct people's movement within bounded spaces—bed to dresser, sofa to coffee table, domestic room to domestic room. The mazelike design of these rugs suggests that there is something more to these spaces than their boundedness and something more to these paths than their straightness. Moreover, their woolen pile looks uncomfortable to lie on. If a patient sought comfort on this couch, she or he was also made to itch a bit. I do not know whether this gesture of aggression on the part of the therapist-host was conscious or unconscious. However, it does bespeak the duty of the analyst to provoke movement by unsettling the ego. Indeed, rugs also direct people's movement into and out of the house. These particular rugs, though, are ill-suited to the needs of people *entering* the house. For example, one cannot wipe one's feet on them. If anything, they point outward, evoking the exotic destinations and sexual adventures depicted in the orientalist paintings of the day. These rugs seem to analogize the exploration of the unconscious to foreign exploration, substituting the colors of the seraglio and the mazelike imagery of the souk for the equally current imagery of the recesses of the Western mind as our "inner Africa." Yet, alongside these rugs, Freud's frequent references to his patients as his "negroes" leave little doubt about the colonial structure of psychoanalysis, and they reveal a glimpse of the repressed but fundamentally Afro-European focus of that structure.

In sum, Freud's upright chair and chaise longue not only endorsed the bourgeois heterosexual model of psychosexual normalcy but also, as critics of psychoanalysis feared, invited its transgression. Yet the notion of transgression suggests, in the first place, the normalcy of the nuclear family and its boundedness as the cradle of the self. Psychoanalysis and its furniture are monuments to Freud's inner and hidden transgression of the normalcy that he outwardly performed. By contrast, the Yorùbá-Atlantic religions start with the premise that the self is innately the crossroads of forces extending to the ends of the cosmos.

Like his statuary, his cigars, and his consultation of Frazer and Tylor, Freud's Middle Eastern rugs bear witness to the making of nineteenth-century central and northern European bourgeois identity through its militarily conquests and increasingly unequal terms of trade with the Mediterranean, East Asia, and the Caribbean. The exclusion of signs of Europe's lively but increasingly unequal trade with Africa and the visual nonspecificity of such signs from the Black Americas (i.e., the cigars) call to mind the same avoidance that one sees in the preserved manor houses of the slaveholding US South. Elites who are vulnerable to the low status associated with Black people are the least comfortable about using signs of Blackness in their household iconography of the self. Further evidence of this point is that Freud willingly joined in the nineteenth-century and fin-de-siècle French-mediated fashions of *chinoiserie* and *japonerie*, and conspicuously avoided the French and German Afrophilia that had become popular in the 1910s and '20s. The fact that Freud's hero Hannibal and his Egyptian statuary were also African seems to have escaped him. Like Greece itself in the eyes of the more northerly Europe, Africa has a "classical" face with which Europeans and wannabe Europeans can identify, even as they cast its contemptible and dark contemporary counterpart as the constituent other (Herzfeld 1987).

Freud's Artifact Collection

Much of psychoanalysis is an archaeology of the human mind, reconstructed through the cross-cultural study of mythology, the colonial ethnology of contemporary "savage" life, and the dreams of Freud and his patients. Freud also used antiquities as a source of evidence and as prompts in his myth-based "talking cure" (Jones [1953] 1961: 356).[2] Yet, like Freud's interpretations of mythology, ethnology, and dreams, his collection of purchased and gifted antiquities offers hints about the self to which Freud aspired, as well as the self that he feared being identified as.

As a collector myself, I experience the thematic assembly of things intended for viewing as a commemoration and display of my ideas, tastes, travels, and friendships (see Matory 2016 and the SABA Collection). Like one's spouse, one's children, and one's books, they are an extended portrait of the self. They also fill a void, materializing aspirational dimensions of the self. If one's collection is protected from the elements, from breakage and theft, and from sale as separate items, it can become one's posthumous legacy and proxy. Everything else that is publicly known about Freud's ambitions suggests that he, too, intended for his collection to serve the purposes of aspirational self-fashioning and posthumous self-commemoration. I think of the books I write, similarly, as my "children"—not nearly as valuable or as beloved as my flesh-and-blood offspring but, still, as extensions of myself that I hope will long outlive me. In this sense, too, Freud's published theories—like Marx's—must be thought of as elements of a distributed, aspirational self, and not as abstract, perspectiveless truths from on high. It is useful to read Freud's artifact collection in this light.

According to Jones, Freud's nearly lifelong fear of death was matched by a lifelong aspiration to worldly wealth, fame, and power, as well as a pharaonic desire to monumentalize himself and his idea for immortality (Jones [1953] 1961: 56, 173, 226, 277, 409, 488). His obsession with the collecting of Greek, Cypriot, and Egyptian "antiquities," which he called his "national gift" (*Nationalgeschenk*), dramatized his aspiration to such an enduring and influential legacy. He displayed these items in his waiting room, his consultation room, his study, and on his desk (281, 264, 266, 356), where they also appear to have been advanced as evidence of Freud's deeply historical difference from the paradigmatic "savage" victims of Europe's nineteenth-century overseas empire.

Hundreds of imported statuettes crowded Freud's workspaces and, consequently, the visual environment of Freud, his acolytes, and his patients (see figure 6.2). Among the gifts he received, he particularly cherished the ancient Greek antiquities that he received from Marie Bonaparte (e.g., Jones [1953] 1961: 331, 356, 460, 474, 482, 489, 527). Indeed, his ashes are stored in an ancient Greek urn that she gave him (530). The Freud Museum London

FIGURE 6.2 Freud's office, featuring his armchair, couch, and "Oriental" rugs, as well as part of his artifact collection. PUBLISHED WITH THE PERMISSION OF THE FREUD MUSEUM LONDON.

website shows that he collected not only Greek, Cypriot, and Egyptian artifacts but also a number of Japanese and Chinese pieces as well, not to mention Middle Eastern rugs. At the same time, fauvists, cubists, and surrealists were famously referencing sub-Saharan African spirited things in their art and publicly debating their significance. Freud could not have been unaware of the real-life African spirited things in his environment as he formulated his theory of the fetish. Yet, contrary to the prevailing fashions, African art was conspicuously absent from the forest of statuary that he displayed on his desk and in his waiting room.

This artifact collection suggests that this effort at clarifying his difference from Africans was not unconscious. Freud and the late Hegel were separated by almost a century, and, while Marx's work was a direct response to Hegel's, Freud's was not. Nonetheless, the real-life African referent of the term "fetish" must have been on Freud's mind, too. From the mid-nineteenth century until Freud's time, thousands of anthropomorphic sub-Saharan African consecrated or once-sacred things entered central and northern Europe through the efforts of European missionaries, colonial administrators, and the sort of "explorer" with whom Freud expressly identified. Among the more famous explorations concerned with Africa and its objects was the Dakar-Djibouti Mission (1931–33). From 1907 until the mid-1950s—that is, for much of Freud's adult life—the real-life African fetish was at the center, and was arguably the foundation, of modern art. In 1907, twenty years before Freud's

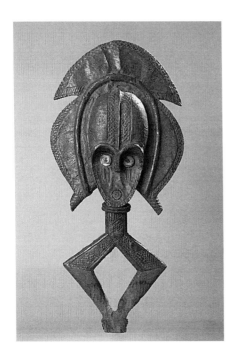

FIGURE 6.3 Kota reliquary statue (SABA COLLECTION EO12). Such statues were among the African sacred things imitated by the cubists and fauvists in the early twentieth century and still widely admired by European and Euro-American modern art collectors in the twenty-first century. See, for example, Pablo Picasso's painting *Les Demoiselles d'Avignon* (1907) and Stepan 2006: esp. 10, 74, 75.

most comprehensive article on fetishism, the so-called African fetish had already become a formidable physical presence at the center of European cultural life.

It was in that year that Picasso first visited these made beings at the Musée d'Ethnographie du Trocadéro in Paris and, according to his own report, learned from them "what painting was all about."[3] Figure 6.3 is a Kota reliquary figure from Gabon and an example of the sort of African spirited things at the heart of the actor-network of European modern art virtually throughout the time that Freud was writing about the fetish and assembling his collection.

In this historical context, the exclusion of African things from Freud's sculptural self-fashioning and archaeology of the human mind cannot have been an oversight. Given Freud's literacy and the career-changing influence of his Parisian sojourn with Charcot, neither such later disinterest in nor unawareness of Parisian trends would seem a likely explanation. This conspicuous gap in Freud's collection suggests an unfashionable but motivated and psychoanalytically understandable denial. The *assimilé* is usually the last to buy into the recognition of the elite's fashionable embrace of Black people's culture: he fears giving the elite the opportunity to say, "I told you so; I knew you were Black all along." However, the *assimilé* also has the choice of embracing and riding this fashion toward a recognition of his own distinctive, and possibly African-like, value. Like Freud, many of the leaders of European Afrophilia were, by the standards of the eighteenth-century Enlightenment and of nineteenth-century scientific racism, only ambiguously European or white—such as the swarthy Roman Catholic Andalusian Pablo Picasso and the Sephardic Italian Amadeo Modigliani. They might also be compared with another hero of this revolution in the European spirit—the light-skinned African American Josephine Baker, whose famous "banana dance" and resistance to the Nazis gave living, breathing, heroic form to Europe's "inner Africa."

Freud chose the usual, and opposite, defense mechanism of the *assimilé*—the evasion and studious denial of his likeness to black people. The question of why southern European artists in Paris identified positively with Africa awaits another study. But the Europe-wide fame of their choice highlights the elective and remarkable nature of Freud's contemporaneous choice to exclude African things from his archaeology of the human mind and from a collection that physically dramatized and extended his own public persona.

Freud's study of and most important article on the fetish coincided with Josephine Baker's years-long and world-famous "banana dance" on the Parisian stage, as well as the height of the Jazz Age, when many Europeans and Euro-Americans sought relief from their repression in the mimesis of a sort of Blackness and Africanness designed for this very purpose, a mimesis resembling in function the sort of Blackness propagated in the most popular styles of rap music today—that is, a caricature.

It may well be that, already in fear of misrecognition by his gentile colleagues as a woman and an unassimilated eastern Jew, Freud felt he could ill afford to give further credence to his alleged likeness to the African as well. Freud's disavowal of his "inner Africa" may also demonstrate his argument, in *Totem and Taboo*, that compulsive neurotics studiously avoid things that remind them of their own forbidden desires. Getting near them entails the dual risk of personal temptation and ostracism by those who have kept their proper distance from the forbidden object. I would add that racially ambiguous people and socially ambitious members of stigmatized races have an amplified incentive to avoid association with such forbidden racialized objects and practices. They risk being identified with the id of the dominant race—an identification that leads periodically to fashionable celebration but daily to a heightened level of policing, repression, and persecution.

Like his patients, Freud could repress but not extinguish his own inner African demon. The ego-defensive intent behind his public expression of pity for the "poor naked savage" in *Totem and Taboo* was made evident, at least since 1886, in his repeated joke about the lion eating the negro—a far earlier, longer-running, and intimate revelation of his hostility toward and fear of recognizing his own human connection to Africa. As both Böhme ([2006] 2014) and Apter (1993) have suggested, the fervor of Europe's accusation of fetishism toward Africa has made that very "Africa" an inescapable touchstone within European identities, including Freud's.

Freud apparently identified with the historical and social position of the European oppressor of the "negro," just as the well-socialized son identifies with the castrating father. The idea-monument left behind to "justify [Freud's] existence" (Jones [1953] 1961: 226), psychoanalysis was broadly structured around the derogatory language that his fellow nineteenth-century social evolutionists in England employed to establish their superiority to non-Europeans. Freud not only eschewed the more liberal nineteenth-century ethnology in his own mother tongue but also generated a tendentious rhetoric that subliminally disambiguated him from women and Africans. Freud's response to the antisemitic put-down that he and his kind were no better than Africans and women was not a disavowal of such hierarchical judgments but an embrace of that hierarchy, with the caveat that Jewish men (and especially the assimilated among them) *are* better than women and Africans. His rhetoric seems to suggest that assimilated Jews should be spared the cruelty and exclusion that Europeans had become accustomed to inflicting upon women, unassimilated Jews, Africans, and other dark people.

Freud's own theory of projection enables us to recognize his theory of "fetishism" as just that, a projection of not-quite-white Europeans' anxieties about their social status onto people with an even less secure claim to dignity and rights in a European gentile-dominated world. It is already well understood that fetishism can be a projection of *value* and *agency* onto a disputed repository thereof. However, I would add that a further dimension of fetishism is the projection of inherent *worthlessness* and *disability* onto some people and things by people who wish to draw attention away from their own vulnerability to the same sort of negative projection by others.

It might be inferred that Marx's and Freud's reactions to racial ambiguity were also shaped by the similar ambiguity of Roman Catholics in central Europe. It should not be forgotten that the intercultural encounter between Africans and Europeans was not the only early habitat of the fetish problem. The problem was also at home in the wake of the Thirty Years' War—the murderous clash between Protestantism and Roman Catholicism, particularly in the German- and Dutch-speaking lands. The Dutch Calvinist merchants in West Africa who branded African gods "fetishes" branded Roman Catholic sacramental objects, with the exception of the Eucharist, with the same expletive.

Thus, in more ways than one, Marx's and Freud's theories reveal the multiple and successive forms in which stigma was displaced from one European group to the next, often through the proxy of Africans and through the vocabulary of "fetishism." As Jews, they were, like Catholics and Africans, implicated by the Protestant critique of fetishism, of which they were all accused. I have argued that the "negro slave," the "savage," and the unassimilated Jew are themselves fetish elements that personify Marx's and Freud's fears about the undervaluation of the assimilated male Jew—and possibly of the male Catholic as well. In this act of fetishization, Marx and Freud themselves mime and normalize the castrating role of the white Protestant European pater.

Marx and Freud also help us to see that fetishism affects at least three parties in its semiotic and social process. While one party or thing is supercharged with value or agency, another is denied a corresponding amount of value and agency. The third party is the speaker, who is redefined by these positive and negative displacements of value and by his assumption of the posture of the unmarked knower in the upright chair, as opposed to the marked and known party on the couch, whose non-normalcy highlights the knower's normalcy. Marx and Freud both illustrate the defensive motive of the stigmatized to flatter some, to stigmatize others, and to sidestep the question of their own positionality. Such passing on of stigma is itself a form of fetishization and a normal corollary of the social process in hierarchical societies (Matory 2015b). The theories and gods made by these processes are especially enduring and supercharged with affect because they look both ways. Theory assumes an additional fetish power by obscuring the social position and interests of the knower.

Freud's Cigar

From the photos in their biographies—which are read far less often than their photo-free theoretical treatises—a Black North American like me would not immediately guess that Marx and Freud had been born dark haired and would be considered black- or mulatto-looking by their European relatives, friends, frenemies, and enemies. But so they were, affirming, once again, my point about symbolism and representation that physical realities do not determine how the people who live them interpret or use them. Conversely, both Marx and Freud described themselves as white men. Their carefully posed photographs deserve a close reading in the light of this interpretive struggle.

Freud's photographic portraits are self-consciously designed elements of his distributed aspirational self—that is, the idealized persona that includes his network of things and closely identified people. His characteristic photographic pose included a three-piece suit, a cravat, a watch fob, and a cigar in hand (see figure 1.3), conveying, perhaps intentionally, the sort of self-possessed bourgeois masculinity that he wanted to project. Yet, unintentionally, it also hints at the psychological and physical power of his tobacco addiction and the sacrifice to his health that it entailed. Freud's theory of human nature suggests that his proud display of the cigar reflects both a level of denial about his fatal addiction and his investment of that cigar with conflicted feelings that he himself did not fully understand.

During Freud's exile from Nazi-dominated central Europe, he died a slow and painful death from oral cancer, which he knew had been caused by his passion for cigar smoking. Yet throughout his illness he continued smoking. Freud's cigar extended his fetishization of the penis with a phallus-shaped, human-made thing that smoked him. This pleasurable indulgence was both proof of his bourgeois whiteness and a multidimensional threat to it. On the one hand, Freud stared critically at the viewer and pointed the burning tip of the cigar outward as though it were a cocked gun aimed at a third-party.

On the other hand, the cigar's dark staff and light tip make it look like an erect uncircumcised penis. Freud's compulsion to display this thing that was dominating him chemically and literally killing him seems masochistic, dramatizing his internalization of the gentile pater's threat to castrate him, and do worse. Freud ([1927] 1961) ascribed such self-destructive behavior to a universal "death wish," resulting from the father's suppression of the son's infantile feelings of aggression and the boy's internalization of the father's attitude. We know that Freud derived pleasure from sucking this highly cathected thing even as it injured him fatally. But there is a further sense in which the cigar undermines Freud's efforts to don the crown of the gentile pater. It may be ironic or it may be perfectly consistent with Freud's theory of the Janus-faced nature of the fetish that the cigar is the tone not of white but of black flesh.[4] The dark brownness of the cigar (not to mention the likelihood that it was produced by Afro-Latin Americans) made Freud's "inner Africa" public, reminding us of his equal proximity to (and indeed possession by) the dark side of humanity. Indeed, Freud's photographic display of this constantly stiff thing suggests his compulsive wish to release the unsocialized and excessive libido that he has attributed to brown and black men and, as a condition of gentile acceptance, has worked so hard to repress in himself.

There is every reason to believe that Freud's representation of his patients' psychodynamics was also a projection of his own racialized psychodynamics. For his part, Freud recognized the humanness of the "savage" and understood "civilization" to be a painful distortion of human nature. In his acknowledgment of civilization's discontents, one must assume that—as a scientist who employed his own dreams as evidence about all human psychology—he was reporting the especially unhappy contradictions of his own situation as a Jewish parvenu. At the same time that Freud identified the dark "savage" as the embodiment of the his own unadulterated, socially unacceptable inner self, he also made the "savage," the "neurotic," and the Western child into parallel antitypes of the "civilized" adult sovereign he wanted to be. The strongest impulse within this ambivalent posture—the expiation of Freud's own "inner Africa"—also expressed a "death wish" for real-world Africans and pariah Jews. For Freud and for those who study his work, the great power of his fetish (despite its lapses as an empirical science of healing) may lie precisely in its Janus-faced qualities. Freud bore elegant witness to the reality of human ambivalence in hierarchical societies at least partly because he himself suffered from it so acutely.

While it is widely rumored that Freud once said, "Sometimes a cigar is just a cigar," there is no actual evidence of his ever having said that, and there is much to contradict the idea that he would believe it, either.[5] Freud's cigar might be interpreted, after the fashion of his own theory, as a fetish both acknowledging and disavowing Freud's own potential castration—or, more credible, his murder—by the white German-speaking gentile pater with whom he so intensely identified. With that cigar, Freud defiantly—and self-destructively—asserted the phallic white manliness and national citizenship that nineteenth-century European antisemitism and, in the end, Nazism had denied him. Concomitantly, the cigar both acknowledged and disavowed the blackness with which his mother had lovingly credited the young Sigmund and of which gentile Europe had, with hostility, accused Freud and his fellow Jews.

Canonical Books

The foremost fetishes of historical materialism and psychoanalysis are the translated and mechanically reproduced books of Marx and Freud, which give the impression that these men created ideas abstracted from any particular time, place, language, writing system, or social position and that theory comes from an Other world, where people think in the absence of company, where they do not eat or shit, hawk or spit, and where their shoes do not pinch or rub specific parts of their feet.

For example, the translated black-and-white and mechanically reproduced text of Freud's *Totem and Taboo*—in English language and Roman print, despite Freud's German mother tongue and enjoyment of Gothic script—alienates his social evolutionist personality theory from the social context of its production and fortifies the illusion of abstract thinking far removed from the influence of, among other things, sick and crying children, loans and gifts from friends, cushy apartments, personal insecurities, the weather on the way to the library, the juggling of bills, the distractions of horniness and shame about one's desires, the aspiration to get married, the needs of elderly parents, book subventions by acolytes and fights over which of one's acolytes would translate the book, the pain of oral cancer, alcohol and cocaine intoxication, wars and fluctuations in the book market, the deaths of loved ones, and the anticipation of one's own death. When we read Freud's mechanically reproduced books and essays, we cannot hear him hawking and spitting, as he habitually did.

When we read Marx's worshipfully cited *Capital* in English, we cannot feel the cold of their underdressed author on his way to the British Museum, see where and how he managed to have sex with the maid, or directly witness the hopes he heard in his daughters' halting piano chords, as he funded their lessons with a stream of alms from Engels. The printed text is normally as silent about the conditions of its production as is, according to Marx, the factory or the coat about the source of its value in the labor of eating, breathing, sleeping, shitting, and sexually reproducing white-skinned workers under the sway of competing ideas about their ontological status in an age of European overseas empire, much less in the labor of their Black counterparts.

No more than other things are books and essays infallible spirits. The cleanliness and rectilinearity of the page creates but a false impression of transcendence and infallibility. The boundness of books, like that of other scriptures, too easily lends itself to the fiction of their internal consistency from one page to the next, their timeless truth, their universal applicability, and their disinterested authorship. It is time for Marxists, Freudians, and other partisans of European social theory to recognize the thingness of books. Like other things, they are materializations of mental and social experience, as well as hieroglyphics of social relationships. Like other things, they are made of matter and can be made into touchstones of communities, which need physical foci precisely because those communities, too, are made of matter.

Ideas are inseparable from material forms. Even the most abstract ideas begin as synapses enabled by respiration and digestion. Even the ideas of Marx and Freud travel through sound and light waves, and their most enduring ideas are also grooves in a lithograph or ink on a page. Those inscriptions, like the magnetic ones on an internet server, depend on large networks of people and equipment to fund, inscribe, disseminate, store, and endorse them. The utility of seduction in the spread of ideas is further proof of their materiality. Whether we read psychoanalysis as a movement, a science, or a cult, the revelation of its mundane and immanent rituals of social bonding will still come as a surprise or an affront to those who regard European social theorists as a species distinct from and inherently superior to Afro-Atlantic priests and their ideas. The fact remains, though, that Freud's psychoanalysis was not only an idea but also a dense network of social relationships physically embodied in colonial-era mythical models, racialized desires, sexual insecurities, professional referrals, gift-exchange, chaises longues, rugs, statues, cash, cocaine, alcohol, and tobacco.

Conclusion to Part II

My aim here is not to make Marx and Freud look ridiculous or to reduce their arguments to mere reflexes of their material conditions. Rather, it is to show that Marx and Freud were not disembodied theory machines but human beings embedded in the real anatomy of frail bodily life and required to negotiate their uncertain fates within the emergent nation-states and empires taking shape around them. Historical materialism and psychoanalysis are not the products of a transcendent universal consciousness. The actor-networks from which they emerge were, like the so-called fetishes of their erstwhile African antitheses, grounded in culture-specific furniture and symbolic systems. The enormous insights in the work of Marx and Freud are apprehended all the more clearly when we recognize the fraught cultural, social, economic, and political ecology from which they arose. Our treating *Capital* and *Totem and Taboo* as God-sent scripture might well have pleased Marx and Freud, insofar as doing so advances their political agendas. However, if the goal is to use them in the project of enhancing our understanding of social life in general, we had better reread Marx and Freud within a broad ethnographic context, which is what I am attempting here.

I am calling attention to a set of facts about Marx's and Freud's humanity of the sort that tend to be overlooked when social scientists apply the insights of European thinkers from a particular place to people and situations in other places and times—facts that we would hardly be inclined to neglect if we were analyzing the insights of other human beings, such as the priests of African religions. Indeed, Marx and Freud themselves have taught us better than to ignore their own unconscious or private motives. Much less should we give Marx and Freud a pass when they casually embrace and strategically amplify their fellow Europeans' just-so story that Afro-Atlantic priests are the world's antitheses of rationality and exemplars of unenlightenment about the real value of material things. There is nothing ethereal about the epistemology behind this anti-African story or behind the various European social theories that emerged from it.

Much as Marx embraced the Enlightenment's use of the Guinea Coast as the paradigm of unenlightenment and fetishized the "negro slave," Freud fetishized the white penis and displaced the allegation of assimilated European Jews' unworthiness of citizenship onto unassimilated Jews, European women, and non-European "savages." However, I have argued that Freud's own interstitial gender, sexual orientation, and race caused an ambivalence that is well explained by his description of the most powerful and enduring of fetishes—that is, as hypercathected material objects that embody the fetishist's identification with both the castrated and the castrator. Articulated in the context of the rise of central European antisemitism, European overseas imperialism, and US American lynching—as well as Freud's own ambivalence about his Westernness and his caginess about his personal life—Freud's theory of fetishism invites interpretation as a model of Freud's own tandem ambivalence about his birth family and about his own precarious role in the family of the central European nation-state.

Psychoanalysis is a set of insights and a form of social organization intent on solving the problems of a specific time, place, and social position. Its cultural and positional specificity, far from diminishing its worth as a method of scholarly analysis, amplify its worth as a case study, illuminating and illuminated by historical materialism, Afro-Atlantic religions, and itself. Both in its materiality and in its logical structure, each of these phenomena might be described as a fetish—that is, as the material embodiment of a proposal about proper socioeconomic relations self-consciously arrayed against rival proposals and embedded with the perspectives of rival positions in a social hierarchy.

Viewed in Afro-Atlantic perspective, the fetishes of Marx and Freud ambivalently problematize the normativity of white subjectivity. White subjectivity is actively embodied through the lopsidedly ambivalent excoriation and appropriation of blackness. Marx and Freud answered doubts about their whiteness primarily by othering the "negro slave," the "savage," and the "fetish." Yet they begged fellow whites to join them in recognizing that assimilated Jews were not alone in resembling the "negro slave" and the "savage" or in their taste for the "fetish."

Through the accusation of "fetishism," Marx and Freud joined exponents of the Enlightenment in the ironic accusation that Africans and their kind inappropriately attributed value and agency to things, in contrast to an aspirational European who conducted his social relationships, worshipped his god, and formulated his theories without undue reference to material things. However, the truth is that while all of these parties were debating the value and agency of bodies and other material things, these theorists and their followers have simply taken for granted, naturalized, or been anxious to obscure the physical things, material circumstances, and social interests that shaped their choices about what to value, how to measure its value, and whom to credit for that value.

Like Herder, Hegel, Boas, Luschan, Frobenius, and me, Marx and Freud were material beings in a material world, moved by biological, economic, political, cultural, and social forces beyond their unique control. But they also made choices, assembling people, ideas, and physical things that addressed their culturally, historically, and biographically specific needs in a manner that others have subsequently found convincing and useful. They reinterpreted people and things, as well as the relationships among them, in full knowledge that their interpretations were contested and had different material implications for the well-being of different parties in the debate. It is for that reason that they and their followers have so often endeavored to abstract their choices from the circumstances of their genesis and thereby evade scrutiny about the socially positioned interestedness of their choices.

Although a knowledge of those circumstances potentially amplifies, clarifies, or corrects the truths that they tell, I cannot deny the real-world power of theoretical and theological principles that have been abstracted from the circumstances of their genesis. They are highly useful in advancing goals that rely on mobilizing and organizing people, rather than on the empirical management of facts and causation. Social relationships are too complex to rely on mere facts and causation, much less syllogism. Discourses and deeds based upon these modes of reasoning are uninspiring to most people. Conversely, faith in the implausible story of Mary's virgin conception has successfully mobilized billions and helped to consolidate a European-centered empire that now dominates the world. So when we advocate or criticize a theory, we must be clear and intentional about whether we are concerned with its empirical aims or its social objectives. There is perhaps a measure of wish fulfillment in even the most empiricist of scholarship and theorizing.

But the most powerful social theories, like the most enduring fetishes of other sorts, are perhaps those that embody the ambivalence of the theorist's social objectives in a sharply graded social hierarchy.

I take the supercathected material things in the lives of Marx and Freud to be the most radical proof of the likeness between social theories and the more conventional referents of the term "fetish." Marx's coat and factory embody the ambivalence of Marx and other European wage workers about whether they are better served by joining forces with the victims of European overseas imperialism or by standing on the backs of Blacks to achieve equality with the gentile European bourgeoisie and aristocracy. Freud's intaglio rings embody the conflict between assimilated Jewish men's desire to join the bourgeois brotherhood of the European nation-state and their awareness that the Christian roots of that brotherhood threaten long-term subordination and even death to Jews. I have argued, too, that Freud's collection of antiquities is an element of his distributed self, assembled in a collective project to deny his "inner Africa," while the upright chair aggressively accentuates his outward whiteness in contrast to the inner "negro"-ness of his patients. To me, the message of his cigar is somewhat more subtle, fully embodying both the sadism and the masochism of a person precariously suspended between blackness and whiteness, femaleness and maleness, heterosexuality and homosexuality, vulgarity and sophistication.

Next I turn these insights toward the spirited things of the Afro-Atlantic religions, based upon the hypothesis that, like Marx and Freud, the priests have made their fetishes at a cultural and class crossroads, and most influentially so at the same cultural crossroads where the European "problem of the fetish" arose—on the Guinea Coast, where, I will argue, African merchant-monarchs' relationship-building exchange of African people and things for European things and distilled substances produced the paradigmatic altars of the Afro-Atlantic world.

The real-life African and Afro-Latin American referents of the term "fetish" also embody socially positioned understandings of value and agency. We may learn a great deal about them by considering their own debated meaning in the intercultural spaces they occupy, the class interests they articulate, and their Janus-faced embrace of the oppressed and the oppressor alike. The Afro-Atlantic gods are hardly the wrongful repositories of agency and values that European merchants and "theorists" constructed in an effort to illustrate their own rightness. But they do regularly include European commodities to which European merchants attributed very different degrees of value. And, once consecrated, they embody a degree and type of agency that the sixteenth- and seventeenth-century Dutch merchants on the Guinea Coast and their Enlightenment scions found difficult to understand. The implication of this conflict of understandings is not—as in the conventional use of the term "fetish"—that Afro-Atlantic priests were wrong but that they and their Dutch interlocutors held *different* understandings of value, agency, and what social relationships are implied by the proper valuation of things.

Most ethnographies of African and African-diaspora religions ignore the historical dynamism and the tradition of debate that shape all of these traditions. Perhaps partly as a function of the authors' brevity of contact and shallowness of friendship with the priests, much of the literature on African religions limits itself to the documentation of stereotypical patterns. However, my analyses concern not only the patterns but also the situational debates that complicate these patterns and the historical changes that unsettle them.

What follows is an analysis of the semiotic patterns, pragmatic dilemmas, and transformative debates that animate the sacralized material things of orisha-, *vodun*-, and *nkisi*-worship around the Atlantic perimeter. Like historical materialism and psychoanalysis, Afro-Atlantic liturgical objects and altars propose forms of social relationship that answer the rival interpretations of and prescriptions for real life propagated amid the rise of global capitalism and the nation-state. The focus of the following analysis is beads and cowrie shells, currencies of the devastating Atlantic slave trade that have been incorporated at the heart of the redemptive social projects and icons of the Afro-Atlantic priests. To the same degree that Western social theorists and their acolytes attempt to conceal the social origins and driving interests behind theory, the priests of the Afro-Atlantic religions historicize their gods and identify their making and investment with power as a collective social process. Yet when they suspect that the exposure of these processes will be used to undermine the reality of the gods and the social programs embedded in them, they, too, react with words of denial.

PART III

POTS, PACKETS, BEADS, AND FOREIGNERS

The Making and the Meaning of
the Real-Life "Fetish"

The real-life African, Afro-Latin American, or Afro-German referent of the term "fetish" assembles material objects—some natural, some home-crafted, and some industrially manufactured commodities—according to strictly observed rules and under the supervision of authorized expertise. And it does so in a way that guides people's thoughts and inspires communities. Yet those rules and the shape of the communities so inspired are not timeless and unchanging. Black and Yorùbá nationalists seeking an anchor for our collective pride and central European nationalists seeking an antitype to their own collective dignity and deservingness tend to share the premise that African indigenous religion is primordial and exempt from a history of human ingenuity and real change over time. On the contrary, I suppose that, like the theories of Marx and Freud, all religions address historically specific problems.

The breadth and depth of my observation of consecrated social relationships and ritual conduct—as well as my three and a half decades of conversation and ritualized conviviality with priests of West African Yorùbá religion, Cuban Ocha/Santería, Brazilian Candomblé, and Haitian Vodou—leave me profoundly skeptical of the reports of arbitrary African foolishness left by Dutch Calvinist merchants for the champions of the Enlightenment. Like the ways that Enlightenment *philosophes*, the later Hegel, Marx, and Freud chose to use them, these reports were often deliberately satirical and seldom well informed or merely reportorial (see, for example, Pietz 1988: 118). And, as I have argued, their satire needs to be read in historical context. These satires were shaped by the intent to skewer the writers' European rivals by comparing them to the most contemptible image of the African that they could construct. But even when intended partly to document West African beliefs and practices, these accounts lacked any basis in firsthand communication in the native language of the priests.

Contrary to Pietz's summation of the Dutch merchants' reports, it is very unlikely that the beings whom Hegel dismissed as "fetishes" and their latter-day counterparts around the Atlantic perimeter were either capriciously found objects or mere objects of any sort. What the European satirists of African religions, Roman Catholicism, and European royalty represented as caprice might be read more fruitfully as a moment in the intercultural semiosis that defined the Afro-European encounter on the Guinea Coast, a process that has provided a model for the present analysis of consecrated things. The fetish embodies rival perspectives on the same physical thing and on the social relationship mediated by this supercathected thing. The supercathected referents shared by the Enlightenment and the Afro-Atlantic religions—such as beads and "negro slaves"—encode rival perspectives on the proper relationships among people, and they depend for their significance on the shared European and African experience of the Atlantic trade and its commodities.

Perhaps the crux of the difference between historical materialism and the Afro-Atlantic religions is their opposite positions concerning the value and agency of the enslaved. It is entirely plausible to imagine that the master's expropriation of the slave's labor is the model of alienation. However, the model of the inept and unproductive slave in the work of Marx derived neither from Hegel nor from Marx's abstract logic but from Marx's opportunistic borrowing of the propaganda of southern US opponents of abolitionism, propaganda that relied on the denial of what every slaveholder knows—that no machine or commodity is as profitable as a person. The made gods of the Afro-Atlantic religions affirm this truth. The gods are made, and the chief metaphor that defines a thing as valuable and powerful is nomenclature and ritual that treats the thing like a person engaged in a relationship of mutual dependency with the worshipper—usually a relationship analogous to mastery and servitude, in which the worshipper may be the involuntary servant or the master. Such nomenclature and ritual include feeding the god, calling him or her by a human name, and asking him or her for favors that result in reciprocal obligations. Moreover, the worshipper's relationship to humanized things invariably embodies and is defined by relations of mutual dependency with the worshipper's fellow living and breathing devotees of the god.

PLATE 1 A circum-Atlantic party of Eshus cooling down at the end of a meal. In the background (LEFT to RIGHT) are an Exu (SABA COLLECTION CO47) and an Exua from Bahia, Brazil, and a Nigerian sculpture of Èṣù. In the foreground are a Beninese Legba and a Cuban American Echú Allé. On the first throw by the diviner (that is, by me), the four round coconut pieces fell in this combination—*Alafia* (in Cuban Spanish), which indicates the gods' satisfaction, predicting peace and balance.

PLATE 2 House for Elegguá (SABA COLLECTION B037). The number three and the juxtaposition of red and black are emblematic of this god. Made in South Bronx, New York (Cuban Santería/ Ocha), it was built to house an Elegguá, along with his warrior companions Oggún and Ochosi.

PLATE 3 French tapestry of a Kongo queen being carried in a hammock (SABA COLLECTION E018; 1008). The Dutch court portraitist Albert Eckhout originally painted the image that inspired this one based on his 1642 encounter with ambassadors from the Kongo kingdom of Soyo. Note that a virtually identical Eckhout-inspired tapestry depicts a *king*, rather than a queen (Fromont 2014: plate 29). See also plate 7.

PLATE 4 My necklaces (*collares* or *elekes*) for seven Cuban *orichas*, which also establish my membership in the temple of the priest who created my Afro-Cuban gods (SABA COLLECTION B357). Clockwise from twelve o'clock are (1) Oricha Oco (lord of the farm), (2) Ochún (goddess of wealth, love, and beauty), (3) Changó (god of thunder and lightning), (4) Yemayá (goddess of the sea), (5) Obatalá (lord of purity, wisdom, and age), and (6) Elegguá (lord of the crossroads and of communication). At the center is (7) the necklace for the owner of my head, Oggún (god of iron, war, and revolution). Each necklace features bead combinations in the numbers and colors emblematic of the god it invokes.

PLATE 5 Idè Ifá necklace for a priest of the divination god Ifá (West African Yorùbá indigenous religion, SABA COLLECTION D099). This is a stunning example of the type of bead necklace worn ceremonially by a novice or priest of the Yorùbá divination god Ifá. Through the color of the beads or the combination of beads of contrasting colors, each of the seven segments divided by round white beads evokes an òrìṣà or a special ritual function: clockwise from twelve o'clock, Ìbejì, Ṣàngó, Ifá, Ọbàtálá, Ọya, Alájere (an avatar of Ọbalúayé), and ifà. The strands of the tassels evoke additional gods or special ritual functions, such as Nàná Bùrùkú, Èṣù, Ọbà, Ọ̀ṣun, and itún. Though virtually all of these tiny beads were imported from Europe—many of them long ago—each type of bead has a time-honored African name and is valued for its embodiment of the sacred legacy of the African gods it evokes and the antiquity of the wearer's family's devotion to that god.

PLATE 6 Beaded votary oars for Ochún, normally placed near the goddess's altar as a devotional gift (Cuban Santería/Ocha, SABA COLLECTION B013). They also invoke her power to guide the worshipper and to propel him or her forward in life. The yellow and amber colors of the beads are emblematic of this goddess.

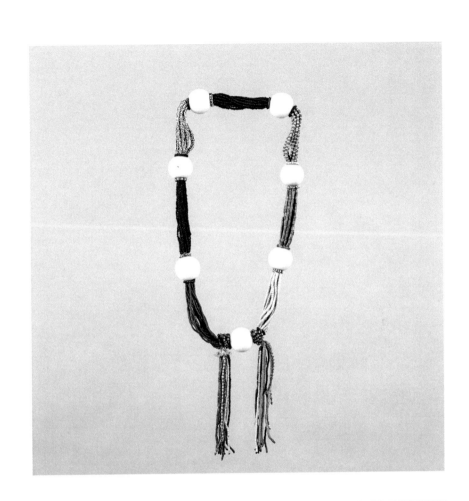

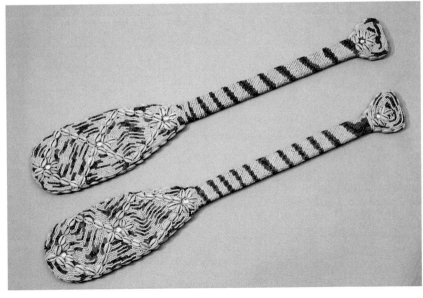

PLATE 7 The Haitian Vodou goddess Rèn Kongo, meaning "Queen of Kongo," in the form of a *pakèt kongo* (SABA COLLECTION A003; cf. FIGURE 8.21). Manmi Maude made her for me. Consider in figure 8.21 the similar form of a historically related being from West-Central Africa and, in plate 3, an elite European interpretation of the queen of Kongo. Combining the usual Kongo-Atlantic and Yorùbá-Atlantic styles of containment—the sack and the vessel, respectively—the body of my *pakèt kongo* for Kafou (SABA COLLECTION A014) is a ceramic teakettle (*chodiè*) filled with the combination of substances that gives him life and then cloaked in cloth and ribbons. Kafou is the lord of the crossroads in the Petwo "nation," or denomination, of Haitian Vodou. Manmi Maude also made him for me. See also figure 9.6.

PLATE 8 A spectacular family of sacred Abakuá drums (SABA COLLECTION B347) and scepters (B348) crafted in 2014 by Manuel Martínez Navarro and his acolytes in the Afro-Cuban Abakuá initiatic society. These drums have been "baptized" with animal blood, which, in Afro-Atlantic religions, is understood to bring a whole range of previously inanimate objects to life.

PLATE 9 Small urns (*tinajitas*) of the Mellis, the Cuban Santería/Ocha twin gods, in the emblematic colors and numbers of Yemayá (LEFT, seven blue beads alternating with seven clear beads) and Changó (RIGHT, six red beads alternating with six white beads). These altar vessels were precisely crafted by Ádys Álvarez and Bárbara Rodríguez of Artesanía Yoruba in Hialeah, Florida (Cuban Santería/Ocha, SABA COLLECTION B008).

The Contrary Ontologies
of Two Revolutions

Hegel's denunciation of African gods and animated things was not entirely devoid of empirical content, but it does more to reveal his inattention to his own projections than to prove that Africans' dialectical approach to the divine is wrong.

Hegel wrote in his *Philosophy of History* ([1822] 1956: 94):

> As the objectivity [of the fetish] is nothing other than the fancy of the individual projecting itself into space, the human individuality remains master of the image it has adopted. If any mischance occurs which the Fetich has not averted, if the rain is suspended, if there is a failure in the crops, they bind and beat or destroy the Fetich and so get rid of it, making another immediately, and thus holding it in their power. Such a Fetich has no independence as an object of religious worship; still less has it aesthetic independence as a work of art; it is merely a creation that expresses the arbitrary choice of its maker, and which always remains in his hands. Hence there is no relation of dependence in this religion.

Indeed, such conditional skepticism is common in African religious traditions: if a god does not work, it may be threatened or abandoned. Such skepticism may look silly from Hegel's point of view, but from the perspective of a third party, it seems less ridiculous than Hegel's apparent preference to stick with a god whose functionality is equally unverifiable and his apparent unawareness that his own god is also a function of his projected wishes, fears, and ritual efforts.

What is more surprising is that Marx, as a critic of Hegel's and others' projections, gave Africans no credit for a degree of the wisdom that he urged Hegel's followers and the rest of Europe to embrace: that it is people who make gods, and that, like other products of human effort, the gods are elements of the human self and projections of our own collective agency. Marx's recalcitrant failure to notice that the African "fetishists" resemble him suggests that he could not see past the Enlightenment's perennial fetish: the African, or black, antitype of all that is or should be good in Europe.

At a greater distance from the Enlightenment legacy, psychoanalysis also reifies elements of the self—the id and the superego—and gives them a reality outside of the socially recognized but fictitious ego. Like the Yorùbá- and Fòn-Atlantic gods, these elements are offered up for professional and collective reflection, and these aspects of the self—including those that one might once have feared that others would not accept—become objects of communal caretaking and respect. Together, the Afro-Atlantic priests and Freud illuminate what is culture specific and equally reified about the entity that Hegel called the "individual" and that English speakers tend to call "the mind," as though it were an internally integrated thing entirely endogenous to its owner. Out of date with the neurology of his day, Freud never seems to have gotten over the religious fiction that the object of his "talking cure" was some range of ghostly entities hovering inside the head. In the tradition of Hegel and Marx, and equally out of date in the golden age of cubism and jazz, Freud also continued to propagate the flattened image of the African priests as the antitype of the kind of European he hoped to become.

The Afro-Atlantic gods and spirits embody avowedly human-engineered networks of relationship linking this world (ayé in Yorùbá) and the Other (Òrun), and worship is also the management of those networks. These human-constructed gods are portals of affect and structures of apperception, as well as switching stations in the relationships among the worshippers. Since 1982, I have purchased—on behalf of Harvard University, Duke University, or myself—or received as gifts some 1,200 human-made things and human-constructed gods that embody Afro-Atlantic ideas about the makeup of a human or divine being and about the nature of value and agency. They can be seen on the SABA website. Here I document some of these spirited things, rituals, conversations, and debates among participants from which I infer the meaning and through which I have experienced the power of the gods.

Just as I have examined Marx and Freud from an Afro-Atlantic perspective, I devote this and the next section to illuminating the Afro-Atlantic gods and their priests from the vantage point of Marx, Freud, and a number of allied European social theorists. Marx's suspicion about the class interests embodied in religion and Freud's insights into the collusion of the castrator and the castrated in the most enduring fetishes underlie the following analysis of Afro-Atlantic empowered things. Both the fin-de-siècle French sociologist and rabbi's son Émile Durkheim and the turn-of-the-twenty-first-century French Catholic anthropologist of science Bruno Latour enter into this intercultural debate about the ontological nature of the Afro-Atlantic gods. For them, as for Marx, it is people who make gods. Indeed, for Durkheim ([1915] 1965), gods are among our most powerful experiences of the social. Phenomenally, what makes these material things and living altars vehicles and realizations of the Afro-Atlantic gods are the actions of the social networks that assemble them, keep them sacred through continual and concerted ritual action, and thereby, in a word, "make" them.

The ritual communities that keep the gods effective in our lives are also hierarchical relationships of selective tutelage among people and echelons of access to knowledge about symbolic signs, songs, dances, recipes, rules of food presentation, gift giving, labor exchange, and other procedures that continually and simultaneously reactivate both the god and the social unit that serves him or her. It is for this reason that Esteban Quintana, a priest of the Santería/Ocha, tells me, "This is not a religion you practice alone; you need people" (personal communication, October 26, 2016). For example, a *santero* priest consults his elders on ritual procedure, he or she enlists a team to make the workload bearable, and a priest depends on the witnesses of his or her initiation to authenticate his or her authority. Countless ritual procedures demonstrate that one's connection to the gods is created and conferred by the collective. Plate 4 shows the bead necklaces that both embody my membership in the Casa de Obatalá in Roxbury, Massachusetts, and authorize my possession of the gods that the chief of the House, Babá Steve, has created for me. These necklaces, like those of every member of the House, were strung by a team of previous recipients of necklaces from the House (Esteban Quintana, personal communication, October 28, 2016).

Gods and the Iconography of Membership

The detection and management of the Afro-Atlantic gods' actions in this world rely on the knowledge of an intricate iconography of symbolic numbers, colors, clothing styles, geographical features, and animals that highlight the connections—such as complementarity and association—among dissimilar peoples, species, and things. For example, in plate 4, the color combination of blue and clear in the necklace at the bottom (4), as well as its alternating sequence of seven beads in each color, it as an embodiment of Yemayá, the goddess of the sea. By contrast, the necklace made up of different shades of yellow, each in sets of five (2), belongs to Ochún, the goddess of fresh waters.

In many ways, the essence of the gods is membership. However, that membership rests on a conception of people and their relationship to the rest of the universe that is as articulate about transcorporeal, transgenerational, transspecies, and transgeographical subjectivity as post-Enlightenment social theory and practice are about the ideal autonomy of each individual from the human and nonhuman objects of his or her perception, from history, from nonhuman species, and from people of other races and ethnic groups. This conception of the interdigitated relationship between each person and the rest of the universe is as articulate about the human engineering of these connections as post-Enlightenment Western social theorists are about the enduring difference between insiders and outsiders and about the essential antagonism between the individual and the collective.

Typical of Enlightenment thinking, social-contract theory assumes that human beings started out as individuals and, out of rational self-interest, agreed to join in a society of mutual respect. On the contrary, and more consistent with the Afro-Atlantic insights that emerged from the Afro-European encounter on the sixteenth- and seventeenth-century Guinea Coast, the rebel Jewish sociologist Émile Durkheim argued that people are products of the collective and society, even though, he assumes, most religious people falsely experience society as a self-existent and presocial divinity that exercises a power over them. Yet to the degree that Afro-Atlantic priests have long recognized that it is humans who make their gods, it is difficult to credit Durkheim with the unveiling of a collective illusion, unless we focus on the fact that he is legitimately correcting a collective *European* illusion. His critique of the Abrahamic religions and of Enlightenment social theory certainly confirms Afro-Atlantic ideas about the social nature of religion, but these ideas are already far more advanced in this line of reasoning than Durkheim's own.

A full-scale Afro-Atlantic social analysis of Durkheim is beyond the scope of this book, but anyone who wishes to improve upon Durkheim's analysis would do well to take seriously the Afro-Atlantic idea that people make the gods but the gods make us, too. Similarly, parents and other ancestors make their descendants, but a person cannot be a parent without having a child.[1] It is also worth noting that even Durkheim was more interested in classification and the reification of discrete societies than in the connections between classes or between societies. Arguably, an Afro-Atlantic analysis of Durkheim has a great deal more to teach us than does a Durkheimian analysis of the Afro-Atlantic religions. However, this book, I hope wisely, addresses its audience from the audience's own most likely point of entry.

FIGURE 7.1 Votary sculpture for the god of thunder and lightning, Ṣàngó (SABA COLLECTION DO36). It is better interpreted as a dramatization of the relationships that make up the god than as a portrait of an anthropomorphic being in the manner of Western conceptions of gods. The main human figure here is kneeling and holding a chicken that is at once an offering vessel. She wears the hairstyle most emblematic of Ṣàngó possession priests (àgògo), and she carries on her back a baby holding the god's conventional scepter and weapon, the double ax (oṣé), which represents thunderstones and whose name also means "thank you." Hence, the main subject of this sculpture, like most of the anthropomorphic images of the orishas, is not a humanlike otherworldly being but the gestures dramatizing the multidimensional hierarchical relationships among humans, animals, and meteorological phenomena that constitute the god.

The Afro-Atlantic gods do have some anthropomorphic representations. However, only an untrained eye will mistake these representations for portraits, as opposed to models of the typical relationship between the god and his or her human vehicles. In West Africa, the shrine sculpture on an òrìṣà altar is definitely part of the òrìṣà. However, it is seldom clear whether its visual form is intended to represent the god or, alternatively, a worshipper of the god. Such sculptures look like people but typically depict horseback riding, the carrying of babies on the back, children's following their mother, subordinates' flanking dominant figures, and so forth—all dramatizing the *relationship* between the god and the worshipper or between the god's medium and the viewer. Among the most common images is a woman kneeling and offering her breasts or, alternatively, a simple lidded bowl or one in the shape of a fowl (figure 7.1).

FIGURE 7.2 Cuban Santería/Ocha image of selected orichas, made in China (SABA COLLECTION B281). See also SABA COLLECTION C147, a beach wrap representing twelve major Brazilian *orixás* in the Brazilian Candomblé religion. Each one wears the colors and carries an allegorical object emblematic of that god. At the center of the textile is an overhead view of the pate of a person undergoing initiation in the possession priesthood.

In the Americas, the most common visual representations of the god are statues or lithographs representing a Roman Catholic saint who "syncretically" corresponds to or is an aspect of that Afro-Atlantic god. In ritual practice, such figures evoke the appropriation, cannibalization, and transformation of European power (Apter [1991] 2004). Furthermore, the use of statues of the female Saint Bárbara as an embodiment of the male god Changó, for example, highlights the irony that things are not as they appear, that the appearance of subordination can conceal enormous craft and power, and that power manifests itself in the world through the merger of opposite parties that had once been constructed as starkly opposed.

A more recent and less ironic genre of depiction has arisen from the need of Western primitivist, Negrophile, or environmentalist tourists to give a single anthropomorphic form (see figure 7.2) to the network of objects, animals, meteorological and geographical phenomena, personality types, and conventional types of relationship that actually make up an Afro-Atlantic god. Such tourist art is not unimportant. It also circulates among believers and their friends as mementos of friendship and reminders for visitors to remember the love of their hosts and to keep in touch. However, the ontology of these gods is much more complex than any single portrait or object.

History and the Making of the Gods

In this section, my main concern is the historical specificity of the mutual making of gods and people. The anthropologist Karin Barber (1981) identified the diverse degrees to which West African indigenous religions recognize human agency in the creation and sustenance of divine beings, specifically analogizing the gods of the Yorùbá people of Òkukù to the "big men" of nineteenth-century Yorubaland. She shows that the òrìṣà-worshippers in that town during the late twentieth century regarded themselves as having "made" their gods in the same sense that nineteenth-century big men were made by their followers: in order to become and remain powerful, big men needed numerous devoted followers, whom they had to reward in order to keep their support.

My analysis is also inspired by the Swedish Covenant Church missionary Karl Edvard Laman and US anthropologist of religion Wyatt MacGaffey, who conducted astonishingly detailed investigations of the materially embodied gods worshipped by early twentieth-century Kongo people of West-Central Africa, in what are now the Democratic Republic of Congo and the Republic of Congo. These well-documented spirited things, or *minkisi*, reveal early twentieth-century Kongo people's desires and their assumptions about value and agency in a time of early-colonial violence and political transformation. Laman employed a score of BaKongo catechists to investigate the *minkisi* and their priests, as well as document the practices, verbal formulas, and explanations associated with these gods. MacGaffey invaluably mined Laman's publications in his own detailed and history-conscious analysis of these West-Central African power objects.

Most of the Afro-Atlantic gods I have known come not from West-Central Africa but from the locus classicus of the fetish problem—West Africa, between what are now Ghana and Nigeria. The indigenous spirit-possession religions of the Yorùbá and Fòn peoples manifest themselves in small-scale West African domestic settings. However, in the form through which we know them today, they appear to have been elaborated intensely by merchant-monarchies and African-diaspora entrepreneurs during and after the Atlantic slave trade (Matory 2005). Now these gods also live in the great capitals of Brazil, Cuba, Haiti, Suriname, and the United States, where they have multiplied and acquired a level of popularity and material elaboration unprecedented in West Africa. The African gods of Latin America now also dance in Kreuzberg, Berlin, as well as Lisbon and Amsterdam.

Here, I focus on a set of material things and sacred beings collected between 1982 and 2017 and housed in the Sacred Arts of the Black Atlantic Collection at Duke University. Most were created by priests or commissioned artists and craftspeople with the theological conceptions, material needs, aesthetics, and social relationships of Afro-Atlantic worshippers in mind. The accretions and attachments on them also reveal a history of their transformation in collective ritual use. The collection encompasses empowered things from the mid-nineteenth century, as well as every time period since. Although the materials and names of visually similar things from different places and times may differ, the earlier pieces are easily recognized by contemporary worshippers as the ancestors of extant sacred things and beings. Moreover, in the Yorùbá-Atlantic traditions, beads and cowries are a constant reminder of commonality and continuity among these traditions. Yet I do not presuppose the continuity of meaning and use over time. Collectively, these consecrated things embody a genealogy of changing meaningful forms, political conditions, and social projects. I tap previous archival research (Matory 2005, [1994] 2005) and participant observation of how priests live and work in multiple countries today in order to reconstruct a history of the changing political economy and of the changing interest groups that have contributed to the present-day form of Afro-Atlantic altars and relationships.

This comparison among West African Yorùbá and Fòn religions, West-Central African Kongo and Yaka religions, Brazilian Candomblé, Cuban and Cuban American Santería/Ocha, Caribbean and Caribbean American Spiritism, and Haitian and Haitian American Vodou, or Sèvi Lwa, in a capitalist age offers a real-time, real-world corrective to what Hegel, Marx, and Freud supposed about the thinking of other, pre-twentieth-century Afro-Atlantic worshippers who, we now know, also manipulated the conditions and materials of Atlantic capitalism to create sacred value and agency in their own interests.

These religions, their gods, and their priests are not things of the past but our coresidents in the great cities of the US, Latin America, and Europe, which host a lively industry devoted to the making and the maintenance of Afro-Atlantic gods. The Mercado da Madureira in Rio de Janeiro, Brazil, is probably the world's greatest emporium of the herbs, natural substances, and manufactures required for the practice of these religions, but smaller versions of this huge shopping complex are found in Bahia, São Paulo, Havana, Mexico City, Port-au-Prince, New York City, and Washington, DC. In the front window and on the shelves of shops called *botánicas*—typically owned by Jewish natives or immigrants from the Caribbean, El Salvador, Guatemala, or Mexico—the crucifixes and the statues of Roman Catholic saints and the Buddha will look familiar to many Westerners, but they are surrounded by other items either unfamiliar or seemingly out of place, such as cowrie shells, soup tureens, cauldrons, bead necklaces in a bewildering array of color combinations, safety candles with exotic labels, bottled po-

FIGURE 7.3 A *ño* and a *ña*, senior house slaves worshipped in Caribbean Spiritism (SABA COLLECTION H002).

tions, bunches of herbs and sticks, horsetail fly whisks, wooden and sheet-metal crowns, leather whips, and burning incense that sensuously invoke an ontology unfamiliar to most Westerners. Some customers pray and leave money at a bristling altar while others throng the front counter or cluster in the aisles deliberating in low tones over which candles to buy or which bunch of leaves looks the freshest. Still others deferentially await the attention of the merchant or the diviner. These emporia are a nexus of exchange between countries, between religions, and between worlds.

One pair of spirited things in the collection embodies a conventional image of house-slave spirits esteemed in Latin America (figure 7.3). Though I bought them from a Caribbean Latino *botánica* in Spanish Harlem—El Congo Real—they bear "made in China" stickers. In this pair, the female house slave—a *madama*, or *ña*—has *X*'s penciled on her shoes and, on her knees, the inscription *Vovó Maria*, or "Granny Maria," suggesting that before arriving in the US they had once done ritual duty in Brazil. The open question of whether I attribute their arrival to the invisible agency of "the market," as Adam Smith might have done, or to the more visible networks of people, things, signs, natural forces, and rituals that constitute the gods is what makes it instructive to call them "fetishes." So does the third life of such spirited things, as vehicles of Western self making in the museum.

The sacred beings who sit behind the vitrines of European and Euro-American museums do not simply die there: they gain a new life as fetishes of European bourgeois and national identity. Something similar might be said of the spirited things in the SABA Collection. These sacred Afro-Atlantic beings certainly acquire a life in the ethnographic and art-historical imagination of the academy. But they also retain their lives in networks directly akin to the ones that gave them birth. As an element of my "Afro-Atlantic Religions" classes at Williams College, Harvard University, and Duke University, and related educational programs at the University of Vermont, priests of these religions have repeatedly fed and feted the gods whose embodiments and other sacred paraphernalia make up the collection. Students, professors, administrators, and neighbors of the university join in the singing and dancing, as well as feasting and feeding the gods, building on the network of relationships that made the gods and keeps them alive—networks that the gods have made in their own image.

On the campus of Duke University, the gods in the collection have been energized by struggles between anthropologists and laboratory scientists about the relative applicability of the First Amendment of the US Constitution and the Animal Welfare Act of 1966, which justifiably urges the humane treatment of laboratory animals but fails to address the religious uses of animals and expressly excludes farm animals from its scope. In violation of the requirements of the traditions I study—as well as the rules of kosher and halal butchery—the Animal Welfare Act prohibits the killing of a fully conscious animal by the cutting of its throat. The laboratory scientists at my university conventionally overenforce this legislation in order to guard against the loss of federal funding. So months of negotiation were required to secure the conditions for these gods to thrive on campus. In this analysis, the conflict required to secure those conditions is as important as the victory they won. This conflict has created and undone friendships, alliances, hierarchies, and avoidance relationships across a remarkable array of departments and schools on campus.

It should be noted that sacred paraphernalia and spirited things of the sort depicted in the following chapters are seldom seen by nondevotees, and they seldom live or act in isolation from dozens of divine companions. They normally live on restricted-access altars crowded with other human-assembled beings, gifts, food and beverage offerings, books, lithographs, perfume bottles, flowers and herbs, candles, oils, cloth, feathers, scribbled prayers and curses, smoke, and dust. They smell of perfume, incense, and patinated blood. They echo or muffle the tintinnabulation of bells. Degrees of rank, knowledge, and trust normally limit one's access to these empowered things and the associated sensations, and, for most laypeople, direct encounters with these quickened things occur only at times of distress, when those laypeople need help or healing. Otherwise, laypeople are more likely to encounter the gods in the dancing bodies of their "horses," or possession priests. Hence, the present photographically mediated encounter with the gods circumvents a number of normally gnostic stages and multisensory contexts in order to highlight certain taken-for-granted but cross-cultural themes that would otherwise continue to be overlooked, or, as in Enlightenment philosophy and post-Enlightenment social theory, would remain "pedestals" for the aspirations of low-status white people who feel that they deserve more out of life.

Fetishism and Semiosis in Social Context

I am not the first scholar to see in West African and Afro-Latin American gods an alternative to contemporary European fictions about the ostensibly objective character of value and about the exclusively human and individual nature of agency. With the briefest of references to West African and Brazilian Candomblé gods, Bruno Latour (2010) launches his argument that the division of agency between people and their creations is culture specific. To him, the contemporary West is the stingiest and most delusional of all cultures in its denial that the things we make have power over us. But even in the West, our ideas about this matter remain murky and confused. Contemporary Western critics of other peoples and classes tend to assume that people who attribute power to icons are just mistaken, forgetting that even laboratory science creates not unmediated, objective truths but consensual, human-made images mediated by human-made machines. These machines isolate variables generated by the human imagination, variables that had not existed as discrete realities until the moment of their artificial and conceptual isolation by people. Yet we mistake the results of laboratory experiments for independently truthful snapshots of a self-existent reality (Latour and Woolgar [1979] 1986).

  In Latour's view, reality never speaks an unmediated truth about itself to us humans. As a liberal Catholic, Latour affirms that the icons of religions like his are not intended to report an objective reality but to instill a *way* of seeing reality and a *posture* toward reality. He similarly takes African and Afro-Latin religious icons seriously as embodied ways of seeing and effecting human cooperation in the world. In support of his argument, I affirm that things do participate in a collectively and historically human-made world that—because of a history of concerted human action, habit, and reaction—affect people as powerfully as I am affected by a red traffic light or by the umpteenth celluloid tear-jerker about two white people overcoming, against all the odds, the many obstacles to a life "happily ever after." However, partly because I am a child of the West, I also resist Latour's wish to attribute such a degree of agency to things. I cannot resist my doubts that things intend, dictate, or act. But Latour does move us a step closer to understanding the *dialectic* of subjectivity and objectivity implicit in Yorùbá language and in orisha-worship generally.

My historical and biographical analysis of fetishes contradicts a recent trend in the literature on material culture to attribute agency to things and landscapes—a trend emphasizing their power to *dictate* and *constrain* what we do with them, how we do it, and what we do in general. By establishing that our behavioral interaction with things is physically overdetermined, we are led to assume that our semiotic interpretation of them is also overdetermined (e.g., Hodder 2012). I am uncomfortable with the degree to which these models shift agency and even volition away from human beings.

I do not agree with the recent rejection of the concept of "symbols," as opposed to "embodiments" and agents of our "entanglement" with them (see, for example, Hodder 2012 and Böhme [2006] 2014 for excellent articulations and defenses of the literature on this antisymbolic, or antirepresentational, position). Human beings always have a choice about how to use and interpret things. Things affect us, to be sure, but always in a manner shaped by the culture, momentary interest, and creativity of people. Unpredictable contingency related to natural and social occurrences powerfully affects our plans. However, there is enormous plasticity in our ability to interpret and respond to even these disruptions of our norms and expectations. The cross-cultural, transtemporal, and interclass polysemy of objects—that is, the phenomenal character of the fetish as Freud, Pietz, and I have outlined it—proves that it is people who determine the meaning of objects and who make conflict-ridden decisions about what to do with them in any given instance.

Things do not reciprocally determine the meaning of people. It takes a sentient perceiver to confer such meaning. This fact is the motive behind my dialectical historical analysis of the things, people, and conventions that comprise Euro-Atlantic and Afro-Atlantic fetishes. It should be noted that Afro-Atlantic priest friends and I sometimes disagree—more often about race, gender relations, and the price of a sacred thing than about the nature of the gods. But they also disagree with each other, and these debates are in the nature of the gods. The discourse of the fetish enables us to recognize the ethnographic salience of the debate itself.

Another contributor to the antirepresentational wave in the interpretation of artistic and sacred objects is Alfred Gell (1998). On the one hand, there are approaches to material production that prioritize aesthetic appreciation or the communicative meaning of the work. On the other hand, based on the example of what he calls "primitive art" in South Asia and the South Pacific, Gell proposes a revision of the anthropology of art and art history generally. He argues that the practitioners of the traditions he studies are little interested in aesthetic appreciation and that, for them, the question is not what an object *means* but what it *does*.

For Gell, art is a technology that does more than communicate meaning. Rather, it tantalizes and beguiles. Within an existing field of actors, expectations, and understandings, an artwork points at and causes social effects by motivating inferences, responses, and interpretations. Within a chain of commissioning agents, artists, and viewers, the art object—and particularly a ritually consecrated one—so powerfully stands for a human actor or his or her patient that it acquires almost the same type and level of agency as a person.

Nor, says Gell, does an artwork merely sustain class structures or legitimize dominant ideologies. The aesthetic motifs within an artwork do bear an elective affinity with the social order that produced it, affecting the visual form of, for example, an apotropaic object in a setting of omnipresent violence and instability—as they do in the case of the late nineteenth-century Kongo *minkisi* gods analyzed by MacGaffey. However, Gell adds that no single such object explains or reveals a whole picture. Like psychoanalysis and the Afro-Atlantic religions, the South Pacific ontology implicit in the artwork Gell studies assumes that the person is "fractal," or "distributed," terms that Gell borrows from Strathern (1988). The South Pacific person is understood not to be contained within the body but to be made up of a network of bodies and transactional objects. Homologously, no single artwork acts by itself. It is not only an element of the network of a person and a network of people but also part of an ensemble of chronologically and synchronically related artworks. Such networks and ensembles are key to the efficacy of an artwork.

Gell's antisemiotic proposal resembles Viveiros de Castro's (2004) critique of the "epistemological" approach that he regards as typical of anthropological analysis. That approach assumes that people of different cultures simply represent the same self-existent, natural world in culturally diverse terms. On the contrary, Viveiros de Castro argues that the ontologies of different peoples are so different that different peoples can be said to inhabit different worlds. For example, he describes the "Amerindian" world as discrete from the "modern" or "Western" world.

However, my conception of the fetish and the intercultural social context of its genesis belies the premise of these antiepistemological, antisemiotic, and antirepresentational arguments. The notion of the fetish calls attention to a context of interaction, rivalry, melding, antithesis and, in a word, "dialogue" (Matory 2005) between cultures, worlds, or value codes that their partisans construct after the fact as opposites. Amid this interaction, rival human agents not only act in conjunction with material things but also epistemologically contest the legitimacy of the projects of their rivals, of what their rivals do with things, and of the value that their rivals attribute to things. And their own projects and valuations of things anticipate reciprocal dissent.

The accusation of fetishism usually arises in situations in which rivals are in a tug-of-war over the meaning and use of the *same* physical thing, human body, or human body part. It might not be a fact of nature that different actor-networks occupy the same world. However, in the encounters that produce accusations of fetishism, the rivalry between projects produces a shared world, which it is difficult to describe without attention to epistemology and without the vocabulary of "representation." Every exchange is a repurposing and resignification of the thing exchanged. And relationship is always the repurposing and resignification of the interlocutors and of the things in between them. An actor's accusation of fetishism re-presents his rival's thing as proof of the correctness of the accuser's own emergent project in contrast to a parody of the rival's. Yes, rival actors and actor-networks *do* different things with different art objects, but they also debate over the value, use, and meaning of the same art objects. Hence, pace Gell, doing and meaning are not mutually exclusive. The accusation of fetishism is a put-down and an attempt to shift the balance of power among rival actors, in what is usually a highly complex, multiparty field of actors. And the put-down can be a highly effective political act (consider Said [1978] 2003). In sum, semiotic dilemma, the investment of networks of people from opposite social positions in the same objects, the investment of the same meaning in opposite objects, the dwelling of opposite populations in the same place, and the alternating of opposite roles to the same body are what gives the fetish its endurance and its flash. The Afro-Atlantic religions assume the fractal nature of each person, the intercultural and dialogical nature of semiosis, and the network-like character of—as well as the presence of contrary traits in—each god.

The supercathected things of central European social theory and those of the Yorùbá-Atlantic religions embody differently positioned but equally thoughtful and interacting takes on shared circum-Atlantic political and economic conditions. For their respective devotees, those things solve different sets of problems. At the height of nineteenth- and early twentieth- century Atlantic capitalism, Africans and their American descendants faced the problem of how to deal advantageously with exogenous and often European powers. In many ways, they modeled their ritual solutions on a long history of trade and cultural exchange with other African peoples and with the Islamic world. Assimilated central European Jews such as Marx and Freud faced the problem of how to deal advantageously with their doubly ambiguous position in the social hierarchy of European empire. In many ways, they modeled their theoretical solutions on gentile Europeans' treatment of Africans. Now, Babá Murah is among the thousands of Afro-Atlantic religious practitioners—including immigrants from Cuba and Brazil, as well as native Germans and Norwegians—who dance on the now-common ground of African gods and central European social theory, Berlin.

The dawn of Atlantic capitalism was an encounter among several multireligious European, African, and Native American societies. However, coming from highly marketized societies, Africans and Europeans encountered each other with a level of mutual understanding about commodities that was alien to the contemporaneous Native American societies (Graeber 2001). Each of these continents was host to a heterogeneous array of parties competing to control resources and people. In the pursuit of safety, comfort, love, and self-fulfillment, there were winners and losers. Or, from what may be a more fetishist perspective, which treats hierarchy as a normal condition of relationships, there were parents and children, husbands and wives, masters and slaves.

As in Marx and Engel's project and in the Afro-Atlantic religions alike, the central question has concerned how to convert intercultural market relationships into more stable social ties promoting safety, comfort, love, and self-fulfillment. On the Guinea Coast and in the racialized societies of the Americas, this conversion regularly involved the use of commodities (such as captives, cowries, beads, and rum) produced, received, or furnished through market-based alienation, as well as their conversion into tokens of secure relationships, such as the beads and cowries whose exchange long mediated enslavement, marriage, and clientelism. By repurposing such tokens, the priests have reengineered the relationships among potentially rival persons, peoples, and nations, turning them into a power exchange.

The aesthetic and the anthropology of assemblage in Afro-Atlantic altars commemorates this human-orchestrated détente, and ritual continually recapitulates it. Rituals involving songs, poetry, incantation, herbal fusions, and blood continually reenergize the altar and the détente that it embodies. However, the efficacy of the rituals that create new beings, install a being in an altar or in a human body, and consolidate the relationships among beings does not depend on materials and priestly technology alone. It also depends on the *loudest* possible singing, the *hottest* possible dancing, and the *most effervescent* possible interaction among the participants in the ritual. The strength of the gods depends on the force or, as Haitians describe it, the "heat" of these interactions. Moreover, on each ritual occasion, participants recall the past history of such periodic ritual performances, the people who have participated in them, and the consistency of their efforts to protect the spirited thing from profanation. In doing so, the participants heighten certain exclusive social relationships, fortify the network of mutual obligations, and protect these relationships and obligations from ever-possible decommissioning. To treat the assemblage as sacred is also to treat the network of relationships as sacred. Songs remind the participants of the strength and audacity of the gods in defending the sacred community, in punishing apostasy, and in rewarding the community's perseverance. These practices stand in contrast to the rituals of European fetish theory, whose signature is the excoriation and excommunication of the African other.

On multiple occasions during my periods of teaching or public lecturing at Williams College, Harvard University, Duke University, and the Free University of Berlin, I have cotaught with Doté Amilton, Babá Steve, Manmi Maude, Ìyá Òṣun Òṣogbo, Babá Murah, and Babá Danny Rodríguez, an *oriaté*, or master of ceremonies, of the Santería/Ocha religion. Every few years at each of these institutions, usually in tandem with my "Afro-Atlantic Religions" class, my priest friends not only fete the gods they have given me but also lead discussions in my classes and deliver public lectures. Secrecy, apprenticeship, and gradual, gnostic revelation—rather than exposition—are the normal modes of instruction in these religions. But, for the past thirty-seven years, my trial-and-error identification of the most articulate of priests, my friendship with them, and my coteaching with them have enabled me to test my understandings of these religions in the context of our collaborative explanation and demonstration of them to students, faculty, and administrators at these leading US American and German guardians and incubators of Western social theory. These priests and I have also worked together in populating the SABA website with information about the spirited things displayed there. In the course of these joint efforts, I express my own understandings (as well as those of Hegel, Marx, Durkheim, Weber, and Freud), they correct me, and I record both the consensus and the remaining tensions in our journey of mutual transformation. The following account is structured by an unfolding dialogue, which is also the typical phenomenal form of the religions whose actor-networks I document here.

Commodities and Gods

In the Afro-Atlantic religions, beads, cowrie shells, schnapps, gin, and rum are powerful and omnipresent metonyms of the enduring relationships between the worlds that constitute people and gods. And the most powerful beings are defined by the strength and multiplicity of these relationships. As items produced or harvested for the purpose of exchange, Venetian- and Bohemian-made "African trade beads," cowrie shells, and rum are commodities akin to those whose value Marx debated. Indeed, they were among the foremost goods with which European traders bought Africans. The intercultural struggle over the value of these commodities and over the agency of Africans has long been a touchstone of the both the post-Enlightenment nation-state and the Afro-Atlantic religions.

In this chapter and the next, I emphasize two distinctive aspects of the Afro-Atlantic religions that follow from the peculiarities of the times, places, and classes that have hosted these religions:

··· their full embrace of the realities of globalizing merchant capitalism, money and profit; and

··· the apparent irony that, in host countries that officially venerate republican democracy and avow the equality of all citizens, these religions propagate spiritual families steeped in the hierarchical imagery of royalty and slavery, with the conviction that such relationships are alive with intimacy and personal efficacy.

The material focus of my fetishist analysis of Marx was coats, factories, the piano, and the "negro slave," and of Freud it was couches and upright chairs, intaglio rings, the Acropolis, Rome, the "negro," the "savage," and so forth. The focus of my fetishist study of the Afro-Atlantic gods is (1) pots, calabashes, mortars, and soup tureens; and (2) cowries, beads, and sequins.

But of course the argument that follows chiefly concerns the ideas and social relationships embedded in those material things. What the linguistically incompetent Dutch Calvinist merchants and the sarcastic propagandists for the Enlightenment chose to represent as "trinkets" and ordinary but arbitrarily sanctified things are better understood as the furniture of an intrinsically intercultural and interclass debate over value, agency, and, concomitantly, over the proper nature of social organization.

While Marx and most European social theorists focus on production as the main source of value, what turns merchandise and gifts from distant African kingdoms, Europe, Asia, and elsewhere into gods is not the production of those objects but their assembly and their repeated consecration through the ritual exchange of labor, cash, and other material things. In the Afro-Atlantic religions, the paradigmatic site of value production is not the European factory but African royal marriage.

In the long-distance network of alliance and compound selfhood proposed by the Afro-Atlantic religions, cowries and beads are the generalized media of exchange. Yet the herbs, feathers, and stones that are equally important elements of Afro-Atlantic altars demonstrate the same principle. They come from the wilderness and enter human society through processes of exchange, including offerings of food, animal blood, and cash to the beings embodied in the far-flung places from which those things are gathered. Like the most powerful agents making up the self, the cowrie shells and beads in altars usually originate in places far away from the local body and the local polity. Cowries and European beads demonstrate these religions' nearly originary involvement in the trans-Saharan trade and, indeed, in circum-Atlantic capitalism. They also demonstrate the very non-Marxist priestly conviction that value does flow from exchange and not just the timed labor of production. The value and meanings of things are not determined by production alone—

much less the fraction of any given society's labor time employed in their production—but also by the availability of the raw materials, the symbolic meaning of materials and manufactured goods, the conventions of exchange, and the relationships effected and affected by such exchange, all of which are subject to continual bargaining and debate. These often-imported physical things are further supercharged with additional value by the local relations of gifting, inheritance, affiliation, ordination, and slave trading that they commemorate.

In the Afro-Atlantic religions, divine beings and social relationships are constructed through the slow-return exchange of symbolically coded physical things, just as marriages are. Indeed, both divinities and people—like children—are outcomes of slow-return exchange and compounds of exchanged things. Each divinity or person is a set of relationships materialized through commerce, ritual gifting, and souvenirs of long-term debt. Like communities, gods are assemblages animated and kept alive through such repeated exchanges.

Making a god—and thus remaking the worshipper—requires an enormous amount of cooperation and financial exchange. Afro-Atlantic altars demonstrate not only the productivity of economic exchange in a person's life but also the translocal nature of the person or agent. For example, the vessel altar that both represents the worshipper's head and is her god is full of cowrie shells. Altars also often contain beads, which are typically imported from Europe or from distant African locales. Perhaps for the same reason, the diverse and prestigious origins of the beads of a monarch, priest, or god are metonyms of the owner's tandem wealth in people and goods. In all of the Afro-Atlantic religions, the practitioners mark their devotion by wearing color-coded bead necklaces whose exotic origins are much-discussed features of their quality.

Initiation into the Yorùbá-Atlantic religions is dominated by the incision of the human body and the simultaneous and parallel insertion of things into both the body and a ceramic, wooden, or metal vessel, as well as symbolically coded exchanges of labor, money, and materials among the initiand, her fellow worshippers, and the god. It is normal for the intended beneficiaries of ritual to pay the presiding priest and other members of the ritual team. Cash payments are often denominated in conventional amounts, corresponding to the emblematic numbers of the relevant god. It is equally normal for members of a ritual family to buy and sell materials among themselves. Commerce among friends and kin is no source of embarrassment. Through the years, a whole ensemble of exogenous beings is thus made and installed in heads and pots, thus becoming active in and through a priest or priestess. And such installations involve an intricate series of payments and exchanges of labor that occur at least annually.

Hence, the making of gods is at once production and exchange. And this exchange is no more extraneous to capitalism than are slavery and the formation of corporations. Throughout its known history, the making of Afro-Atlantic gods has depended on cash-ridden translocal exchange and has served to generate material profit for insiders through the deft management of trade in goods produced expressly for exchange and often produced far away. In the Afro-Atlantic religions, the making of a god is also a self-conscious immobilization of commodities and their conversion into permanent nodes of social relationship—namely, a fully spirit-stocked senior priest and the score of vessel-altars through which he or she and the community of followers are managed.

Despite Marx's premise to the contrary, it is difficult to identify an intellectual tradition more emphatic than the Afro-Atlantic religions about the indispensability of human knowledge and effort in the making of gods. And it is difficult to name an intellectual tradition more embarrassed (and therefore less reflective) than post-Enlightenment central European Protestantism about the inspiring, constraining, and empowering character of the material things (especially the human-made and human-consecrated ones) in people's lives (Latour 2010). By contrast, the Afro-Atlantic priests make high technology of transforming consciousness through the manufacture and animation of things, and they do so with great awareness of the human role in this process. Yet, in mocking the spirit of capitalism, Marx counted on the likelihood that his fellow mid-nineteenth-century Europeans would cower before the calumny that they resemble Africans in our ostensible unsophistication. Lost in his own irony, Marx joined his fellow Europeans in overlooking the richness and insightfulness with which West Africans understood—long before he did—that people make themselves and remake others through their labor. And, for reasons that are difficult to deny (in the absence of a blindered advocacy for the European industrial worker), Afro-Atlantic priests also recognize the importance of *exchange* in people's self making.

In the United States, where the descendants of Germans are a plurality of the population, and Protestants the plurality of religious practitioners, the Germanic Protestant embarrassment about the charisma of human-made things might help to explain why erotic fetishism is so simultaneously embarrassing and titillating to us (Matory in preparation). Out of such embarrassment comes a failure of introspection and sometimes mere confusion, perhaps helping us to understand why US American construction companies and realtors get away with claiming to sell "homes." It seems that most of their customers are easily persuaded to overlook the fact that only the effective long-term relationship building of the occupants can animate a house with the spirit that makes it a home. That charismatic spirit is real, but it is not the con-

struction company that created it. Nor can a realtor sell it. The people who
create that charisma are the parties who share time and exchange resources
in the house, the residues of which sharing and exchange are materialized in
the building, its furnishings, their arrangement, and the maintenance of the
building and of the landscape that surrounds it.

To an equal and opposite degree, West African Yorùbá consciously create
the *ilé* ("house" or "home") through the ritually coordinated invocation of
genealogy, through family attributive poetry (*oríkì*) and *òrìṣà*-worship, the
burial and feeding of dead ancestors in and around the buildings, and the
burial of empowering and protective substances in its floor. Indeed, until
recently, houses tended to be made of laterite, a material needing more
constant structural maintenance by its occupants than cement, stone, or,
in temperate zones, wood. Ironically, the European thinkers most emphatic
about pointing out the human source of divinity have made Africa into the
paradigm of a form of ignorance that seems more typical of Europe and Euro-
America, where the ideally even-Steven exchange of cash for labor and goods
is intended to strip a person's material belongings of any residue of obligation
toward the maker or supplier of those belongings.

Marx falsely distinguished "negro" slavery from capitalism as though
these institutions belonged to distinct and noncontemporaneous evolutionary stages. Similarly, Freud constructed the "savage" as some evolutionary
stage antecedent to "civilized," white Europeans. On the contrary, the obvious historical truth is that the Africans and the Europeans at the foundation of both the "problem of the fetish" and the Afro-Atlantic religions were
coeval, foundational, and central participants in circum-Atlantic capitalism.
The prototypical African "fetishists" and the prototypical European critics
of fetishism were not, respectively, the forebears and the subjects of human
history but, instead, contemporaneous interlocutors and actors with rival
perspectives on capitalist production, its products, the exchange of its products, and their legitimate uses in the making of communities.

Initiation in the Afro-Atlantic religions tends to be costly. In Cuba and
Brazil, it usually requires gifts in cash, labor, and physical things from a network
of supporters. It requires clothing, fresh sacred herbs, sacrificial animals and
other foods, beads, cowries, distilled alcohols, vessels, and the intensive services of scores of priests and musicians. The commercial nature of sacred
power is evident in the sacred stories about the gods' lives and in the omnipresence of commodities in the ritual remaking of selves. However, even
more important than commodities in this process is money removed from
circulation—especially foreign money.

Food matters, too. Like Christendom, the metaphorical family of
an *òrìṣà*, *orixá*, *oricha*, or orisha priesthood is called into being through

transubstantiation and commensality. The animal blood decanted over the assembled emblems of the god quicken those emblems with life, turning them into divine people. Blood from the same animals is applied to the heads of initiands, creating and quickening the same god in their heads (Matory [1994] 2005). This blood also creates a "blood" kinship among the priests and their god. Further establishing their status as a family, the priests and their gods eat the sacrificial foods together. To most Westerners, the role of commensality in the consolidation of kinship is relatively obvious, and this metaphor of "blood" kinship is almost as comprehensible. This verbal metonym of kinship is found equally in English, in the Romance languages spoken by Afro-Atlantic worshippers in Cuba and Brazil, and in Yorùbá.

However, the omnipresence of foreign cash and commodities in this form of West African family making might be surprising. In the nineteenth century, cowrie shells were a major currency of not only slave trading but also bridal payments. Bridewealth—owó orí ìyàwó (literally, "money/cowries for the head of the bride")—confers upon the husband's lineage not the ownership of the wife but the membership of the children in that lineage. Long the monopoly of royals, beads imported from Europe and from distant West African places highlight the metaphorically royal nature of the lineages constructed through priestly initiation. Such signs of international commerce have been prolific in the Afro-Atlantic religions since the date of our earliest written documentation of their practice.

Marx's labor theory of value endorses the equality of the participants in the production process and, with the term "fetishism," charges capitalism with violating its own avowed ideal. Freud's Oedipal scenario posits the ultimate equality of the son with the father, as the son will ultimately have a woman of his own. To an equal and opposite degree, the Afro-Atlantic priests posit a permanent, gerontocratic inequality in the sacred family, and they do so on the model of the mundane African family. For example, while the Western metaphor of "brotherhood" implies the equality of male fellow citizens of the nation-state, Yorùbá kinship terminology and ethics imply that a younger sibling or cousin permanently owes deference or obedience to a senior sibling or cousin, regardless of his or her sex. In this mutually empowering relationship, the junior party may expect wise advice, protection, and generosity from the senior party. Similarly, the altars of the Afro-Atlantic religions presume an often unequal but mutually amplifying power exchange (Weiss 2011; Matory in preparation) between long-term interlocutors modeled on the relations between husbands and wives, ancestors and descendants, monarchs and subjects, big men and their followers, riders and horses. By contrast, Marx detects in unequal exchange a relationship of exploitation dependent on confusion. The form of these altars suggests that the unequal relationships between gods and humans, rulers and ruled, foreigners and locals is as potentially fruitful as the unequal relationship between husbands and wives. Indeed, through various verbal and visual metaphors, possession priests are constructed as wives of the gods in a manner that also seems to commemorate the role of royal wives in the Ọ̀yọ́ palace's trade with the Europeans on the Guinea Coast.

And, in the manner of power exchange, these relationships are at times reversible, in the sense that wife-takers must show deference to wife-givers and possession priests reshape the character of the gods who possess them.

The religious vocabulary of horsemanship also commemorates a political history of horsemanship in the Ọ̀yọ́ Kingdom. Ọ̀yọ́ was the northernmost of the kingdoms that would eventually be identified as Yorùbá, and its unique geographical access to the trade in horses from the Hausa emirates farther north in the savannah enabled them, between the mid-sixteenth century and the early nineteenth, to assemble the largest empire in Yorùbá history (Matory [1994] 2005: 8–13). Indeed, when Ọ̀yọ́ conquered the Fòn kingdom of Dahomey, horsemen and wifelike possession priests were the Ọ̀yọ́ monarch's omnipresent viceroys in that region, as well. The collapse of the Ọ̀yọ́ Empire had equally momentous consequences. Through the enslavement and overseas dispersion of Ọ̀yọ́'s subjects, the collapse of that kingdom spread this politically and religiously supercharged vocabulary of horsemanship and wifeliness, along with the royalist logic and commodity-based iconography of Ọ̀yọ́ religion, to Brazil, Cuba, Trinidad, and Haiti.

The iconography and the sacred stories about the goddess Ajé illustrate the centrality of transoceanic commerce in these religions, even within West Africa. The West African Yorùbá goddess of trade and wealth is Ajé—the master of money. She is cognate with the Cuban goddess Allé and with the Brazilian goddess Ajé. As the West African Yorùbá priests of Ifá tell the story, she is the daughter of the sea goddess Olookun Ṣeniade. Consequently, even in far-inland city-states like Ilé-Ifè, her altars are full of seashells. Jacob Olupona writes, "This Yoruba narrative may signify the emergence of trade and commerce across the Atlantic Ocean. . . . The Atlantic Ocean trade made possible the ensuing prosperity because without trade and commerce this wealth would have been impossible" (2011: 131). "In another Ifá [divinatory] narrative regarding Ajé," he adds, "the goddess is credited with the invention of money or cowry shells. . . . The narrative thus explains the change from barter to trade as well as the development of the use of money" (ibid.).

And what are cowrie shells? Hogendorn and Johnson (1986) call cowries "the shell money of the slave trade" (see also Matory [1994] 2005). When returning from South Asia with light cargoes, European shippers used cowrie shells from the Maldive Islands as ballast and then traded these shells for people in West Africa. Because of their distinctiveness, limited supply, and relative durability, West Africans in the region of the Niger River found them useful as currency. Thus they became the generalized medium of the slave trade around the Guinea Coast and in its hinterland. They were the chief denomination of a unit of labor value far more fundamental, even in the capitalism of Marx's day, than Marx was willing to recognize in more than a metaphorical sense—real-life slaves.

Virtually all orisha altars contain numerous cowries (e.g., figures 8.9, 8.16, 8.17, 8.19; plates 1, 2, and 9; and SABA Collection D123), the main divination kit of orisha priests consists of sixteen cowries, and they decorate a fantastic array of liturgical clothing and art (e.g., figures 7.2, 7.3, 8.1, 8.2, 8.5, 8.6, 9.1, C.1; plate 6). In addition, the Santería/Ocha goddess of wealth, Allé, resides in a conch or whelk shell, while the Candomblé goddess of wealth, Ajê, is full of conch shells (see also figures 8.11 and 8.21). In these religions, the association of wealth with shells and the Atlantic trade is joined by a further element of the altars of the goddess of wealth. From the late fifteenth century, Venetian chevron beads became the most valuable alternative medium. Also partly because of their blue-dominant color scheme, they are prominent among the insignia of Yemoja, the West African Yorùbá river goddess most closely associated with the maritime trade.

West African Ifá oracular texts also tell the story that Ajé went out one day looking for a new slave. Having consulted with an Ifá diviner, she made a wise choice. When she recognized the right slave to buy, she asked his name. *Owó*, he replied—"Money." Olupona summarizes, "Owó was so serviceable that even before he was asked to do something he had already done it. Because of [Owó's] intuitiveness and faithfulness, Ajé summoned all the people around her and instructed them that if they wished to have dealings with her they must first consult with Owó, who would function as an intermediary between her and her clients" (2011: 132). The complete dependency of the god and his or her worshippers on a slave or low-status intermediary between them is a common theme in these religions. Another Ifá oracular verse adds that Ajé "was tired of roaming about and having no permanent abode" (ibid.). So an Ifá diviner instructed her to assemble sixteen large black pots, two hundred cowries, and hundreds of sacrificial animals, guaranteeing that, once she made the sacrifices, she would prosper, have a permanent home, and gain followers on both sides of the Atlantic. It is because of Ajé's sacrifice that people realized they do not have to carry their wealth around with them. They could keep the cowries they did not need to spend immediately inside black pots (232–33). These pots were in effect savings accounts for the profits of the Atlantic trade.

FIGURE 8.1 Raiment of the god of thunder and lightning, Ṣàngó, when he mounts his possession priestess or priest (SABA COLLECTION D124). See also Matory ([1994] 2005: 196), as well as SABA COLLECTION D129.

One might view these oracular stories not only as parables about the depth of the Afro-Atlantic religions' embeddedness in the shared political economy that Westerners call capitalism but also as origin tales about the form of most òrìṣà altars in the Yorùbá-Atlantic world—cowrie-filled pots. Hence, faith in the Nigerian and Beninese òrìṣà, the Cuban *orichas*, the Brazilian *orixás*, and the Trinidadian orishas is also a continued or resurrected faith in the value of the currency of the slave trade, which indeed translates the most total and literally defining form of purchased human labor power—the slave.

European-style coinage and banknotes are also important in the Afro-Atlantic religions. The altars of certain gods contain imported coins, as well. For example, the altar embodying the Cuban goddess of wealth, Allé (cognate with the West African Ajé), must contain seven foreign coins. The coin-festooned scepter of the West African Yorùbá god Ṣònpònnón (seen in SABA Collection D069) is a further case in point. On this fly whisk–like object, the tassels are strips of colonial Nigerian coins. Even the forest leaves used in the construction and maintenance of the gods are purchased with European-style coins, paid on the forest floor to the Yorùbá god Ọ̀sanyìn and the Brazilin Ossaim.

As in figure 8.1, the attire of Ṣàngó manifest in his Nigerian possession priestess or priest is normally covered with cowries, the money of the slave trade, and his undergarments (*yèrì*) feature a coin purse.

Yet, as wealth removed from circulation, the white cowries inside black pots become embodiments of the communal self (Matory 1986; see Böhme [2006] 2014: 279–95 on the constitution of the self in the form of stationary wealth, much as museums and gold stores embody the subject of the nation-state). I would add to Böhme's argument the idea that this stationary self is not, even in the state museum or reserve bank, a monad but a self constituted dialectically by its internalization of imports. Few worshippers in Africa or the Americas are aware of slavery's role in establishing cowries as money in West Africa. In the American forms of these religions, cowries tend to be identified as "African" in origin, and, among African American Black national-ists, the type of Venetian and Bohemian beads that came to circulate in Africa during the slave trade are appreciated as "African trade beads." Similarly, in West Africa, as in Suriname, Dutch schnapps and other old-fashioned Euro-pean beverages are identified, instead, as the favored drinks of our African or Black ancestors. Black pots full of white cowries and, almost as often, Euro-pean beads give physical form to the ostensibly wealth-generating marriage between Africa and Europe. It is difficult not to read the blackness of the pots and the whiteness of the cowries as an allegory and commemoration of the intercontinental relationship that defines the Afro-Atlantic self.

Today, the form of Afro-Atlantic altars remains an heir to the Afro-European coastal trade. That form still expresses confidence in the value-producing and subject-producing character of exchange with radically different kin or ethnic groups, eras, and altitudes of the cosmos. However, amid the novel social ruptures characterizing its twentieth- and twenty-first-century context, the social corollaries of the contrasts of kinship, ethnicity, era, and altitude that constitute the self-other relationship may be quite different from what they were at the time of the slave trade.

Foreigners in One's Head

A glaring contrast between post-Enlightenment European and Afro-Atlantic models of personhood remains instructive. The paradigmatic subject of the Enlightenment, psychoanalysis, and historical materialism is the white male antithesis of the African. By contrast, the paradigmatic subject of the Afro-Atlantic religions is a black woman introjecting multiple exogenous others defined by their origins in or connections to distant peoples, eras, or altitudes of the cosmos. By "altitudes," I mean the height-associated dif-ference between this world (ayé) of the living and the Other (Òrun), which is sometimes identified with the above but is understood more often as a netherworld from which gods and ancestors arise. The internationalism of these sacralized others suggests a history of mythmaking by merchants and migrants. Indeed, translocalism is a key metaphor of the network and hierarchy of cosmological relationships that constitute the ideal Afro-Atlantic person (Matory 2009).

The networks that make up gods, people, and temple communities are often global. Even the gods hosted by Yorùbá worshippers in West Africa are commonly said to come from the north, from the Middle East, from foreign African ethnic groups, and from distant Yorùbá towns. For the Ọ̀yọ́-Yorùbá, this person from a distant time and place is often Nupe (that is, a member of a largely Muslim ethnic group residing to the north of Old Ọ̀yọ́) or is indexed by antique European trade goods. In Santería/Ocha and Candomblé, the deity is typically "African" and is indexed by specific African, Asian, and European trade goods. In Haiti, the Rada gods are defined by African origins as well as European manners and trade goods, while the Petwo gods commemorate the enslaved ancestors' eighteenth-century suffering and rebellion against the French. These interethnic, transhistorical, and often explicitly commercial transactions are also a power exchange and an exchange of identities, both of which leave their participants deeply fulfilled (Matory in preparation). Contrary to Marx's position, one aspect of the value of a commodity derives from the translocal commodity exchange that brought that exchangeable thing to Africa. Perhaps that value is not intrinsic to the physical thing, but that value does not, in any case, derive uniquely from the quantity of labor time that had been invested in its creation, even if it was produced by wage labor. It derives from the promise of long-term, long-distance, and, even better, intercultural connection to others.

Hence, our religions embraced and adapted the Roman Catholic saints rather than rejecting them, after the fashion of the Abrahamic religions' response to religious others, as a contamination (see, for example, the African–Roman Catholic hybrid figure of San Lázaro and Babalú Allé shown in figure 8.2).

In 2000, Marta Moreno Vega published a memoir called *The Altar of My Soul*. It describes the multinational score of beings whose convergence— as much within her body as upon her domestic altar—makes up her soul. "Among my ancestral spirit angels," she reports, "are the Native Indians of the Caribbean, the Moors, Kongos, and Yorubas of Africa, Gypsies and Europeans from Spain and the Caribbean" (Vega 2000: 17). This conception of the self is concretely embodied in ancestral altars called *bóvedas*, which arise from a Caribbean and especially Puerto Rican interpretation of French Kardecist Spiritism. Practitioners called *espiritistas* maintain them in honor of their ancestors, but they are among the multiple types of altar maintained by Puerto Rican and Cuban *santeros*, as well. A *bóveda* normally features a monstrance commemorating the ancestors, a ritually prescribed number of glass water vessels to attract them, and candles to enlighten them, as

FIGURE 8.2 San Lázaro/Babalú Allé, a hybrid African god and Roman Catholic saint clad in African-inspired cowry shells (Cuban Santería/Ocha, SABA COLLECTION B040).

well as photographs of the family dead. It also commonly includes ethnically stereotyped images dramatizing the racial and cultural hybridity of the worshipper, such as statues of a slave identified as a *congo* (see figure 8.5, for example), a North American Plains Indian, a fan associated with a gypsy (*gitana*), candles in honor of Lucumí gods, and a doll embodying the spirit of a dead *santera* priestess consecrated to one African-inspired oricha god or another. The doll's skin color, dress, and head tie typically identify her racially, geographically, and historically distant origins. Specifically, many such dolls are usually identified as a type of spirit of the dead known as a *madama*, whose French-inspired name suggests her Haitian origins. After the Haitian Revolution, thousands of Haitians moved or were forcibly taken to Puerto Rico, Cuba, other Caribbean islands, or Louisiana. Rum and *àgua florida* (floral water) cologne are among the commercial products given to these spirits to keep them present and alive in our homes. Even the cologne bottle typically features an orientalist image of a Turkish or Arab odalisque.

Thus, the Afro-Atlantic worshipper's spiritual completeness and efficacy are measured not in terms of the solidity of his or her "identity"(which is a favorite trope of personhood in the Anglo-American university) or the purity of his or her "race" (long the pride of the dominant classes in the Americas) but in terms of the multiplicity, breadth, and historical depth of his or her internalized translocal connections. Note that this emphasis on the cosmopolitan and the translocal did not originate in the conditions of the Atlantic trade. The ancestors of Yorùbá have long been urbanized, and the palaces that elaborated what we now called "Yorùbá indigenous religion" sit at the center of cities specializing in trade-oriented manufacture and exchange across African regions, across the Sahara, and across the Atlantic Ocean. The West African Yorùbá cities most influential on orisha-worship in the diaspora—Ọ̀yọ́, Abẹ́òkúta, and Lagos—sit on terrestrial, riverine, maritime trade routes and were privileged by their intermediary positions. Like their priestly servants and allies, West African merchant-monarchs drew great power from the breadth and continuity of their interregional social and commercial connections. The endurance of equestrian imagery as well as imported horses, beads, cowrie shells, conches, foreign cultigens, and European alcohols in these religions suggests the powerful historical influence of Guinea-Coast merchant-monarchs and their strategies during the Atlantic trade.

Cosmopolitanism remained a hallmark of these traditions in the Americas and in the ongoing dialogue among orisha-worshippers in Nigeria, Cuba, Brazil, Haiti, and the United States. For example, nineteenth-century Chinese immigration to Cuba brought into Santería/Ocha additional icons of the foreign and of relationships with the foreigner. The Chinese martial artist and culture hero Guan Gung, also known in Cuba as Sanfancón, was adopted as the Chinese avatar of Changó (SABA Collection B011/0007). He, too, often appears on *bóvedas*, invoking the worshipper's Chinese forebears. Today, a cosmopolitanism much like that of the sixteenth- and seventeenth-century merchant-monarchs of the Guinea Coast remains elemental to the efficacy of Ìyá Ọ̀sun Ọ̀sogbo as a high priestess of the Nigerian river goddess Ọ̀sun and as a social mediator among adoptive family and tens of thousands of followers (including several anthropologists) around the Atlantic perimeter.

Hence, both east and west of this great ocean, Yorùbá-Atlantic altars are surrounded and filled with sacred images and artifacts from faraway places. Initiation and the construction of the Afro-Atlantic gods, even in their American contexts, create and continually reanimate such relationships through signs of the foreign (see figure 8.7 and SABA Collection B052, J067). (See also Beliso-De Jesús 2015 and Matory 2009 on the transnational nature of divinity.) In sum, the altars and devotees of the Afro-Atlantic religions are monuments to mutually profitable relations of exchange and cooperation with beings from the Other world—not only ancestors and members of other families but also divinities who personify our relationship to foreigners and

commercial trading partners from far away. This logic of the human relationship to the divine and to other human beings bears countless residues of
West African merchant-monarchs, strategic management of the trade with
the emirates of the northern savannah and the trade on the Guinea Coast.

Divinity, Wifeliness, Slavery, and Power

Jean-François Bayart (1989) makes a related point in his critique of the "extraversion" of African political economy. Deliberately sidestepping the positive implications of the term "extroversion," from which most foreigners
seeking friendship in sub-Saharan Africa benefit, Bayart observes that political power in Africa has long rested upon leaders' privileged access to foreign
powers and resources, as well as control over their distribution, rather than
on local "development," leading to dysfunctional levels of extraction, exploitation, and underdevelopment. There is much truth in this critique. But Bayart's
vision is as partial and motivated as that of Willem Bosman before him.

Bayart assumes that outward orientation is the cause, rather than the cir-
cumstance, of Africa's exploited and underdeveloped condition. As Mauss
([1923–24] 2000) points out, exchange among heterogeneous parties (including
intermarriage) is a positive alternative to the equally available alternative of
warfare, and such exchange with outsiders is not inevitably extractive and
exploitative. Through most of human history, orientation toward the Other
has led to mutual obligation, responsibility, and even beneficence.

Over the decades, I have received extraordinary kindness from Africans,
Brazilians, and Haitians who would have no way of commanding proportional
recompense from me. Our continuing friendships have been motivated as
much by my hunger to reward their kindness as by my desire to learn more
about their traditions. As a middle-class US American almost accustomed
to friends of long standing who insist on splitting the restaurant bill every
time or, worse, paying only the precise cost of their own food, I was at first
shocked by the Afro-Atlantic disposition to extend generosity to the Other
for the pleasure of it and of assuming that Others, too, delight in helping
their own Others when they are able. Now, in a hybrid way, I delight in extending the most lavish possible generosity to people who have extended
me such faithful and uncalculated kindness. Because my (re-)Africaniza-
tion at the hands of my many benefactors was delayed by two uninterrupted
decades of the finest education in post-Enlightenment Westernness that a
black-skinned parvenu could receive, one of my greatest regrets in life is
that, while I was receiving the benefits of Afro-Atlantic extraversion, I was so
focused on getting tenure and providing for my nuclear family that I failed

to keep in touch with some of my Afro-Atlantic benefactors and have lost the means of contacting them. Sadly, some of them now live only in my heart and in the altars kept by the living. Their corporeal vessels are no more.

So, in my view, the problem with African extraversion is not that it is inherently dysfunctional but that it has been paired with Europe's own style of extraversion—the delight in and idealization of profit at the Other's expense, of which overseas imperialism was the grossest form. For example, Indian friends tell me that their compatriots despise the Western imperialist in a way that they do not despise the Islamic imperialist, since the Muslim conquerors became part of South Asian society. By contrast, Westerners remained apart and established a system in which deep intercultural and intercommunal connections chiefly subserved the purpose of extraction. Africa paid a major price—even higher than India's—for the benefits that this typically post-Enlightenment European form of extraversion conferred upon Europeans, subsidizing Europe's own halting transition from poverty and despotism to social democracy. Even more fundamentally than Orientalism (Said [1978] 2003), the anti-African subjectivity of post-Enlightenment reasoning about the European self is the ideological groundwork of Europe's predatory extraversion. European extraversion has been as much to blame as African extraversion for Africa's impoverishment since the late eighteenth century. Africans' aspiration to long-distance partnership may have been a good idea, but geographical circumstances brought it a bad partner.

Bayart overlooks a further cultural backdrop to West African extroversion and extraversion—one equally related to the entanglement of the merchant-monarchs with European maritime traders since the sixteenth century.

Decades ago, a Harvard graduate student and initiate of Santería/Ocha noticed that, at the time, crowns made up a plurality of the items in the SABA Collection. "This could be a crown show!" she exclaimed. Hereditary rule has long been at the center of West African Yorùbá social and political organization. Appropriate to Africa's extroversion and extraversion, horses imported from the north, beads imported from the south, and a marital logic of communion and delegation are among the symbolic touchstones of Yorùbá royalism. In fact, beaded crowns, necklaces, and fly whisks are omnipresent elements of the pageantry and the technology of both Yorùbá monarchy and the Yorùbá-Atlantic spirit possession religions. With their extraordinary bouquet of multicolored bead embroidery, the Yorùbá crowns of the past five hundred years reveal the recent and cosmopolitan roots of what is often assumed to be primordial in the West African-based civilization.

The defining emblem of Yorùbá monarchy is a conical crown adorned with thousands of diversely colored glass beads sewn onto them, including

FIGURE 8.3 Yorùbá royal crown. Note the typical beaded veil and hierarchical organization of birds. Photograph reproduced with the kind permission of the Hamill Gallery of Tribal Art, Roxbury, Massachusetts.

an especially distinctive veil of beaded strands that obscure the monarch's face (figure 8.3). A little-noticed fact is that this form is absent from the rich twelfth- to fifteenth-century archaeological record of this region.

Glass beads of the type used to embroider modern Yorùbá crowns and òrìṣà priestly paraphernalia were unavailable in West Africa until the era of the Atlantic trade, and the earliest extant examples of the face-concealing conical crown date only from the late seventeenth century. Cowries and indigenous striated blue glass ṣẹgi beads may have adorned crowns during an earlier period, and a few extant crowns from before that period are decorated with brass sequins or beads cut from bone. At the end of the fifteenth century, Portuguese merchants made coral beads available to the non-Yorùbá Kingdom of Benin, whose merchants made them available for incorporation into the paraphernalia of the ancestors of today's Yorùbá monarchs (Beier 1982: 24–35).

The prerogative to assemble diverse varieties of beads imported from far away is apparently an old feature of royal and religious iconography in this region. However, the sudden proliferation and diversification of glass beads on the crown and the emergence of the beaded veil coincide with the growth of the Atlantic trade and suggest a profound change in the gendered logic of sovereignty in this region, a change directly related to the Afro-European dialogue of the sixteenth and seventeenth centuries. Far from being mere "survivals" (Herskovits [1941] 1958) of some primordial African tradition, defining features of Brazilian Candomblé and Cuban Santería/Ocha are also direct products of this change.

There is evidence that the proto-Yorùbá kingdom of Ilé-Ifẹ̀ mass-produced glass beads from the eleventh century to the fifteenth. However, 90 percent of the thirteen thousand glass beads from this period examined by Babalọla are blue (Babalọla 2017; Babalọla et al. 2017; Babalọla, personal communication, November 7, 2017). The fifteenth- to sixteenth-century collapse of industrial bead production in Ilé-Ifẹ̀ coincided with the rapid growth and diversification of glass bead production on the Venetian island of Murano, from the fourteenth century onward. The massive importation of diversely colored Venetian glass beads and their later Bohemian counterparts revolutionized the iconography of royalty and divinity among the ancestors of the Yorùbá and apparently aided in the simultaneous reorganization of political power around the Gulf of Guinea.

Somewhere between the fourteenth century and the seventeenth, not only the form of crowns but also the basic logic of governance materialized in them seems to have changed. On the one hand, the brass and terra cotta portraiture of twelfth- to fifteenth-century Ilé-Ifẹ̀ is highly naturalistic and individuated, apparently depicting royals without veils and with highly individuated faces. In these pieces, dignitaries' bodies are often covered with beads, from the neck downward and on top of the head, leaving the face the visible focus of attention. On those few representations with remnants of paint, there is no evidence that the beads on their bodies varied significantly in color (Beier 1982: 33). By contrast, the defining element of royal self-presentation among the Yorùbá and their ancestors over the past three to four centuries has been the emblematically Yorùbá veil of diversely colored glass beads, which obscures the monarch's face and suggests the erasure of his or her personal identity in favor of the institutional power of the monarchy itself. Drewal, Pemberton, and Abiọdun vividly describe an exemplary twentieth-century monarch and the depersonalizing logic evoked by the beaded veil: "The King's face is not only covered by a veil of beads but is concealed by a beaded shield held over his mouth. In the past the faces of kings were not to be seen, for it is in the crown, not the face[,] that royal power resides" (1989: 30). Of course, the "past" described by these authors had a genesis and has a history of its own.

The faces typically embroidered on this genre of royal crown also reveal the Atlantic historical setting and cultural logic of this change in proto-Yorùbá religion and polity. The one or more bead-embroidered faces on the cone of the crown invoke Olókun, the òrìṣà of the sea. Closely associated with the Atlantic Ocean, he or she is credited with inventing both beads and crowns (Beier 1982: 24–35). The local variation in and ambiguity of this god's gender is perhaps a hint of the gender-transforming technology employed in royal strategies to exploit the coastal trade with Europeans. The color coding and the arrangement of beads on such crowns are highly important, as they specifically invoke not only Olókun but a whole range of gods and other spirits that came to animate the monarch's person and conduct. Color- and numerically-coded glass beads animate the paraphernalia and persons of not only royals but priests as well. Royal and religious ritual is a parade of bead-covered crowns, necklaces, scepters, and pouches defining the relationship among gods, the palace, priesthoods, guilds, families, and their human personnel. This modern sacred iconography of community-shaping things depends on the availability of large numbers of imported glass beads—in not only blue but also white, black, green, yellow, pink, and red.

Unlike their twelfth- to fifteenth-century antecedents, modern Yorùbá crowns also typically feature a hierarchically arranged circle of birds, soliciting the cooperation of the potentially malign forces known as the àjẹ́. An àjẹ́ is an inner avian genius animating each of those wonderful women whose cooperation is necessary if we wish to survive and prosper (see also figure 8.13). These women are politely called "our mothers" (àwọn ìyáà wa), as only a fool would insult them by calling them witches. The omnipresent circling-birds motif on the post-seventeenth-century crowns is entirely absent from the twelfth- to fifteenth-century brass and terra cotta figures exhumed in Ilé-Ifè̩.

The extant prototypes of these now typically Yorùbá crowns date back to the late seventeenth century (Babalọla, personal communication, November 7, 2017). Though this crown form might predate this period, it is unlikely to have predated the availability of large numbers of diversely colored Venetian beads brought through the Atlantic trade starting in the sixteenth century.

If a new beaded iconography of sacred power emerged from the sixteenth- to seventeenth-century Afro-European encounter on the coast, indigenous gender transformations and the Ọ̀yọ́ palace's importation of horses from the north made the empire's sixteenth-century surge toward the Atlantic coastal ports possible. Indeed, this period is associated with the earliest importation of horses from the north, enabling Ọ̀yọ́ to conquer a tsetse-free corridor—the Benin Gap (also known as the Dahomey Gap)—toward the Atlantic coast. In that region, possession priests analogously known as "horses" (ẹsin) or "wives" (ìyàwó) of the gods, as well as messengers prepared ritually after the manner of possession priests and wives of the monarch, served as delegates possessed by the will of the palace. Indeed, the gender of the monarch himself appears to have been transformed by these new arrangements. Palace historians report that the kingdom's imperial expansion began with the reign of Ọrọ̀mpọtọ, a monarch who turned from a woman into a man (Matory [1994] 2005: 10).

The revenues of the Guinea Coast monarchs long derived largely from their mastery of heterogeneous streams of long-distance trade—especially, since the sixteenth century, the transoceanic commerce—helping us to understand why, to this very day, not only Yorùbá royal attire but also the contents of the vessel altars of the gods come from a transoceanic array of locales. It should also be noted that this sort of mastery is not principally patriarchal, following the father-son succession ideally imagined in European monarchies and in Freud's Oedipal scenario, not to mention his attempt to recruit Jung as his successor as the patriarch of psychoanalysis. In fact, because Yorùbá royal titles usually circulate among the *multiple* founding families of the jurisdiction, few sovereigns have actually succeeded a parent.

The monarch's sovereignty is constructed, instead, in terms of husband-wife relations and motherhood. In the Yorùbá terminology of affinity, a woman is considered the "bride" or "wife" (ìyàwó) of all of her affines—that is, not only her connubial bed partner but also of all of his kin, particularly his patrilateral kin. She owes them deference, just as they owe her protection and financial support. Concomitantly, each woman or wife is also a "husband" (ọkọ) to the wives of all of her male consanguineal—and especially her male patrilateral—kinsmen. Similarly, the monarch is configured as "husband" to his subordinates, including "our mothers." At the same time, he is ritually configured as a "bride" or "wife" to the dynastic god and a wife-like possession priest of the heterogeneous powers materially encased in the crown and inserted into his body during coronation rituals, many of which are also invoked by the emblematically colored beadwork of the royal crown, necklaces, robes, shoes, thrones, footrests, and fly whisks. As "wives" and "mounts" of the god, Ṣàngó possession priests (see figure 8.1) dramatize and facilitate the monarch's own role as a vessel and vehicle of the ancestral, divine, foreign, and Other-worldly forces that cascade through the whole hierarchy of priests, delegates, and subjects who make up the polity (Matory [1994] 2005, 1994, 1986). In a 1989 interview, the Aláàáfin, or king of Ọ̀yọ́, told me that his rituals of coronation indeed made him a "wife" (ìyàwó) of his dynastic god, Ṣàngó. Indeed, the beaded crown is regarded as a divinity in its own right, and the monarch may never apply it to his own head; like the attire of Ṣàngó possession priests, it is always applied by a committee of officials standing behind the wearer, where the wearer cannot see the committee. The crown and the dynastic god—made, managed, and maintained by palace personnel—possesses the monarch himself.[1] Rather than a heroic individual personality in his own right, the monarch is the apex in a nesting hierarchy and network of wifely human vessels.

In this system, the paradigmatic vessels and vehicles in the delegation of power are not men but women, or wives and mothers. Just as "farmer" (àgbè) is the normative profession for a man in Yorubaland, "trader" (*oníṣòwò*) is the normative profession for a woman. Indeed, historically the chief of the marketplace in most towns is a woman bearing the title of Ìyálóde. Moreover, to this day, women from certain Yorùbá subethnic groups dominate the long-distance trade in foodstuffs, and both women and men participate in small-scale import and export exchanges with Asia and the West. Both independent female long-distance merchants and wives trading on behalf of their merchant-monarch husbands were critical to the political economy of nineteenth-century Yorubaland and emblematic of a cultural logic of value that prioritizes exchange (Matory [1994] 2005). For example, Clapperton (1829: 21) encountered the wives of the Ọ̀yọ́ monarch "every place trading for him." In 1830, the Lander brothers observed "not less than a hundred" Ọ̀yọ́ royal wives in "Jadoo" (probably Ìjèbú, a distant southern neighbor of the kingdom). The Landers described the women as follows: "They have all passed the bloom of life, and arrived here lately with loads of trona and country cloth [handwoven cloth, likely from the Ọ̀yọ́ North region] which they barter for salt and various articles of European manufacture, particularly beads; with these they return home, and expose them for sale in the market and afterwards the profits are taken to their husbands" (Lander and Lander [1832] 1839, 1: 122; also Matory [1994] 2005: 21).

Some of these "wives" may have been literal bedpartners of and coparents with the sovereign, but others may have been the widows of antecedent monarchs, who continued to be considered "royal wives" (*ayaba*) and therefore mothers of their husbands' successors. Some may have been messengers (*ìlàrí*) of the monarch, delegates ritually prepared as possession priests of the monarch's personal will (Matory [1994] 2005: 10–11). These trading parties may also have included not only female but also cross-dressing male *ìlàrí*.

That these wives were reportedly all postmenopausal may mean that the social status of postmenopausal wives was distinctive in the nineteenth-century conduct of royal commerce, as it is in the service of the gods. Both menstruation and recent sexual contact with human husbands are defiling to people immediately engaged in some Yorùbá- and Fòn-Atlantic rites, and women are eligible for certain offices or to sacrifice birds (they are still typically ineligible to sacrifice four-legged animals) only after menopause.

Twentieth-century studies of Yorùbá women in commerce may cast doubt on Clapperton's and the Lander brothers' contention that the palace "wives" handed their profits over to their husband. What is evident, though, is that a large number of women and possibly cross-dressing men traded on the Guinea Coast or governed the Ọ̀yọ́ Empire's provinces in the savannahs of the Benin Gap under the aegis of the monarch, that they were authorized to do so by their status as literal or metaphorical "wives" of the monarch, and that the palace derived material benefit from their activities. The palace had thus adapted norms of plebeian gender relations to the project of state sovereignty and metaphorically extended them in the service of managing distant imperial provinces and the Atlantic trade. This revolutionary gendered and metaphor-laden technology of royal bureaucracy, in tandem with the related technology of Ọ̀yọ́'s Benin Gap colony of Dahomey, is prolifically evident in Brazilian Candomblé, Cuban Santería/Ocha, and Haitian Vodou, as well.

Like the integration of equestrian symbolism into the ritual construction of Ọ̀yọ́ royal and divine authority, the iconography of the monarch's feminization may have had some northern sources. During the sixteenth and seventeenth centuries, Ọ̀yọ́ was in dialogue with both Europe and the Islamic world. Muslims were then a common presence at the Ọ̀yọ́ royal court. It is therefore worth wondering whether the *veiling* of monarchs drew some part of its intended symbolic significance from the veiling of wives in Islam. This may also be the period when monarchs came to be sequestered in palaces, not unlike the wives of many prosperous Muslim men. Stories told about the pre-sixteenth-century arrival of Ọ̀yọ́ monarch in the city of Ìgbòho suggest that the proto-Yorùbá monarchs had not always been confined to their palaces or capitals.

The bureaucratization of the Ọ̀yọ́ palace and the de-personalization of royal authority were also a feminization—or, properly speaking—a uxorialization—of the monarch. This feminization includes what seems to be an equally new association of the monarch with "our mothers." Although the monarch is expected to be the *chief* of these powerful women, his crown suggests that he is also one of them. At its late eighteenth-century peak, Ọ̀yọ́ royal authority—which was also the principal source of Santería/Ocha's and Candomblé's iconography and technology—was more like a nesting hierarchy of wifeliness and motherhood than like a patriarchy. Ọ̀yọ́'s collapse in the early nineteenth century propelled hundreds of thousands of kidnapped subjects of Ọ̀yọ́, including many priests, into a maritime slave trade bound for Brazil and Cuba.

It is already common sense that the Atlantic slave trade transformed the politics of the Gulf of Guinea Coast and its hinterland. However, in the discussion of so-called Yorùbá indigenous religion, the omnipresence of diversely colored glass beads, the veiling and sequestration of monarchs, and the plethora of literal and metaphorical wives and horses in the palace and the priesthood tend to be taken for granted, as though they were primordial features of political and religious life in Ọ̀yọ́, its West African colonies, and its American diaspora. No. Like the Enlightenment, they are revolutionary changes demonstrably indebted to the sixteenth- and seventeenth-century Afro-European encounter on the Gulf of Guinea Coast. They reveal the centrality of the sixteenth- to seventeenth-century Afro-European commerce to the transformation of religion and politics—in truth, one and the same thing—in the Ọ̀yọ́ kingdom and its diaspora, a transformation that took place not only in parallel but also in dialogue with the European Enlightenment.

Yorùbá kinship, kingship, and religion are no isolated idylls to be romantically contrasted with the world of Marx and Freud. Rather, those worlds have been deeply enmeshed with one another since the sixteenth century. From different social positions in the same circum-Atlantic dialogue, European social critics and Yorùbá-Atlantic priests have formulated radically different ideas about the role of exchange in creating value and about the gender of the efficacious human subject. For example, in the Yorùbá-Atlantic traditions, wifeliness and motherhood, rather than the father-son relationship, are the ultimate inflections of power in action. This comparison is made all the more vivid by analogy to the naming of Yorùbá-Atlantic drums, which transform the subjectivity of priests during rituals of spirit possession. Indeed, as the reader will see below, the lead drum in most Afro-Atlantic sacred drum ensembles is called the "mother." Neither of these revolutionary articulations of value and agency through the management of things is self-evidently wrong or right. What we can say is that each is far better understood as a culturally conditioned and interested set of strategies for in pursuit of well-being than as an ethereal cogitation transcending the cultural suppositions and material projects of its exponents.

Unlike the extroverted and extraverted African merchant-monarchs of the past, the devotees of the òrìṣà today share the common experience of being under siege by Christian and Muslim critics and by the outmigration of family members who had historically united, for their mutual benefit, around the òrìṣà. In this context, European and Asian beads, shells from the Indian Ocean, and European alcohols and perfumes become emblems of not only centuries-old foreign trade connections but also genealogical antiquity and the primordial and thus ostensibly inescapable obligations animating the family and the ethnic group. By commemorating a long history of local circulation, once-imported beads, shells, and distillates come to encode the interests of those who wish to hold a fissiparous family and ethnic group together or who wish to claim rights to manage the collective resources of religiously and class-heterogeneous families (Weber [1922–23] 1946; Matory [1994] 2005: 133–78, esp. 158–61; consider also Richman 2005).

Hence, Yorùbá-Atlantic altars, too, are deeply ambivalent, simultaneously commemorating both extroversion and extraversion, royalty and slavery, fusion and fission, voluntary and involuntary solidarity, voluntary and involuntary dispersion, and the tandem benefits and injuries of hierarchy. Like the attire of Yorùbá monarchs, other Afro-Atlantic spirited things commemorate a past cross-pollination and embody a prayer for its endurance in the future. But they also embody the history of the slave trade. The West African domestic altar styles that monarchs and merchants adapted to their own purposes were also adopted by and later adapted to the purposes of enslaved Afro-Latin Americans, and their free descendants, the most influential of whom traveled back and forth across the Atlantic in the conduct of pilgrimage and trade (Matory 2005). These altar styles were also adopted, adapted, and greatly elaborated by Cuban refugees in the US, African Americans, and non-Cuban Latin Americans and Latinos all over the Western Hemisphere. In these sacred memorials and portals of translocal exchange, I see the sacred strategies of West African merchant-monarchs and of people victimized by these monarchs and their European trading partners. These are the people kidnapped, enslaved, and then proletarianized, who then made an effort to establish value-producing links of mutual obligation among their oppressed fellows and with the powerful.

In the Candomblé religion, the goddesses Iansã, Oxum, and Iemanjá are all queens, or "royal wives" (*ayaba*). SABA Collection C134 shows a mannequin wearing festival attire for Oxum, the goddess of fresh waters, gold, honey, and sensuality. Her emblems are yellow and gold, the sword, the royal crown, and the *abebé* (a combined fan and mirror that dramatizes both her vanity and her cooling powers). In most cases, the goddess's crowns occlude the face of the possession priest with a beaded veil (see, for example, figure 8.6 and SABA Collection C023, C027, and C037). (For Cuban variants on this form, see B001 and B043, which are not worn by possessed priests but placed atop the goddess in the form of her ceramic vessel altars, such as B167 and B383.)

People who play subordinate roles in the capitalist economies of the nation-states where they live understand themselves somewhat differently in the context of the Afro-Atlantic religions. They participate in the dignity and reputation of the temple, receive care and protection from the leaders of that community, enjoy upward mobility through the temple's quasi-gerontocratic hierarchy, and, on the occasion of festivals, demonstrate their essential inner dignity. Often servants by day, they are queens and kings by night. Throughout the day, in the end, they merge the potentials of both.

And yet Afro-Atlantic priests also attribute great power to divine slaves. The capture and sale of fellow human beings has been an empowering strategy for white, black, and Native American denizens of the Afro-Atlantic world. Apparently embodying such a strategy, the *bociɔ* (pronounced "boh-chaw"), or charm, shown in figure 8.4 was made by descendants of the most voracious slave-trading kingdom in African history—Dahomey.

Dahomey secured its freedom from domination by the Ọ̀yọ́ Empire by trading in slaves, many of them from Ọ̀yọ́ and other regions that are now part

FIGURE 8.4 *Bociɔ* charm (Fòn, Dahomey, SABA COLLECTION J023). Note that he is bound up and that part of the binding is a releasable plug through his neck.

of Yorubaland. Probably crafted after the end of the Atlantic slave trade, this wooden but nonetheless living agent appears to have been activated by the removal of the spike from his neck. The ropes binding him suggest that he is under someone else's command and that he is possessed of powers that the owner would benefit from controlling but, if careless, could lose control of and be destroyed by. The *bociɔ*'s wide-open eyes, well-defined ears, and bent knees suggest alertness and agility. Though bound, he is quite different from the incompetent "negro slave" conjured by Marx.

Though he is visibly wizened, the muscularity and pose of this Cuban- or Puerto Rican–inspired *congo* spirit (figure 8.5) emphasize the power and efficacy of the enslaved Black man. He is bursting out of his work clothes, and his rolled-up pants suggest that he is ready to move. White streaks suggest the lightning-fast power of his crotch and thighs. His arrow-straight gaze says that he knows what is going on, while his jewelry, the cowrie shells, and the chicken show that he knows what to do about it. His white hair highlights his experience and wisdom. His red lips, scarf, waistband, and toenails pose an incendiary threat, in lieu of the cowardice that white North Americans typically attribute to the slave and the nonrevolutionary contentment that Marx implies (see also the *ño* and the *ña* in figure 7.3, whose bowls and necklace hint at the Afro-Atlantic sources of their power).

FIGURE 8.5 A *congo* spirit (Caribbean Spiritism, SABA COLLECTION H006).

Thus, in the interpretation and management of conditions both east and west of the Atlantic, royalty and slavery remain central themes in the iconography of the Afro-Atlantic religions and will be taken up further in my *Zombies and Black Leather* (in preparation).

Beads and Sequins

Both altars and initiates are typically a treasure trove of beads, mostly imported from far and wide (figures 7.2, 7.3, 8.1, 8.5, 8.6, 8.18, 8.21, 9.1, 9.3, and C.1; plates 2, 4, 5, 6, and 9; and SABA Collection B205 and D105). Yorùbá-Atlantic altars are literally full of the artifacts of global trade and commemorations of trade relationships. Beads, coins (e.g., SABA Collection D069), and sequins (e.g., figure 8.6) are metonyms of a commerce with the foreign that is both secular and sacred. In the eyes of the sixteenth- or seventeenth-century Dutchman or the Portuguese who brought it from Venice or Bohemia, a bead may have been a worthless tchotchke or a reminder of the inferiority of Dutch or Portuguese manufactures, but for the African merchant who bought it, it was likely a thing of beauty, technical finesse, and invocatory power—a souvenir of a long-distance connection with a trading partner or god of wealth, and, when gifted by a fellow African, a token of local solidarity.

FIGURE 8.6 The Brazilian goddess Oxum dancing with my daughter, Ayò, during an October 1992 festival in São Paulo. The goddess is adorned with Maldivean cowries; Venetian, Bohemian, and Ghanaian glass beads; Mediterranean coral beads; sequins; and gold lamé (Brazilian Candomblé). SABA COLLECTION D008 is a further example of the Nigerian goddess's elaborate beadwork. Please also see the beaded "fans" (*abèbè*) of the Nigerian Yorùbá goddess Ọ̀ṣun at D010. Fans embody the vanity and cooling power of Ọ̀ṣun, as well as her Brazilian counterpart, Oxum, and her Cuban counterpart, Ochún.

The preservation and display of beads commemorates a privileged partnership with a well-connected emissary of the Other world and dramatizes the desire for that relationship to endure and evolve in the service of future projects. They may look like mere adornment, but beads also map out in standardized codes the connections and open the paths between people and between worlds (see figures 8.6 and plates 4 and 6, for example). The hard imperishability of beads—like that of the stones and coins that also make up altars of the networked self—also appears to dramatize the permanency that trading partners and worshippers hope for in these relationships. The durability of glass beads is of a piece with their reflective smoothness, qualities also evident in the cowrie shells, sequins, mirrors, enamel, polished sheet metal, whitened calabashes, and highly glazed ceramics with which Afro-Atlantic priests give material form to spirit and relationship. These materials reflect light, even in dark surroundings, visibly suggesting an emanation from elsewhere (Thompson 1983).

Once reworked, strung or embroidered, inherited, repaired, and re-strung or re-embroidered in the proper color and numerical permutations, imported beads ultimately came to embody connections to social networks much older, wider and deeper than trade connections to the European merchants. Indeed, the Venetian or Bohemian bead and the European merchants who brought them become but metonyms of these African-centered gods of networking. In this way, even though cowrie shells become brittle and visibly thin over time, their agedness testifies to the antiquity of the legacy-bearing altars, artworks, and relationships to which they are attached.

The Afro-Atlantic religious appreciation of beads and cowries is no more foolish than the equally religious Euro-American appreciation of gold and dollar bills. Each form of appreciation mimes confidence in the continuity of one set of relationships between people and between peoples who habitually rely on these materials to create social relationships, while explicitly or implicitly casting doubt on a rival program of relationship-building and -regulation through things. The European origin of glass beads and the Maldivean origin of cowries were as easily forgotten by African priests as the Guinea-Coast origins of the fetish problem was by recent social theorists and kink practitioners—that is, incompletely and in ways that continue, subliminally, to inform Afro-Atlantic gods, European social theories, and kink alike. Also forgotten are the African and Amerindian origins of Europe's gold.

Haitian sacred art is particularly famous for its use of sequins. Reportedly, their use proliferated because seamstresses were able to sweep up and repurpose them when they had fallen on the floor of foreign-owned clothing manufacturers. The makers of Haiti's famous Vodou flags and of bottles for the gods' beverages delight in the appropriation and repurposing of Roman Catholic images, as well, but not these images alone (see, e.g., figure 8.7; SABA Collection A008). Cosentino (1995: 28) summarizes: "fragments of Africa, certainly, but also bits and pieces from the Taino, from Celtic and Enlightenment France, from the Jesuits and the Masons and all the emporia of twentieth-century capitalism."

In sum, the gods and their material embodiments are products of a network of exchange, assembly, and production whose unity as value-producing dimensions of capitalism Marx was anxious to deny. At the same time, Freud suggested that, in embedding powerful collective affect in things, the "savage" exemplified a childlike or neurotic act that "civilized" adult Europeans have learned to moderate. I have made the case that Freud himself was highly vulnerable to the same accusation and that there was nothing particularly childlike about this form of semiosis and materialized sociality. For their part, Afro-Atlantic priests are aware that they have been singled out for othering by Bosman and his intellectual heirs, and the priests' enlightening retort is embedded in their theology and their elaborate iconography. The rich material culture of the Afro-Atlantic religions calls attention to the rival codes through which the value and agency of the commodity have been

FIGURE 8.7 Sacred flag for Lasirèn (Haitian Vodou, SABA COLLECTION A055). Note the typically European forms of the mermaid, the trumpet, and the handheld mirror. Even her hair, in dreadlocks, seems to suggest the latest in foreign hairstyles. See also SABA COLLECTION A008, a bottle for Èzili Freda, a goddess of love, beauty, and European-style luxury. On that bottle, the European symbol of the heart evokes this goddess's association with heterosexual seduction and alludes to her murder at the hands of her jealous sister, Èzili Dantò. Note the small L-shaped black dagger in the upper left corner of the heart.

constructed and to the universal role of such intercultural rivalry and personal ambivalence in the making of social life.

Pots, Calabashes, Mortars, and Soup Tureens

Easily overlooked as background, filled vessels are perhaps the clearest metaphor of Afro-Atlantic personhood (Matory [1994] 2005, 1986). Most òrìṣà altars, particularly in the spirit possession cults, are filled pots, calabashes, bowls, and mortars, which are, in altar configurations and ritual action, made analogous to the heads of the possession priests (see especially figure 8.8). Indeed, the Yorùbá word for "skull" (àkòtòrí) analogizes that body part to a type of wide calabash vessel (àkòtò) that is also commonly used as the vessel in the vessel altar that embodies an òrìṣà god (figure 8.9). Like Ajé's black pots full of white cowrie shells, human bodies—and heads in particular—contain multiple beings, virtually all of which are exogenous to their container and even foreign to the human vessel's homeland.

This ontology and iconography parallels and exceeds the psychoanalytic understanding that the self hosts multiple and even conflicting agents. The "talking cure" was, by Afro-Atlantic standards, Freud's underdeveloped way of helping people to manage their internal heterogeneity. In the poverty of his introspection and failure to recognize forces beyond the two-generation nuclear family, Freud is the childish one. However, Freud's insight was a considerable advance on the Enlightenment notion of individuality, whereby the ideal human body is the province of but a single agent with autonomous volition and a machinery of perception and consciousness that is objectively separable from its social and natural environment.

In the Afro-Atlantic religions, vessel altars embody a technology to manage the human head, body, and community with the assumption that the same agent can crosscut and make itself present in multiple bodies. Various types of vessels employed mimetically to manage the multiple sacred contents of any given head, body, or community are shown in figures 8.8 through 8.11, 8.15, and 9.2 through 9.4, as well as plate 9 (see also and SABA Collection B036, B052, J067, and J070). This chapter adds to a substantial and expanding literature detailing the analogy between people and pots in West Africa (e.g., Warnier 2007; Matory 1986, 2005, [1994] 2005; Barley 1994; David, Sterner, and Gavua 1988). The logic that people are vessels emerges most shockingly—at least to a newcomer—through the omnipresent leitmotif of soup tureens, which are the vessels most commonly used in Santería/Ocha and Candomblé altars.

The Afro-Atlantic religions continually rehearse the embodied idea that neither the worker nor any other kind of actor—be it a son, a patriarch, a wife, or a mother—is born an atom, autonomous from and predating exchange-based social relationships. Nor will she ever be an atom. A person is constituted through the value-producing work of long-term exchange. A person is a crossroads of the connections constituted by multiple exchange partnerships. The ritual and commercial assembly of flesh-and-blood people and of divine people who incarnate in multiple human bodies are old phenomena in West African religion, with an important role in the governance of families and of states.

Like psychoanalysts, Afro-Atlantic priests tend to think and act in defiance of the individualist fiction embedded in the Enlightenment—that a person is a single bounded and internally integrated being. For Freud and his followers, the human personality is a struggle among the id, the ego, and the superego. To Freud, the dominance that the ego attributes to itself is delusional. The bounded integrity that the nation-state and the banking system attribute to the person is also fictional. Similarly, the Afro-Atlantic religions represent and act upon the body—and especially the head and the womb—with the understanding that it is a vessel temporarily housing multiple beings. Indeed, Yorùbá people's parlance and accounts of their spiritual anatomy expressly compare a person's head to a pot or a calabash. Elsewhere

FIGURE 8.8 Headlike Yorùbá water pot, probably employed in the worship of the river goddess, Yemoja (SABA COLLECTION D033). **FIGURE 8.9** A *koto* calabash altar and embodiment of Yemoja in the town of Ìgbòho, Nigeria, opened as her worshippers prepare to feed her in 1988. The small lidded metal and ceramic vessels within her head- and womb-like calabash are Yemoja and other gods inherited, worshipped, and fed by this family, such as Òsun and Obàtálá (Yorùbá indigenous religion). Each is filled with consecrated stones and cowry shells. The two long-necked calabashes in the background are *sérè* rattles used to salute or call the goddess. Two *koto* calabashes of Yemoja in the royal palace of the Onígbòho chief are shown in their lidded state in Matory (1994) 2005: 163.

in the Yorùbá-Atlantic world, soup tureens are the preeminent ritual metaphors of heads and wombs (see, e.g., figure 8.10 and 8.11; Matory [1994] 2005). In Yorubaland, the payment of bridewealth (literally, "money for the head of the bride" [owó orí ìyàwó]) by the husband's family to the wife's gives the husband's family title to the subsequent proceeds of her womb. This title is verbally equated with the ownership of the wife's "head." Brazilians draw this comparison more subtly, calling altar arrangements like the one shown in figure 8.11 a "lap."

Yorùbá people analogize the head to a vessel in various ways. First, it is said to have been made in the Other world (Òrun) by a divine potter known as Àjàlá. A good "head," which is equivalent to a good destiny, is said to have been well formed and well fired. A bad "head," or bad destiny, is said to be flawed like a badly formed and badly fired pot. Some stories report that a person chooses his or her own head, or destiny, before coming from the Other world, while others report that an ancestor helps one to choose it. In either case, one's head is the outcome of choices individual, ancestral, and communal. Even posthumously. Whereas good people go to the "good Other world" (Òrun rere), bad ones go to Òrun the "Other world of potsherds" (Òrun àpádì)—suggesting the termination of the cycle of reincarnation into the family.

Like the head and the womb of a worldly wife, the head of a possession priest and the vessel altar of the òrìṣà god are homologous portals of exchange and instruments of production. Priestly initiation and vessel altars make certain women and men expert managers of such exchange, production, and reproduction. Material signs of exotic, foreign presences are also important metonyms of wealth. Even the altar vessels themselves reveal such foreign presences (e.g., SABA Collection B052 and B167). The foremost desideratum sought from the òrìṣà gods is children, to which many other forms of wealth are analogous (Matory 1986, [1994] 2005).

The payment of cash bridewealth was an important part of West African Yorùbá marriages in the nineteenth century and continued to be so in the Òyó North region during my intensive research there in 1988–89. Bridewealth legitimized the children born to the marriage and made those children members of the father's lineage. With some logical and symbolic consistency, Yorùbá-Atlantic altars tend to be full of such money, much of it the old money that was exchanged for people during the Atlantic slave trade—that is, cowrie shells (owó eyo, literally "pieces of money"). But old coins are also common in altars. In a well-maintained altar, the cowrie shells are said to multiply, and so are the stones that also make up part of the god. In this respect, sacred money and stones share in the nature of children in

FIGURE 8.10 Deep-blue soup tureen altar for the goddess of the sea, Yemayá (Cuban Santería/Ocha, SABA COLLECTION, yet uncatalogued). Note the handles shaped like the heads of ducks, these aquatic birds being emblematic of the goddess. See also SABA Collection B036, an urn (*tinaja*) of the *oricha* Olocun, the gender-ambiguous god of the ocean depths. Covered with brain coral and whelk shells, this vessel might also be used to house Yemayá. **FIGURE 8.11** A "lap" (*colo*) of the Brazilian Candomblé goddess Oxum (SABA COLLECTION C028). The gold trim and aquatic shells of this porcelain set invoke this goddess.

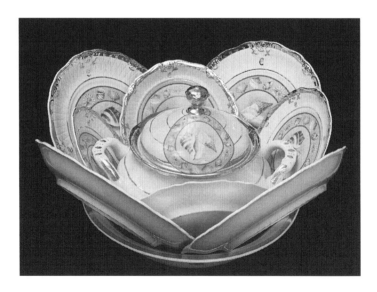

a well-maintained Yorùbá family, of followers in a well-maintained temple, and of money under capitalism.[2]

In the eighteenth and nineteenth centuries, those who managed the slave trade could supercharge the multiplication of the lineage by kidnapping more wives and by acquiring more bridewealth in the form of cowrie shells. The cowries and beads that African monarchs and merchants acquired in exchange for their mostly male human merchandise filled and empowered the womblike altars of the òrìṣà gods. Òrìṣà altars thereby recall an era of supercharged lineage reproduction, but one in which the stakes and the chance of losing were high. Under today's circumstances, the reportedly invisible self-multiplication of the stones and cowrie shells in an altar goes unexplained, but they seem to embody—in the sublimated imagery of the Atlantic slave trade—a prayer for more wealth in people. Stories told closer to the Atlantic coast are even more textured by that history: cowries are said to have been harvested from the Atlantic by fishermen who used human bodies as bait. Nowadays, the hope that the contents of altars with increase themselves seems to encode the òrìṣà priesthoods' hope for renewed prosperity and population growth. In the late 1980s, amid rising Muslim aggression and limited opportunities for education, Ìgbòho's possession priesthoods were doing little better than maintaining their populations. Matters might have improved since the establishment, in recent years, of a school for the òrìṣà-worshippers unwilling to convert as a precondition to attending school.

The succession of sacred marriages and births forms and extends a priestly lineage. To be a priest is to join a genealogy of priests whose gods have been made in the same conventionalized tradition of practice. Even if one lacks initiatic brothers and sisters, ritually born of the same initiatic parents, one invariably has the equivalent of ritual cousins. And, as in the West African Yorùbá kinship systems, not even kinship within the same generation rests on the assumption of equality. A person is outranked by a person initiated even a day earlier than herself. These always-vertical social relationships are, in principle, based upon hierarchy and unequal exchange between gods and people, among those who are consecrated to the same god, and among those who are initiated in the same network of temples. Moreover, no level of interpersonal conflict is allowed to undermine the respect and mutual obligation stipulated by these hierarchical spiritual relationships.

The Many Who Dance in Me

West African Yorùbá priests report that everyone is born containing a number of entities, which the person has prenatally selected, has been assigned, or has inherited in the Other world (Òrun). Hence, these natural denizens of the Other world are also closely associated with the inner world, as opposed to the visible, outer world:

- ··· *orí*, the inner head, or destiny, is made by the heavenly potter and chosen by, or assigned to, the person before birth;
- ··· *esè*, the spirit of the leg, which drives one's progress in life and enables the fulfillment of one's destiny;
- ··· *òrìṣà*, the gods;
- ··· and so forth.

Some Yorùbá people ("our mothers") reportedly also have in their bellies an *àjẹ́*, a creature that sometimes flies out at night and, in cooperation with its coven of fellow *àjẹ́*, consumes other people's life force. However, even the inner head (*orí inún*) of a normal person—the most essential aspect of the self—can travel outside his or her body. For example, one of the most benevolent of Yorùbá prayers beseeches, "May your mother's [inner] head follow you" (*Orí ìyá ẹ áá sìn é lọ*). Because they travel between this visible world and the invisible inner or Other world, the elements of the self are often analogized to winds, merpeople, or birds.

For example, many Brazilian Candomblé priests say that the *orixá* gods are—or that they resemble—"winds" (*ventos*).[3] And initial or incomplete moments of spirit possession are specifically called "taking in a *sea* breeze" (*tomar um barravento*). Strikingly, like gods and the ships of European merchants, such breezes from the sea are apparitions from one world actively taken into another. However, the Cuban parlance reminds us that these entities are not lacking in concreteness and solidity. At the moment of initiation, an actual being called a *bicho de santo*, or "holy beast," is surgically inserted into the head, to be surgically removed only at the time of the burial of its human vessel. Also at the time of death, the soup tureens containing the gods of the deceased are typically smashed and thrown into the river. Similarly, a calabash is smashed over the grave of a deceased West African Yorùbá possession priest.

Not only wind but also water dramatizes the dynamics of the vessel self. Other metonyms of the oceans further highlight the role of the Guinea Coast encounter in the making of the Afro-Atlantic self. The god of the sea, Olókun, is considered the inventor of beads. And, like the aquatic cowrie shell itself, fishlike beings seem to dramatize the shore-like sacred intersection of African and European worlds. Afro-Atlantic ichthyanthropic spirits amalgamate African images of the divine with images from the prows of European sailing ships, as well as a famous poster from a German "people show" (*Völkerschau*) during the 1880s about a "Hindoo" woman snake charmer (Drewal 2008: 36, 49–52; also SABA H003 and H004). In the SABA Collection, item J067 is Ghanaian movie poster depicting a Mami Wata, an aquatic goddess closely associated with the wealth flowing from trade with Europeans.

However, birds are the preeminent image of the Other/inner world, especially of beings who travel between worlds, such as *àjẹ́*. Even by themselves, feathers may express the same idea. These visual motifs are also found in the Abrahamic images of angels, who, like birds, have feathered wings (figure 8.12). Such foreign images are easily borrowed, indigenized, and resignified by Afro-Atlantic priests.

Birds appear on a range of Yorùbá-Atlantic spirited things—crowns, ceramic vessels, and staffs embodying the powers of healing. They can also embody a person's fate. West African Yorùbá royal crowns, staffs of personal fate (*ọ̀pá òsùn*) (figure 8.13 and in the SABA Collection D040 and D056), and staffs of the god Ọ̀sanyìn (*ọ̀pá Ọ̀sanyìn*, D062 and D063 in the SABA Collection) are the most famous examples. Ọ̀sanyìn staffs materialize the persuasive power of the priest or herbalist to bring our mothers (*àjẹ́*) into alignment with the client's goals, the priest and the prayer that he or she may succeed by enlisting the *ajẹ́* in an orderly power exchange much like a marriage. The priest or herbalist becomes a polygamous "husband" (*ọkọ*) to our mothers (e.g., Olupona 2011: 101, also 52). Standing in his or her front yard, the Ọ̀sanyìn staff advertises the herbalist priest's ability to enter into such a relationship with these powerful women for the benefit of the client. These bird-topped or -centered staffs must always remain upright, dramatizing the continuous alertness of the owner and his or her spirits, including the inner head. Indeed, the term *ọ̀pá òsùn* contains a prayerful pun: the phrase *ò sùn* means "does not rest or sleep" (figure 8.13).

A similar Brazilian staff stabilizes in another way. Oxalufã, the elder of the two most common avatars of the lord of purity, Oxalá, employs the *opaxorô* as a cane (figure 8.14). This god is so old that, when he possesses a priest, he walks around the sacred festival area of the temple (*barracão*) in a low crouch and, without his *opaxorô*, could hardly move forward at all. To Brazilians, the bird at the top of the staff is a dove and represents peace. The crown suggests his preeminent royalty, and emblems of the many gods to whom he is the father hang veil-like from the crown and from each umbrella-like canopy on the staff. These canopies recall the white cloth that covers his possession priest, underlining his seriousness and the respect one must show in his presence. The West African counterpart of Oxalá is called Ọbàtálá—usually translated as "The King of the White Cloth." This parlance also alludes to the caul, as this god is responsible for forming the fetus in the womb.

In sum, what might heuristically be called the Yorùbá-Atlantic fetish constructs each person as a vessel of *multiple* exogenous spirits, each of which

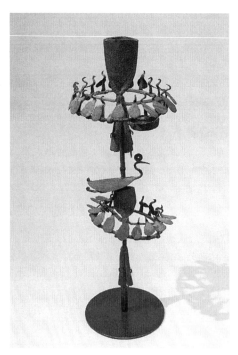

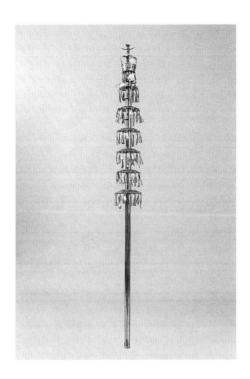

FIGURE 8.12 Roman Catholic effigy of Saint Michael the Archangel (SABA COLLECTION F020). Note his feathered wings, which contrast with the batlike wings of the African- or Moorish-looking devil. As spirits that similarly transit between this visible world and the Other or inner world, they both fly. This saint is associated or identified with several Afro-Atlantic gods, such as Ogou in Haiti.   **FIGURE 8.13** Yorùbá staff of fate (ọ̀pá òsùn, SABA COLLECTION D027). It embodies the long-term orderliness and stability of a person's life and must never be permitted to fall down, lest its owner succumb to misfortune. Such staffs usually feature one circle of small and often highly abstract birds surrounding a larger, more visibly birdlike image above them and at the center of that circle. But this unusually complex and vivid staff of fate underlines the same point: good fortune and progress in life depend upon bringing order to—rather than expunging or suppressing—the potentially conflicting and destructive forces, including but not limited to witchcraft (àjẹ́), that normally populate our lives. That the staff of fate can easily fall down dramatizes the constant threat of human failure, particularly because the social forces that make up the person and his or her surroundings are often in tension with each other and can fall out of balance. See also SABA COLLECTION D105, B078, and B089.   **FIGURE 8.14** Opaxorô (Brazilian Candomblé, SABA COLLECTION C001) by the late Mário Proença. This type of staff is used as a cane by the elderly god Oxalufã when he perambulates the festival space. The dove at the top of the staff resembles several types of West African Yorùbá sacred staffs (e.g., figure 8.13), but this bird is usually identified with the Christian high god. Oxalufã is syncretized with a particular Bahian apparition of Jesus Christ, Nosso Senhor do Bonfim. The staff was commissioned by Candomblé priest Amilton Sacramento Costa, who, for my benefit, forewent the opportunity to buy this rare and sought-after piece. Upon his first visit to me in the United States, Doté Amilton became alarmed when he did not immediately see it in a prominent place in my home. In fact, it was standing next to my bed, so it was the first and the last thing I saw every day. Both he and I understand that careful and sustained attention to the spirited things he has given me—including the Exu and the Exua that he made for me—reflects and embodies the depth of my commitment to him.

has been constructed or is potentially managed through the manipulation of a vessel filled with multifarious material things characterized by their foreignness, their mobility, and their history of exchange. Yet their iconography and their handling also anticipate threats to the fulfillment of the owner's destiny and well-being. Vessels are fragile and permeable to unwelcome forces.

As suggested by their aeolian, ichthyanthropic, or avian iconography, gods come and go, and the contents of vessel altars are not long stationary. They ebb and flow. Just as spirits can move in and out of the body, they can move in and out of the altar vessel. Indeed, a certain cyclical ebb and flow is necessary for the recharging of the god. Every week, every month of twenty-eight days, or every year, the vessel altar is emptied out and its contents re-animated by the gathered priests with life-giving fluids, typically including water from the body of water sacred to that god, herbal infusions, distilled spirits, perfume, or animal blood. These rituals mime the departure of the god for his or her foreign, extrasocial, or extraterrestrial abode, his or her renewal by the wild energies there, and his or her reempowered return to the consequently reempowered community of worshippers. Note that in this cosmology the West is cast not as "civilized" but as "wild." Media reports of rampant gun violence in the US confirm this conception.

Afro-Atlantic gods typically incarnate in multiple people and in a network of natural and manufactured things. In turn, one person usually hosts multiple gods and spirits. Yet relationships between spirits and their human hosts can expand, break down, or, when they are deleterious, be restricted. Both people and things can join or leave the body of the god. Another way of putting it is that people are slowly shifting configurations or assemblages of spirits and animated things, and gods are also ever-shifting configurations or assemblages of people, animals, plants, and animated things. So virtually every personal or community altar is covered with vessels intent on creating, stabilizing, and managing these dynamic configurations and assemblages, and, as circumstances change, modifying them appropriately.

Hence, histories of the gods focus on the making and breaking of relationships. For example, tales about the river goddess Yemoja in the town of Ìgbòho report that she came from that town but moved to Ṣakí to become a wife (ayaba) to the king there (figure 8.15). The two agreed that she would remain married to him as long as he never spoke ill of her large breasts and as long as she never spoke ill of his large testicles. But one day they argued, and he insulted her breasts, whereupon she insulted his testicles. She then put her water-carrying pot (orù) on her head and ran away from the palace, followed by a hostile crowd. By the time her pursuers reached her, she had vanished, leaving only her breasts or her orù pot (note this further instance of the tendency of West Africa òrìṣà priests to analogize women and their reproductively important body parts to vessels). And it is from her breasts or from her pot that the River Ògùn issued forth.[4]

Since then, her worship has involved a cycle of emptying and refilling the sacred water pots and calabash-altars in the palace shrine. In late August or early September, after the major harvest of corn and yams, the priests of Yemoja bring the calabash-altars out of the shrine room, spill them out onto a floormat, divine over them, and refresh them with an herbal infusion, sacrifices, songs, and prayers. Then the priests go to the river, offer food there, and retrieve water. The possession priestess known as the *arumi*, or "water carrier," carries the filled *orù* pot back from the river on her head, whereupon the entity animating the river also fills her head. The *arumi* becomes the goddess Yemoja. On the way back to the palace shrine room, the priestesses and their accompanying drummers call upon the monarch of the quarter, who has sponsored and funded the rituals. This ritual process annually re-energizes the shrine, the priesthood, the palace, and the town at large with the goddess's *àṣẹ*, or "sacred power and authority" (Matory [1994] 2005: 133–76). These rites simultaneously clarify the membership and hierarchy of the priesthood, as well as the nature of its power exchange with the monarchy.

In 2014, Ìyá Ọ̀ṣun Òṣogbo, Ìyá Ńlá from Kìsí, and Àǹtí Kẹ́hìndé from Ìṣẹ́yìn gathered together in the town of Ìṣẹ́yìn to "give birth to" (*bí*) my Yemoja Olówó Kan—"Yemoja-of-the-One-Cowry-Necklace" (see figure 8.15). Indeed, their own Yemojas are also said to have given birth to mine.

One reason is that my Yemoja's white-chalked calabash body contains ancient marine clamshells, cowries, and river stones drawn from their respective altars, just as their altars contain items inherited form the gods who gave birth to them. In parallel, I am a grandchild to the priestesses who gave birth to the Yemojas of Ìyá Ọ̀ṣun Òṣogbo, Ìyá Ńlá, and Àǹtí Kẹ́hìndé. In this way, my Yemoja gives material form to my membership in the ritual families of all three of these priestesses.

My beloved Yemoja-of-the-One-Cowry-Necklace also contains assorted items of worship (*ibọ*, literally "fed things") that were crafted especially for me. They embody my goddess's powers of defense, cooling, and beautification. Among these items are miniature manacles (*ṣẹ́kẹ́ṣẹ́kẹ́*), a sword (*idà*), a comb (*òòyà*), a fan (*abẹ̀bẹ̀*), tools for parting and plaiting hair (*gariga* and *ikótí*), an axe (*àáké*), and an arched nail to secure things in place (*ààbà*). Altogether, the three precious bead necklaces in the Onígbòho chief's palace altar of Yemoja in Ìgbòho boast a dozen chevron beads (in Yorùbá, *jìngbìnnín*), supplemented with long braided strands of white seed beads (*ṣẹṣẹ efun*); centuries ago, they likely cost a fortune in captives (Matory [1994] 2005: 163). Of equal antiquity,

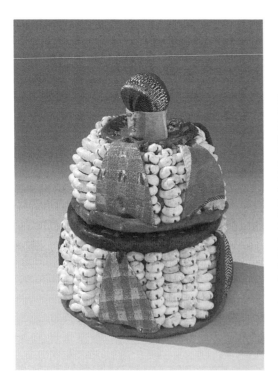

FIGURE 8.15 Ìyá Òṣun Òṣogbo Talabi Adedoyin Faniyi, chief priestess of the goddess Òṣun in the Nigerian city of Òṣogbo, posing beside my December 2016 altar honoring Yemọja (goddess of the River Ògùn; see also SABA COLLECTION D123), Ṣàngó (god of thunder and lightning), Ajé (goddess of maritime wealth), Ẹgbé (our heavenly mates), Àyàn (god of the drums), Ìbejì (the god of twins), and Orí (my divine inner head), as well as my wife, Bunmi's, Òṣun (goddess of the River Òṣun, *far left*). **FIGURE 8.16** *Ilé orí,* altar of the head (West African Yorùbá indigenous religion, SABA COLLECTION D022).

the one exceptional necklace that I gave to my Yemọja Olówó Kan comprises twenty-eight Venetian chevrons interspersed with eight lion claws (SABA 1030).

My devotion to Yemọja began in 1981, when I learned of her importance as a personified link among Nigeria, Brazil, Cuba, Trinidad, and more broadly, the Afro-Atlantic diaspora. Hoping to study her there, I first went to Nigerian in 1982 and, over the years, became friends with three elderly priestesses of Yemọja and a dozen priests of her son Ṣàngó in Ìgbòho, an ancient capital of the Ọ̀yọ́ Empire, and published my first book (Matory [1994] 2005) based upon my experiences there. For these reasons, the altar in figure 8.15 is laden with memories not only of my newer friend Ìyá Ọ̀sun Òṣogbo but also of my old friend, the late Yemọja priestess Ìyá Elégbo of Ìgbòho, and of the tears she shed during the 1989 festival procession as we visited the graves of her own late priestly foremothers. In the form of antique blue ṣ̀ẹgi beads from Ilé-Ifẹ̀, antique Venetian chevron beads, old marine shells, cowrie shells dull and thin with age, brass manillas, British colonial coins, bright-red sashes (ọ̀já ororo) handwoven from synthetic thread, Ajé's large incised pellet of kaolin (ẹfun) from Benin City (a non-Yorùbá capital of ancient transoceanic connections, which are embodied in its focal devotion to the sea god, Olókun), and Chinese-made yellow seed beads (oyindẹ) strung for the river goddess Ọ̀sun by Ìyá Ọ̀sun herself (SABA D008). This altar gives material form to my translocal connections with the present generation of Yemọja priests and with a dynasty of priests and priestesses who came before us. Ultimately, they also link us to a changing network of trading partners that probably preceded and certainly endured beyond the sixteenth- and seventeenth-century Afro-European encounter on the Guinea Coast.

The bottle of Gordon's gin on the altar illustrates the use of imported things to activate and celebrate deep and ancient connections among people. We use it to wash, feed, and salute Yemọja. Imported from Scotland, it is frequently used in Nigeria in prayers for longevity because, as long as it is protected from the open air, it never decays and for communion with the ancestors because Yorùbá elders have consumed it for generations. In naming ceremonies, this favorite of the ancestors is used to pray for the long life of newborns. A locally produced substitute, Seaman's schnapps, is equally acceptable for these purposes, but we could not find it in Durham. Along with the use of such European-style distillates, Yemọja's taste for hominy (ègbo) made from corn—a grain first domesticated in the Americas—underlines the great debt of what is usually called "Yoruba indigenous religion" (ẹsìn ìbílẹ̀) to the Triangular Trade.

In the Afro-Atlantic religions, packages, bundles, and leather containers often serve the same functions as pots. For example, figures 8.16 and 8.17 show a leather-brocade-and-cowrie-shell container of the sort used as a Yorùbá

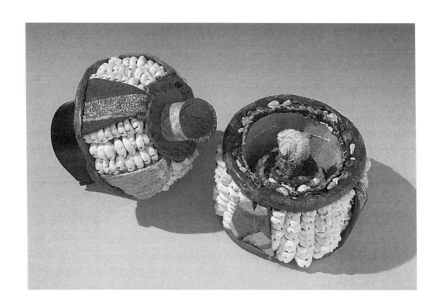

FIGURE 8.17 *Ilé orí* with *Ìborí* shown.

FIGURE 8.18 Doll for Òsanyìn, god of herbs (West African Yorùbá indigenous religion, SABA COLLECTION DO37). According to Ìyá Òsun Òsogbo, Talabi Adedoyin Faniyi, this finely beaded, mid-twentieth-century doll was probably an insignia of authority belonging to a high-ranking herbal healer and priestess of the god Òsanyìn. Its green and ochre color themes refer to leaves and earth. Stuffed with empowering substances and mimicking the priestess in appearance, this doll not only represents the power of the priestess but also imbues her with the power of her god.

altar of the head (*ilé orí*). This container mimics the physical, or outer, head (*orí òde*), while the abstractly anthropomorphic object within (*ìborí*) materializes the inner head—that is, the owner's fate and intelligence—in ritual operations to maximize his or her success in the world.

Afro-Atlantic technicians of the sacred also sometimes use conspicuously anthropomorphic figures to construct the beings who act in and around the body. For example, figure 8.18 shows an unusually elaborate sacred doll. This doll features a rich array of European glass and African stone beads, which, like the more conventional cowrie shells, commemorate the commercial and translocal constitution of the Yorùbá-Atlantic human being. The neat stringing and application of these tiny beads to the doll required considerable labor, skill, and time.

Such anthropomorphic figures are also designed as containers, as they normally feature hollow spaces filled with animating substances and then sealed or stitched closed as the creature is assembled and activated. The Òsanyìn doll (figure 8.18) is probably packed with consecrated substances that materialize this power. These made anthropomorphic beings are no less vessels than pots and humans are (see also figures 8.19 and 8.20).

A chiefly West-Central African variant on the theme of containment—found, for example, among Kongo and Yaka *nkisi* power objects—is the bundling and packing of things into the belly of an anthropomorphic figure (figure 8.21; see also SABA Collection E015), or the use of a cloth sack charged with consecrated substances as the base of the anthropomorphic figure (for Haitian examples inspired by this West-Central African variant, see plate 7 and SABA Collection A002, A063 through A066). The reliquary statue in figure 6.3 embodies the collective ancestors of a Kota family in what is now Gabon. Normally, its base would be a sack of the ancestors' bones. More often packets, bundles, and boxes, West-Central African altars and their American counterparts imply the made, compound, and vessel-like nature of personhood in an idiom slightly different from their Yorùbá-Atlantic counterparts and others in dialogue with the Guinea Coast.

In the Afro-Atlantic traditions, pots, calabashes, cauldrons, bottles, urns, soup tureens, bundles, figurines with fillable cavities, and other containers animated by a consecrated combination of material things are not only gods in their own right but also metaphors of the vessel-like nature of the human person. Hence, such containers are also machines for the deposition of beings in the human person that make him or her effective, prosperous, and safe. Such containers are also machines for the removal of improper beings that reduce the person's effectiveness, prosperity, and safety. For example, in Brazilian Candomblé, rough earthenware vessels known as *alguidares* are commonly used in rituals of expiation known as *ebós*. In these complex rites, animals,

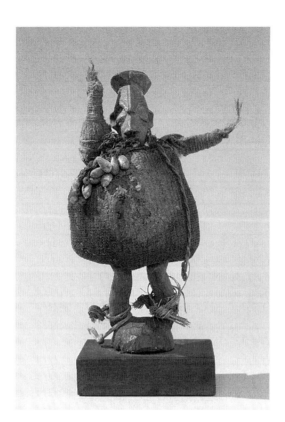

FIGURE 8.19 Elegguá, lord of the crossroads and of communication between humans and gods (Cuban Santería/Ocha, SABA COLLECTION B143, B145). An opening beneath him is stuffed and sealed with the substances that give him life and endow him with his specific powers. **FIGURE 8.20** Oché (Cuban Santería/Ocha, SABA COLLECTION B327). The substance of his life and of his specific competencies is deposited in a cavity in his head, beneath the double ax. **FIGURE 8.21** A Yaka *nkisi* god (West-Central Africa, SABA COLLECTION E003). See also SABA COLLECTION E015.

foods, cloth, twine, and other such substances are used to "cleanse" (*limpar*) the person by absorbing the malign beings and forces that have entered or bound him or her. Having absorbed these malign beings and forces, these items are immobilized and then deposited in the *alguidar* vessel, whereupon they are wrapped, carried to a place far away from the patient, and released where they are least likely to reenter the patient's body.

And while any given priest might describe a particular spirit or force as malign, such talk is highly situational. Any being or force might be perceived as acting harmfully, depending on whether the speaker has fulfilled all outstanding promises to the spirit and is therefore in his or her good graces, whether that spirit or force is present and active in an appropriate place, and whether he or she is acting there at an appropriate level. In general, each person hosts multiple spirits and is subject to multiple forces, and each such person must interact effectively not only with all of those spirits and forces but also with other people—each of whom is moved by his or her own equally idiosyncratic permutation of spirits and forces.

The Drums, Too, Are Alive

The cowrie-, bead-, and herb-filled vessels of the Afro-Atlantic religions are alive with the same spirits that fill people's heads. It is the drums that orchestrate the spirits' most dramatic arrivals into and departures from their human and nonhuman vessels. In order to do so, the drums themselves must be alive. If the chief metonym of Enlightenment ethics is a set of impersonal laws that limit everyone's potentially nefarious conduct in the same way, the chief metonym of Afro-Atlantic religious ethics is the dance, whereby people with diverse styles and mutually affecting inspirations interact intensively for each other's joy and progress. The measure of the success of a human life or of a festival for the gods is not the conformity of all to a fixed standard of behavior but the intensity of our interaction and the amplification of our cooperation and well-being.

So in most of the Afro-Atlantic religious traditions, drums, too, are animated with consecrated substances and thus with spirits that turn them into a type of people. Although each drum also embodies a being generic to its type of drum, each sacred drum must also be born, and, in many cases, it acquires a name of its own. Once animated, drums are fed like every other person or human-made being. In the West African Yorùbá and in the Afro-Cuban Santería/Ocha traditions, drums can literally speak. When beaten, they produce the same rhythms, stress patterns, and tonal patterns as human beings do in liturgical pronouncements, enabling insiders to understand the melodies and rhythms they produce as speech. Indeed, Afro-Atlantic sacred drums are often described as "the voices of the gods." Yet each is an animated being with a will of its own.

This family of Nigerian Yorùbá *bàtá* drums (figure 8.22) is animated by Àyàn, the *òrìṣà* of drumming. Illustrating the compound and concrete nature of such gods, Akìwọwọ and Font-Navarrete (2015: 38) explain, "Àyàn . . . can be understood as an integrated spiritual and sonic collective, which includes its disembodied voice and spiritual energy, its tangible musical and ritual vessels, and its drummers and devotees." In figure 8.22, from left to right are the *omele*, the *gúdúgúdú* (the father of the drum ensemble, also known as *Kútanyín*, or "It-Is-Death-That-Exposes-the-Teeth"), two *kúdi* drums, and the *ìyá ìlù* (the "mother," or chief, of the drum ensemble).

The set of Cuban *batá* drums in figure 8.23 was crafted by the highly respected master drummer Mililián Riverí Galís, popularly known as "Galí," of Santiago de Cuba. They are animated by an *oricha* known as Añá, who might be regarded as the ultimate, common progenitor of these particular drums. These drums are said to have been "born" from Galí's set of drums, just as his set of drums was "born" from those of Galí's godfather (*padrino*), Chachá, who according to Galí was the great ancestor of all *batá* drumming in the Cuban city of Matanzas. At the same time that a set of consecrated drums is "born," the owner and chief player of these drums is "born" to his new role as the consecrated player of these drums. Moreover, like the ensembles in figure 8.22 and plate 8, each ensemble of drums is described as a family (Akìwọwọ and Font-Navarrete 2015: 44, 45), but, once consecrated, it is also treated ritually as one compound person, and a high-ranking person at that.

Every drum ensemble is a female-headed household. The largest drum (in the center of figure 8.23) is called the *illá ilú*, or "mother drum," in the Yorùbá-related Lucumí language of Cuba. Ideally, each of the straps on the *illá ilú* to which the bells are attached is a belt that once belonged to a flesh-and-blood person, whose personal energy helps to empower the drum to do her work. The second-largest *batá* drum (*far right*) is the *itótele*, also known as *omelecó*, *ómele*, or *omelé*. The third-largest (*far left*) is the *ocóncolo*, or *oconcoló*.

The drums speak, and they do so as both a family and as a regiment. Each Cuban *batá* drum has a smaller head and a larger one, the larger being known as the *enu*, or "mouth," of the drum and the smaller one known as the *chachá*. Yet in some Cuban traditions, a metal ring (*agoya/agolla*) worn at the smaller head of a consecrated drum is regarded as the drum's mouth "for ritual purposes." This ring implies the drum's membership in an initiatic brotherhood akin to the Òyó-Yorùbá military brotherhoods that these drums accompanied

FIGURE 8.22 A family of Nigerian Yorùbá *bàtá* drums (SABA COLLECTION D017).

during nineteenth-century warfare and in caravan processions during that time (Marcuzzi 2013).

The drums eat together, too. They are normally fed each time they are played. And together they produce offspring. The smallest drum in figure 8.23 (*foreground*) is called the *elecotó*. It is not played but will be held under the arm or around the neck of a novice drummer during his initiation, when he is first presented to a family of consecrated drums (*tambores de fundamento*) and to the priestly community (Akìwọwọ and Font-Navarrete 2015: 44). Elecotó will also be used in the birth of other drums.

Although they have not been consecrated as *tambores de fundamento*, the *batá* drums in Duke University's SABA Collection were "born" just like any others. The maker of these drums, Galí, told me that he ritually prepared them before releasing them to me, and he directed me to undergo a secret swearing in (*juramiento*) authorizing me to play *batá* drums in general and to handle these drums in particular. At Cabildo Rosa Torres/Changobumí, the oldest Ocha temple in the eastern Cuban city of Santiago de Cuba, I underwent the *juramiento* under Galí's sponsorship, whereupon he became my ritual drumming godfather.

However, my confusion over the nature of this ritual preparation caused some tension between my friend and Duke University colleague David Font-

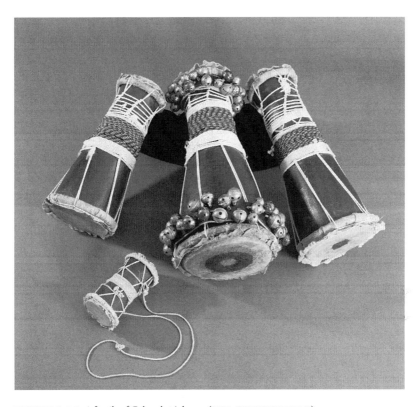

FIGURE 8.23 A family of Cuban *batá* drums (SABA COLLECTION B351).

Navarrete and me. Based on Galí's information that these drums had been ritually prepared and on the ritual that I had undergone, I mistakenly told David that the drums had been consecrated, making them *tambores de funda-mento* (or "consecrated drums").

David, who is an Añá priest, told me that the only such consecrated *batá* drums that are normally in collections, rather than being played by communities, are those that have been impounded by the police (David Font-Navarrete, personal communication, October 28, 2015).[5] Ultimately, I had intended these drums for inclusion in the SABA Collection, but I reassured David that, far from being prisoners, all of the animated things in the SABA Collection are used ritually, fed, and kept alive by the visiting priests who come to campus and by the best ritual care that I am able to provide (personal communication, December 21, 2015). For example, pursuant to the most faithful possible fulfillment of Galí's instructions, I had gone to great lengths to acquire fine sleigh bells and secondhand belts for the drums that he had sired. Moreover, I had every intention for these *batá* drums to take part in future rituals held at Duke in conjunction with my course and lecture series on the Afro-Atlantic religions.

However, David explained to me that a consecrated *batá* drum ensemble is, in itself, a high-ranking and ritually well appointed priest subject to the unique protocols of its membership in a specific drumming dynasty.

Beyond a generic name for each drum, indicating its size, shape, and role in the ensemble, each family of drums bears a single, overarching personality and a collective proper, personal name, such as "Añá Cholá"—which appears to mean, in the Lucumí liturgical language of Santería/Ocha, "The Spirit of the Drum Creates Honor." Like West African Yorùbá names, the consecration names of drum ensembles and the initiatic names of priests have literal meanings related to the circumstances of their birth and to the hopes of the parents for the child or, in the Cuban case, of the godparents for the godchild. Like a novice during her initiation, a *batá* drum ensemble during the process of consecration undergoes a divinatory reading of its fate (called the *itá*), which also indicates the ensemble's taboos and the requirements of its proper use and handling. In Gali's *rama*, or dynasty, of drummers, the *itá* of the drums must be read specifically by a *babalao* diviner.

Though it is optional for most human novices to have it, every family of consecrated *batá* drums must possess its own "hand of Ifá," the initial order of consecration to the divination god Ifá and the beaded bracelet that signifies and gives material form to that consecration. Also like an initiated priest, a consecrated family of *batá* drums has an Echú (that is, the Ifá-related counterpart of the trickster and messenger god Elegguá) and an *osun*, or staff of fate, which must never fall over. The *osun* staff of a set of drums must be as tall as the mother drum is long, just as the *osun* staff of senior priest or a *babalao*—a high-ranking type of priest, indeed—must be as tall as he (SABA Collection B296; my own *osun*, resembling SABA Collection B089, is only about ten inches tall. Cf. the Nigerian *ọ̀pá òsùn* in figure 8.13.) The bathing of drums and priests in consecrated herbal baths is similarly critical. This preparation is governed by the lord of herbs, Osain. And, like a priest, each family of drums also possesses its own Osain, a consecrated gourd that is the initiand's—in this case, the drum ensemble's—god of herbs.

Though David had previously consented to affix the bells to the straps for me, once the controversy over the drums' ritual status arose, he clarified that he could not touch the drums themselves, as he was not part of Gali's initiatic dynasty, did not know its rules, and could not violate the standards of conduct required by the spirit of his drums' and his own drumming dynasty.

I doubt the existence of ghostly, immaterial spirits—whether in material things or in people. So I continually question my Durkheimian conclusion that these consecrated material things apotheosize human relationships. Perhaps it imposes an exogenous cultural model on the Afro-Atlantic religions. Spontaneously, though, David's words reassured me that I am on the right track. Although there is no doubt in his mind about the aliveness of a family of drums, he, too, regards the proper treatment of a drum ensemble as a metaphor and a metonym of proper participation in a drumming dynasty. Cuban *batá* traditions and practices vary slightly from one dynasty (*rama*) of drummers to the next. Moreover, acknowledging the legitimacy of a family of drums is like acknowledging the legitimacy of a human priest's ordination and, therefore, of a person's or drum's legitimate membership in the priesthood. However, for him, the Durkheimian hypothesis about the nature of gods by no means demands a demystification of these animated things.

He said that he does believe in the existence and the power of immaterial, ghostly beings who can benefit you or, if you deliberately violate their ritual prescriptions, cause you equal and opposite harm. And he does believe that an immaterial, ghostly spirit occupies drums and the drummers. He also believes that if he violates its precepts, this ghostly being can (like other spirits and gods) harm him in the same material ways that it will reward him for keeping his ritual commitments to it. He adds the caveat that the actor's intentions matter, and that my demonstrable efforts to care for these and the other living things in the collection will protect me from harm. In fact, I add, my good fortune in life so far suggests that they appreciate my efforts.

However, his worries about handling my drums resulted not from the view that the immaterial, ghostly spirit in *my* drums could harm him but that the spirit in *his own* drums would harm him. His reasoning rests firmly on the principle that his community is delineated by shared standards in the treatment of these animated things and that those things are animated precisely by the concerted nature of their treatment by people. He is accountable to the community of Cuban drums and drummers as a whole. His level of accountability does not require total, blind obedience to the elders, but, before he acts, he is obligated to consider carefully what the elders would do under similar circumstances. His giving legitimacy to a set of drums that he cannot be sure is legitimate would impugn his reputation in this highly competitive community. Moreover, if he applies any given ritual procedure to these drums, there would be a sacred expectation for this procedure to continue in the future, forever altering the nature of these drums and disrupting the community indexed by the standards and procedures of the drumming community from which these particular drums were born. Yet David's preeminent duty is to the dynasty that gave birth to him as a drummer and therefore to the genealogical spirit residing in him and in his drums. This is the spirit to which he is most accountable and vulnerable should he violate the precepts given by his dynasty's elders and materialized in his drums (Font-Navarrete, personal communication, January 15, 2016).

For David, Añá is real but is also inextricable from the communities assembled by the god's oaths, precepts, and performance. Moreover, we both disagree with the implication of Marx's and Durkheim's shared premise that Afro-Atlantic priests are ignorant of the social source of the gods' value and agency. For David, the gods' power, their will, and their presence in their physical vessels are of a piece with the conscious choice of the worshipper to enact and uphold the reality of the god (see also Barber 1981 regarding a virtually identical West African Yorùbá conception). The power and the will of the god to punish a worshipper for his or her infractions depends on the consciousness and will with which the worshipper has agreed to obey the rules and on the intentionality of the worshipper's violation.

Our discussions also helped me to understand better the continual vacillation of most Afro-Atlantic priests between the conventional Afro-Atlantic parlance that human beings "make" gods and, for example, Babá Murah's insistence, in the midst of our debates, that gods are self-existent. David confirmed that one source of his and some other priests' discomfort in avowing the human-madeness of the Afro-Atlantic gods is the fear of the post-Enlightenment accusation that these gods and their worshippers are manipulative. However, David and I also agree about the far greater manipulation potentiated by the premise at the heart of the Abrahamic religions: that the social rules, preferences, and interpretations propagated by Jewish, Christian, and Muslim leaders originate from an entity beyond human comprehension and legitimate scrutiny (personal communication, January 15, 2016).

It is clear, then, how seriously many Afro-Atlantic priests take both the personhood of these spirited things and the social bonds that are inherent in them. And that seriousness is in no way diminished by their conventional acknowledgment that these spirited things are human made, and that their endurance and their effectiveness in our lives flow from and require collective human effort.

The Afro-Atlantic sense that spirited things derive their value and agency from the social relationships they embody is perhaps most explicit and least ambiguous in the Cuban men's secret society known as Abakuá.[6] The most important drums in the Afro-Cuban Abakuá tradition give material form to the role of particular office-holders in the actor-network of gods, people, and things (plate 8). In a sense, they dramatize the trance-free possession of the officeholder and dancer and of his consecrated regalia by the spirit of his office.

The Abakuá secret society is historically related not to the peoples now known as "Yorùbá" but to the multiethnic Ékpè, or "Leopard," society of the

Cross River region, in what is now southeastern Nigeria and southwestern Cameroon. Ékpè was the sort of trade cartel that must have frustrated European traders on the sixteenth- and seventeenth-century Guinea Coast. This men's initiatic society was brought to Cuba during the first half of the nineteenth century by enslaved Efik and Ibibio people, who employed it as a sort of labor union and mutual aid society in the port cities of the provinces of Havana and Matanzas. In Cuba, Abakuá members are known alternately as *ñáñigos* (see SABA Collection B030) and as "the leopard men" (*los hombres leopardos*). Hence the artificial spotted cat skin on the largest drum in plate 8. In Abakuá sacred performances, a drum, the associated masquerade, and the leopard man dancing that masquerade are all, in a sense, the same person. Each scepter bears a similar relationship to a masquerade and to a dancing officeholder.

The maker and animator of these drums and staffs is Manuel Martínez Navarro. Best known as "Manolo Escaparate," he is a *babalao* diviner and the leader (*nasakó*) of the Isún Efó chapter of Abakuá in Havana. The chapter's name, La Cara de la Brujería Abakuá, means "The Face of Abakuá Sorcery." He and his assistant Elier Macías del Valle told me, "Men speak of the drums as though they were people. Yes, each drum is a person who holds an office, or a responsibility, in the religion." (*Hablan los hombres de los tambores como si fueran personas. Sí, cada tambor es una persona que tiene cargo en la religión*; personal communication, July 10, 2014.) Like Jacob Olupọna in his description of Ọbàtálá and his "icons" (2011: 155; also see below), Elier and Manolo speak to me in the subjunctive about the personhood of the drums, as though they are trying to bridge the gap between Enlightenment and Afro-Atlantic ontologies. But nothing else in their conduct or parlance reveals any doubt that the spirited things in their midst are alive.

In plate 8, from left to right, are (1) Empegó (sometimes spelled "Mpegó"), (2) Mosongo, (3) Embácara, (4) Encrícamo, (5) Eribó (6) Illamba, (7) Mocongo, and (8) Ecueñón. The largest drum, Eribó (*center*), is also known as "Sesé Eribó" or "Obón-Entuí." Manolo translates this last name as "the Mother of Abakuá." During the sacred processions of Abakuá, such drums are carried side by side in a consistent order, with the largest drum on the right.[7] Empegó and Ecueñón are normally turned a bit toward each other in order to "protect the secret" (*guardar el secreto*). Like a "bishop" or the "pope," say Manolo and Elier, Eribó wears a crown, the cross at the top—concealed in this photo—being a further reference to his high rank in this religion. (In analogizing Eribó to male officials of the Catholic Church, Manolo and Elier seem, again, to be bridging rival ontologies. In the Afro-Atlantic traditions, the lead drum is almost always identified as the "mother.") Like most other important Afro-Atlantic rituals, Abakuá processions are accompanied by drumming, but these most sacred, plumed drums are not beaten musically. The music is provided by a wooden bell known as Ecón and consecrated drums known as Bíapa, Oró-Apá, Cuchillerma, and Bongo-Enchemi. While Bíapa, Oró-Apá, and Cuchillerma play fixed rhythms, Bongo-Enchemi improvises.

Both the crown with its cross and the chalice shape of the illustrated Eribó drum—like the official drum of Manolo's chapter—mark its makers as members of a "white" chapter of the Abakuá society: their lineage originated from the controversial but strategic admission of whites to this mutual-aid society in the mid-nineteenth century (Miller 2009). According to Miller, whites used Abakuá to guarantee the secrecy of coconspirators in the resistance to Spanish imperial rule. These gorgeous "fetishes" are anything but capriciously found and arbitrary in the authority they express. They were born at the intersection of semiotic histories, political initiatives, and roles in capitalist commerce. They are finely crafted from industrially manufactured and imported rope, velvet, artificial jaguar and ocelot skins, tacks, beads, cowries, glue, salvaged sheet metal, and lathe-turned wood, as well as the skin of the goat and the feathers of the roosters whose blood gave them life. All of the raw materials entered this assemblage through purchase, gift giving, and a highly specialized division of artistic and priestly labor. Under the dire conditions of Cuba in the "special period" since the loss of Soviet subsidies, these spirited things are an extraordinary testament to Manolo's ingenuity and to the heterogeneity of his social connections near and far.

Like the gods of Haitian Vodou, who are invoked with *vèvè* drawings, each type of drum in an Abakuá drum ensemble has its own named "signature" (*firma*), which is inscribed on the front. It is also the signature of the officeholder corresponding to that drum. Each of the four meticulously assembled dusterlike rooster-feather staffs (*muñones*, *isúes*, or *plumeros*) on Eribó corresponds to and embodies one of the four ranking offices (*plazas*, or *títulos*) in the Abakuá chapter that normally owns it. And each one has a signature of its own. According to Manolo and Elier, the cowries adorning Eribó represent wealth because they were once money. Eribó contains within its resonating chamber several empowering items: a further cowrie shell, an amulet (*resguardo*), and several seeds, including *quita maldición* and *carolina*.

Manolo tells me that each of these feathered staffs, like those on the other drums, took four months to make. He harvests the feathers from the beautifully glistening and multicolored sacrificial roosters that he himself raises in the rear courtyard of his house. Then he meticulously secures thousands of tiny feather bouquets with thread, attaches them to a wooden rod, and upholsters the hilt of this staff with leopard-patterned cloth and the signature appropriate to it. These bantams also appear to be one source of the blood with which these sacred drums are fed. Goats are another.

Eribó's own special *muñón* (5a) is called Isué—its own special pope- and bishoplike status marked by the peacock feather on its head—and it bears the same signature as Eribó. Although multiple *muñones* remain with Eribó during the processions of other chapters, as depicted in a number of publications (e.g., Thompson 1983: 258, plate 157), Elier told me, perhaps describing an idiosyncrasy of his chapter, that only this Isué feathered staff remains with Eribó during processions. The other feathered staffs—identified clockwise around the drum—are (5b) Illamba ("owner of the sacred voice" or "the voice of Abakuá"), (5c) Isuécue ("Iyamba's assistant" or "the representation of Sikán, the secret of Abakuá"), and (5d) Mocongo, or Mongongo ("the chief of the tribe"). According to Elier, these feathered staffs are carried by dancers without drums. Also borne or danced during processions, the scepters (*bastones*), from left to right, are (2) Mosongo, (3) Embácara, (6) Illamba, and (7) Mocongo. Each feathered staff and each scepter has a "signature." Note that Illamba is embodied in both a feather brush and a scepter bearing the same "signature," as is Mongongo (Elier, personal communication, July 10, 2015; Manolo, personal communication, July 11, 2015).

Each of these plumed drums plays a specific and important role in the ceremonies of the initiatic society. For example, Encrícamo "is responsible for bringing out the *íremes*, or sacred masquerades" (*es encargado de sacar a los íremes*—see SABA Collection B030). Empegó "opens the meetings" and "opens the ceremonies of Abakuá" (*es él que dá inicio a la religión; le dá abertura al inicio del plante de Abakuá, el inicio de la ceremonia*). He is "the drum of order" (*el tambor del orden*) and is struck (slow-slow-quick-quick) to begin and end the ceremonies of the chapter. Three hits on Ecueñón is a call for silence, but Ecueñon is also "the executioner for the religion" (*el verdugo de la religión*). He is responsible for the sacrifices (*es encargado de los sacrificios*): it is he who "kills the animals for Ekpé [Abakuá]" (*mata los animales para Ekpé*) (Manuel Martínez Navarro, personal communication, July 11, 2014). Manolo was not speaking the language of post-Enlightenment ontology: he did not say that this drum is the symbol of the authority of the man who sacrifices the animals. Drum, masquerade, and sacrificer are one organic subject.

Elier holds the office of Encoro in the Isún Efó chapter, also making him the dancer of the masquerade called Encoro, which, he brags, is "the keeper of the greatest number of secrets" (*el íreme que más secretos guarda*). Elier also keeps and takes care of the chapter's own Eribó drum. Thus, during ritual processions it is also his Encoro masquerade that dances in front of Eribó. When the Encoro masquerade rises, the Eribó drum must rise (i.e., the drum's bearer must lift it up); when Encoro crouches to the ground, Eribó must do so (i.e., Eribó's bearer must lower that drum), as well. There are between ten and twenty masquerades in each procession. But only two are followed by the living, sacred drums—Encoro, who is followed by Eribó, and Eribangandó, who is followed by Encrícamo.

In the Afro-Atlantic religions, most other drums are beaten, and, at the height of ritual intensity, they induce trance-possession—that is, spirit possession that displaces the consciousness of the medium. In their ensembles of three to six drums, along with gongs and beaded gourds, Afro-Atlantic sacred drums normally play polyrhythms, and the dancer, with his or her steps and other body-part isolations, selectively mimics or syncopates over these polyrhythms. In the multiplicity of their coincident rhythms, the drums reflect the heterogeneity of personal rhythms in society and of the multifarious beings in each dancer's head (see also Chernoff 1979; Brown 1987). With artful repetition, surprising turns, feints suggesting the loss of balance, and dramatic pauses, the dancer seems to mime the ego's improvisatory management of his or her inner heterogeneity and the conflicting expectations of the communities of which she is a part. In turn, the drummers respond to the dancer's improvisations, similarly miming the role of each person's improvisations on the social order as a whole. Executed by lifelong insiders to these traditions of self making, even the most basic of these existential performances are breathtaking in their stamina, drama, and poise. The most locally admired of performances are so complex in their violation of the 4/4 expectations of my R&B, funk, and even reggae musical upbringing that, at times, I simply do not understand them. They are so polyrhythmic and layered with syncopation upon syncopation that they exceed the term "syncopated." It is often difficult for me, as a spectator, to identify the fundamental beat.

John Miller Chernoff (1979) identifies this embodied logic of music and dance as the most dramatic illustration of a broader emic representation and ethics of social interaction in the West African societies that practice these forms of polyrhythmic drumming. Karen McCarthy Brown (1987) reads Haitian and other African-inspired forms of spirit possession as further illustrations of a sophisticated embodied personality theory, social psychology, and morality.

Unexamined, Marx's parodic use of African spirited things blinds us to the complexity of Afro-Atlantic social ideals without clearly adding to our understanding of how most Europeans assign value and agency to things. Instead, he uses stereotypes about Africans to show Europeans how different they should be from those stereotypes. By Afro-Atlantic standards, Freud's decentering of the self was at least a baby step in the direction of elucidating the complexities of human will and consciousness. Of course, the ego is not in control, but there are far more beings animating a person than the id, the ego, and the superego. And the interaction among them is not simply a struggle between the ego and the superego to control the id. The operation of the compound self is more like a dance or a dialogue that extends a history of ancestral dialogues and overlaps with the dances or dialogues that constitute one's contemporaries.

Our gods are intimate parts of us, but they do not dominate us except with our consent. In support of this point, Candomblé priest Amilton Costa contests the assumption, widespread among the lay admirers of his religion, that a person's personality duplicates the mythic personality of his or her tutelary god (*o dono da cabeça dele/a*). Rather, a person's character emerges from a lifelong pattern of choices to follow or to resist one's received disposition, the result of which is often an outward personality that is the opposite of the god's reputed character. David Font-Navarrete added that one's ancestors play a similarly nondeterminative role in one's character, and that one's ritual family is often the setting in which a person replays his or her relationship with birth parents and siblings and then makes adult choices about whether and how the personal conduct trained initially by those familial relationships needs to change (Font-Navarrete, personal communication, April 16, 2016).

Afro-Atlantic ritual comprehends the beings who make up the self not as idiosyncratic like the ideal US American bourgeois individual but as socially produced personifications of the dilemmas experienced by people with shared ancestral histories and in similar social roles. Spirit possession constructs and draws out these personified dilemmas for collective recognition and for recalibration to current circumstances. Among these current circumstances are the entry of people from different cultural and historically backgrounds into the religion and, just as often, adversarial attacks by the partisans of neighboring fetishes.

The height of this public recognition and calibration of compound selves is the festivals of spirit possession, in which drumming and singing coordinate the public manifestations of related spirits in multiple people. In the dialogue between the drums and the dancers, there is usually a contest of wills. The lead drummer repeatedly uses "breaks" (Thompson 1983) in the music's established metarhythm to destabilize the ego control of the dancer, while the singer, in many of these traditions, insults the god (for example, in Santería/Ocha, with songs called *puyas*), provoking the divinity to abandon his or her aloofness and fully manifest him- or herself in the body of the dancer. As a partner to the Candomblé drums in calling the gods to mount the priestesses and priests in the Ilê Axé Opô Afonjá temple in Salvador da Bahia, Brazil, one drummer friend of mine called his fellow drummers to arms at the start of a ceremony by shouting, "Let's go kill some people!" (*Vamos matar gente!*) Of course, he was not speaking of a literal homicide but of so totally unbalancing the dancers that they would lose all semblance of ego control, giving way to the will of the gods and their rhythmic voices. The aggression in his words, as in Freud's, revealed his own inner struggle. Unlike most drummers, he had felt the "sea breeze" (*barravento*), making him vulnerable to the accusation that he was a *bicha*, or a sexually penetrable male (see Matory 2005: 188–223).

The Madeness of Gods and Other People

The question of whether the Afro-Atlantic gods are human-made arises in the context of an intergenerational and intercultural frisson. But the same can be said of the Afro-Atlantic gods themselves. The answers to this question emerge from intergroup rivalry and intragroup ambivalence. At this generational and cultural crossroads, the Afro-Atlantic priests are anything but the exemplars of unawareness, projection, and befuddlement that the theorists of the fetish have made them into. Marx's fundamental concern was to criticize forms of European social life that turn people into objects and things into subjects (Michael Hardt, personal communication, March 2017). To him, fetishism was the false transfer of agency from people to commodities and the denial of European workers' preeminent role in creating the value of those things. Compared to the Afro-Atlantic priests, Marx is shockingly non-dialectical in his perception of the reciprocal making of people and things.

Dueling Ontologies

For the Afro-Atlantic priests and for me, the distinction between subjects and objects is situational and far from coterminous with the difference between people and things. For example, at the simplest and most obvious level, when I love my child, teach my student, or pay taxes to the government, my child, my student, and my government are the objects of my actions and I the subject of the action. Moreover, the oblong conference table around which I teach my class makes my students and me feel certain things and inclines us to behave in certain ways. It embodies a set of relations of semiequality between my students and me, enabling all of them to see and to address each other and me in a way that rows of chairs facing a lectern do not. In this way, the table is a subject doing something to us and we are the objects of its action. In removing my litter and wiping up spills from it, I demonstrate my respect for and membership in the community that shares it. My inner impulse to do so at the end of my classes is powerful, almost involuntary, like the guilt that I feel when I eat more than my share of a collective meal.

What may seem to many of my readers the weakness and nongeneralizability of this example simply illustrates the transience of US American bourgeois networks, in which, for example, the house that is one's home is likely to be sold or rented to someone else in one's lifetime. Imagine, on the other hand, physical things that have been invested with generations of accumulated meaning, affect, memory, and traditions of mutual obligations related to their shared use. Such accumulated psychic and social power can affect a person's thoughts, feelings, and sensory perceptions in a way that may be unimaginable for most nonreligious US Americans, unless, for example, military experience connects them in this way to the US flag or regional shame and pride connect them in this way to the Confederate flag. Even some US Americans are similarly moved by the books of Marx and Freud. Similarly, intense rituals like Afro-Atlantic religious initiations can quickly establish powerful relationships between things and people, thus powerfully affecting the relationships among the people themselves.

For me, the problem lies not in treating people as objects or things as subjects but in ignoring the potential subjectivity of *anything* around us. To many people, the greatest crime of Western capitalism lies in its nearly total objectification of the earth, its failure to consider that we belong to it rather than it to us, that our stripping it of saleable resources for short-term profit does and will continue to harm us. Not only can things do things to people, but the processes of subjectification and objectification are dialectical. For example, when the students in my spring 2017 "University as a Culture" course became convinced that I really wanted to hear their voices, they proposed that we rearrange the rows of desk-chairs in that classroom to form a circle. They volunteered to do so before each class session and, out of respect for the wider community of users, to return the desk-chairs to their original grid pattern afterwards. In doing so, they have recognized their power to rearrange the desk-chairs and the power of the desk-chairs, as they arrange them, to transform our interaction. The fatal flaw in the post-Enlightenment West's and Marx's aspiration to a sharp, humanist separation of human subjects from ostensibly nonhuman objects is the denial of the subjectivity of the things around us, such as the earth, as though human beings and a few species of domestic animal are the only actors and the only subjects with rights that legitimately limit our own individual claims. This aspiration also tends to mask the dependence of the erstwhile human subject on other humans and the power of subordinates to drive the behavior of their social superiors.

The Afro-Atlantic positions that I have been able to discern are dialectically related to Western humanism and Abrahamic monotheism, but they also offer distinct lessons. In agreement with Marx, much Yorùbá-Atlantic parlance and ritual strongly imply that it is people who make gods. Yet the Marxist critic of fetishism will also find in some Afro-Atlantic rituals and priestly pronouncements evidence for a critique of these religions, such as the denial by some Afro-Atlantic priests that people make their gods. This seeming contradiction between avowal and denial may involve a defensive reaction to Christian and Muslim criticism. But it also may reveal a dialectical ontology at the heart of Yorùbá language and of orisha-worship generally. In a way that is difficult to understand within conventionally Western linguistic and theological frames, Yorùbá gods and people, like erstwhile subjects and objects generally in the Yorùbá grammar of experience, are assumed to make each other reciprocally.

Jacob Olupona's account of an *òrìṣà* procession illustrates this apparent internal contradiction:

> The next phase [of the festival for the god of purity Ọbàtálá and his wife Yemòó] was to *bring the deities into the temple* and to place them in their shrines. . . . To prevent the frequent theft *of icons of the Yorùbá deities,* [the] *representations of Ọbàtálá and Yemòó* were kept in the National Museum. . . . In the late afternoon, a number of young men holding àtòrì (striped canes) set out for the National Museum, *where the Ọbàtálá and Yemòó icons "live" (are safeguarded),* to bring them to their Ìdìta Ilé home. . . . As these men walked toward the palace, they gestured at onlookers to go indoors to avoid exposing themselves to the danger of *beholding the deities with the naked eye.* Passersby who were caught unawares covered their faces. In the museum, two men collected the *two icons* already wrapped

in cloths, and the party headed back to the temple. This time the warning shout was louder. A few men preceded the party, clearing the way and warning onlookers. As I was later told, the convoy had cast charms on the road (*wón ti ró ònà*) *to prevent evildoers from neutralizing the power of the god and goddess*. As they proceeded toward the palace, the young men uttered threats of sudden death to those who defied their warnings to keep indoors. (Olupona 2011: 155, italics mine)

In the culturally hybrid context of the marriage of convenience between òrìṣà religion and the Ilé-Ifè branch of the Nigerian National Museum, Olupona understandably wavers between describing the painted stone sculptures at the center of this ancient priesthood as "representations" and "icons," on the one hand, and as "the deities" and "the god and the goddess," on the other. It is not clear whether he vacillates between the vocabularies of two radically different ontologies because his priestly companions did so or because the confusing differences between the ontologies of the priests and of his anticipated readership were beyond the scope of his argument.

This account can be read for evidence of the importance of material things as loci of debate not only over real value and agency but also over proper social conduct. The physical icons described by Olupona bridge the contrasting roles of Ọbàtálá in the state museum and in the priestly procession, as well as the contrasting perceptions of òrìṣà priestly families and of the Pentecostals competing for influence in the royal palace of Ilé-Ifè. This case of rivalry between perspectives demonstrates the utility of the term "fetish," calling attention to the animation of socially important things by conflicting value codes, including the Janus-faced ambivalence of even their most devoted worshippers. Ọbàtálá and Yemòó share with the putatively transcendent gods of Christianity and Islam both the bold claim that they can strike dead those who offend them and the reality made patently obvious by daily episodes of Islamic and Christian terrorism that it is people who carry out the vast majority of punishments for the violation of their gods' taboos. These devotees of Ọbàtálá and Yemòó simultaneously reveal the human-enforced authority and the human-induced vulnerability of the gods. Such authority and vulnerability have also been made evident each time Romans, Christians, or Muslims destroyed or reconsecrated the temples of their enemies and met with successful or failed resistance. Iconoclasm is no less concerned with the power of sacred material things than iconophilia is (Latour 2010).

At such cultural and commercial crossroads, there is much to be misunderstood and debated, including the quantitative value of things, the nature of people's responsibilities to each other, and the distribution of agency, or credit, among people and things. The divergent ways in which different languages represent feelings further illustrate how value conflicts animate the so-called fetish. For example, in Yorùbá, bodily states and feelings are subjectified and externalized, and the verb for experiencing a feeling is usually transitive. For example, cold or heat "grabs" (*mú*) a person. Similarly, hunger "strikes/kills" (*pa*) a person, thirst "dries" (*gbẹ*) a person, longings (such as missing home) "hit" (*sọ*) a person, and pride in one's beauty or wealth can "mount" (*gùn*) a person, just as a god can (see also Lienhardt 1961 on the Dinka). In Yorùbá, each of these bodily experiences is a reciprocal interaction between the person and an agent that cannot act—or, therefore, exist— without its grammatical or its sentient object.

Linguistically, Yorùbá constructions of human feeling differ sharply from their semantic counterparts in English and Mandarin Chinese with respect to where they place the boundary between the self and world, as well as who is accorded the responsibility for feelings.[1] On the one hand, in English and Mandarin, it makes sense to say, "*It* is cold," which means something very different from "I am cold." By distinguishing between the two, we English speakers avow faith in the idea that temperature exists independently of how people experience it. Indeed, the variable artificially isolated by thermometers has long convinced me of the possibly absurd view that the "cold" is self-existent. On the other hand, to my wife, Bunmi, this distinction makes no sense. In her Yorùbá manner of speaking and thinking, to speak of the cold being self-existent is as absurd as speaking of "hunger" as self-existent. It seems that, for many an *òrìṣà*-worshipper, it may be equally absurd to speak of a god as though she or he were self-sufficient. Our difference of opinion is food for thought about what is culture specific not only about the phenomenology of gods specifically but also about the phenomenology of experience generally. The reality of the *òrìṣà* rests at least partly on what Yorùbá speakers assume—no more or less empirically than English speakers—about the phenomenal structure of the interaction between interior and exterior realities in the making of experience, which also has implications for how people of different cultures assign agency to people and things more generally.

Expressions of feeling in German and the Romance languages call attention to further conceptual possibilities. For example, like Yorùbá speakers, German speakers appear not to distinguish emphatically between *my* being cold and the general, perspective-neutral claim that "*it* is cold." In German, the statement that *it* is cold must also name the *perspective* from which the observation has been made: that is, for example, "it is cold *to me*" (*mir ist kalt*). Like an English speaker, a Portuguese speaker can name coldness as a perspectiveless phenomenon, the Portuguese counterpart to "*it* is cold" being "*it* does makes cold" (*faz frio*). But Portuguese indicates perspectival cold in terms of the cold person's *proximity to* or *companionship with* the cold: that is, the cold person "is *with*" (*está com*) coldness. Hunger, thirst, shame, or longing are expressed with a similar grammar. By contrast, in German, Spanish, and French these states are constructed as the affected person's *possessions*. One "*has* hunger or thirst," rather than "*being* hungry or thirsty."

Thus, in a range of non-English languages, feelings are described as transitive actions enacted by one party upon another. Some languages are more inclined to identify the experiencing person as the *subject* of the feeling (and of the predicate), while others are more inclined to identify the experiencing person as the *object* of the feeling (and of the predicate). Dinka and Yorùbá will strike many Westerners—but English speakers far more than most—as especially inclined to identify people as the *objects* of their feelings and of predicates about those feelings. This African linguistic disposition may also lend itself to a clearheaded denial of the autonomy of experiential phenomena like gods from the humans who experience them and to an emphasis on the dialectical interaction that jointly produces gods and human people. Conversely, the English linguistic disposition may lend itself to some particularly clumsy dichotomies between subjects and objects.

This reflection has some instructive implications regarding the meaning of Western spiritual concepts like "charisma." For example, US Americans tend to attribute "charisma" to John F. Kennedy, as though his popularity, attractiveness, and persuasiveness arose from some immaterial *quality* or ghostly *substance* internal to him and simply perceived by others. However, my discussions with Afro-Atlantic priests recommend the idea that "charisma" actually describes a particular quality of *relationship* between, say, Kennedy and the segments of the public who attribute this quality to him. Similarly, Afro-Atlantic daily talk, priestly parlance, and ritual practices suggest the possibility that a god is less an immaterial or ghostly being than a particular quality of people's relationship to other people and things.

African and European perceptions of divinity and material reality are hardly opposites, but they do arise from different linguistic families and histories of thought that may lend themselves to different notions of the goals and ethics of social life. There are parallels between, on the one hand, the dialectics of divinity and experience and, on the other, the dialectics of price bargaining in West Africa—both of which processes may have contributed to misunderstandings during the Afro-European encounter on the Guinea Coast of the sixteenth and seventeenth centuries. I can see how these misunderstandings became a useful allegory in intra-European debates about personal autonomy, the fixity of value, and the rule of impersonal law—central debates in the efforts of the rising European merchant class and bourgeoisie to redefine their relationship to the aristocracy (and to the workers) in the run-up to the Enlightenment.

The fundamental unit of Afro-Atlantic actor-networks is not the intentional actor moved by internal states to act upon nonintentional objects but the highly specific transitive action whereby a suprahuman, interspecies subject and his, her, or its human vehicle constitute each other, often through the proxy of consecrated things such as altars, clothing, and accessories. In the Afro-Atlantic religions, the construction of gods and that of humans are parallel, tandem, and dialectical processes. Both gods and people are made up of preexisting materials assembled through exchange, and each god or person serves as a densely bundled switching station in a network of relationships and processes. Priestly rituals are a technical effort to rearrange and control those relationships and processes through the proxy of exchanged things.

Making Ritual Families

Possessing these things is not an end in itself. Rather, people use them consciously to embody, activate, and prioritize certain relationships and processes. Like most religions, the ones I research borrow commonsense role categories from the local cultural system of biological reproduction—such as mothers, fathers, sisters, brothers, husbands, wives, lovers, ancestors, lineages, heterosexuals, homosexuals, *bichas*, and [real] men—and then adapt those categories tendentiously to the crafting of thing- and substance-mediated metaphorical families that are not quite predicted by the conventional local family structure alone. Such families are called "houses" (*ilé* [Yor.], *ilês* [Brazilian Nagô], *casas* [Sp.]), sharing their name with the building or collection of buildings normally inhabited by the same family. In West Africa, the collective that worships the same *òrìṣà* is often coterminous with a kin group that shares the same house. This physical house is empowered and protected by the mundane efforts of its inhabitants and by substances planted in the floor and in the rafters. So is a Brazilian or Haitian temple, which may unite many *nonliteral* kin and otherwise fissiparous branches of a literal family in a tightly knit sacred family. Nowadays, the *casa* of Cuban and Cuban American Santería/Ocha is often metaphorical. It is a lineage centered on a single ancestor, rather than a single shared and permanent architectural headquarters.

However, just as basic to the building of Yorùbá-Atlantic sacred families is the use of literal animal blood to turn initiates into the ritual and metaphorical "blood" kin of the other temple members. These sacred families are further consolidated through the sharing of meat among gods and their followers (Matory [1994] 2005: 200). The self-described "families" created by initiation, worship, and commensality differ conspicuously from "natural" or biological "blood" families in that these sacred families are manufactured through harvested animal blood and literally set in stone. Cuban priests call their fellow initiates in the same temple "stone family" (*familia de piedra*), with reference to the consecrated and blood-fed stones that sit in the vessel altars of the house.

Through daily parlance and ritualized forms of dressing up, purchase, gift exchange, and long-term, thing-mediated vows regarding the devotee's sexual behavior, the devotee is constructed as a the child or the spouse of the god and, simultaneously, as the child or the spouse of the god's temple community (Matory [1994] 2005). Committed relationships between gods and living humans (and between priests and their initiands) are regularly constructed as instances of birth by or marriage to the gods and are mediated by material things associated with child rearing and weddings. In Cuba, the priest who initiates a person is said to "give birth" (*dar a la luz*) simultaneously to a new god and to the god's new priest. And the new god is also said to "be born" (*nacer*) from the preexisting god, or empowered things, of the initiating priest. All at once, the vocabulary describing these cathected things identifies them as instruments of communication with the gods, as temporary repositories of the gods' power, and as the gods themselves.

Dressing up is a key behavioral metaphor in the phenomenology of the Yorùbá-Atlantic gods and monarchs, who, like the priests, embody the gods. Yorùbá monarchs (*ọba*) are usually selected from the ranks of a set of families credited with the earliest settlement of the jurisdiction, making even the charter for their authority a function of human activity and history. Then a committee of electors, in collaboration with diviners, whose decision making is always iterative, selects the monarch. Initially and on a daily basis, the monarch is always crowned by a committee of others, who literally stand behind him or her, preventing the monarch from seeing the empowering substances that another committee of people, the crown makers, has placed inside the crown. A god, too, is always dressed from behind, and others apply the human-designed substance of the god's power to the medium's head. Some language suggests the primordiality and self-existence of the god that has inhabited the person, but both the practice and the usual language describing divinity in the world focus on the multigenerational continuity of the human technical activities and active concurrence that have created whatever is compelling or inescapable in the god's power. In other words, the gods are something like our ancestors: we are born from them and by the efforts of each generation of their human embodiments.

And, like other genealogies, this one is not simply a matter of biology. It is a matter of selective acknowledgment, active commemoration, the cultivation of consensus, and coordinated activity. In Yorùbá, even the most seemingly biological of descent relationships evade merely biological definition. For example, the closest translations of the English-language terms "mother" (*ìyá*) and "father" (*bàbá*) refer not only to the woman who gave birth to and the man who is understood to have sired the speaker; they also refer to any kinsperson or non-kinsperson of a higher generation to whom the speaker chooses to show respect. Descendants play a further role in the creation of their ancestors. The birth of a child radically changes the social role and status of the parent, such that a Yorùbá parent is more likely to be addressed as "Mother or Father of [First Child's Given Name]" than by that parent's personal name. Even childless adults benefit from this actively suprabiological construction of genealogy. It is common to address them as "Mother" or "Father" of a close niece or nephew.

In the city of Jacmel, Haiti, Vodou participants recognize their biological kinship to an unbounded but, in principle, exogamous network of siblings, half siblings, parents, their siblings and half siblings, grandparents, their siblings and half siblings, and the descendants of all of the above. As a cognatic network, this unit has no particular genealogical center, although people do tend to be closer to their mothers' relatives than to their fathers'. Immigration and conversion to Protestantism tend to fracture this network, while the worship of the *lwa*, as the gods of Haitian Vodou are known—which is sometimes motivated by the sense that the supplicant's problems in life have resulted from their neglect—draws people together around relatives with special expertise in *lwa*-worship and in solving the problems caused by any given person's neglect of them. Because nonrelatives also find the services of these experts useful and are willing to pay for them, their leadership within the family is also facilitated by their ability to redistribute much-needed food, shelter, clothing, and employment opportunities. It is common for nonrelatives and even foreigners to undergo initiations that mime their rebirth into the ritual family or their literal marriage to the ancestral gods of the household.

In theory, each person and each temple hosts all of the gods. However, national history, town identity, family history, and biographical experience prioritize certain gods over others in any given person's or temple's pantheon. Indeed, the worship of the *lwa* gods is a metonym of the selective construction of genealogy and kinship among the living. A well-equipped Vodou devotee brags that she or he has inherited twenty-one gods from his or her mother's family and twenty-one gods from his or her father's family and, in the same breath, that she or he is surrounded by 201 gods on each side. As in West African Yorùbá parlance, these numbers are not literal but evoke countless multiplicity.

They hail from every African "nation" that supplied captives to Haiti and from the Roman Catholicism of both the French colonizers and the Polish mercenaries who reportedly fought for the Haitian Revolution. One entire nation of gods—Petwo—is largely made up of archetypal figures from the Haitian Revolution, and the Ogou gods embody the spirit of military leadership in the Haitian Republic, even wearing its conventional uniforms. Vodou is a religion of Haitian nationality.

Yet any given worshipper or temple prioritizes and is chiefly governed by a subset of Haiti's ancestors. For example, the first person buried in the local cemetery is worshipped as a god—a *bawon* (or "baron")—and his or her tomb is a special source of help. Moreover, certain gods are peculiar to certain regions of Haiti—as, for example, the god Agawou is worshipped proudly as a mark of Jacmel's religious distinctiveness—and people are expected, foremost, to ensure that the inherited or made and bought gods of their parents and grandparents are not neglected, lest those gods cause trouble in the generations of descendants left behind. Yet a temple assembles the gods so inherited and brought by all of the worshippers initiated into the temple family or wedded to one of the temple's gods. Hence, Vodou is, phenomenologically, a manner of keeping the spirits of the community's ancestors alive and of unifying a network of cognatic kin and allies around their maintenance.

So, to the same degree that Islam emphasizes the self-sufficiency of the high god and his autonomy from kinship relations (he has no parent, partner, or children), Vodou emphasizes the reciprocal dependency of and kinship among people, gods, and, by extension, communities. The well-being of people depends upon the gods in the same sense in which our existence and character depend on our ancestry, and our gods would weaken, go away, and cease to unify networks of family and ritual kin if we ceased to worship them. They depend on our unity, and they unify us. In sum, a successful temple is the product of genealogical selectiveness, human ritual knowledge, financial resources, and leaders' persuasiveness in assembling spirits and people.

Gods as Products and Producers of Assembly

In contrast to the stereotypically iconoclastic Protestant conviction that divinity is self-existent and transcendent, a casual assumption to the contrary is common in Afro-Atlantic parlance. For example, in Yorùbá, an altar is called the "face of the god" (*ojú òrìṣà*), which may also be translated as the eyes, surface, or location, of the god. This term suggests that the larger part or more general dimension of that god exists elsewhere, but the altar is the focus of a given person's or community's interaction with that god. But much parlance also indicates that the altar is, in itself, a god. This place of human interaction with the gods is clearly human made. The items that make up any given altar have come together as a result of the specifications of initiatic and divination procedures, inheritance, gifting from fellow priests, and commissioning in honor of the god. And what seems to make it a god is the fact of its being assembled and of its being a continual locus of assembly by people.

Asked what any given item on the altar is, every West African Yorùbá priest I have ever asked replies, "It is the god" (Òrìṣà ni), unwilling to give that distinct item in the assemblage a discrete and particular noun—that is, unwilling to say, "That is a stone from the river, that is a shell from the sea, that is a woven cloth from Ìgbétì, that is a cast figurine from Òṣogbo, and that is a beaded image from Ogbómọ̀ṣọ́." If forced to itemize, they name a few things and then quickly put a stop to it, concluding, "Òrìṣà ni gbogbo ẹ̀" (The god is the *entirety* of those things together). A gestalt logic of ritually coded juxtaposition both defines the assemblage as the god and makes it effective. To put this another way, the god him- or herself seems to exist in the fact of *assemblage*, or in the form of the *relationship* among the things, phenomena, plants and animals, ancestors, deceased possession priests, and living people who make it up. The presence of the divinity is chiefly identified in places where multiple constituent or associated objects, phenomena, and processes have been brought together by people. According to such commonplace parlance, the god is not a mere material thing. Nor is the constituent item the mere repository of an exogenous force.

In Yorùbá, Spanish, and Portuguese, the tandem acts of assembling altars and initiating priests are called "*making*, or *doing*, the god" (ṣe òrìṣà [Yor.]; *hacer el santo* [Sp.]; *fazer santo* [Pt.]). It involves the making and the insertion or the realization of an additional being in the body of the new priest. This being is regarded as a unique instance or enactment of a broader power and ensemble of elements, including samples of material things belonging to the god's network, a proper name, personal likes and dislikes, and specific rules for the conduct of the god's human host. Initiation simultaneously constructs that god in the human body of the devotee and in a vessel-altar, simultaneously reanimating and amending the broader power that is the god.

The daily parlance of worshippers in Yorùbá, Spanish, and Portuguese makes no distinction between what English speakers would call the "making" and the "doing" of the god. That is, the god may be regarded equally as a made being or as a series of actions—that is, the human-performed actions of assembly and invocation themselves. For example, the verbs ṣe in Yorùbá, *hacer* in Spanish, and *fazer* in Portuguese can all be translated as "to make" or "to do," perhaps further explaining the hesitancy of most Nigerian priests I ask to name the objects within an altar separately.[2]

The sense in which the gods are "made" is ambiguous in other senses, as well. Hence, the term is the touchstone of debates and dueling discourses.

In Brazil, for example, the description of Candomblé as a "religion of nature" (*religião da natureza*) is common and is made more plausible by the widespread Western representation of black people as closer to nature than are whites. This discourse suggests that unmediated nature is the foundation of Candomblé. However, when the gods appear in their possession priests on the occasion of public festivals, the gods themselves are typically configured and addressed like royals and knights.

The multifarious phenomena identified with a god—in the case of the Nigerian god Ṣàngó, thunder, lightning, royalty, justice, the punishment of thieves, the combination of ochre and white, thunderstones, the ram, the double ax, the tortoise, the leopard, the mortar, the phrase *Káwo Kábíèsílè*, and so forth—all predate the initiation of any given priest. And indeed, virtually every altar contains stones, seashells, herbal infusions, minerals, and animal blood that predated the initiation. However, it is also noteworthy that these "natural" items are almost all processed by human hands. The backs of the cowrie shells have been broken off, the herbal infusions prepared by strict procedure and verbal incantation, the camwood ground, the river lime dried and compacted into standardized forms, the stones scrubbed in lye soap and ritual infusions, and the animals exsanguinated through expert procedure, all amid songs, prayers, and incantations without which these individual items would be powerless and without which the effort to "make" or "do" the god in the altar and in the novice would be ineffective.

And virtually every altar contains not only items conceivably attributable to "nature" but manufactures embodying the attributes and competencies of the god (see, e.g., SABA Collection D004). The "tools" (e.g., *herramientas* [Sp.]; *ferramentas* [Pt.]) of the gods include tiny hammers, scissors, swords, slippers, rings, bracelets, ploughs, and axes—manufactured items that enable and illustrate the god's skills in the transformation of the worshippers' world (e.g., figures 8.14, 8.20, 9.1, 9.2, C.1, and SABA Collection B080, B100, B106, C025, and C046). In Yorùbá, similar tools are called *ibo*, or "worshipped/fed things." In addition, each god manifest in his or her possession priest carries in hand an allegorical staff or other item (e.g., *atributo*, or "attribute," in Spanish)—that is, a tool that demonstrates and embodies that god's characteristic method of defending the devotees and, when necessary, punishing (*castigar* [Sp.]) or "passing sentence" (*dictar sentencia* [Sp.]) on them.

Spirited Things as Embodiments of Human-Made History: Oggún, Yemayá, and Changó

The Santería/Ocha god of thunder and lightning, Changó, carries a double ax. This *hacha* represents lighting, which is understood to be a hurled stone (figure 9.1).

The doubleness of the ax invites further reflection on the Janus-faced ambivalence of the fetish.[3] Babá Steve Quintana tells the story of the goddess of

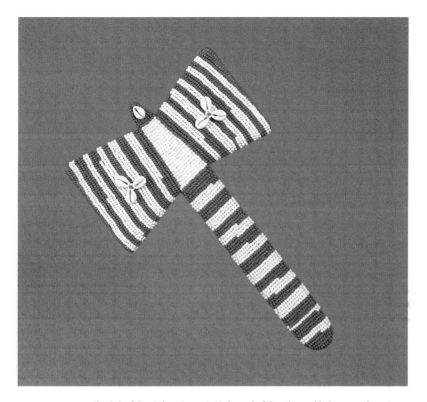

FIGURE 9.1 Ax (*hacha*) of the Cuban Santería/Ocha god of thunder and lightning, Changó (SABA COLLECTION B283). Red and white is Changó's emblematic color combination.

the sea and dark-skinned Ur-mother, Yemayá, who was raped by the god of war and iron, Oggún. Oggún embodies the long history of iron smelting and empire building in West Africa (Barnes 1989) and of the slave trade, which brought guns and initiated an arms race in the region (figures 9.2 and 9.3). European-style guns are among the preeminent symbols of Oggún (as they are of Yemọja in West Africa). The fruit of this rape, Babá Steve tells me, was Changó, a *mulato*. Since he learned of that rape, Changó has detested his father, just as lighting, when it descends, strikes iron first. The red beads on Changó's double ax evoke fire, Changó's element, while the white beads invoke the peace and coolness of his companion god Obatalá, the lord of peace, wisdom, and purity. When Changó is not raging, he is the bon vivant and the most charming of womanizers. He has multiple wives, some of whom married him after abandoning Oggún. Changó is the most popular god in the Yorùbá-Atlantic religions.

And he is deeply devoted to his mother. Whither Yemayá goes, he goeth. Like him, she both joyfully froths (in the white caps and foam at the seashore) and rages (in the white-hot hurricanes of the Caribbean and the tsunamis of the

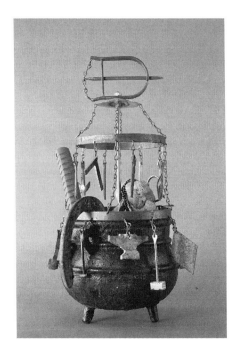

FIGURE 9.2 My Oggún, god of war and iron, made for me by Babá Esteban Quintana. Oggún's iron cauldron brims with his "tools," which include, among other things, knives, scythes, rakes, railroad ties, and a toy gun. My *chibiriquí*—the rack of pendant tools above the cauldron—was made by the famous artist of sacred ironwork, Totico. At the top is the bow and arrow of Oggún's brother Ochosi, the god of hunting and criminal justice. Because of my history of orthopedic surgeries, my Oggún also works with a scalpel and surgical scissors. See also SABA COLLECTION B239 and B100 (Cuban Santería/Ocha).

FIGURE 9.3 An Oggún fully dressed alongside his worshipper at an altar in Havana (1999). His cauldron is draped in shredded palm fronds (*marió*), a favorite outfit of the god. This suit is exceptionally well made. Note the toy gun at the center and the Elegguás at this god's feet. The multicolored paper mask atop Oggún invokes the god's former wife Ollá, the goddess of wind and storm. Some sacred stories (*pataquines*) report that Changó either cuckolded Oggún or took Ollá from him altogether, one of the multiple reasons for which, according to *santeros*, Oggún and Changó do not get along (Cuban Santería/Ocha).

western Pacific). In Cuba, their unity is manifest in the sacred twins: ideally, the vessel of one wears the colors of Changó, and the other wears the colors of Yemayá (see plate 9).

The interaction of Yemayá and Changó—the Ur-mother with her cosmopolitan son—and his wives—defines the long-distance cross-cultural, trans-oceanic cross-fertilization that is the Afro-Atlantic world. It resembles the Oedipal narrative of the son displacing the patriarchal father. Combined with the fact that Cubans consider Changó a *mulato*, this story invites reading not only as an Oedipal drama of filial ambivalence but also, and even more vividly, as an allegory of Europe's rape of Africa and the ambivalent mediating power of the merchant-monarchs. With its contrasting hot and cool colors and its blades that cut both ways, Changó's double-bladed ax is a study in ambivalence.

The preeminent merchant-monarchs of the Guinea Coast were the rulers of the Ọ̀yọ́ Empire, of which Changó's West African cognate, Ṣàngó, is the tutelary god. For such coastal merchant-monarchs, their priests, and their followers, the Afro-European trade was a source of arms and goods that could be used to consolidate African social relationships, build African empires, and defend their own African communities. However, those merchant-monarchs who participated in and benefited from the slave trade, as the rulers of Ọ̀yọ́ did, sometimes victimized their own followers and could themselves always fall victim to the slave trade. Ọ̀yọ́ collapsed by the hand of its northern trading partners, the Hausa-Fulani emirates, but, as Ọ̀yọ́'s subjects fled southward, rival coastal merchant-monarchs delivered tens, if not hundreds, of thousands of them into the Atlantic slave trade.

The assemblage of processed nature and manufactures into a technologically manageable unit, focused on a body or an altar, is the product of human activity, without which these materials would not be a god. And without such concerted attention to the general spirit of the same name, says Ìyá Ọ̀ṣun Òṣogbo, this spirit would have no affect on human life. Indeed, one Yorùbá proverb declares, "Kòsí ènìyàn, kòsí òrìṣà" (If there were no people, there would be no gods). Moreover, a dictum known almost as well among the *orixá*-worshippers of Brazil as among the *òrìṣà*-worshippers of Nigeria declares, "Kòsí ewé, kòsí òrìṣà" (Without leaves, there are no *òrìṣà* gods). This dictum does not mean that leaves are a constituent of each self-existent, prehuman entity known as an *òrìṣà* but that, in order to make and maintain an *òrìṣà*, the priests must gather the leaves appropriate to the assembly of that being. In order for any of these leaves to be ritually effective, the priests must pay for them in the forest and collectively activate them by singing as they steep the leaves. Hence, leaves are indispensable to the life of the gods, but so are the well-informed collection and processing of these leaves by people. This assumption is shared by the Fòn-Atlantic caretakers of the Haitian *lwa* gods.

Priests seldom draw any verbal distinction between the god as a disembodied spirit and any of its physical manifestations—for example, the river is Ọ̀ṣun, and so is her priestess. Nor do worshippers normally distinguish between the god as a general spirit and the human-assembled and ritually maintained altar of the god. The altar is also Ọ̀ṣun, as is any item consecrated to her on that altar. Of exceptional events, such as powerful lightning or the flooding of a river, worshippers also say, "It is the òrìṣà/orixá/oricha/orisha." But the most normal referent of this phrase in daily life is the altar assemblage or a possessed person, who is him- or herself also a ritually prepared and iconically clothed assemblage. But even the unpossessed priest of a god may be called the god. For example, in the city of Ọ̀ṣogbo, the followers and clients of the high priestess of the goddess Ọ̀ṣun call her by the title associated with her priestly office—"Ìyá Ọ̀ṣun," meaning "Mother, or Senior Woman, of Ọ̀ṣun." However, they may also call her by the name of the goddess herself—"Ọ̀ṣun." And they are correct, the priestess tells me. In turn, she calls the possession priest of the god Ṣàngó "Ṣàngó," even when that priest is not possessed.

All of these daily ways of speaking call attention to the central role of *people* in the making of the gods. People and consecrated things constitute the god, they assemble any given instance of the god, and they enact, or "do," the god.

However, my conversations and debates with priests about this commonplace parlance have elicited diverse opinions about whether gods predated the existence of people, about whether people made the gods, and about whether the gods would have any effect upon human life in the absence of human ritual activity. Of course, the "problem of the fetish" is part of the context of the priests' response to my interpretation—that is, they are aware that the Afro-Atlantic gods have been accused of factitiousness and their priests of manipulation.

Most of the priests mentioned in part III declare belief in the transcendence and self-existence of certain immaterial beings, such as God Almighty. They tend to express greater uncertainty about another range of beings—such as the òrìṣà gods. Some priests, especially in socialist Cuba, forthrightly recognize their gods as made by and dependent on human effort. In other traditions, only some beings are expressly acknowledged as human-made, such as *gad* and *pwen* in Haitian Vodou and *adumakama* in the Surinamese and Dutch Winti religion. Other priests from some traditions frontally question the everyday parlance that gods are "made," condemning it as a vice of language. Yet virtually all of the Afro-Atlantic priests with whom I have talked agree that rituals cease without practitioners, that altars become inert without rituals, and that, without ritual care, gods run amok and eventually die. Some priests' hesitancy to confirm the madeness of most gods—despite the daily, casual parlance that strongly suggests it—teaches us important lessons about the conflicting value codes that animate these animated things.

On the Reciprocal Making of People and Gods

In July 2014, I presented my argument about Marx's bias and the construct-edness of the gods to a circle of *santera* priestesses and a spiritist in socialist and once-officially atheist Cuba. The head priestess of Casa-Templo Changó Bumí, the most renowned temple of Santería/Ocha in Santiago de Cuba, spoke first and most fervently. "Marx did not consider *us* people," declared Oggún Fumi, "But Lenin recognized that black and white are the same, equal." She continued, "And, *of course*, people make their gods."

But Ìyá Ọ̀ṣun, the High Priestess of the Ọ̀ṣun shrine complex in Òṣogbo, Nigeria, told me that, as forces of nature and as forebears to human beings, the *òrìṣà* do predate humans and exist independently of us. However, humans' feeding and application of herbal solutions and blood to the shrines "strengthens" the gods, and, in the absence of human ritual action, the gods withdraw from their altars and from involvement in human lives generally. Then everything goes wrong, says the priestess. In sum, the *òrìṣà* and their worshippers "depend on each other" (Adedoyin Talabi Faniyi, personal communication, April 14, 2014).

The material and commodity-rich embodiments of Yorùbá-Atlantic divinity are encoded with signs of not only Yorùbá speakers' extrabiological, volitional, and dialectical conception of parenting but multiple other human-made relationships unrelated to descent, as well—such as marriage, horsemanship, slavery, and monarchy. These signs encode a history of changing political and economic exigencies affecting particular times, places, and classes. All over the world, religious models tend to seem anachronistic and foreign relative to present-day conditions of the worshippers who adopt them. By implying the inevitability of the social relationships embodied in spirited things, the apparent primordiality and Other-worldly transcendentalism of these models seem intent on exempting them from defiance by reason of short-term and pragmatic self-interest in the present day. But these models also give clear evidence of the distinctive cultural suppositions and material interests of the class that have founded and, up until the present day, transmitted any given religion (Weber [1922–23] 1946).

Contrary to Marx's presupposition that fetishists fail to recognize that it is people who make gods, there is a great deal of talk among Afro-Atlantic worshippers to the effect that people make, or "do," gods; that people and gods are "born" through human effort; and that it is people who enable gods to function.

It is true, though, that many leaders and spokespeople of these religions stop short of declaring the gods fully human made, and their testimony—in a mirror reflection of Olupọna's—vacillates between pronouncements that the gods are human-made and self-corrections that then deny it. Ìyá Ọ̀ṣun Òṣogbo resolves this seeming contradiction with her observation that gods and human people "depend on each other" (Adedoyin Talabi Faniyi, personal communication, April 14, 2014). She adds that gods make people, but people make gods, too.

Just as Marx's and Freud's assertions about the fetish contested rival positions on the distribution of the rewards of labor and citizenship, the Afro-Atlantic making of gods contests rival positions on the proper arrangement of relationships, loyalty, and authority. So a further reason for this seeming contradiction is that Afro-Atlantic priests are aware of the Western critique that African gods are *uniquely* human-made and are therefore merely efforts to manipulate other people. Moreover, even within the Afro-Atlantic religions, the active pursuit of power is generally considered hubristic and is associated with the pursuit of personal profit at others' expense, as in the avowed making of spirits like the Haitian *pwen* and the Surinamese *adu-makama*. For these related reasons, a high-ranking priest's acknowledgment that the gods are made potentially delegitimizes his or her authority. Perhaps for the same reasons, it is far less difficult for the lower-ranking followers of these priests than for the high-ranking ones to say that the gods are made by people, and they do so all the time. That is, most priests of Yorùbá indigenous religion, Santería/Ocha, and Candomblé speak of initiation as the "making" of a god. The minority most likely to refute this parlance—even after having spoken it regularly in their daily parlance—are chief priests.

For example, the chief of Berlin's Candomblé temple, Babá Murah, reacted to my question about why West African Yorùbá òrìṣà-worshippers, Cuban *santeros*, and Brazilian *candomblecistas* all normally describe initiation in the possession priesthood as the "making of the god." While he himself regularly and casually employs this term *fazer santo* (to "make," "do," or "perform" the saint) and also welcomes the title "Babá" (short for *babalorixá*, from the Yorùbá "father-who-owns-the god"), Babá Murah's answer to my question in 2014 seemed to defend his religion from the possible accusation that its gods lack the prestigiously transcendent and preexistent nature of the Protestant high god prevailing in his host city of Berlin. Indeed, the main thrust of the Dutch Protestant and Hegelian critique of African religion is that its gods are made by humans and are, for that reason, *ridiculous*. And Candomblé priests are aware of the accusation. Thus, Babá Murah dismissed the term *fazer santo* as a misnomer and a linguistic error, saying, "We don't *make* a *santo* because people are already born *made* [i.e., deeply connected to the gods]!

Initiation simply sets them on the path of the religion." In other words, he emphasizes the inborn connection of a person to his or her tutelary divinity; that connection is not made but merely regularized and strengthened by the initiand or the priest.

Babá Murah added, in a conventional speech I have heard from other Brazilian chief priests—many times and unprompted by me: "And I'm not a *pai-de-santo* [i.e., "father-of-the-saint," a term that most Brazilian Candomblé-participants consider correct], because *santo* [the collectivity of the gods] doesn't have a father, or a mother. I'm a *caretaker* [*zelador*] of the saint!" It did not dawn on me to ask him why a god needs to be taken care of. But Brazilian Protestants even critique the need of *orixás* for caretakers, calling the Candomblé gods *seres alimentares*—"beings [who need] to be fed." The Cuban Ocha parlance that a new Ochún altar is "born" from a preexisting Ochún altar or priest is unfamiliar to Babá Murah. He does, however, acknowledge the similarity of the new novice to a baby born by human efforts, but he explains this representation in terms of the *newness* of the novice to the way of the *orixás*, who are to him self-existent forces of "nature" (*a natureza*). He says that Xangô is the thunder, Iansã the wind, Oxum the river, and Iemanjá the sea. He says nothing about Ogum being technology or Oxóssi being the hunt, much less about Xangô being epicureanism and royal governance.

Yet, at Babá Murah's May 2014 festival for the god of war and technology, Ogum, and his brother Oxóssi, the lord of the hunt (figure 9.4) (although it could have been the festival of any god), I was struck by a scene that I had witnessed many times in Afro-Atlantic temples. On the one hand, Babá Murah's manifest goddess Iansã chose the dances she would dance, directed the drummers to play appropriately, and instructed Babá Murah's visitors and followers on where to move, what to do, and when. On the other hand, a conscious Babá Murah seemed to *instruct* the gods manifest in his followers on how to dance and where to move. These gods appeared to obey the conscious chief priest by whose talents and efforts they were being trained. Indeed, their subordination to this human person seemed to be part of their education.

In observing such scenes, my best friend in Brazil, the Candomblé high priest Doté Amilton, has explained to me that it is not the initiand but literally the god him- or herself who is being trained in this process, explaining that the new god of an *iaô*, or novice priest, has to be taught to dance and respond properly and promptly to verbal, gestural, and musical cues. And the results are astonishing. I have seen Doté Amilton induce possession by uttering the briefest of phrases and clapping his hand, whereupon dozens of gods manifest in people who had been chatting, playing games, or doing their chores involuntarily converged upon Doté to receive instruction. Doté tells me that he cannot employ this awesome power too often; his human

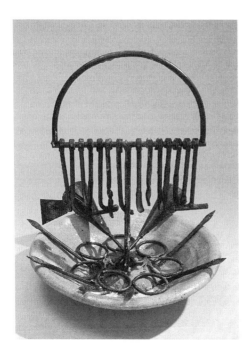

FIGURE 9.4 My Ogum, god of war and iron (Brazilian Candomblé, SABA COLLECTION C020). He is the Brazilian counterpart of the Afro-Cuban god Oggún. For comparison, see the tools (*herramientas*) of Oggún in (figure 9.2).

charges would resent him for it. But his power over the gods he has made is real and can be used to discipline both them and their hosts. The most cultivated of Afro-Atlantic gods certainly direct, train, and rule people, but the most cultivated of Afro-Atlantic priests also direct, train, and rule the gods. In reaction to my interpretation—and, implicitly, those of Ìyá Ọṣun Ọṣogbo, Oggún Fumi, and Pai Francisco, as well—Babá Murah reasoned, it is *the body of the initiate* that has to be trained to receive the god's energy properly and not the god who requires training.

Because they are thoughtful people living in diverse cultural and political environments, Afro-Atlantic priests hold diverse opinions about the received parlance of their religions. Because they are neither the fetishists constructed by Hegel, Marx, and Freud nor the "people without history" (Wolf [1982] 2010) constructed by an earlier anthropology, we should not expect otherwise.

Babá Murah offers a brief sermon and blessing at the end of each festival, before we donate money for the meal and then eat together. He concluded the 2014 Ogum and Oxóssi festival with these words: "Só com a fé nos orixás é que os orixás vão aparecer em nossas vidas" (Only with faith in the *orixás* will the *orixás* appear in our lives). The language of active "faith" as the key to divine intervention hardly separates Candomblé and Santería/Ocha from contemporary European Christianity, but it does highlight the indispensability of human will in the efficacy of the Christian and the Afro-Atlantic gods alike. Yet the self-fashioning of the Abrahamic religions has long depended on the exaggeration of their difference from Canaanite, Roman, and pre-Islamic Arab religions. Since the Enlightenment, Afro-Atlantic religions have taken the place of these other non-Abrahamic traditions as litotic proof of the self-evidence, unique truth, and inevitability of the European speaker's position on society, history, and the universe.

Far more than the talk of "faith," which they share with the Abrahamic priests, Afro-Atlantic priests' alternating talk about the self-existence and the "madeness" of the gods brings the ambivalence of the fetish consciously to mind. The gods make, do, or perform us, and we make, do, or perform the gods. In the face of the social relations that we reify as gods, as laws, or as scientific facts, we are both subjects and objects of those reifications. Even at their most defensive, Afro-Atlantic priests are far more dialectical than the Guinea-Coast fetishist imagined by Bosman, Hegel, and Marx. Indeed, they are, in the same sense, more dialectical than Bosman, Hegel, Marx, and Freud themselves.

On the Human Sources of the Other World

Babá Murah's assertion that the gods are self-existent finds much support in Afro-Atlantic talk about an Other world that predated earthly life and unpredictably intervenes in it. Spirit possession is living proof of ritual experts' understanding that human life is continually structured by that *Other* world. Even noninitiates often find these reported interventions from the Other world uncanny and difficult to deny.

For example, in 2015, Bárbara Valdés, the co-owner of the now-defunct Artesanía Yoruba in Hialeah, Florida, and designer of sacred beadwork, told me that although her late parents were and all of her siblings are initiates of Santería/Ocha, she is not. However, like those of most initiates, her doubts about spirit possession are conditional: while spirit possession may be real, she regards many people who claim to be possessed as fakers. For example, years earlier, in the midst of the supposed possession episode of one man by the oricha Oggún, Bárbara whispered to her friend, in a voice that the supposedly possessed person could not possibly have heard, that she would believe this man's possession was real only if he picked her up and spun her around. In her explanation to me, she added that she is about 200 pounds, while this possession priest was skinny and looked weak. However, minutes later, the body of the man whose possession she had doubted walked up to her, picked her up in his arms, and pirouetted all around the room. Later on in the *bembé*, or festival, the god dropped a dollar bill that he had collected from a worshipper, and Bárbara bent down to pick it up. Someone shouted a warning for her not to touch it, but the Oggún intervened and said it was OK, whereupon he picked the banknote up and plastered it to Bárbara's forehead, saying, "Don't forget me." And she did not. Bárbara has kept that dollar bill ever since. For Bárbara, not every apparent possession performance is real, and she leaves open the question of how these forces have come about. But the occasional spirit possession performance is proof positive. It is no mere coincidence that money was involved. As we have already seen in a half-dozen less familiar currencies, money is, in the Afro-Atlantic religions, the foremost souvenir and invocation of contact with the Other world.

According to West African Yorùbá sacred lore, the visible world was founded by an òrìṣà and ancestor—Odùduà—who came from heaven and, with the aid of a domestic chicken, created the land. Like this one, the origin stories of virtually every Yorùbá town describe an arrival from some Other place. Similarly, the daily inner world of living people is populated by spirits brought from the Other world during gestation and ritual initiations. Dreams are often regarded as the manifest workings of this Other world, workings that cause events and enable predictions in this world.

West African Yorùbá of various religions also report the return of the dead from the Other world. For example, some people who die prematurely are said to live out their normal lifespans far away from the people who knew them in life, such that the abnormality of their continued presence in the world of the living usually goes unnoticed. Yet many Yorùbá tales report accidental or unanticipated encounters between the living dead (àkúdàáyà) and their relatives, giving dramatic proof to the permeability of the boundary between this world and the Other. Further proof lies in the signs of invisible or obliquely visible visitations by those who died in old age, such as noises in the house or wet footprints discovered on the otherwise dusty floor of an unoccupied room once inhabited by the deceased. Ìyá Òṣun Òṣogbo reports such encounters with her deceased adoptive mother, the Austrian òrìṣà priestess Susanne Wenger.

The gods sometimes reportedly materialize as flesh-and-blood bodies in order to rescue their followers from potentially harmful circumstances, such as kidnapping and war. Ìyá Òṣun said that as a child, her father was rescued from kidnappers by the goddess Òṣun herself, in the flesh. However, possession-trance in the context of sacred drumming is the most dramatic, regulated, and regular of appearances and interventions from the Other world. During festivals, the gods take over human bodies, dancing, singing, healing, and dramatizing the connected streams of ancestry, meteorology, geography, botany, ethology, and human technology that link this world to the Other one.

Hence, on the one hand, like Marx's futurist prophecies and the early psychoanalysts' divination of each other's unconscious hostility, the Other world guides the conduct and structures communities of Afro-Atlantic adepts in this visible and present-day world. On the other, by welcoming, feting, and training the gods—and by constructing the indispensable physical vehicles of their appearance in this world—Afro-Atlantic ritual experts also transform the Other world. As all orisha-worshippers know and most say—in these very terms— "Jorge's Oxum" differs in appearance, affect, seniority, and power from "Alberto's Oxum," "Adeniran's Ṣàngó" differs from "Aiyé Gbajéjé's Ṣàngó," and Babá Murah's Iansã is equally unique. As the possession priest rises in rank, that priest shapes the god as much as the god has influenced that priest.

Babá Murah insists that his denial of the "madeness" of his gods is not intended as a defense against German and Protestant prejudices. It's simply what he believes. However, it is difficult to ignore the oppositional context of his articulations of belief. For example, he and his followers are highly aware that many Germans stereotype Brazilians as highly sexual, frivolous, and primitive. So even his discussion of the photo of Forum Brasil's Carnaval performance in Berlin—displayed on the wall of the temple's dining room—emphasized the clothedness and respectability of the posing dancers. Other items on the temple's display walls showcase the authority conveyed by his priestly genealogy and its Other-worldly sources, including group photos with Mãe Beata in her immaculately white *baiana* outfit (see figure 9.5), ritual gifts from her, statues inherited from deceased relatives, and sculptures from Africa.

Babá Murah is also highly aware that the German state and most of the neighbors around his Kreuzberg courtyard are hostile toward animal sacrifice, a hostility requiring the *justification* of sacrifice that he offered to me and had apparently offered to others even before he felt the need to refute the parlance that the gods are made. He asked me socratically why, in Brazil, where it is legal, animals are sacrificed to the saint, or god. The answer he gave is usually intended to unsettle outsiders' excessive and prurient focus on animal sacrifice in Candomblé, but it also unintentionally revealed a subtle vision of the relationship between the gods and their caretakers, one *supportive* to the view that people make gods.

When I answered that the spilling of animal blood on the altar transfers the life force of the animal to the altar and to the god, he corrected me, saying that the god is "made of" (*feito de*) four types of blood, all of which are essential to giving life to and sustaining the life of a person, as well— green blood (which comes from leaves), black blood (charcoal and minerals from the earth), white blood (water; breast milk too, he says, is a white blood necessary for human life), and red blood (animal blood). People and the altars of the gods are "made" (*feitos*) similarly, he told me, through the *assembly* of these four types of blood, each of which existed and contained life-giving force before an altar was assembled and before a child was born and nurtured. In his argument, Babá Murah underlined the preexistence of

FIGURE 9.5 In the context of Berlin, this Bahian women's outfit projects exoticism (SABA COLLECTION C152). However, it is the typical attire of street vendors of Afro-Bahian delicacies and Candomblé priestesses—historically, overlapping professions—and it is rich with readable signs of its wearer's spiritual and liturgical status. The finest of these suits, like this one, are cut-work cloth (*rechiliê*), visually suggesting the wearer's permeability to the windlike gods. This particular arrangement of the outfit would mark its wearer as a chief priestess or the holder of an elevated office in the temple and, as is typical of chief priestesses, a devotee of a male god. Her blouse is a *batá*, rather than a *camizu*, and she wears the "cloth from the African Coast" (*pano da Costa*) over her shoulder rather than around her breast. Moreover, she is not wearing pantaloons, which a low-ranking priestess needs to protect her modesty as she prostrates herself before her superiors. During a festival for the gods, the skirt of a low-ranking priestess should be supported by numerous stiffly starched slips (*anáguas*) so that it looks round and buoyant as she dances. By contrast, a chief priestess remains seated for most of the ceremony, making it uncomfortable to wear numerous slips. Here, the head tie (*torço* or *ojá*), is wrapped like a turban, marking the wearer as a devotee of a *male* tutelary god. By contrast, the head tie of a priestess consecrated to a female divinity would be tied so that wings extend upward from the sides.

a person's, a god's, and an altar's contents, but without realizing it, he also said repeatedly that gods and people are "made" or "done" (*feitos*) through the human assembly of raw materials. He added that ritual exchanges—such as the payments to the god of leaves, Òsanyìn, for the herbs indispensable to the high ritual of animal sacrifice—"make the god grow," inducing and further empowering the god to grant the worshippers' wishes. However, Babá Murah then corrected his initial word choice: the exchanges cause the "efficacious power [*axé*] of the *altar* to grow."

Babá Murah normally calls the altar itself a god. For example, in his reply to a draft of this book, he insisted that there is no distinction among the god, the elements of nature identified with the god, and the altar, since the god is present in all of these places. However, in reply to my queries about the madeness of the gods, he preferred to *distinguish* the altar from the god—the god being a self-sufficient entity and the altar a place of more-or-less concentrated and effective *access* to the god.

Elaborating on the distinction between altars and gods, Babá Murah then said that an altar is a place to which the god comes because a worshipper places there the things that the god likes, such as sacrifices and prayers. Gods dwell in altars for the same reason that a person goes home at night—because the home contains the things that he or she likes. Babá Murah describes sacrifice and the food offerings to the gods as a communal feast among people and the gods, because, he says, the people eat same foods that are offered to the gods. Eating together is always more enjoyable, he says, than eating alone: the food tastes better. That is why gods keep coming back to a well-tended altar and, through it, keep granting the wishes of the worshipper. Thus, the sacred feasts build the community of humans and gods through commensality.

In common, the priests of the Afro-Atlantic religions seem to agree that the differentiated raw materials and forces with which a primordial high god populated the universe predated human beings as we know ourselves and were people of a sort in their own right—bundles, vessels, or types of energy, each with a character of his, her, or its own. Countless years later, our relationship to them is not merely chemical or biologically hereditary. It is a relationship created partly by the human marriage and procreation that selectively and socially reshuffle these bundled energies within a line of descendants and within each descendant. But, just as important, this relationship is created by our choice to prioritize, worship, and, in a word, feed certain energies within and around us, to participate in those energies, and to cooperate with communities of people who prioritize, amplify, and participate in the same types or bundles of energy.

Much like Spanish, Portuguese, and English speakers, Yorùbá speakers describe shared ancestry as shared "blood." The priests of the Afro-Atlantic religions employ the blood of sacrificial animals to create a set of non-kin relationships analogous to "blood" kinship, prioritizing the kinship of sacrificial blood over that of family and inviting blood kin to prioritize some biological "blood" relationships—that is, the ones reinforced by sacrifice—over other "blood" relationships. The vitality of gods correlates with the vitality of the largely optional communities that worship them, and the death of gods correlates with the death of those communities.

The energies and social units that constitute the gods would dissipate and cease to structure relationships if people chose no longer to embody them. The death of a god is coterminous with the death of a worshipping community, and a calling or a haunting is the resurrection of a past genealogy of communal relationship. Gods can reassert themselves following the lapse of their worship, but the misfortunes that are interpreted as the demands of the gods are redressed through sacrifices that assemble old and new communities in the name of the god.

Whereas Protestants prioritize the posthumous survival of the individual, Afro-Atlantic priests prioritize the posthumous survival of the literally and metaphorically genealogical communities that constitute and are constituted by the gods. Ìyá Ọ̀ṣun Òṣogbo explained to me why alcohol, including and especially archaic European alcohols, are, like blood, omnipresent features of the rituals creating and fortifying the Afro-Atlantic gods. It is because such alcohols do not decay with age and because they are associated with the foreparents who have drunk them since time immemorial (Adedoyin Talabi Faniyi, personal communication, December 2016). I would add that the antiquity of these types of alcohol in Nigerian òrìṣà-worship and Surinamese Winti, for example, is highlighted by the fact that these brands of alcohol are, like Venetian chevron beads, now difficult to find in the colonial metropolis. Their commemoration of present-day people's relationship to distantly past ancestors simultaneously commemorates the historical depth of African priests' relationship to the European merchants who conducted the maritime portions of the Atlantic trade.

The death of ancient gods is the death of ancient, human-made communities that have long been circum-Atlantic, interspecies, and suprabiological in scope. To acknowledge the gods' human-madeness is also to confess the fragility of communities, communities that, like every community, are under constant threat by centripetal forces, such as the claims of rival communities to worshippers' and merchants' allegiance. There are reasons for some Afro-Atlantic religious leaders' hesitancy to confirm the everyday parlance that their gods are made. Yet the priests' debate and apparent vacillation over whether the gods are made may bespeak a deeper consistency in these religions, one that both upsets the Enlightenment caricature of the fetishist and may have been key to these religions' endurance in an adversarial world—that is, a dialectical ontology of gods and human beings. It is as evident to most priests that people make gods as it is that gods make people.

FIGURE 9.6 Vodou ceremony led by Manbo Asogwe Marie Maude Evans at my home in Durham, North Carolina, March 2015. See also plate 7.

The Spirited Things of Manmi Maude

My Haitian priestess friend Manbo Asogwe Marie Maude Evans spoke with a similar ambivalence about her and my *pakèt kongo* (figure 9.6 and plate 7). She makes these god-animated vessels and bundles with specific secret ingredients and procedures, harnessing the "heat" of the drumming, singing, and dancing in the neighboring *peristil*, or public ceremonial hall, to empower them. Once a *pakèt kongo* is made, she freely calls it by the name of the god it embodies. However, like Babá Murah, she emphasizes that the god (*lwa*) dwells in the *pakèt kongo* because we welcome the god with things that he or she likes and that the god will depart from a *pakèt kongo* that is not regularly "entertained" and asked for favors. Figure 9.6 shows the beginning of a *fèt Vodou*, or "Vodou party," at which priests and admirers of Vodou "entertained" the gods embodied in the *pakèt kongo* that Manmi Maude has made for me. Although Manmi Maude surrounds the various *pakèt kongo* with foods "for the gods," which people may not eat until the ceremony has ended, she hesitates to say that the gods or the *pakèt kongo* "eat" per se. What they mainly require in order to remain in the *pakèt kongo* is not food but perfume and lit candles. They are attracted by the light.

This shared theme in the accounts of Babá Murah and Manmi Maude mirrors Afro-Atlantic ideas about the relationships between humans. For almost all of my Yorùbá, Haitian, Brazilian, and Cuban friends, friendship is not a merely abstract feeling of long-term affection. Like the relationship between gods and people, human friendship rests of a consistent history of reciprocal requests, gifts, and joyfully rendered services.

Speaking of her goddess more generally, Manmi Maude says that if she stops "entertaining" and making requests of her Èzili Dantò, she supposes that the goddess will go back to the wilderness. Yes, she agrees, the *pakèt kongo* of Èzili Dantò is shaped like a person and, specifically, like the goddess, because the goddess dwells in the cloth packet. But, pressed to say whether the *pakèt kongo* is the goddess, Manmi Maude prefers to say that the *pakèt kongo* is like a "telephone" to the goddess (personal communication, March 2015).[4]

Allied with the debate over the relationship between gods and made, or assembled, things is the debate over the relationship between people and their gods. When I showed Manmi Maude footage I had filmed of ritual activity and interviews in her temple in Jacmel, what most fascinated her was the deeds and words of her own gods as they performed in her body. She had seldom seen them in action as they possessed her. During these screenings, Manmi Maude denied any recollection of what the gods manifest in her body had done or said. Where the drumming made it impossible for us to hear what the gods had told one or another follower of Manmi Maude's, she could not fill in the gap from memory. She also explained, in abstract principle, that her gods predated her existence and consciousness and that no matter how much she has resented or resisted the demands of these gods, there is seldom much room for negotiation with them. In the end, she usually obeys them. In the Vodou, or *Sèvi Lwa*, religion, these gods and a person's responsibility to take care of them are typically inherited, and, though Manmi Maude and most other devotees have initially resisted the calling, they eventually submit and are glad that they did. They say that doing so saved their lives.

When I explained to Manmi Maude Marx's idea that it is people who make gods and not gods who make people, she firmly rejected the proposition. Trying to persuade her, I mentioned the fact that many of the gods of Vodou are historical or archetypal figures from the time of the Haitian Revolution. In my view, such relatively recent, eighteenth-century origins imply that people had a hand in the gods' making or at least in the transformation of archetypal Revolutionary characters into gods. In response she told me the following story about how the *lwa* had demonstrated their reality to her long before she had even known consciously of their existence, proving that the gods act autonomously from people and independently of their will.

Though her single mother served the *lwa* gods inconspicuously and without explaining her ritual practices to Maude, Maude has had dreams about the gods since she was a small child. In one dream, a *lwa* "appearing in the image of her father" told her that she would one day meet her father and that, soon thereafter, someone would give her a red car. Decades later, when she had emigrated from Haiti to the US, events unfolded just as that god had predicted in the dream. Manmi Maude had long forgotten the dream, but it came back to her with shocking force on the day that a friend handed her a set of car keys. At first, she was incredulous about such a generous gift, but it was real. Then she saw the car, and it was indeed red. Manmi Maude goes a step further than Bárbara Valdés. For Manmi Maude, there is no other explanation for this series of events than the self-existence of the *lwa* gods.

In the light of this conclusion, Manmi Maude's spontaneous story of how human worshippers can change their gods is especially surprising. Manmi Maude frequently tells the story of one reason that she long resisted the calling of her goddess, Èzili Dantò: the goddess had a deeply disturbing way of getting her attention. In Maude's dreams, the goddess appeared waist-deep in the ocean as a naked dark-skinned woman with both female and male genitals. In this dream, the hermaphroditic goddess was having sex in every conceivable way with a light-skinned woman, who was also waist-deep in the water. Intervening in that dream, Manmi Maude protested loudly, screaming that she could not accept this lesbian overture or the efforts of a lesbian goddess to claim her. Dantò then reassured Manmi Maude: yes, the goddess acknowledged that she is a lesbian, but "only because her other worshippers had made her that way." Dantò said that she had come to Manmi Maude in this form in order to get the future priestess's attention, but she added that, because of Maude's objection, she could become heterosexual. Yes, Manmi Maude affirmed, Manmi Maude herself had changed her goddess's sexual orientation by fervently rejecting the goddess's prior, human-created character.

Though both Babá Murah and Manmi Maude deny my inference that the gods are made and affirm that the gods are self-existent, their spontaneous discourse and stories in other contexts at the very least upset any notion that this self-existence resembles the unchanging self-existence that Abraham and his followers tend to attribute to their god. In heavily Christian environments, Afro-Atlantic priests internalize and react against the question of whether their gods are factitious. Of course, I am not entitled to explain their convictions away on this basis. The sound-proofed coach house that is Babá Murah's Ilê Obá Silekê is surrounded on three sides by stacks of apartment windows in the surrounding high-rises, which is perhaps the most extreme instance of the Islamic, Christian, and post-Enlightenment capitalist or socialist gaze that has been an important context of Afro-Atlantic religious practice for at least two centuries. And the reality of its influence on us does not depend on a deterministic argument, any more than my argument about Marx and Freud does. Ìyá Òsun Òsogbo observes of gods and people that we "depend on each other." And, as Fanon observed, so do Black and white—in religious practice and in theory. Hegel, Marx, Freud, Babá Murah, and I are all men with a special stake in defining the line of difference between these two anchor positionalities in the tragedy of circum-Atlantic life, which is why we are the central characters in the story that I tell. But Babá Murah has been the more delightful interlocutor, because, unlike the parvenu, he accepts, without embarrassment and most often with a hearty laugh, the many spirits who dance in him.

Just about all Vodou practitioners seem to acknowledge that at least *some* spirits are human made, such as *pwen, gad, lougawou,* and *zonbi.* Within communities of Vodou practitioners, the emically salient question is usually not *whether or not a god has been made* but whether a god has been made for the benefit of the community or *for the benefit of a selfish individual.* As in Surinamese Winti, the accusation of madeness tends to be reserved for the latter case. According to some Vodou priests, *pwen* are material beings made by disreputable priests and sold to people who use them for selfish and often malevolent purposes. They are powerful and effective, drawing wealth, godchildren, and crowds of spectators to the temples of the priests who own them, but they violate the *Ginen,* or honorably ancestral (literally, "Guinea" or "West African"), moral traditions that Manmi Maude holds sacrosanct. In these ways, *pwen* resemble the *adumakama* spirits of Surinamese and Dutch Winti as they are described by Surinamese people in Amsterdam.[5] Through their madeness by ambitious people, such noninherited spirits dramatize the disruption of the collective family group through selfish individualism (Larose 1977).

However, once a *pwen* has been inherited and has entered the pantheon of its maker or buyer's descendants, a *pwen* can become a communal and respectable—or Ginen—*lwa,* making the well-known history of its madeness irrelevant to moral judgments about it (Larose 1977). Moreover, Haitian priests widely agree that made and bought spirits (*pwen achte*) tend to work faster and with greater respect for the worshipper's precise wishes than do Ginen spirits. For priests who make or buy such spirits, they are therefore defined not by their malevolence or selfishness but their efficacy, their profitability, and the ferociousness of the punishments then inflict if the worshipper or owner fails to fulfill his or her reciprocal promises to the spirit. The avowed makers and owners of such spirits emphasize that any spirit—even an honorably ancestral, Ginen spirit—can become malevolent under such conditions.

Haitian *vodouisants* also widely acknowledge at least one species of spirit that is bought or made without being malevolent. A *gad* spirit is typically made by rubbing certain ritually prepared substances into incisions on, for example, a person's upper arm. It defends its owner from any type of danger that approaches. It is known to be working when, for example, the host's arm spontaneously and involuntarily rises up. Manmi Maude once knew a man whose arm did not go down for three days, until after the danger had passed.

Gad in other parts of the body cause other, similarly involuntary actions. For example, when the host has unknowingly swallowed a poison administered by an enemy, a swallowed *gad* will quickly cause its host to vomit. Though *gad* are clearly human-made beings and Manmi Maude makes them, she and her followers tend to reserve the marked attribution of madeness for *lougawou*, *zonbi*, and *pwen*, which they associate with evil. Among priests in Jacmel, Manmi Maude is reputed to be unusual in her choice not to work with made-and-bought spirits in her temple.

Manmi Maude and her Haitian *ti fèy*, or "godchildren," gave me details about the most feared of human-made beings. Perhaps the most horrible and frightening of beings in the Vodou universe is the *lougawou*, which is terminologically cognate with the French term for werewolf. According to my acquaintances in Jacmel, the *lougawou* is a human-made and always female spirit that has acquired too much power and thereby escaped the control of its master. Like other spirits that are openly recognized as made or bought, the *lougawou* is initially made in order to enrich its selfish owner at the expense of other people. The *lougawou* feeds on people in a most extreme and fatal way. It walks around during the day looking like a normal human being. However, after uttering certain prayers and incantations at the crossroads, it turns into one or another kind of animal and "walks in the night." Most often, it looks like a turkey (*kòdèn*) but fire shoots from its eyes, ears, nostrils, underarms, and anus. Around 2008, in her private home next to the Jacmel temple, Manmi Maude herself and several of her highest lieutenants saw a *lougawou* in the process of taking on its nighttime form.

A *lougawou* can reportedly kill children or adults with its beak, but its typical modus operandi is to alight on the roof of a house so as not to be seen, whereupon it kills a child in the house by sucking his or her spirit out through a window. Seven days after the child has been buried, the *lougawou* exhumes the child, turns the child into a fish, a pig, or a cow and either sells it at market or takes it home for consumption by the *lougawou* and her coven of fellow *lougawou*.

Lougawou are even more frightening, it seems, than the other major villain in the Haitian cosmos, the typically male *bòkò*, or priest who, for selfish purposes, creates *zonbi*, in the form of living-dead people or of disembodied spirits captured from the graveyard and imprisoned in a ritually prepared bottle (Matory in preparation).

Thus, Manmi Maude's followers in Jacmel typically focus not on the debate over whether spirits are human made and preexistent but on the contrast between *recently* made spirits and *inherited* ones, because recent manufacture implies selfish motives on the part of the maker and buyer. Manmi Maude's explicit denial of the human-madeness of gods might be understood in these terms, since she fully admits that, once inherited and cared for across generations, a human-made and bought *pwen* spirit will become a *lwa* god, recognized as *eritaj*—that is, something made inherently respectable because it is associated with the ancestors.

An Afro-German Dialogue

Ìyá Ọ̀ṣun Òṣogbo, Babá Murah, Oggún Fumi, David Font-Navarrete, and Manmi Maude practice different national traditions and speak radically different mother tongues. Among them, only Ìyá Ọ̀ṣun and Manmi Maude have met each other, on the occasion of our week-long collective lecture series at the University of Vermont in 2014—an acquaintance too brief to explain the remarkable degree of overlap among their conflicted but contextually understandable explanations of the ontology of gods and other sacred beings. They all upset the premises of the allegory at the center of Enlightenment thought and the late or post-Enlightenment models of Hegel, Marx, and Freud—that Afro-Atlantic priests assign value and agency arbitrarily, that they merely project their individual will onto spontaneously found physical objects, and that they are unaware of human agency in the creation of the value and efficacy of consecrated things.

In dialogue with these late or post-Enlightenment hypotheses about the value and agency of gods—through my words, through their experience of antagonism from the Abrahamic religions, and through their exposure to the environmentalist and animal-rights critique of animal sacrifice—Ìyá Ọ̀ṣun, Manmi Maude, and Babá Murah offer a number of overlapping positions about whether and how the gods are human-made. Afro-Atlantic altars are assemblages of preexisting substances with a value and a personality of their own. However, it is human effort that activates, consecrates, and sustains them in a concrete and visible form than makes their constructive intervention in human lives possible. Each sacred altar is a specific entity with a uniqueness, originality, and human authorship of its own. During spirit possession, that god manifests him- or herself in the body of the altar's owner. Through possession, dreams, and ritual action upon the altar, the god and its human worshipper are each other's authors, transforming each other over time.

However, unlike Oggún Fumi in Santiago de Cuba, these three priests challenge any suggestion that the gods are made from scratch. Their anxiety to make this point clear to me may be a reaction to the Abrahamic critique of idolatry and, even more likely, to the Afro-Atlantic suspicion that gods made by lone individuals embody a community-destroying selfishness. In this context, Babá Murah and Manmi Maude seem to be arguing less against the proposition that the gods are made than in favor of the idea that the madeness of legitimate gods is collective and ancestral, rather than individual. Ìyá

Òṣun resolves the paradox in terms confirmed by the spontaneous stories and ritual conduct of the other three priests: people construct gods, and gods construct people. In the words of Ìyá Òṣun, people and gods "depend on each other" but ideally do so in a collectively and ancestrally sanctioned way.

I am reminded of Marx's assessment that the factory is an accretion of the surplus labor power alienated from generations of workers and that it facilitates the further alienation of present-day workers' labor. Alternatively, from an Afro-Atlantic perspective, one might conceive of the present-day worker's relationship to the factory as an intergenerational process in which the factory and generations of workers have progressively remade each other. If Afro-Atlantic altars are an allegory of anything, it is the principle that a person is not an ideally autonomous and purely self-willed subject in a world of things. Rather, a person and the things around her are crossroads of inheritance, mutual obligation, circumstances, and personal will affecting each other.

In sum, people make people. People are made in the same sense as gods are, and they are made of virtually the same substances. People are born through thoughtful recombinations of ancestors' biological materials and of other bloods collected by the parents and fed to the child, as well as guidance by and the acknowledgment of biologically unrelated forebears and mentors. Each newborn and each new initiate is a recombination of things, substances, powers, alliances, and loyalties that have made up and continue to be part of the gods. A child's body and person are products of assembly, of bringing together the elements that make a person a functional actor who is present in and helpful to his or her community. In sum, a human being is an assembled, or constructed, portal of exchange. And so is a god. As Viveiros de Castro (2004) said of lowland South American peoples, the Afro-Atlantic religions surely accord greater value to the raw materials of production and reproduction than does a capitalist-era European thinker like Marx. However, just as Marx argues that the prevalence of slavery in ancient Greece inhibited Aristotle's recognition of the true nature of value, we might also conclude that Marx's advocacy of the wage laborer inhibited his recognition of the value- and agency-producing character of genealogy, hierarchy, and exchange.

There are clearly endogenous debates and differences of opinion among Afro-Atlantic priests, just as there were among Hegel, Marx, and Freud. For example, does initiation "make" gods and their devotees, or simply establish a fruitful relationship between them? Are high priests "fathers" and "mothers" of the gods, or merely their caretakers? In the end, however, the diversity of opinion about the madness of the gods and any given priest's vacillation over the issue is as insignificant to most Afro-Atlantic priests as is the difference between the anthropomorphic form of the god and his or her nonanthropomorphic interventions through floods, earthquakes, healing, military routs, and the like. This difference is insignificant to them as the difference between "its being cold" and "her being cold" is to my wife, Bunmi.

There are other ambiguities in the language of Afro-Atlantic priests. For example, though the members of a temple are called "children," "fathers," "mothers," or "wives" of the divine, the prepositions and verbs linking these people to the gods and each other are always ambiguous. Do priests and initiates belong to the god, or does the god belong to them? Are they the containers of the god or the gods the containers of the people? Are the personnel parents and children *of* the god or *in* the god? The upshot of all of this is a conception of divinity in which the ensemble of the personnel of the god, along with the material things and phenomena associated with the god all over the world, *are*—in a way that can be interpreted variously—the god. The difficulty of translating this parlance into consistent English vocabulary and syntax confirms the notion that Afro-Atlantic priests assume a level of dialectics in the making of people, gods, and their communities that is not easily translated into English. The networks that make up people, gods, and their communities are not easily parsed into discrete or fixed subjects and objects.

Marx recognized the social nature of production but not the central and prior role of exchange in the social production of the producer. The Afro-Atlantic religions highlight the central and prior role of exchange in the production of the producer. Moreover, for the priests, deferred compensation and the hierarchy that results are not inherently suspicious. They inhere in the nature of marriage and childbearing. So why should they not inhere in less important moments of the production process, as well?

The spirited things of the Afro-Atlantic religions are demonstrably products of both labor *and* exchange, heavily influenced since the sixteenth century by the larger context of circum-Atlantic capitalism. In West Africa, naturally, the domestic forms of these religions overlap with but differ from the ones elaborated by monarchs and merchants who—as conditions of profit making and survival—participated in the Atlantic slave trade, which dispersed the antecedents of the Yorùbá-Atlantic religious traditions around the Atlantic perimeter.

These religions depend and always depended on the extraction and processing of natural products, as well as human artisanship. However, they also depend and depended on long-distance commerce in products such as cowrie shells, beads, rum and schnapps, red palm oil (*epo pupa*), shea butter (*òrí*), kolanut (*obì*), bitter kola (*orógbó*), horses, cloth, herbs, river lime (*efun*), camwood powder (*osùn*), alligator pepper (*atare*), books, and so forth—many of them imported into the place of worship. These religions are conventionally understood as the "survivals" of changeless African practices transported to the Americas in the hulls of slave ships. I have argued elsewhere (2005) that these religions have also been transformed profoundly by the interests and efforts of free Black travelers and merchants, nationalist folkorists, bourgeois patrons, and international feminists, all of whom sustained clientelistic relationships with the priests. Here I have added that the dominant form in which these religions arrived in the nineteenth-century Americas was profoundly influenced by the projects of Ọ̀yọ́'s merchant-monarchs, accretions of which are found in the altars of Santería/Ocha and Candomblé.

The altars, or thrones, of the Yorùbá-Atlantic gods materialize the idea that people and communities reflect and depend on economic and monetary exchange. On the one hand, these religions mobilize the power of capitalism. On the other, they invest their resources in the construction of people—that is to say, in Marxist terms, in the construction of workers—who are not individuals with the obvious right to be paid in proportion to the hours of labor that they have contributed to social production. A person is, instead, a crossroads and a nexus of translocal connections and long-term debt. And her body is only a temporary vessel, or conduit, for these connections. The person is not sufficiently discrete from others to accommodate the logic of the even-Steven exchange of labor for its time-based equivalent in cash or goods.

To the present day, the practice of these religions continue to generate a major industry and distribution network in São Paulo, Bahia, Havana, Miami, and New York. Initiations and other spiritual services also attract pilgrims, religious tourists, and copious remittances to Cuba. Sacred and secular commerce nourish communities of mutual assistance all around the Atlantic perimeter. Thus, these religions continue to reflect the history of their involvement in circum-Atlantic commerce, and they make no apology for their use of commodities and paid services, as well as the artifacts of old commercial ties, in the improvement of individual and communal human life. These ties have generated a new world religion that, more and more over time, unites a dozen countries around the Caribbean and the Atlantic in a continuous network, or web, of exchange.

But a shared paradox underlies these seemingly divergent perspectives on the forces guiding human life. Just as US American parlance frames charisma as the quality of a person rather than of a relationship, many Westerners are inclined to attribute an autonomous life, momentum, and trajectory to the market, as though some form of that material assembly of cleared land, buildings, roads, goods, and crowds hovered over the actual people who define its purpose and its conventions, inexorably dictating the momentum and trajectory of human conditions and actions. Yet without people there is no market. Adam Smith's foundational political economy is an argument about how best not to interfere with that momentum and trajectory, with the understanding that every nation does so in one way or another, and that the very choice not to implement a policy of production or exchange is itself a human choice. Like the people who populate, conduct, and are animated by markets, the people who make, worship, and are animated by gods tend to experience these forces as suprahuman and self-willed. Just as Afro-Atlantic priests debate the meaning of the "madeness" of the gods, so do Marxists debate the degree to which Marx universalized the labor theory of value and the balance of human agency and teleological inevitability that he attributed to history. Marx is fundamentally a reformist heir to the tradition of the market as an "invisible hand" (à la Adam Smith), while the priests of the Afro-Atlantic priests either embrace or pull against an opposite anchor—the human-madeness of the gods. Yet contemporary Western ambivalence about the nature of "the market" might, for a Western readership, provide the clearest analogy to the ambiguous ontology of the Afro-Atlantic gods.

The questions that a class- and race-challenged Marx has inspired me to ask of the priests are not the stuff of everyday conversation among Afro-Atlantic priests or Marxists, but the subtlety of the priests' response illustrates a fundamental commonality between the Afro-Atlantic religions and historical materialism—the understanding that gods are grounded in material reality in a manner obscured by the Abrahamic religions, particularly in their royalist and bourgeois implementations. And, though they speak from different racial positions and gendered priorities, Freud and the Afro-Atlantic priests enter the Afro-European dialogue with a range of shared assumptions about personhood. However, Marx's and Freud's dilemma as potential victims of the gentile West made it easier for them to stereotype the African other than to recognize these commonalities. In any case, even by the standards of Marx and Freud, the paradigmatic "fetishists" are no fools about the nature of value and agency. In fact, they have a great deal to teach Marx and Freud about both.

The most elemental point of this exposition on the ambiguous madeness, or constructedness, of the Afro-Atlantic gods is that, if eighteenth- and nineteenth-century orisha- and lwa-worshippers are anything like their twentieth- and twenty-first-century successors, then the anti-African metaphor at the shared root of Hegelian, Marxist, and Freudian social theory is tendentious and interested, not ethereal and beyond the material constraints of social life in these men's respective times and places. Unlike Bosman's, Hegel's, Marx's, and Freud's fetishist antitype of good governance and reasoning, the makers, or constructors, of the Afro-Atlantic gods are not given to projecting divine power into arbitrary things, and they are not unaware of people's role in making valuable goods, social orders, or gods. In fact, my own insights about racially and class ambivalent Europeans' self-fashioning through social theory is deeply indebted to the Afro-Atlantic reasoning about the reciprocal making of people and gods.

Conclusion to Part III

No more than other European theories are those of Marx and Freud abstract statements of truth neutrally applicable to the interpretation of all times and places. Rather, they are socially situated proposals for the resolution of culturally informed and historically specific political and psychological dilemmas. And so are the Afro-Atlantic religions. The most visible difference is the bodily postures and material forms in which those proposals are embodied. The difference between European theories and Afro-Atlantic religions is usually constructed as the difference between the observer and the observed, between the subject and the object of knowledge, and between the ruler and the ruled. We see this contrast most clearly in the difference between the post-Enlightenment European book and the Afro-Atlantic vessel, packet, or filled-cavity anthropomorphic altar.

Afro-Atlantic spirited things reveal a history of extroversion, extraversion, and a concomitant conception of the self as a vessel and a crossroads of heterogeneous long-distance relationships under the conditions of the Atlantic trade. By contrast, the mass-produced, translated, and reprinted book of European social theory typically conceals the human history of its genesis in a specific culture and time, and in the author's class insecurity, ethnoracial marginality, and unspoken sexual desires. It has no "aura" (Benjamin [1936] 2002). But books do not inevitably conceal their human history or the social relationships that give them life. For example, each copy of the Torah and of the Qur'an is invested with sacredness and surrounded by rules of proper treatment. In northern Nigeria, people are regularly killed based upon the accusation that the murder victim had mishandled a Qur'an, a book thereby constructed as more valuable than a human life because it stands for a contestable configuration of community.[1] A product of mass translation and the culture of mechanical reproduction, not even the most sacred book in the English or German language generally possesses the aura to demand such respect, much less the death of a human being. But Engels did call *Capital* "the Bible of the working class," and the credulous abstraction of Marx's and Freud's theories from the social context of their production does at times convey an air of worship and has come at a cost to Black people.

By contrast, the vessel, packet, or cavity-filled anthropomorphic altar of the Afro-Atlantic religions reveals the historically, personally, and situationally specific convergences of often rival forces that make up the Afro-Atlantic person and constitute both her rivalries with others and her own intrinsic ambivalence. Each one of these altars is filled, surrounded, and patinated with gifts (including shells, beads, animal blood, bones, and artwork) that commemorate a history of relationship between gods and their priests and between priests and their followers and friends. Moreover, books like Marx's and Freud's are normally read in silence by lone individuals, while altars must be read aloud, as it were, by the collectives that continually maintain them through song, dance, and sacrifice, which equally reveal the rival forces that animate these consecrated things. The mass-produced book substantiates a political amnesia about the material architecture of historical materialism and psychoanalysis, which—in the forms of factories, overcoats, the piano, the "negro slave," the Acropolis, the intaglio ring, the upright chair, the couch, and the "savage"—encodes a fetishism that Western academics normally refuse to see. I have endeavored to highlight the lopsided ethnoracial, class, and gender ambivalence embodied in these fetishes of central European social theory.

Perhaps now is the time for a definition of "fetishism" that follows from the fifteenth- and sixteenth-century encounter on the Guinea Coast and integrates what we have so far learned from the conversation among Marx, Freud, and the Afro-Atlantic priests. Fetishism is the projection of particular values and qualities of agency upon material things, a projection that anticipates rival projections and asymmetrically legitimizes particular claims of value, agency, and social relationships at the expense of other possibilities. An important dimension of the concept derives from the usual contexts in which the term "fetish" is used—settings in which rival and copresent parties disagree about the value and agency of the referent. The relationship between these parties is often hierarchical and mutually dependent, such that the power of the most enduring fetishes lies in their embodiment of the perspectives of both the dominant and the subordinated parties, making the fetish a powerful kind of sign, supercharged with lopsided ambivalence.

Because, in recent centuries, the exponents of the Afro-Atlantic religions have more often been the servant than the master, to invoke the roles in Hegel's dialectic, they have had to be more aware of the centrality of such fetishism in the global political and cultural economy and even in the working of local communities. Whereas the "freedom" sought by the Enlightenment's paradigmatic subject rests on the immediate dischargeability of debt, Afro-Atlantic subjectivity prioritizes long-term connections mediated by asymmetrical, enduring, and even undischargeable debt. The freedom of Protestants relies on the concentration of all irreciprocable debt on God the father and the gift of Jesus's sacrifice on the cross. Islam, a brotherhood founded by a merchant, similarly concentrates undischargeable obligation upon one single god. The Enlightenment sense of community rests atop the now-taken-for-granted assumption that equality among white men, even-Steven exchange, and the short-term nature of obligatory social relationships are the normal conditions of human relationship. By contrast, Afro-Atlantic priests and rituals take for granted the normalcy of intergenerational relationships that result from persistently unequal exchanges and forms of obligation among multiple people, exchanges that are never terminated by a final pay-off and erasure of debt. For Afro-Atlantic priests, hierarchy and unequal social relationships are normal, this-worldly phenomena, the discharging of which is neither normal nor meritorious. However, Western and Afro-Atlantic anxieties about the loneliness of egalitarian individualism and the hierarchical implications of long-term connection meet in the figures of the *zonbi*, the zombie, the *pakèt kongo*, and the toys of bondage, discipline, and sadomasochism. Steeped in the historical vocabulary of the post-sixteenth-century Afro-European dialogue, these materialized anxieties are the subject of *Zombies and Black Leather* (Matory in preparation).

ESHU'S HAT, OR
AN AFRO-ATLANTIC
THEORY OF THEORY

"Fetish!"

What do we learn by hurling this word-weapon back at its originators?

Like Eshu's two-sided hat, this book has provoked a fight not only among Marx, Freud, and the Afro-Atlantic priests but also between canonical social theory and the ethnographic method. Whether they are enemies or friends depends upon the moment and upon the perspective of the reader.

This is my Afro-Atlantic perspective. On the one hand, Europe's post-Enlightenment theorists—including the late Hegel, Marx, and Freud—have constructed themselves and the Europe to which they aspire as the adversaries of Africa—that is, as the European antithesis to the Africa that they have imagined in the service of their own respective classes and races of European. On the other, the Afro-Atlantic priests whose thoughts I have endeavored to document in this book and the spirited things I have interpreted through those thoughts construct exogenous populations—including Europeans, Nupe people, and migrants from the Middle East—as positionally opposite but essential and intrinsic elements of the relational self. To my mind, Hegel and Marx are less wrong, bad, or in need of correction than they are real and powerful exemplars of one widespread response to stigma and marginalization—ethnological Schadenfreude.

Nonetheless, Hegel, Marx, and Freud are weighty among the conflicting spirits that constitute the vessel self of Afro-Atlantic scholars like me, and these spirits are made more alive, manageable, and effective in our lives when we acknowledge the full range of their dilemmas, their powers, their weaknesses, and their blindspots. Those discomfited by my efforts to reveal the malignant and the benign dimensions of Marx's and Freud's theoretical projects may take comfort in the fact that we adherents of Yorùbá indigenous religion, Candomblé, Santería/Ocha, and Vodou tend to treat our gods in the same way. The essence of divinity is not the exemplary embodiment of perfection but the exemplary embodiment of human dilemmas and of the harmful potential of even the most potentially beneficent forces.

Conversely, Africa is weighty among the conflicting spirits that animate Hegel, Marx, and Freud. For example, Freud's insight that the family is not the loving oasis or conflict-free refuge imagined by many bourgeois Westerners, that it is the source of the conflicting spirits within the self, that people are therefore deeply ambivalent, and that their ambivalence often reveals itself in their ritualized use of objects confirms and, yet, is much less cosmopolitan and sophisticated than what the average Afro-Atlantic priest has long known. Freud's linear social evolutionism seems to have blinded him to the extrafamilial and contemporaneous origins of the id. Freud avowed that the "savage" African lurks underneath the "civilized" facade of the European.

Freud may have admitted that his and other Europeans' efforts to suppress the African "savage" within their own souls only fortified the power of that inner "savage" over them, but Freud seemed unaware of how the African "savage" got there. That "savage" was born not in human evolutionary origins or even in the heart of Africa but at the Afro-European trading posts, factories, and forts of the sixteenth- and seventeenth-century Guinea Coast, and that "savage" grew strong on the sentiments of late eighteenth-century gentile burghers and nineteenth-century assimilated Jews, who, by aggressively asserting their difference from and superiority to the "negro," sought to prove their worthiness of enfranchisement in Europe.

Emily Apter (1993) argues that the ostensibly "real" power or phenomenon that European social critics project onto the thing they call a fetish (a "reality" that the ostensible fetishist has failed to understand) is itself imaginary. Apter adds that, though imaginary, the accusation of "fetishism" has great implications for the accuser him- or herself. It calls attention to the contestability of the accuser's own assertions about what is real. Moreover, in order to sustain his or her correctness, the accuser must, in the end, internalize the image of the fetish as an antitype of the accuser's self. Thus, as in the cases of Hegel, Marx, and Freud, the African fetishist and his critic become codependent and mutually constituting phenomena. Before and during the Enlightenment, European royals and aristocrats had seen in black African monarchs a counterpart to their own inherent dignity and potential allies in the struggle against Islam. During and after the Enlightenment, European burghers and racially ambiguous whites saw in the black African slave an antitype and negative proof of their own equality to the European aristocracy. Hence, during the long nineteenth century, Hegel's, Marx's, and Freud's "inner Africa" was not an evolutionary survival but an artifact of the Atlantic trade and of the struggle over its symbolic and material dividends. No less animated by the Atlantic trade are the Cubans, Brazilians, and Germans who, since the 1970s, have brought Ochún and Oxum, Yemayá and Iemanjá, Ollá and Iansã, Changó and Xangô to dance on Hegel's grave.

The fetishes of Marx and Freud instantiate a struggle within the Abrahamic and Western traditions over whether the family and the communities modeled upon it are naturally open or closed. Against the Hebrews' foundational mistrust of neighboring families and tribes, Christianity and Islam endeavored to build interfamilial brotherhoods through the metaphor that the brothers are fellow sheep or slaves to their god. Engels went further by denaturalizing monogamy and the patriarchal family ([1884] 1978), and Marx proposed a pan-European family with reference to its shared and equal stakes in coats, factories, and the "negro-slave." Freud's fetish revolutionized

Western treatments of demoniac possession, neurosis, and the various forms of discontent that he attributed to "civilization." His "talking cure" proposed healing through the revelation and transformation of European family relationships by means of the couch and the upright chair. His hidden transcript (Scott 1990)—with reference to the Acropolis, the fur hat, the intaglio ring, the "savage," the lion and the "negro," the cigar, and a collection of statuary— was the inclusion of assimilated Jewish men in the family that is Europe and its diaspora. In all of these projects, the premise of the family's inherent self-containment and closure is the foundational assumption, and the solution to the problem is its internal rearrangement or the adjustment of its boundaries.

The Afro-Atlantic religions emerge from the opposite premise—that the antecedent condition of life and the precondition of production is exchange. The exchange between people and between families is intrinsic to the existence of each person and every family. And so it is between peoples. For the Afro-Atlantic priests, the acknowledged sources of the internally heterogeneous self vastly and expressly exceed the boundaries of the nuclear family. In fact, Yorùbá kinship terminology acknowledges no such unit; in it, all males of a higher generation are called "father" (bàbá), all females of a higher generation are called "mother" (ìyá), all siblings and cousins senior to the speaker share the same designation (ègbọ́n), and all junior siblings and cousins share the same designation (àbúrò). Perhaps concomitantly, there are vastly more conflicting spirits than the three named by Freud—the ego, the superego, and the "Africa in us" that is the id. The Afro-Atlantic counterpart to Freud's family drama encompasses multiple networks of social and environmental forces—including meteorological events, geographical features, herbs and trees, animals, human-made things, dead people, money, germs, diverse races, and diverse occupations—each of which networks animate other people as well.

The Afro-Atlantic priests are way ahead of Freud (and even ahead of the allopathic physicians who have recently recognized that the body is a biome) in realizing that there is no way to expel or suppress the many seemingly exogenous elements of the self. Those elements will just come back. They are intrinsic to the biome that is the person. Hence, the ritual drama of the Afro-Atlantic religions enacts and manages these elements of the self through the physical metonyms of not only what we Westerners would call the nuclear family (such as blood, the house, and the wife/mother) but also extrafamilial relationships (such as slavery, equestrianism, pottery, ecology, and the translocal commerce in coins, cowries, and beads).

The Fetish as a Clash between Middle Kingdoms

In 2015, the Department of Comparative Studies and the Diversity and Identity Studies Collective at the Ohio State University hosted a discussion of an earlier draft of this book. There, one Marxist scholar demanded clarity about the difference I draw between self-evident truths, such as global warming, and religious phenomena, while another scholar, who specializes in German-African relations asked me to clarify the distinction I see between religion and philosophy. I replied that clarifying such distinctions was not the aim of this book. Personally, I have many strong convictions about what is true or false, about what is right or wrong, and about what is delusional or empirical. In the past, I have been willing to say, for example, that one particular scholar told blatant untruths about Yorùbá history and society (Matory 2003). However, facts are never found ready-made in the world. The reality of the cosmos is inchoate, and no aspect of that reality is discrete from its other aspects. Within that inchoate reality, every variable that we discern is a construction based upon selective attention, as is every variable with which we can correlate that variable. As Latour and Woolgar ([1979] 1986) put it, even the facts produced in laboratories are a "middle kingdom" between a reality "out there" and our culture-specific, socially conditioned apperception. By extension, I argue that every theory or god is the outcome of the ongoing and mutually transformative confrontation between such apperception and the world.

Equally shaped by our selective attention and awareness is our willingness to describe the relationship between any two or more variables as causal rather than correlative. All we can really say is that the correlation upon which our practical efforts depend has been effective in a certain percentage of cases and under certain conditions. For that reason, as an *anthropologist*, I am unwilling to concede my OSU interlocutors' insinuation that there is something more real about global warming than about, say, the resurrection of Christ or the labor theory of value. However, I do believe that these facts are useful in the pursuit of different practical goals and in the realization of different communities. Whatever facts I may chose to believe, I have repeatedly discovered that my sense of the true and the right very seldom determines how other people think and act. Contrary to the reigning supposition in the university, people are very seldom persuaded to change their minds by arguments based upon evidence and syllogism. Multisensory rituals and vivid anecdotal accounts about one's own experiences and feelings are usually much more persuasive. This book concerns the signs that people use to reshape social life, the experiences that inspire that effort, and the cultural-historical backdrop that makes these signs persuasive.

I have definite opinions about the truth. However, the task I have laid out for myself in this project is not to determine the truth about the world "out there" but to examine the conditions under which "middle kingdoms" clash and the nature of the signs—namely, "fetishes"—that emerge from this clash. Contrary to Marx and Freud, I have argued that fetishism is not primarily an error assignable to the speaker's Other but a central semiotic touchstone of social life at its most normal—whereby people of different ranks and social backgrounds struggle to define their relationships with each other through the mediation of contested material things.

Marx and Freud—like their fellow Europeans, from Pieter de Marees to Hartmut Böhme—apply the term "fetish" to the inter- or intrasocietal Other in a manner that only inadvertently calls attention to the debatability of the social reforms that the critics themselves are recommending. By tossing that epithet, the speaker normally means to establish a hierarchy of truth, value, and competency. And, naturally, the speaker places himself in the superior position. Instead, I consciously employ the term to show that Western theories of fetishism (including my own) take shape in a coeval dialogue with the Other. It is not the wrongness of the Other's value code but the *tension and conflict* between Marx's, Freud's, or Böhme's value code and that of their European and Afro-Atlantic interlocutors that makes their shared referent a fetish. This book is therefore an extended meditation on what things and their designation as "fetishes" teach us about social hierarchy and its inherent debatability. Commodities, noses, white people's other erotic fetishes, and Afro-Atlantic empowered things are magnets of conflicting, socially positioned, and historically specific visions of self, society, and who owes what to whom—complementary and rival visions that have emerged in tandem from the conditions of Atlantic slavery and capitalism, European and European-inspired nationalisms, and European overseas imperialism.

Therefore, the aim of this book is not to rank the relative correctness of Marx, Freud, and the gods Black people make. Nor is it to prove that either Sigmund Freud or Karl Marx was essentially racist. Rather, I wish to show that by quoting them as sources of abstract truisms about the all times, places, and social positions, we are actually canonizing as universal truth variables constructed by some people who occupied specific social statuses in specific cultures during specific historical periods, as well as the correlations that they selectively and interestedly chose to emphasize. The very idea of treating specific central Europeans' thoughts as abstract, universalizable theory is an act of fetishization, always worth viewing in the hierarchical social context in which one party's assertion of the abstractness and universality of its truths rests on the projection of all concreteness and specificity onto its dark Other. Describing this semiotic practice as "fetishization" is a call to investigate the concrete and specific furniture that the white cloak of "theory" has hidden in the service of its contestable cause and in the interest of its discreditable advocates. Such fetishization is neither right nor wrong, but it does embody a canonical though debatable proposition about whose agency counts and about the relative value of people of different genders, sexual orientations, classes, races, and religions. Perhaps the most intriguing theories and other fetishes are those that simultaneously dramatize the threats from above and those from below. Like Freud, Marx is both lion and negro, roles also materialized in the couch and the coat.

Since the Enlightenment, "theory" has embodied an aspirational positionality of which black women are the ultimate antitype. The irony is that, in the Afro-Atlantic religions, the paradigmatic self is an African royal wife, but the white man is not the antitype of that ideal subject. Rather, what makes the dark, vessel-like wife an ideal model of the self is her potential complementarity to an unlimited range of foreign interlocutors, including white men. When well managed, this role complementarity is the ideal model of exchange and productivity. Yet the creative powers of wives are of a piece with the destructive powers of "our mothers," just as the slave can destroy his or her master.

This book will not change any Marxist into an anti-Marxist or any Freudian into an anti-Freudian. Rather, by illuminating the particular material, cultural, and social conditions under which these models of and for social life have been made, this book is intended to enhance the usefulness of historical materialism, psychoanalysis, and the Afro-Atlantic religions. Of course, the material, cultural, and social context of each of these actor-networks is ultimately the whole universe, but I have highlighted the microcontext that historical materialism, psychoanalysis, and the Afro-Atlantic religions most obviously share—the patterns of production and exchange, enslavement and emancipation, reproduction and extermination defining Atlantic capitalism. Though long forgotten or taken for granted, this shared context is implicit in the term "fetish" and continues to shape the networks of concepts, practices, and animated things that make up historical materialism, psychoanalysis, and the Afro-Atlantic religions.

The Materiality of Theories and Gods

The gorgeous material gods of the Afro-Atlantic religions have here provided a touchstone and a reminder of the material, cultural, and social processes that go into the formulation and materialization of *all* ideas, even the ones that seem most abstracted from the circumstances of the thinkers' personal lives. Not even the most high-flown theory should be regarded as immaterial or disinterested in its genesis, formulation, or interpretation. Every theory and every god is an act of construction and a performance with social and material roots, implicit intentions, unexamined implications, and variable outcomes.

One implication of using the word "fetish," and the repeated touchstone of my analysis, is the discovery of the mutually clarifying and mutually edifying similarities between psychoanalysis and the Afro-Atlantic religions—specifically regarding the role of ambivalently charged material things in the unfolding of the social relationships proposed by Marx and those instituted by Freud. To a degree, historical materialism, psychoanalysis, and the Afro-Atlantic religions all recognize the historical nature and human-madeness of subjectivity. But, to the same degree that the Afro-Atlantic priests are articulate about the human-madeness of their own gods, Marx and Freud are either oblivious to or in denial about the human-madeness of the subject they have constructed and about interested priorities underlying their constructions.

It is a mistake to treat European social theory as a form of pure, ethereal logic. Even when described as philosophy, subjected to open debate and criticism, and formulated in enclaves of prosperity seemingly removed from the influence of the European theorist's obvious hunger, thirst, hypothermia, and economic dependency on materially interested patrons, the thought of such theorists—just like everybody else's—is shaped by the social conditions, personal insecurities, and goals of the thinker. Like Afro-Atlantic religion, European social theory is grounded in historically specific conditions, culture-specific presumptions, and local struggles over the distribution of wealth and honor in daily life. Like other scholarship, much of post-Enlightenment European philosophy is an effort to distinguish the writer flatteringly from antecedent writers, and much of European social theory is an effort to distinguish the West from the rest in the context of a European overseas imperialism that had ambiguous material implications for both Guinea-Coast merchant-monarchs and assimilated central European Jewish men. Marx and Freud were not speaking their truths from above the fray.

Marx and most Afro-Atlantic priests agree on the premise that such fetishes, for all the power they embody and project, are assembled, animated, actuated, and, in a word, constructed by people themselves. Freud and most Afro-Atlantic priests acknowledge that multiple poorly understood forces—whether conceived as psychic or spiritual, inner-worldly or Other-worldly, latent or ancestral, fluidic or anthropomorphic—govern the life of any given person, that these forces are social, that they are regularly in conflict with each other, and that they are best managed through ritually mediated social interaction. In common, Marx, Freud, and the Afro-Atlantic priests agree that ultimately the ego is not in control. Conscious will is but one of the forces negotiating the outcomes of life and history. Most bourgeois West-erners, like me, live in denial of this conviction. Yet with their sense that the gods are made and are kept alive through a genealogical process, Afro-Atlantic priests invite scrutiny about the human sources of the gods and suggest a dialectical model of their power. Marx's and Freud's suppositions about the subject of history deserve similar scrutiny.

The Freudian-influenced Marxist Louis Althusser (1969) underscores the idea that the ego—that is, the meeting point of one's divided subjectivity and history—is itself a fiction. Indeed, we might call the "ego"—metonymically defined by the apparently bounded human body it occupies—the most fun-damental fetish. Althusser notes an intriguing parallel between Marx and Freud, one that brings them close to the Afro-Atlantic priests, as well. Marx recognized that history has no center, just a series of people's misrecogni-tions of who history's true agents really are. In sum, history for Marx, like the human lifespan for Freud, is a dialectic propelled by contradictions between who is accomplishing things and who most people think is accomplishing them. Just as Marx recognized that history is not propelled by great men, Freud recognized that the self is no single, self-guided agent. Like the misrecognized subject of great-man history, the ego is a product of a misrecognition produced by the surrounding ideological formation. Inspired by both Marx and Freud, Althusser asks us to examine the taken-for-granted ideological formation that has produced Marx and Freud—an examination that I have extended to the Afro-Atlantic priests, as well. What subject and whose history do Marx and Freud and the Afro-Atlantic priests conjure with their respective ontolo-gies and cosmologies, for what audiences, through what cathected material things, for whose benefit, and at whose expense? What kind of individual or collective self does the European social critic conjure through the instru-mentality of the fetish, and what power does the fetish then hold over him? Althusser recommends that we investigate the material-historical conditions that generated the popular misrecognition of the self as such an ego. What this book does is historicize and socially contextualize three alternative pro-posals about the shape of human agency, as well as the social relationships and the material things that embody them.

Because all new social relationships arise from and react to older ones, the fetishes of Africa and Latin America and the fetishes of Europe begin with culture-specific and inherited vocabularies of self and social relationship that precede and surround those fetishes. Fetishes competitively reconfigure and build on those vocabularies in ways shaped by time, place, class interests, and the gravity of rival fetishes. Like the usual real-life Afro-Atlantic referents of the term "fetish," Marx's and Freud's theories of history and personhood propose new actor-networks that reconfigure old ones in response to the demands of specific times, places, class interests, and rivalries. The choice of the term "fetish" to describe another population's affectively potent things and actor-networks was itself a form of fetishization that Marx and Freud adopted from the champions of the Enlightenment.

What Ìyá Òṣun Òṣogbo said about the Afro-Atlantic gods bears application to European social theories as well: they may predate their worshippers, but if people stop worshipping them, they cease to affect human life, and whole networks of expected social relationship go awry. In other words, society depends on fetishes, but fetishes acquire their strength and their efficacy in social life from people's material investments in them. Ideas depend on our social and material enactment of them, such as speaking, debating, publishing, reading, interpreting, denouncing, transforming, and enforcing them. This fact benefits dictators and liberators alike. But nothing is more helpful to a dictator than the conviction that truth comes from somewhere beyond the physically positioned material experience of particular perceivers and conceivers who are just as human as you or I. In today's academia, a scholar's deficit of pigment and lack of a vagina—and the temporal distance that prevents us from seeing, touching, and smelling their human bodies and possessions—facilitate the impression that their writings convey perspectiveless, universal truths, and inevitable social outcomes. Prohibitions on the visual depiction of Mohammed facilitate a similar impression about the Qur'an.

Such depersonalization of authority facilitates a sort of academic possession-trance, as described by a graduate student of mine from Hong Kong:

> The argument that theories, similar to the gods in Afro-Atlantic rituals, are made by people does not mean that they, as well as the gods, are not valid or real. They are valid in the sense that they help us better understand the world from a certain perspective which may have been overlooked. More importantly, they are real in the sense that they . . . involve a power exchange, and they are able to affect the way we think and behave toward each other. This in fact reminds me of some experiences I had at Duke. After learning about a certain theory that they strongly like or agree with, such as Nietzsche's superman or Lacan's the Real, some of my friends here would look at everything around them through the lens of that theory and involuntarily adopt a theoretical language in daily conversation, sometimes even with people who had no idea about that theory. . . . I realize that this may be how theory, as a fetish itself, especially in academia, could have power over us, even though the original intention should be to utilize theory in our understanding of the world. (Jin Ling, CA 801 reflection paper, week 13, November 22, 2015)

Such states of possession-trance resurrect the likes of Marx and Freud as transcendent gods rather than real-life human interlocutors.

The so-called fetishes of the Guinea Coast and its diaspora were conceptual linchpins of the European Enlightenment and of the Yorùbá-Atlantic religions alike, and the taproot from which this book has grown. The assembled commodities of which these African gods were made may have appeared to the Dutch Calvinist merchant-adventurers of the sixteenth and seventeenth centuries as the endpoint of the relationship between trading partners, to Marx as misrepresentations of the relationships among producers, and to Freud as symbols of a boy's identification with both the child victim and the paternal agent of castration. However, to Yorùbá-Atlantic worshippers they seem to have enshrined the beginning of hoped-for relationships across the clarified boundaries between worlds, tribes, nations, and bodies. By its very nature, the so-called fetish also highlights the tension between European and African positions. It is a thing between worlds that compels consciousness of and reflection on contradiction.

Afro-Atlantic and especially Yorùbá-Atlantic priests consciously assemble and manage the self and the divine subject through the vivid sign of thing-filled, womblike vessels. These vivid, multisensorial signs call attention to the materiality of the coats, the factories, and the "negro slaves" that Marx employed in reformulating the subject of history and to that of cigars, fur, noses, couches, and intaglio rings in Freud's redefinition and management of the bourgeois citizen. These material foci of cathexis, worship, and the hope of revised social relationship are best understood in the context of the gender, sexual orientation, class, and race of the fetishist, as well as the aspirations and anxieties inherent in such social positions in the host society and the historical era. For example, I have tried to explain in these terms why psychoanalysis represents women as deficient, while the Yorùbá-Atlantic religions treat them as paragons of agency and value production. The distinct projects of Marx, on the one hand, and the Afro-Atlantic priests, on the other, also shed light on why the slave is an antitype of the effective producer and historical actor in Marx, while she or he is, according to the Afro-Atlantic priests, perhaps the most effective and productive of actors.

Hierarchy, Ambivalence, and "Balance"

No less than the Afro-Atlantic priests, Marx and Freud bring valuable analytical ideas to this discussion. For example, Marx teaches us a great deal about the forms of social inequality generated by exchange, and the role of the commodity in naturalizing them. For his part, Freud establishes ambivalence as a defining element of the self and of the most enduringly seductive material things. Marx and Freud share the idea that social hierarchy is oppressive and painful, and, therefore, that the normative relationship between the self and the other is mutually exclusive and antagonistic—even murderous—rather than mutually edifying. These racially ambiguous men illuminate an important feature of our shared experience in predominantly white societies.

For their part, the Afro-Atlantic religions normalize hierarchy (Matory in preparation) and sacralize difference, with the assumption that oppositely defined parties will—when their relationship is managed properly—interdigitate, interpenetrate, exchange power, and, at the height of ritual efficacy and satisfaction, merge. In the physical things and forms of conduct that he called "fetishism," Freud also intimately described a similarly intense cathectic blending of subjectivity between dominant and subordinate parties. However, he began with the premise that this process is pathological, leaving room for only throwaway lines about the presence of fetishism in normal romantic love, as well. So, through their morally exemplary and dramatic rituals, the Afro-Atlantic priests go much further than Freud in illustrating how, when deftly managed, social stratification lends itself to power exchange and to the satisfying interpenetration of complementary subjectivities. Marx's labor organizing might have benefited from a recognition of the interpenetration of workers' and capitalists' subjectivity in Europe. And, had Marx and Freud been aware of this process in their own self positioning and self making, they might not have stripped the "negro slave" and the "savage" so thoroughly of their value and agency.

Much like the supreme being depicted in the Hebrew Bible, or Old Testament, each constituent of the Afro-Atlantic self can have opposite valences. For example, it is key to her character that many an Afro-Atlantic goddess typically dances with a fan in one hand and a dagger or a sword in the other and that many a god first threatens his worshippers with a weapon and then turns it on him- or herself. If I could ever bear to part with these precious, spirited things, I might indeed have opened a crown shop. But the second most common merchandise might have been weapons. Weapons embodying the power both to protect and to harm are among the paraphernalia of virtually every Afro-Atlantic god. Consider, for example, figures 8.12, 8.20, 9.1, 9.2, 9.3, 9.4, C.1, and plate 1. In the SABA Collection, items B038, B110, B277, D014, D122, and J033 also breathtakingly dramatize the same point.

Even the lord of peace and purity—Obatalá in Santería/Ocha and Oxalá in Candomblé, both of whom are syncretized with Jesus Christ—also wields a sword (see figure C.1). And the best-known sacred implement in the Afro-Atlantic religions, Shango's double ax, cuts both ways: with its two blades, it can either defend a person or punish her. It also resembles a penis with its two testicles, reminding us that the penis itself may be an instrument of either love

FIGURE C.1 Beaded sword (*alfanje*) embodying the warrior aspect of the Afro-Cuban Santería/Ocha god Obatalá, who is normally associated with peace, age, and purity and is "syncretized" with Jesus Christ (SABA COLLECTION B019). Such a sword is intended to adorn the vessel altar of the god.

or violence. Afro-Atlantic leaders defend their acolytes from our mothers but also possess threatening, witchly powers. Indeed, African witchcraft bears the lesson that ambivalence is to be anticipated in all social relationships.

Each Afro-Atlantic person is the vessel for multiple gods and other spirits, each of which embodies its own culturally and historically specific dilemmas in the conduct of human relationships. For example, tales of the West African Yorùbá god Ṣàngó report the glory and wealth of his sovereignty, as well as his inevitable abuse of power. The *mulata/mulâtresse* goddesses of Cuban Santería/Ocha, Haitian Vodou, and Brazilian Candomblé—Ochún, Èzili Freda, and Oxum—apotheosize the character gestalt of sexual desirability, wealth, vanity, and childlessness, while their *negra/nwa* counterparts in these religions—Yemayá, Èzili Dantò, and Iemanjá—apotheosize the character gestalt of fecundity, caretaking, abandonment by men, and brooding anger.

Moreover, as religions of the crossroads, Yorùbá indigenous religion, Candomblé, and Santería/Ocha are rich in examples of interreligious polysemy—that is, the rival meanings of the same thing in neighboring religions. For example, the ram belongs to both the Afro-Atlantic religions and Islam (Matory 1994). In the Americas, the statues and lithographs of Roman Catholic saints are often also the faces of African gods, while the cross can stand for Jesus Christ, for the lord of the white cross, Obatalá/Oxalá, or for the dead (see, e.g., SABA Collection B320). These signs are electrified by the rival priorities of rival traditions and those traditions' opposite ranks in the circum-Atlantic world. The tension between the perspective of the castrator and that of the castrated is to me an apt, though literally unlikely, image of the binary tension between sons and fathers, wives and husbands, slaves and masters, the Afro-Atlantic and the Abrahamic religions. This tension is palpable in the animated objects of the Afro-Atlantic religions and visible in the social practices surrounding them.

From an Afro-Atlantic perspective, Freud's psychoanalysis is but a rudimentary system in the detection of such ambivalence. And, in its very choice to describe such phenomena as "ambivalence," rather than "balance" (Ava Vinesett, personal communication, October 2016), psychoanalysis underestimates the normalcy and the fruitfulness of this phenomenon, as well as the number of forces that people and communities normally balance within themselves. The Yorùbá ọpá òsùn, or "staff of fate," dramatically illustrates the principle that a life well lived relies not upon the avoidance or expunging of potentially malign forces but upon aligning them in an orderly way and upon enlisting them in the service of personal and collective progress (see figure 8.13). The Haitian Vodou priestess Manmi Maude tells me that all of the gods reside within each of us, but, in any given person at any given time, some gods are more prominent than others, thus constituting not only the internally heterogeneous nature of the person but also that of the social and ecological relationships that constitute the person. The function of ritual is therefore to "balance" (*balanse*), or correct the disproportions in, the impulses of each god or spirit as well as in the relative presence of the different gods and spirits in the person's body and in the ensemble of social relationships that constitute the person (personal communication, November 4 and 8, 2016). Priests of West African Yorùbá and Cuban Santería/Ocha also regularly attribute a similar goal of "balance" to their rituals. While a succession of European social and intellectual movements—from the Reformation and the Enlightenment to Romanticism—have progressively elaborated a logic of personal individuation and autonomy, the Afro-Atlantic religions have elaborated an increasingly complex social and ritual model of balancing the multiple relationships that constitute each person-in-community.

Like Marx, Freud, and the Black people who make gods, most people are driven by forces and value conflicts that they do not fully understand or control. By tradition or invention, any given community finds certain material forms—such as cowries, beads, pots, crowns, drums, clothing, houses, couches, rings, books, "negro slaves," and "savages" (not to mention cauldrons, chains, padlocks, and bentwood rockers, among the subjects of this book's sequel)—appealing arenas in which to work out emotional, social, and spiritual conflicts through ritual and other symbolic play. *The Fetish Revisited* analyzes the shared structural context and the divergent social positions that have shaped the material forms and the ritual handling of these highly cathected objects, spirited things, or, in a word, fetishes. This comparative analysis of fetishes Afro-Atlantic, historical materialist, and psychoanalytical calls attention to what is material about European social "theory," what is ideational and debated about the made gods of Africa, and what is similarly ambivalent about them all.

Like everyone else engaged in the contrasting representation of self and other in socially hierarchical settings, Marx and Freud speak in the "logic of the trial" (Bourdieu [1979] 1984). That is, what they say about themselves and others is almost never a neutral observation divorced from an existing rivalry. It is almost always a self-defense, a reaction to a known accusation, and a pursuit of advantage over an adversary. Yet, under the spell of concepts like science, philosophy, and theory—which endeavor to abstract general truths from the specific conditions of their construction—Marx, Freud, and many of their readers in the academy are inclined to overlook the culture-specific and socially positioned motives that shape these men's thoughts and those of their antagonists about the same matters.

Thus, the term "fetish" also alerts us to the sort of circumstances that motivate some people to deride others' lifeways, while others choose to respect and learn from them. Following my earlier analysis of a similar phenomenon among African-descended ethnics and middle-class Black people in the United States (Matory 2015), I argue that stigmatized populations enact a variable balance between, on the one hand, protesting against the unfair treatment of all of the stigmatized and, on the other, arguing for their own exemption from stigma and disadvantage by scapegoating other stigmatized populations. I believe that this phenomenon—ethnological Schadenfreude—structures the lopsided ambivalence of the Marx's and Freud's theories. This ambivalence is also embedded in the highly cathected material things that I have described as the "furniture" of their thinking—such as overcoats, "negro slaves," commodities in general, the fur hat, Rome, the Acropolis, the couch, the "negro," and the "savage." Had they understood better the religions that they ridiculed, Marx and Freud might have pursued greater *balance* in their management of the conflicting demons within them.

The Circum-Atlantic Genesis of Theories and Gods

In this book, I have described the relationship-transforming words, deeds, and things of the historical materialist Karl Marx and those of the psychoanalyst Sigmund Freud, setting their theories against the backdrop of the seventeenth-century Dutch Calvinist merchants' rhetorical uses of African gods, the Enlightenment-era amplification of these uses, and the alternative responses to this Enlightenment rhetoric by the likes of the nineteenth-century German burgher G. W. F. Hegel, the turn-of-the-century German ethnologists Leo Frobenius and Felix von Luschan, and the German American founder of twentieth-century American cultural anthropology, Franz Boas.

To put a fine point on it, the divergent fetishes of Hegelian idealism, historical materialism, psychoanalysis, and the Afro-Atlantic religions are all born of the same circum-Atlantic womb, and they are socially positioned.

From the sixteenth- and seventeenth-century publication of Dutch–West African travelogues to the twentieth-century reign of modern art, the West African fetish has also possessed Europe and its settler colonies. Pointing out an overarching theme among these cases, José Romero, a Duke graduate student, observed "Black people are the condition of possibility of Marx and Freud" ("Theories of Cultural Anthropology," November 25, 2015). It is for this reason that *The Fetish Revisited* showcases what Black experts on the so-called fetish—the Berlin-based Candomblé priest Babá Murah, Cuban Santería/Ocha priestesses Coral and her godmother Oggún Fumi in Santiago de Cuba, US-based *santeros* Babá Steve Quintana, and David Font-Navarette, Haitian and Haitian American Vodou priestess Maude Marie Evans, and Nigerian Yorùbá priestess of *èsìn ìbílè* Adedoyin Talabi Faniyi—say back to Marx and Freud. All of these Afro-Atlantic and European interlocutors speak from cultural borderlands where their agency and the worth of their creations hang in the balance between rival value codes and actor-networks.

The spirits of Islam, the Nupe, and the Bariba are also incorporated into the vessel altars and possessed priests of Ọ̀yọ́ religion (Matory [1994] 2005), while the spirits of the Lucumís, the Nagôs, the Jejes, the BaKongo, Allada/Rada, Ginen, and Africa generally—not to mention the *caboclos*—fill the Afro-Atlantic altars and priests of the Americas. Priests and their altars are occupied and crosscut by multiple foreign spirits, and Europe is clearly one of those spirits, materialized in the beads and cowrie money of the Atlantic slave trade, in European alcohols and cloth, and in an iconography blending that of European and African royalism. So, just as the European bourgeoisie is possessed by an "inner Africa," so the Afro-Atlantic priests are possessed by the European merchant, the slave master, and the colonialist. Thus, theorists and priests could be called "fetishists." However, none of these priestly experts I have consulted shows an interest in hurling this word-weapon back at their assailants Marx and Freud. It is I who do so in order to hear what Marx, Freud, and these Afro-Atlantic priests will say back. What do material things and the ambivalence directed toward them in intercultural and hierarchical settings teach us about social life and the role of semiotics in its construction?

The value-coded debates about agency that prompted the invention and still prompt the use of the term "fetish" help us to understand the dialectical formation of people, peoples, classes, genders, sexual-orientation groups, regions, races, and societies around the Atlantic perimeter. In particular, I have argued that the late Hegel's late-Enlightenment fetish displaced the difficulties inherent in democratic change everywhere, including the German-speaking lands, uniquely onto Africanness. The subject Hegel sought to create through this fetishization of the African as an antitype was the legitimate citizenry of a democratic, united Germany—a citizenry that, for a change, would include burghers like him. Marx and Freud, too, employed this African-targeted word but reimagined its marksman as the "wage slave" and, implicitly, the assimilated Jewish man. The locus standi to point the gun dramatized their assertion of full-fledged whiteness and equality with higher-ranking Europeans.

Marx and Freud were born amid the increasing popularity of a binary ranking system that placed white Europeans above dark non-Europeans, two parties increasingly connected to each other by the downward flow of accusation, control, violence, and manufactures, as well as an upward flow of labor, raw materials, and land rights. With the creation of central Europe's nation-states, based as they were on equality with and separateness from other nation-states, Jewish central Europeans faced dangerous questions about where they belonged in such nation-states and in the emergent Christian-dominated global order.

For her part, Manmi Maude speaks of Marx and Freud in tones of charity rather than contempt: "How can they get us? They will never be able to get us. They never lived that kind of life. It's a challenge for them" (personal communication, January 31, 2016).

Manmi Maude excuses Marx and Freud for what she believes was their ignorance. I, on the other hand, think they made a choice. That it was the increasingly dominant choice in their day does not mean that they were unaware of alternatives—alternatives that are, in fact, evident in their ambivalence. Like the late Hegel, Marx and Freud chose to articulate and endorse a logic of social hierarchy that qualified them to join the system as the superiors of black people and therefore as equals to the people who had long oppressed the Jews and wage workers. What I am willing to concede is that people in Marx's and Freud's race- and class-ambiguous positions had few good choices to save themselves. But it should not be forgotten that Franz Boas, a secular Jew and contemporary of Freud's—whose life also overlapped with Marx's and who suffered the same sort of racial vulnerability—resolved their shared dilemma in a virtually opposite manner. The African American philosopher Alain Locke named the approach he shared with Boas "cultural relativism" (Matory 2015).

It should also be remembered that gentile German-speaking scholars, too, suffered an ambiguous status in fin-de-siècle Europe and faced a similar dilemma, and that, for reasons that Hegel's, Marx's, and Freud's stories help us to understand, their collective response ranged from the liberal to the horrific. Emerging from the pall of eighteenth-century French cultural and military imperialism and left in the dust of both France's political progress and the United Kingdom's economic progress in the nineteenth century, a series of middle-class German speakers from Herder to Boas asserted the cultural separateness and moral equality of different ethnic groups.

Assimilated Jewish men were not alone in their feelings of marginalization in Europe. For example, even though many scholars quote Hegel as an unambivalent trasher of Africa and an unambiguous spokesman for the dominant race, he seems in fact to have been ambivalent about the Haitian Revolution. It should also be remembered that the eighteenth- and nineteenth-century central Europe from which Hegel and Marx wrote was, along with Russia, coughing in the dust of France's political advances and England's economic progress. At that time, German-speaking elites believed France to be the pinnacle of civilization (many Germans still appear to think so), and the German language was a mark of social inferiority. Even today, tours of eighteenth- and nineteenth-century German castles—such as Sanssouci, in Potsdam—reveal the regional aristocracy's slavish imitation of everything French. Like Herder, Hegel spoke from a position of German weakness. A half century later, Marx, too, spoke from a position of German weakness and in the face of French cultural hegemony. In the mid-nineteenth century, Marx assumed the backwardness of Russia and Prussia relative to the political evolution of France and the economic evolution of England. In his London exile, Marx joined myriad German labor migrants who, like their confreres all over Europe, were unable to find work at home. They were not unlike the tens of thousands of West African migrants who now seek work in Germany.

Perhaps it was also a sense of Germans' collective vulnerability and empathy with other stigmatized or marginalized population that motivated Herder's idea that different peoples are morally equal, Hegel's apparent early sympathy with the Haitian Revolution, and the art historian Leo Frobenius's dignification of Africa as well. However, not even the *combination* of Jews and German speakers exhausted the ranks of Europeans fearing marginalization. French psychiatry's late nineteenth-century obsession with "fetishism"—a diagnosis of the nonreproductive sexual behaviors that were ostensibly endangering France's demographic advantage over Germany (Nye 1993)—arose from a sense of national disadvantage. Many nineteenth-century French people also shared in the Enlightenment's premise that Africa is the paradigm of Europe's own pathologies and the comforting thought that such problems are therefore not intrinsic to their own society.

Like that of the French psychiatrists, Freud's medical articulation of the fetish problem had a political backdrop and corollary. France rightly worried that the German speakers, who themselves had so much to prove to the world, were rising demographically and politically. However, World War I reinforced the German speakers' sense of failure. Freud wrote of fetishism during a time of defeat for the German culture that he loved. Having trained in France, Freud began writing about fetishism in the early twentieth century but reached the peak of his preoccupation with it a time when German speakers, with whom he identified, were suffering under crippling reparations payments and a loss of national pride. Freud supported Germany against France but also faced marginalization by those German speakers who branded him an alien on account of his Jewishness.

Mein Kampf ([1925–26] 1941) details Hitler's own sense of the German worker, in contrast to the French worker, as lacking in pride. With the announced goal of restoring that pride, Hitler's murderous reaction was to displace the German people's sense of worthlessness onto the Jews. The connection between an actor's social ambiguity and his ambivalence might explain as much about Hitler as it does about Freud. Like Freud, Hitler came from Austria, a place with a bad reputation in the German-speaking world, and, while Freud was reputedly dark, Hitler was visibly darker, with his black hair and eyes, giving his German nationalism and adulation of whiteness the appearance of a reaction-formation. The German fetishization of the Jews is historically related and logically parallel to Marx's and Freud's fetishization of Africans. They are positionally different but dialectically related fetishes arising from five hundred years of circum-Atlantic history.

Through the proxy of Native Americans and African Americans, the answer of the German Jewish immigrant Franz Boas emphasized the dignity and equality of those culturally heterogeneous populations that would eventually assimilate into the broader US American settler colony. On the contrary, by distinguishing himself from the Africans, Marx contradicted those who would exclude him from the emerging bourgeois-dominated class order of central Europe, while Freud qualified himself for citizenship according to the tandem distinction of being neither an African nor a woman. A common theme of Marx's and Freud's subject making is that they joined the dominant parties of their day in an agreement about who truly deserved to be at the bottom of the *globus cruciger*: it was not the assimilated European Jewish men but the black and brown fetishists. As they sought to erase certain intra-European forms of stratification that would have excluded them—according to class, religion, or gender—Marx and Freud also validated the binary hierarchy of white over nonwhite, with African people as the paradigm case of the latter. In the actor-networks proposed by historical materialism and psychoanalysis, Marx and Freud belonged in the upper echelon rather than the lower.

Yet, well into the twenty-first century, repeated losses in war have left many Germans feeling like a people outmaneuvered and bossed around. In pursuit of a solution to its enduring dilemma, Germany remains torn between the most extreme forms of liberalism and the nastiest forms of xenophobia, and traces of both sentiments are often found in the same person. For many Germans, it is difficult to decide whether the love of Germany is an act of egalitarian self-love, consistent with the love of other, non-German populations, or a celebration of xenophobia and genocide.

The ethical dilemma of the Afro-Atlantic priests seems not to rest on uncertainty about the virtue of either hierarchy among nations or inter-action among peoples. Neither seems to be in question. The overarching Afro-Atlantic dilemma seems to concern the balance between selfishness and collectivism in the conduct of one's relationship with other people and with the Other world. The Afro-Atlantic priests seem to take for granted the reality and the virtue of what Bayart (1989) calls "extraversion," as well as reciprocal giving, patronage, and power exchange in which upward mobility is available to all devotees and interlocutors through idioms of seniority, slavery, or royalty. The enshrined and embodied gods of the Afro-Atlantic dramatize this proposition.

During the 1980s, Pietz reminded the academy about the origins of the "fetish" problem on the Guinea Coast. However, with little awareness of the African or African American perspectives on the term's disputed referent, he focused on European opinions about these spirited things. Since the 1990s, it has become increasingly common to acknowledge circum-Atlantic capitalism and imperialism as influential contexts of the history and practice of Afro-Atlantic religions, as well (e.g., MacGaffey 1993; Matory 2005, [1994] 2005; Drewal 2008). Rosenthal (1998) brought the gods of Ewe Vodu into frontal dialogue with Lacanian psychoanalysis. And Latour (2010: 6–7) briefly allowed the Candomblé *orixás* to contest the European modernists' pretense of having disenchanted material things. The present study extends these seminal efforts by bringing Marx and Freud (along with their thing-centered actor-networks) into dialogue with the priests and spirited things of Cuban Santería/Ocha, Brazilian Candomblé, Haitian Vodou, West-Central African religions, and the West African religions of the Yorùbá and the

Fòn. My objective is to understand how these interlocutors might instruct each other about the political, psychological, and semiotic processes called "fetishism."

In the US American academy, the perspectives of Marx and Freud have been privileged for so long that I admittedly feel compelled here to privilege Afro-Atlantic perspectives, which help us to see with greater clarity what is usually hidden from view or ignored—the culture-specific and socially positioned origins of European social theory. The Enlightenment and its successors have had the power to turn the Guinea Coast and Haiti into object lessons in the errors of certain European factions and to turn black people in general into living, breathing "pedestals" for the display of white suffering and symbols of the white id. This book identifies and denaturalizes the social positions and motivations of the European social theories that have so casually imprisoned us in these rhetorical roles.

However, my objective is not retaliation but a twenty-first-century expansion of anthropology's mission. We have long made a point of analyzing the "native's point of view" and identifying its social, material, and comparative context. Since the 1980s, we have been almost as attentive to the social positionality of the ethnographer. What I argue here is that a historical and social contextualization of European social theorists and their theories is just as integral to our ethnographic calling. The effects of Europe's power/knowledge upon Africa are too obvious to need retelling in a book that is already long enough. Less obvious are the effects of this power/knowledge on Europeans themselves. Marx and Freud are the present case in point. I argue that their theories of fetishism are, among other things, reactions to the threat posed to them by their ambiguous racial and class positions in the emergent nation-states of central Europe.

Latin America's in-betweenness and consequent virtuosity with the fetish are equally obvious. Like eighteenth- and nineteenth-century central Europeans, twentieth- and twenty-first-century Latin Americans have struggled to avoid being cast with the goats. For centuries, Latin American elites have sought to rise above Africa, indigenous America, and even their inferior European (that is, Mediterranean) roots in order to achieve the dignity of full-fledged European whiteness. It is no surprise that their ambivalence has also produced not only deliberate "whitening" through eugenics and immigration policy but also the *mestizo/mulato* nationalism of José Martí and José Vasconcelos and the Afrophilia of Fernando Ortiz and Gilberto Freyre (Matory 2005).

Hence, the pattern that the stigmatized endeavor to displace their stigma onto other, ostensibly less worthy groups is not limited to any specific continent, race, religion, gender, or class. The feeling of social inferiority can scale down to the most microscopic differences of rank, and ethnological Schadenfreude is a common behavior, even among ostensible elites. Except for the uppermost person and the bottommost person in a permanent hierarchy—of which there are mercifully few in the world—everyone struggles against the impending threat of devaluation and denial of agency, to which most people and groups respond not by condemning the hierarchy of worth and prerogative but by emphasizing the greater inferiority of the next group down. Such is the ambivalence of in-between populations.

Yet ambivalence about hierarchy itself is not a universal feature of fetishes. In the eyes of most Marxists and most Freudians, it is either inconceivable or ironic that Marx's and Freud's social evolutionist appeals for some people's equality depend on a put-down of Africans. By contrast, in the Afro-Atlantic religions there is nothing abnormal or extrinsic about hierarchy. The typical Afro-Atlantic priest is no race radical, much less an advocate of class-leveling revolution. In fact, many are quite politically conservative. Instead, the Afro-Atlantic gods turn the tools and the metonyms of the foreigner (including the European), the coastal merchant, the slave trader, and the master into the empowering inner agents of the African, the African American, the enslaved, the underprivileged immigrant, and their descendants.

I have argued that even the Afro-Atlantic gods are, as Pietz (1985: 5) describes the fetish, "a novel object not proper to any prior discrete society." They are creatures of commerce between prior ecumenes and echelons. The merchant may be the prime exemplar of the fetish maker, even outside of the context of maritime trade, because, more fundamentally, he or she stands between the manufacturer (who attributes one set of uses and values to the commodity) and the potential consumer (who almost always attributes a different set of uses and values to the commodity). In order to maximize his or her effectiveness, the merchant must recognize the value codes and speak the languages of both parties. The merchant's profits depend on his or her masterful knowledge of the difference between the vantages of the two parties, the social skill to keep those parties apart, and the psychological skill to manipulate the image of each party in order to secure the favor and loyalty of the other party. An element of this manipulation is denying the consumer any knowledge of how little the merchant pays the producer and denying the producer any knowledge of the how much the consumer pays the merchant. The merchant's power lies in the monopoly over such secrets. That price negotiation is so much more common in West Africa and the Caribbean than in central Europe and the United States gives a hint of why the debatability of value and the proteanness of agency have been so much more obvious to Afro-Atlantic priests than they were to the likes of Marx and even Freud.

On the Word-Weapon Now in Our Hands

I have been asked if I am recommending the general use of the term "fetish" in scholarly, analytical discourse. To be honest, I am not sure. I will be content if my readers decide to use the term with the intent to highlight the debated, Janus-faced meaning and social function of certain important material things, as well as the materiality of even the most high-flown social theories. Elsewhere, I have used the similarly tainted word "syncretism" to highlight the fact that elite factions in creole societies are often characterized by alternation between the advocacy of cultural hybridity ("syncretism") and of cultural purity ("purism")—syncretism when they want to enlist the support of the dark "folk" against a foreign threat and purism when they want to assert the authority of racial superiority and Western education over their local social inferiors (Matory 2005). This observation by Stewart and Shaw (1994) acknowledges that no society is pure and that these positions are ideological, factional, and relative, rather than objective or factual. However, it would still be easy for careless readers to assume that the term "syncretism" refers to a real and objective state of certain populations, practices, or things, with the corollary assumption that some populations, practices or things are *actually pure* in race, origin, or meaning.

I fear, then, that careless readers will take the use of the term "fetish" to imply that some physical things—along with the network of people, practices, and ideas associated with them—are *objectively wrong* repositories of value and agency, with the corollary implication that some other things and actor-networks are *objectively correct* repositories. Although that implication would accord with my practical suppositions and conduct in daily life, it runs contrary to my scholarly argument, since I have found that my self-confident reasoning and deeply felt convictions about the real order of things seldom dictate what others think is true or how they live their lives. My aim here is not to convince the reader that my valuation of things is right but to call attention to a general mechanism of value assignment and social organization that is highlighted by the term "fetish."

The proposition at the core of this Afro-Atlantic archaeology of the fetish is that stigmatized white people often bring black people into the analytical frame precisely in order to normalize themselves in the eyes of their whiter stigmatizers. Despite the Enlightenment's accusation that we Africans are confused, the makers of African and African-diaspora fetishes are no more confused than anyone else about the inequality and the materially grounded nature of social relationships. In fact, like the early Hegel's servant or slave, Black people—or at least those of us who have studied, worked, and lived with whites—tend to be *less* confused because we are more aware (doubly conscious, if you will) of the multiple interested positions that structure our shared space. For the last several hundred years, Black people have been in no position to dismiss the interested positions of our oppressors with a contemptuous verbal wave of the hand. Rather, a close knowledge of the value codes of the oppressor and of one's similarly oppressed fellows has been a precondition of survival. It is with both realism and élan that Afro-Atlantic priests perform this epistemological dance between worlds.

As a middle-class African American, I have found in the Afro-Atlantic religions an affirmation in the beauty and human complexity of people who look like me. The spirited things of these religions embody an iconography and invoke a world far away from the iconography and prescriptions by which US racism daily defines me. Indeed, I have been lucky enough to make a livelihood out of the study of that world. Unlike the many Europeans, Euro-Americans, and Pentecostal Africans or Afro-Latin Americans who seek to reconstruct themselves in opposition to the African "fetish," I see in these consecrated things a dramatic revelation of the contrary forces within me.

Like all gods, the Afro-Atlantic divinities are made up of forces that inspire both love and fear—and not only the fear of, say, lightning, floods, diseases, and the allegedly ill effects of coming too close to their consecrated things without being initiated. The fear they inspire in me also relates to the fact that human beings who are little different from me are capable of facilitating and embracing the profits of the Atlantic slave trade and of the cruel "legitimate" trade that supplied so many of the raw materials from which the altar-embodiments of the gods are made and animated. Rather than weeping before the awesome visage of history, Afro-Atlantic priests and worshippers appropriate real-world forces that have terrorized our ancestors—and me. Yet, instead of *merely* frightening me, these gods evoke a world that defies the assumption of intrinsic white agency and epistemological mastery and intrinsic black passivity and deficiency that has been the convenient foundation of five hundred years of European overseas imperialism and of the "Enlightened" theories that are among its reflexes. The Afro-Atlantic religions are socially positioned studies and transformations of the suffering that produced us. And, ultimately, they ritualize the exercise of mastery by the subordinate.

In this book, I do not ultimately endorse or denounce economic inequality, or side with or against Marx, Freud, or the Afro-Atlantic priests. What I want is for my readers to question themselves about issues on which other people have a different, equally flawed, and equally socially positioned point of view. I have argued that each of the thinkers and actors with whom I engage here endorses a model of the human-animal-thing relationships characterized not by its universal truth but by its concreteness and its owners' unique cultural assumptions, historical moment, and socially positioned interests. I find all of these models of and for life interesting, and they have all shaped me deeply. And I argue that, like other people, I will benefit more by acknowledging the cultural, historical, and social positions from which these models arose than by assuming that any of them came down from the sky as a perspectiveless truth about all times and places.

Recent debates about fetishism have usually been conducted without reference to the original referents of the term and in total unawareness that those referents have an ongoing history and a context as richly intellectual and biographical as it is cultural and sociological, belying the cartoonish fixity attributed to them in post-Enlightenment European theory and identity making. The ideas of Marx and Freud actually help to illuminate this rich context, but a view from the Afro-Atlantic equally illuminates the historical and personal dynamics that shape the gestalt of Marx's and Freud's thoughtful intervention in the world. These dynamics have normally been ignored or taken for granted in the contemporary uses of historical materialism and psychoanalysis. Far from debunking the ideas of Marx and Freud, attention to these historical and personal dynamics—as well as the broader political economy that unites them in dialogue with the priests of the Afro-Atlantic religions—potentially breathes new life into these nineteenth-century social theories. The assumption that Marx's and Freud's ideas transcend the author's social conditions and that every apparent contradiction in their words is resolvable into some higher-level truth that the reader must simply struggle harder to grasp is a widespread frame of mind in the academy but one that lends itself better to the consolidation of a community of the faithful than to the pursuit of the most encompassing truths about history, society, and human character. Explanatory models are enriched, not impoverished, by an understanding of the historical, cultural, social, and biographical context from which they grew.

Of course, this argument requires me to take Marx and Freud down from the black pedestals on which scholars in elite US American universities tend to place them and, likewise, to elevate African-inspired priests and worshippers from the ethnographic netherworld to which generations of European and Euro-American scholars have tended to relegate them. We are not pedestals but people. When we address our compatriots about other ways of life, anthropologists usually look as though we are justifying what we are trying to explain and, conversely, as though we are criticizing the lifeways of our audience. Conversely, the people we are trying to explain often regard our accounts as objectifying and dehumanizing, depriving the people described of not only complexity but also free will. The problem is that in both scenarios we are verbalizing what our audience takes for granted and therefore questioning the naturalness and self-evidence of the foundations of their lives. Hence, my efforts to explain the patterns of debate and understanding that arise from my cohabitation, friendship, and apprenticeship with Afro-Atlantic priests should not be mistaken for a justification of the gods who have brought us together. Or a condemnation.

There is no more reason to romanticize these religions than to romanticize Protestantism, historical materialism, psychoanalysis, the Enlightenment, or the other social contracts that white men sign with each other. Serving any of these fetishes sacrifices some people's interests for the benefit of others' and creates moral dilemmas that are impossible to resolve without conflict, ambivalence, and resistance. Protestantism advanced the causes of not only humanism but also slavery, colonialism, segregation, and, currently, the enrichment of many "property gospel" pastors at the expense of the poorest of the poor. Many Marxist-Leninists allied themselves with the struggle against apartheid, US imperialism in Central America, and Portuguese colonialism in Africa but also rationalized Stalin's and Pol Pot's economically disastrous and, indeed, murderous social engineering projects. Many would also argue that the cost of psychoanalysis, which dominated US American psychiatry for a half century, has always greatly exceeded its demonstrable benefit and, through its dogmatism, has forestalled the search for more effective therapies for some severely ill people (e.g., Lieberman 2015).

I am personally uncomfortable with hierarchy and with the taken-for-grantedness of slavery in the religions I research (Matory in preparation). Indeed, I suspect that my report of this reality will greatly upset the many fellow Black nationalists, feminists, and sympathizers with socialism who romanticize these religions. I am not fully initiated in any of them, one reason being my lifelong discomfort with the hierarchy that is central to them. Even on my wedding day, I could not bear to *dòbálè*, prostrate myself, before for my parents-in-law. I will never let a god tell me what to do unless I want to do it and my participation is consistent with my ethical standards. Hence, I am not justifying hierarchy, just highlighting a taken-for-granted reality of religions about which most of my audience knows little.

Nevertheless, I love many aspects of the Afro-Atlantic religions, their gods, and their spirited things. In my house, I lovingly take care of multiple gods from multiple traditions. They mediate and enrich some of the most important friendships in my life, and they are anchors of a psychological world of Black dignity and agency that Bunmi and I have built around our children and their friends. Moreover, each of these religions hosts an extraordinarily intricate network of symbols and a bottomless well of insights about human character, to which I appeal as I analyze US American national politics and navigate social relations on campus and in my neighborhood.

Similarly, there are aspects of psychoanalysis and Marxism that I love, but I'm not a licensed psychoanalyst or a member of the Communist Party either. Marx, Freud, and the Afro-Atlantic gods are among the many who dance in me (Matory 2009). My efforts here are actually an extension of both European social theory and the Afro-Atlantic gods. This text is a wedding between them. My hope is that knowing the human motives from which they have arisen will help me to be a better and more self-aware me. I hope the same for my reader.

In the end, I am as uninterested in canonizing African classics as in delegitimizing European ones. I understand the need for Black people to craft fetishes of Black dignity to counter the fetishes of uniquely white dignity that lie at the foundation of white supremacy in the West, but history and my own ethnographic investigations in Europe have taught me that white ethnic groups also construct their fictional superiority at the expense of other white ethnic groups (e.g., Matory 2015a, 2015d). The pursuit of flawless Black heroes and of transcendently heroic Black ethnic groups may serve a short-term project of refuting the most unsophisticated types of white supremacy. However, I am so deeply convinced of the essential equality of all human beings that I do not feel the need to tell a story of Afro-Atlantic grandeur, much less one of European inferiority, following certain extreme formulations of Afrocentrism. For me, the best way to honor humanity—Black and white; Jewish, gentile, and orisha-worshipping—is to recognize the human complexity of the actors whose stories I tell. Their beauty and worthiness lie not in their awesome dignity or their exemplary superiority to some other people but in the thoughtfulness of their reactions to moral dilemmas of the sort that we all face in life. And this message is, to my mind, the most consistent message of the Afro-Atlantic religions.

In our house, Exu eats first, before anyone else is served at a ritual, a party, or a salon. As the lord of the crossroads and of communication, he lives with us and breathes into us the impulse to plan ahead, to accept the unpredictability of the outcome, and to adapt to—and take full advantage of—the occasional disappointment of our expectations. Across multiple Afro-Atlantic traditions, Eshu's permanent erection is both a prayer for potency and a reminder of the impotency that herbalists in every such tradition endeavor to redress, just at the red side of his hat calls to mind the black side. Each is animated by the possibility of the other and made desirable by the fact that not only impotency but even priapism, like uninterrupted authority and unmitigated extraversion, is agonizing for its bearer. Eshu's polymorphic phallicism also recalls the complementary, sometimes antagonistic, and equally polysemic reality of the vagina—mobilized variously by wives, mothers, and the wonderful mothers who are sometimes called the witches.

In the name of the Crossroads, I pray that Eshu has conveyed with clarity the message that I intended for you. This carefully crafted and commoditized assemblage of paper, ink, thread, glue, and plastic gives physical form to the spirits with which Marx, Freud, and the gods that Black people make specifically animate me and I animate them. However, if a different set of values and agents animates your relationship with this book and these mighty beings, may the contrast between our value codes still bear a useful lesson for you about the role of the fetish in the encounter between people in different social positions and from different social worlds.

Ultimately, my main points are four:

First, theory is not a disembodied, universal truth but a creature dialectically related to the social environment, material surroundings, and material interests of the theorists. Therefore, whosoever calleth another man's god a fetish, look wherefore he buildeth his own fetish. More broadly, the currently fashionable notion of "theory" is mistaken in the presumption that thought is most valuable and instructive when it is alienated from the context of its production. My conclusion here is not that Marx, Freud, and the Afro-Atlantic religions are made useless by the fact that their positions have been motivated by the widely overlooked forms of self-interest that shape their respective fetishes. Rather, I argue that all ideas are actions and are made more meaningful and instructive by an acknowledgment of the circumstances of their genesis and the motives behind their enactment.

Second, the term "fetishism" is a useful way to illuminate the competitive and strategic nature of meaning making in the construction of European social theories, Afro-Atlantic gods, and numerous other socially effective stipulations about where value lies and who owes what to whom in the course of social life. Hence, the fetish is not ultimately a thing in itself but a name that indexes competitive meaning making at the troubled juncture between dominant and subordinate classes of subject: men and women, whites and Blacks, Christians and Jews, Protestants and Catholics, capitalists and proletarians, capitalists and socialists, and so forth. Hence, the African theories embodied in altars and the European theories embodied in coats, factories, pianos, antique statuary, intaglio rings, the Acropolis, and books are not discrete phenomena alien to each other. They might usefully be analyzed as embodiments of positionally different but dialectically related perspectives on five hundred years of Atlantic capitalism. So it is well to remember that each time we add to the miles-high stack of peer-reviewed books and articles that rest on the fetish of Hegel, Marx, or Freud, we extend the life of a fetish with unequal dividends for the diverse participants in Atlantic capitalism. The same is true each time I put my head down on the ground before Yemoja, Xangô, or Oggún. The according of agency and value to one god or theory regularly entails the disfranchisement and devaluation of other socially positioned gods or theories.

Third, like the most powerful and spectacular of African "fetishes," the most powerful and spectacular European social theories embody not only the social ambiguity but also the political and emotional ambivalence of their creators. Clearly subordinate parties find in such fetishes a reminder of their humiliation and a promise of power through identification with the dominant. Surprisingly, some clearly dominant parties find in the fetish both a reminder of their power and the desirable promise of relief from responsibility (Matory in preparation). It is my hypothesis that socially ambiguous people—such as middle classes, racially ambiguous people, ambitious or high-status members of subordinated races, and subordinated members of high-status races—have the greatest stake in contemplating and resolving the structural oppositions and the conflicting values embedded in the fetish.

Fourth, in the making of theories and of gods, the assignment of agency and value to one social location regularly entails the disfranchisement and devaluation of other social locations. For this reason, populations that are vulnerable to oppression are often highly articulate in trumpeting the even greater inferiority of populations that they can conceivably place below themselves in the social hierarchy. I call this phenomenon "ethnological Schadenfreude." Marx's fetishization of the "negro slave" and Freud's fetishization of the paradigmatically black "savage" are vivid cases in point. They alert us that fetishism lies not just in the actor's displacement of *value and agency* onto locations from which it does not originate but also in the fetishist's displacement of *antivalue and incompetence* onto other human beings.

The cases of Marx and Freud suggest that the people most articulate about the fetish—that is, the ones who are most anxious to pin down or liberate its meaning—are not the people who already fall most clearly into the dominant or the subordinate class of actors but the populations who are struggling against their own ambiguity in order to avoid being cast among the subordinate. The first instinct of ambitious members of stigmatized and oppressed populations is not to call for the undoing of stigma and oppression generally but to deflect that stigma onto another group, with the implication that the other group is the one that *really* deserves the oppression (Matory 2015). During the era of European imperialism, these in-between populations have included not only the assimilated Jews of central Europe and the coastal merchants of Africa but central Europeans generally. Latin Americans might best fit this profile in the age of postcolonial nationalism. In the wake of the civil rights movement, when educated African Americans are in constant doubt about whether we are being judged for our color or for our talents and character, the conditions that produce ambivalent fetishes—in

the form of clothing, houses, cars, academic degrees, and art collections—
and the will get to the bottom of their power are highly evident in the Black
middle class, as well.

"A White Woman Lives in the River"

In the 1930s and '40s, Germany and Austria—respectively the homelands
of Marx and Freud—led the world in turning the genocidal violence that
Europeans had once reserved for Africans and Native Americans toward
the extermination of their fellow Europeans—Jews, Gypsies, homosexuals,
and Europeans of African descent. Yet not all gentile central Europeans were
sympathetic to this brand of high-tech racist nationalism. One such dissenter
fled central Europe and became pivotal in revitalizing the embattled river
goddess Òṣun.

The Austrian artist Susanne Wenger reportedly sheltered Jews from Nazi
predators. Her daughter tells me that, against Wenger's wishes, one young
Jewish man who feared that he was putting Wenger at undue risk bravely
insisted on vacating her house. Walking down the street, before he had
left her sight, the young man was shot in the back of the head. Thus, after
World War II, Wenger had had enough of Europe. She decided to leave that
accursed continent and make her home in a more humane place. Already
deeply embedded in the European psychic world, the African and other so-
called "savages" were, to some other central Europeans, not *exemplars* of
the ills that Europe had overcome or concentrated embodiments of what
was wrong with Europe but an *alternative* to Europe's ills. Between Tibet and
Nigeria, Wenger's choice was made by an offer from the University of Ibadan,
in Nigeria, to her German lover, Ulli Beier, another artist. The offer, however,
stipulated that he must marry before he could accept the offer. The decision
to marry was made so quickly that they used a ring from a curtain rod as their
wedding ring.[1]

Together, Wenger and Beier founded an arts workshop in the Nigerian
city of Òṣogbo, which remains famous today for its distinctive style of textile
design and religious sculpture. Indeed, Wenger was initiated as a priestess
and eventually became the chief priestess of Òṣun in the forested temple
grove in that city, which is also the headquarters of that goddess's worship in
West Africa. Wenger single-handedly defended the large, urban grove from
deforestation, dismemberment, and desecration by land developers and hostile local Muslims.

Her daughter tells me that Wenger had a special relationship with the
goddess and with the forest. When she sought healing or solace, Wenger
would repair to the forest and stay there for days at a time, immune to its

nighttime dangers, such as poisonous snakebites. In fact, the daughter tells me, Wenger repeatedly healed others who had been bitten by snakes in that grove. Despite her elevated priestly title, Wenger would walk down the street with a bag, picking up trash around the perimeter of the grove and its surrounds. As a result of her efforts, the Òsun grove and temple complex have become a UNESCO World Heritage Site and the location of the largest annual òrìsà festival in Nigeria. It rivals the February 2 festival for the sca goddess Iemanjá in Rio de Janeiro. Yearly, it draws pilgrims from all over southwestern Nigeria, as well as Cuba, Brazil, Trinidad, and the United States.

Wenger died in 2009. The high priestess now presiding over this resurrection of the goddess and of the Nigerian òrìsà-worshipping community as a whole is Ìyá Òsun Adedoyin Talabi Faniyi, a Yorùbá woman who, as a child, was adopted and reared by Wenger. On behalf of Duke University and the University of Vermont, I have brought Ìyá Òsun to the United States several times, inviting her to lecture and to collaborate with me in filmmaking and in the mounting of an online museum exhibition of the SABA Collection, from which this book derives its inspiration.

During our spring 2014 stint at the University of Vermont (UVM), where I was a James Marsh Professor-at-Large, Ìyá Òsun received a call from an African American follower in New York who asked if any white people had attended Ìyá Òsun's public lecture at the University. Because the vast majority of her and my sizable audiences in Vermont had been white, Ìyá Òsun was deeply perplexed by the question. Until watching Spike Lee's film *Malcolm X* (1992) in a UVM class that we attended together, she had been unaware of the degree of racial polarization and antagonism in US society past and present. So blended was her subjectivity with her Nigerianized Austrian mother's that she was perplexed that anyone would *not* expect white people to be as interested as black people in the gods of Africa. She had never imagined any correlation between skin color and one's character or interests. Indeed, she was troubled by the question's implicit underestimation of her mother's role in giving life to and, indeed, reincarnating the goddess.

I had to explain that many African American devotees regard the orishas as emblems of Black dignity and orisha religion ideally as a Black-only space for healing from the injuries of living in a violently racist, white-dominated society. In the form of a question, I offered an analogy: how would she feel if the president of Nigeria were a foreigner or a white person? In the realm of the spirit, replied Ìyá Òsun, skin color is a nonissue. In this realm, Màmá Susanne was not a white woman but an "incarnation of Òsun." Hence, for the current Ìyá Òsun, Màmá Susanne's embodiment of the goddess was an ontology far more real than the Enlightenment-infused North American reification of "race"—that is, the division of humanity into three to five discrete and permanent biological and social categories—as a defining identity of a person and index of her relationship to the universe.

I did not speak with the person who called Ìyá Òṣun on the telephone, but I do not assume that her position is unreasoned or parochial. For example, W. E. B. Du Bois's *The Souls of Black Folk* ([1903] 2007), written after Du Bois had studied philosophy at the University of Berlin for two years, recapitulated the central European tension between German Romanticism and the En-lightenment, with which Wenger herself may have been familiar. On behalf of Black US Americans, Du Bois implicitly asked, "Are we a distinct people, or a developmentally inferior instance of the globally dominant norm?" Du Bois's answer, which he summarizes as "double-consciousness," is a variant on the dilemmas faced by Hegel, Marx, Freud, and the Afro-Atlantic priests: "It is a peculiar sensation, this double-consciousness, this sense of always looking at one's self through the eyes of others, of measuring one's soul by the tape of a world that looks on in amused contempt and pity. One ever feels his two-ness—an American, a Negro; two souls, two thoughts, two unreconciled strivings; two warring ideals in one dark body, whose dogged strength alone keeps it from being torn asunder" ([1903] 2007: 3).

Du Bois recognized the multiplicity of spirits in our heads, but he was far more explicit than Freud about the extrafamilial and political nature and about the historical specificity of the subjects dueling in our heads. Moreover, like psychoanalysis but far more thoughtfully, Du Bois's model itself bears the mark of its genesis amid the boundary-obsessed nationalisms of Europe and Euro-America, according to which self and other are properly defined by their oppositeness, rather than by their complementarity and ultimate interpenetration with Africa and its diaspora. Like most African American nationalists, Du Bois resolved to borrow Europe's worthwhile inventions—such as print technology and nationalism—and then search for a separate space of our own. Zionists and other settler colonialists have chosen a simi-lar path. Both sets of actors often borrow from their oppressors more than they willingly acknowledge. As in the case of Liberia, they conquer other people's land and treat the conquered as they themselves were once treated. Then they justify their actions in terms of the fear of ever being treated that way again. In contrast to the Afro-Atlantic religions, these movements tend to deny agency and worth to the populations they subordinate.

Nigerians are not unaware of skin color, but Màmá Susanne's white skin was not a disqualification of her sacred role for another Nigerian interlocu-tor of my UVM colleague Vicki Brennan, either. Indeed, it seemed to invoke a quality of foreignness and to exemplify the dizzying interpenetration of dichotomously defined worlds that characterizes the relational ontology in these religions. In explaining why the city of Òṣogbo must not be neglected in Brennan's investigation of Yorùbá spirituality, that Nigerian interlocutor reported excitedly: "In Òṣogbo, there is a white woman who lives in the river!"

If one assumes that whites and Blacks are discrete peoples, that European capitalism, American slavery, and the supposedly noncapitalist social relations of West Africa are discrete social forms, and that central Europe is a world apart from the Black Atlantic, then the "white woman who lives in the river" captures all of the apparent irony of an Austrian refugee's incarnation of an African goddess. If my argument is correct or useful, central Europe and the Black Atlantic may be different worlds, but their interpenetrations and intersections define some of the most influential characters and spirited things acting in each of those worlds.

The Sequel

Finally, because of the limits that my publisher reasonably placed upon the length of this manuscript, two lengthy sections that I have had to excise from this volume will become the foundation of *Zombies and Black Leather*. Those sections expatiate on the irony that, even in the democratic republics that host these religions, the priests of the Afro-Atlantic religions understand the Other world and the core of their own social relationships in terms of monarchy, marriage, and slavery. Among the material touchstones of these relationships are the crown, the fly whisk, the bentwood rocker, the chain, the whip, and the padlock. These embodiments of relationship and their ambiguity will be a major topic of the next book.

Ethnographically, *Zombies and Black Leather* will focus on the empowered things at the core of my relationship with the Haitian American Vodou priestess Manmi Maude and her transnational community of followers, as well as a tandem analysis of power exchange in the white American bondage, discipline, sadomasochism (or BDSM) scene, where white people describe their practice as both "fetishism" and "kink" (also a term for black people's hair) and dress up in black skins, using this and other highly cathected props to reconfigure their own intimate relationships in terms of the master-slave relationship. Haiti and the United States are united not only by close proximity but also by the relationship between the world's only successful revolution carried out by the enslaved and the mightiest of the world's historically slave-holding regimes. Ironically, Haiti and its national religion embrace extremes of hierarchy, while the steeply stratified population of the US is deeply ambivalent about social hierarchy. Moreover, US troops occupied Haiti for nearly two decades, resulting in one of the most popular tropes in contemporary US culture about the relationship between Blacks and whites, between natives and foreigners, and between human bodies and the diverse forces that can animate them. Ultimately, this next volume will examine one specific web of Haitian and US American things that I interpret as historically and transnationally linked materializations of social connection and alienation: (1) *pakèt kongo*, (2) *zonbi*, (3) the movie zombie, and (4) the "toys" of white American kink.

Pakèt kongo are abstractly anthropomorphic cloth bundles embodying one or another Haitian god, or *lwa*. Yet they are also gifts from the priestess or priest to a follower or protégé. Manmi Maude has given me eight of these spirited things, which embody our friendship and her protection. Their feeding and feting are a regular feature of her lecture visits and the rituals that I have invited her to conduct at Harvard, Duke, and the University of Vermont (see figure 9.6).

The wildly popular US American movie zombie seems to reflect, among other things, a US American fear of the family's frailty and of excessive connection to the foreign Other. It also reflects the history of US American relations with Haiti and the contrast between Enlightenment and Afro-Atlantic assumptions about the proper nature of human social relationships. In Haiti, *zonbi* are bodies stripped of their family spirits or spirits separated from the body of the family—materialized nightmares about the fate of people separated from their communities. The Haitian prototype of this zombie, the *zonbi kò kadav*, is extremely rare but real and much discussed on the island. Such *zonbi* are people drugged in order to create the appearance of death, whereupon they are interred, exhumed, tranquilized, convinced of their loss of self-control, and shipped off to a distant part of the island to work involuntarily for others. From the Haitian point of view, they are inanimate but walking and working things, evacuated of agency, much like Marx's "negro slave." For their part, *zonbi astral* are similarly alienated but invisible spirits of the dead, captured in the graveyard, imprisoned in a bottle, and compelled to work for their new master. *Zonbi astral* are historically related to the West-Central African empowered things, or gods, known as *nkisi* and to the *inquice* gods of the Kongo-related Palo tradition of Cuba. These Kongo and Cuban rematerialized spirits of the dead embody their own history of priestly efforts to rearrange social relationships in competition with rival social projects.

The exaggeration of the prevalence of the *zonbi kò kadav* through its transformation and transposition into the US entertainment industry is historically connected to the long-running fear of Black rebellion in the American republics and to the justification of the US American occupation of Haiti (1915–34). But, even today, some of the most deeply held fears of Haitians and US Americans walk in the figures of the *zonbi* and the zombie.

For Haitians, the forms of spiritual and social alienation that produce *zonbi* are antitheses of the ancestral, familial, and often long-distance connections embodied in the *lwa* gods. The *lwa* are materialized deities normally inherited within families. Indeed, the making of a *zonbi kò kadav* is hardly possible without the agreement of the victim's family, which would allow this form of social execution only if the victim has grievously betrayed the family's collective interests. Thus, the *zonbi* highlights the possibility of losing all of the social relationships that matter and, concomitantly, all of the spirits that would normally occupy and protect the person. It follows that the ownership of a *zonbi* is an antisocially selfish act.

For Anglo-Americans, the zombie materializes an opposite set of fears, conditioned by post-Enlightenment individualism and the normalization of a sharp distinction between subjects and objects—among other things, the fear of the surreptitious foreign enemy in our midst and the vulnerability of the fortress self to the afflictions that lurk just beyond our personal, domestic, and national boundaries, such as Third-World poverty and epidemics (Matory 2015d). These nearly opposite fears also reveal the nearly opposite social ideals of the Afro-Atlantic religions and the Enlightenment—hierarchical social connection as the essence of the self vs. the egalitarian autonomy of the debt-free individual.

BDSM dungeons and erotic Master/slave relationships in the West are as far removed from Afro-Atlantic divination, trance, and healing as they are from the nineteenth-century European labor movement and the fin-de-siècle psychiatric clinic. But Freud's ugly comparison of Europeans' psychosexual pathologies to the sacred rites of black and brown people requires a reply. It is true that both European fetishism and Afro-Atlantic religions resignify material things in a problem-solving struggle over the shape of our personal subjectivity and of our connections to other human beings. But so do the theories of Marx and Freud. Moreover, my comparison of the Afro-Atlantic religions to BDSM is perhaps fairer than Freud's, since—unlike the individual and posttraumatic fetishism at the center of Freud's model—contemporary white American kink is a collective and nonpathological cultural phenomenon intergenerationally informed by Anglo-American and northwest European positions in the racial economy of the Atlantic world. Kink, too, deserves to be understood in circum-Atlantic context. *Zombies and Black Leather* will explore the hypothesis that whiteness and other forms of social dominance are haunted by their own forms of extreme discomfort, such as guilt, loneliness, and the pressure to take control despite the awareness of one's own ignorance and incompetence and their potentially destructive consequences. The daily performance of autonomy, self-determination, dominance, and omnipotence is exhausting, which may explain the fact that the people who play the role of the slave in BDSM dungeons tend to be people who occupy lofty social positions in their daytime lives and that the masters of the dungeon tend to be recruited from subordinate social ranks in the daytime social hierarchy. Yet the most exciting of these erotic performances involve a power exchange and a well-coordinated flipping of roles. To my mind, it is no accident that this form of deeply trusting connection and power exchange between people is performed through the idiom of black skin, masters, and slaves, suggesting its continuity with the legacy of the sixteenth- and seventeenth-century Guinea-Coast encounter.

Hence, *Zombies and Black Leather* will be a detailed ethnography of the empowered things at the center of one transnational Vodou community, comparing them not only with historically cognate Kongo and Cuban spirited things going back to the early twentieth century but also with a range of nonreligious fetishes that rearticulate Haitian and white American social relationships through the medium of fearsome and apparently nonhuman things. Its tentative title is *Zombies and Black Leather: Haitian and White American Connection and Alienation in Haiti and White America*. It will compare how the *pakèt kongo*, the *zonbi*, the movie zombie, and the BDSM toy—each in its own problem-solving struggle over the proper shape of our connections to other people—controversially redefine the value and agency of material things.

ACKNOWLEDGMENTS

The argument is mine, but the book is the product of the labor and mutual regard of multiple networks of people—including the rituals and funding processes that have structured my conversation with the priests of the Afro-Atlantic religions, a genealogy of published conversations in academia that require the ritual citation of great "thinkers," and the collective labor and the ritually structured process of "anonymous" peer review. Like other fetishes, this book is ambivalent, structured as it is by the anticipation and the internalization of contrary positions. One possible measure of the success of this book is the degree to which other people agree with it. Another possible measure is the frequency with which they cite it, taking it seriously enough to agree or disagree with it and, indeed, form communities around its ratification and application or its condemnation and refutation. The best I can hope is that this book will become a commemoration of the communication between such communities and a touchstone of our mutual transformation.

There are those who will see my fetish as a call to solidarity among the worshippers of the Afro-Atlantic gods or among non-Europeans generally. Some of these will consequently see it as a refusal of solidarity with Marxists, Freudians, Jews, ethnically marked populations of African descent in the US, other middling populations in socially stratified settings, or with Europeans in general. Others, still, might see it as an imperialist desacralization of the Afro-Atlantic religions. It may thus call forth a new sense of community among those who feel attacked for their membership in these demographics. I hope that those who react to my fetish in any of these ways will also anticipate and internalize the contrary position that the community of the oppressed and indeed the pan-human community are strengthened when we can discuss openly and empathetically the ways in which those whose hands have been burnt by the hot potato of oppression—an analogy that I owe to my friend Doris Sommer—pass it on to someone else, rather than extinguishing the fire that heated it up in the first place.

For both helping me to make this argument and also regularly disagreeing with me, I thank Karl Marx and Sigmund Freud. Although they, too, have become ancestors, historian Eric Williams and literary critic Claudia Tate have also taught me a great deal. However, the ancestor who most influenced my reading was my mother—child clinical psychologist and race woman Deborah Love Matory, who joined the ancestors twenty-three years ago. And through her I honor the many African-descended people and Jewish people who have risked their reputations or indeed given their lives to advance justice for all, even when it was inexpedient to do so. Without them, I would not have been in a position to write this book.

Yet in this specific project I bear an even greater debt to Babá Murah, Manmi Maude, Ìyá Ọ̀ṣun Òṣogbo, Babá Esteban Quintana, David Font-Navarrete, Doté Amilton, and Oggún Fumi, who have sacrificed the time necessary to mentor me, open my roads, protect me ritually, coteach with me, and correct me face to face. They have also continually fed me and healed me with their hands. The gods they have made for me fill my home and my head with tender feelings and with joyfully embraced social obligations and debates. Above all, this book commemorates the dialogue among the priests, the gods, and me—a dialogue that assumes material form in many of the spirited things shown here.

I also gratefully acknowledge the support of the Humboldt Foundation of the Federal Republic of Germany, which, through the Humboldt Prize, sponsored my intensive, year-long engagement with central and northern European society where it intersects with Latin America and the African diaspora. Most of this book was drafted during that year. In particular, I thank Professor Dr. Ingrid Kummels for the great kindness of nominating me for the prize, for her generous welcome during Bunmi's and my sojourn in Berlin, and for introducing us to Babá Murah. Indeed, we owe a great debt of gratitude to the faculty, staff, and students of the Latin America Institute at the Freie Universität Berlin. Institute affiliates Dr. Claudia Rauhut and Frau Ximena Aragón also deserve special mention for their kindness, as do our dear *berliner* friends Wolfram and Gabriele Nieradzik, Chris and Frauke Spors, Annedore Streyl, and Thomas Rieger. As I lectured and conducted research on Karl Laman's collection of Kongo *minkisi* gods in Sweden, we were received with similar warmth by the director of Stockholm's Ethnographic Museum, Dr. Michael Barrett, and by Professor Ulf Hannerz of Stockholm University. I hope they will all receive this book as a living monument of my gratitude to them.

I have particularly hung on the words of a few individual readers of this manuscript and its antecedents—Sander Gilman, Deborah Heifetz, Frederic Jameson, Juno Parreñas, Doris Sommer, and Noah Tamarkin. Of course, the greatest single contributor to this project has been my wife, Bunmi, who has not only read several drafts of the manuscript and heard a dozen lectures about it but also provided a second set of eyes and ears through which most of the field research behind this book has been recorded and interpreted.

I am enormously grateful to them all. This work is certainly an inadequate representation of their rich lessons to me, but it would have been a very different book had their voices not been in my head.

It would be impossible to calculate the contribution and influence of the score of classes, departments, institutes, and reading groups that have taken the time to respond to my lectures or read and collectively discuss the manuscript with me. These include my classes in the Departments of Cultural Anthropology and of African and African American Studies at Duke University; the Department of Anthropology at the University of Wisconsin–Madison; the Society for the Anthropology of Religion; the Latin America Institute and the Art History Institute of the Free University of Berlin; the Department of Social Anthropology at Stockholm University; the Research Seminar in Cultural Anthropology and Ethnology at Uppsala University; the Casa del Caribe in Santiago de Cuba; the Institute for Ethnology at Goethe University; the Department of Cultural and Social Anthropology and the Department of Religion at Philipps University (Marburg); the History Department of the Leibniz University (Hanover); the Joint Research Programme of the Humanities in the European Research Area Network (Utrecht); the annual Oyekan Owomoyela Yorùbá Studies Lecture, the Department of Comparative Studies, and the Diversity and Identity Studies Collective at the Ohio State University; the Center for Latin American, Caribbean, and Latino Studies at the City University of New York; and the Department of Anthropology, the Department of Human Evolutionary Biology, and the Peabody Museum of Archaeology and Ethnology at Harvard University. As I prepared my lectures in each of these communities, I continually reorganized and bolstered my argument in response to the forms of agreement and dissent I had encountered and internalized after earlier lectures and in anticipation of the forms of agreement and dissent that I might receive from my next audience.

The richest public dialogue shaping this book took place around the "Spirited Things: Sacred Arts of the Black Atlantic" exhibition that Andrea Rosen and I curated in fall 2017 at the Fleming Museum of Art at the University of Vermont around the theme of the fetish (see Jones 2017). This exhibition was made possible by the generosity of the Office of the President of that university and by the genius and hard work of not only Andrea but also Professor Vicki Brennan (who taught several classes around this exhibition), her students (who assisted in its curation), the Fleming Museum director, Janie Cohen, and her magnificent staff: the Collections and Exhibition Manager, Margaret Tamulonis; the Museum Photographer and Graphic Designer, Chris Dissinger; the Curator of Education and Public Programs, Christina Fearon (who enriched the exhibition by coordinating a dozen related scholarly lectures and gallery talks, as well as multiple lectures and rituals by priests); the Exhibition Designer and Preparator, Jeff Falsgraf, and his assistants Lisa Marchetti and Zoe Albion; and the UVM Presidential Communications and Events Coordinator, Susan Davidson. The spirited things displayed in this exhibition are now invested with the spirit of the relationship forged among us and the visiting priests through nearly three years of planning, debate, learning, and conviviality.

It is in this way that a fifty-minute Provost's Lecture at the University of Wisconsin in 2011 turned into this 392-page fetish.

This fetish of paper, ink, and glue also would have looked quite different without the diligent efforts and keen critical insights of my summer-camp mate (forty-four years ago) and now colleague Michael Hardt, against whose great knowledge of Marx I checked the earliest zygote of this project, and of my "anonymous" readers at Duke University Press, Peter Geschiere and Wyatt MacGaffey, two eminent scholars of African religion whose energetic praise and provocations have, I think, made this project dance. The editorial director at Duke University Press, Ken Wissoker, wisely guided me as I threaded the needle between, on the one hand, addressing all of the possible reservations of Marx and Freud specialists and, on the other, keeping the book at a readable length. For her enormous patience, attention to detail, and encouragement when I had just had enough of the press's exacting technical standards, I thank Editorial Associate Olivia R. Polk. And I thank my assistant, Tyra Dixon, for her energy, organizational skill, excellence as a photographer, and cheerful tolerance of my perfectionism.

Without this veritable village of interlocutors, this would have been a much shorter and much less thoughtful and dialectical book. Conversely, without the keen advice of my dear friend Michael Fitzgerald—the articles editor at the *Boston Globe*—this book would have been much longer. The reader and I are both deeply indebted to him.

Needless to say, I alone am responsible for the book's remaining flaws, whatever they may be. I hope that the reader will accept them as a provocation to mutually transformative debate, which is the ultimate purpose of this book and the ultimate service of the fetish.

I salute the òrìṣà, orixás, the orichas, the vodun, the voduns, the lwa, the minkisi, the inquices, the muertos, and the caboclos with respect, devotion, and love. I salute my own ancestors, including the founders of the universities and funding agencies that have made me, and the founders of the universities, departments, and research institutes that have hosted dialogues that continually reoriented this project. I pray that their own cosmopolitan projects may endure in the face of the populist forces have lately risen up to blame destabilizing economic change on foreign enemies. In the name of these ancestors and gods of fruitful exchange, I salute you. If you have finished reading this book, you are now part of them and they a part of you.

I dedicate this book to my dear wife, Bunmi. After twenty-eight years together, we are one person. This book is very much hers, as well.

Papa Legba, ouvri bayè pou mwen!
Alaroyé, Agó!
Láàròyé!
Larôiê!
Ayi bobo!
Aché!
Àṣẹ!
Axé!

Preface

1 See, for example, Mollena Williams, http://risk-show.com/podcast/slave.
2 Sacred Arts of the Black Atlantic, http://sacredart.caaar.duke.edu/.
3 The poetic phrase "spirited things" is also the title of a book edited by Paul C. John-son, *Spirited Things: The Work of "Possession" in the Afro-Atlantic Religions* (2014). With a somewhat different intention, I use the term to describe physical things that have through ritual been animated with sacred value or humanlike agency.

Introduction

1 This sense of inferiority may have been far stronger among the forebears of today's Germany than among the German speakers of the Austro-Hungarian Empire because the latter had an empire whose official language was German (Dr. Richard Kuba, personal communication, November 4–5, 2014).
2 This insight emerged from a videotaped dialogue between Dr. Michael Barrett (curator for Africa, Ethnographic Museum, Stockholm) and me on September 17, 2014.
3 Dr. Richard Kuba warns that this liberal tradition of German ethnology did not enjoy universal popularity in Germany. It did not represent all classes or regions of the nineteenth-century German-speaking world. Nor did it represent the entire nineteenth-century German-speaking academy. More obviously, such liberalism did not remain typical of German ethnology in the twentieth century. Indeed, in the twentieth century, with respect to their degree of liberalism, German ethnology, on the one hand, and British and French ethnology, on the other, seem to have reversed positions (personal communication, November 4–5, 2014). I am also grateful to Pro-fessor Hans Peter Hahn (personal communication, November 4–5, 2014) for his insights about Leo Frobenius and German intellectual history.
4 For example, Böhme ([2006] 2014: 167, 178) shows that Marx was considerably harsher in his condemnation of the alleged African prototypes of "fetishism" than were most of his German-speaking predecessors and contemporaries such as Hegel, Ludwig Feuerbach, Max Müller, and Adolf Bastian, not to mention the French phi-losopher Auguste Comte.
5 For examples of Freud's frequent use of Africa as a metaphor of repressed European sexuality, see, for example, Gilman (1992: 169) and Kramer (1996: 42n1).

6 See Betsy Blumenthal (2017), "New Zealand and India Have Rivers That Are Now Legally Living Entities," *Conde Nast Traveler*, March 29, www.cntraveler.com/story/new-zealands-whanganui-river-is-now-legally-a-human-being.

Chapter 1. The Afro-Atlantic Context

1 The parade of white male superheroes in US American toys, comics, television series, and films appears to reveal ordinary white males' public aspiration to autonomy, self-sufficiency, efficiency, and leadership. But the usually outlandish costumes and masks of such superheroes seem to dramatize the same people's worry that, even when they perform such a posture, it is a masquerade repressing the knowledge of their own very human fallibility and mediocrity, as well as an exhausting expectation even to try to live up to. Consider also George Orwell's essay, "Shooting an Elephant" (1936), in which a white police officer in the British colony of Burma makes a terrible mistake because he fears having his indecision and weakness laughed at by the brown people he had been assigned to police. The private episodes of surrender provided by BDSM must be a profound relief to the many white men who assume the role of the slave in BDSM dungeons and in M/s relationships. Individually, they are no stronger than the rest of us. In fact, they are probably a little weaker, given the relative safely of their circumstances and their overreliance on the fiction of their superiority and the expectation of their immunity to abjection and injustice. Their threshold for disappointment and cracking is lower than for most of the rest of us. The accelerating epidemic of mass shootings by lone white boys and men in the United States provides evidence of this point. It is a sign of decency and humanity that, instead, they sometimes wish deeply to submit.

2 This inference did not cause him to disavow Africans' need or right to be free. Nor did he disavow his conviction that subjection is a necessary stage in the advance toward freedom. Rather, he simply concluded that the emancipation of enslaved Africans should be gradual.

Chapter 2. The "Negro Slave" in Marx's Labor Theory of Value

1 The comparable Brazilian Portuguese phrase is *trabalhado como negros*. Wyatt Mac-Gaffey tells me that this phrase was also common in England during the 1930s (personal communication, spring 2016).

2 This quote appears on the back cover of the 1990 Penguin edition of *Capital*, vol. 1.

3 Defenders and proponents of Marx's message tend to describe his model as an "immanent critique" of capitalism—a critique of capitalism in its own, emic terms (see, e.g., Postone 1993: 21). However, Marx defines value in supraempirical and ways and in expressly spiritual terms that do not originate in the thinking of any workers or capitalists I know. He also attributes an inexorable and nonhuman agency to the historical unfolding of capitalism itself. Like a religious person, Marx continually repairs his vision of capitalism, its fundamental structure, and its inevitable trajec-

tory by denying the observable effects of real-world phenomena like supply and demand, the inequality and nonfungibility of workers (even where mechanization has
reached its most extreme levels), nationalist and race-based loyalty between wage
workers and capitalists, the contemporaneous reality and complementarity of slavery and wage labor within the capitalism of his day, and the unequal buying power
of differently raced or gendered people with the same amount of money in their
respective pockets (see also Harvey 1982: 18, 19, 28, 50, e.g.). Even if we consider
the possibility that Marx is engaged in a thought experiment about what a society *will* look like once it is eventually purely capitalist, or about how, as isolated
variables, labor and profit work within the messy real-world history of industrialization in Europe, we must also acknowledge that his heuristic model is socially
positioned and deficient in its recognition of the interests and sacred priorities of
non-European and nonproletarian actors. Marx's thought experiment concerns
how to liberate the European proletariat from a hamster wheel that the proletariat itself is spinning.

One anthropologist colleague with Marxist sympathies, like a number of
other published defenders of Marx, argued that a critique of Marx based upon
the inadequacies of the labor theory of value is a cheap shot, because Marxists
and non-Marxists alike have long agreed on its inadequacy and because the validity
of Marx's overall argument does not depend on the adequacy of this theory. On the
contrary, I believe that Marx intended for the LTV to be the linchpin of his immanent critique of capitalism. However, I must remind this colleague and others that
my main aim is not to criticize Marx but to demonstrate that his written theories
are no more inherently correct or independent of the author's socially positioned
interests than are the envesseled and embodied theories of the Afro-Atlantic priests.

Nor does this incredulous exegesis of Marxism imply an endorsement of its neoliberal ideological rival. Another friend—a Harvard-trained German economist who,
in 2013–14, held an entry-level position in the European Central Bank—summarizes
why most macroeconomists today disagree with Marx. She summarizes, "Price is a
given," determined, in the long term, exclusively by the financial investment of the
producer, including labor costs, in the product to be sold (anonymous, personal
communication, November 26, 2015). This model assumes that monopolies, cartels, consumer boycotts, consumer negotiation, and state interventions in the market, for example, have only a short-term and ultimately net-zero effect on pricing.
Like Marx's economic model, this neoliberal model averages out and thereby nul-
lifies the real-world variations of culture, momentary need, sentimental value, and
producer-consumer social relationships that affect actual prices. In order for either
of these equations to yield a definitive average value, all trading must have stopped,
since the calculation of averages has no way of including future transactions in the
average. Both models also neglect the degree to which the long-term credits and
debts of the manufacturer, which are the preconditions of the production of a commodity, extend backward infinitely in time, just as the credits and debts that are the
entailments of any act of commodity production extend forward in time until the
end of all production and exchange. The calculation of the average, macroeconomic

value of a commodity—following either the LTV or the current consensus among contemporary Western economists—is impossible and rests on the assumption that the social relationships that make the production of any commodity possible are immediately even-Steven and extremely short-term.

Conclusion to Part I

1 My neologism "supercathected" is inspired by the psychoanalytical term "hyper-cathected," which denotes a person's *excessive* investment of interest or libido in a person, thing, or idea. I prefer the prefix "super-" in order to avoid any implication of incorrectness, which would imply that my own judgment about the amount of interest and libido that a thing correctly deserves somehow transcends the cultural and political specificity of my social position. For related reasons, I retain the use of "hypercathected" when quoting or paraphrasing Freud. He was less circumspect about the cultural and social specificity of his judgments.

Part II. On Freud's Ambivalent Fetish

1 See SABA Collection 1010 for another affectionate image of the blackamoor commonly found in early-modern Europe. One of the most famous blackamoors, *Moor with Emerald Cluster*, sculpted by the Bavarian artist Balthasar Permoser in 1724, has been appropriated as a sacred icon of the Afro-Caribbean god of thunder and lightning, Changó (see, e.g., SABA Collection B107). See also https://en.wikipedia.org/wiki/Balthasar_Permoser.

Chapter 4. The Fetishes Assimilated Jewish Men Make

1 See also www.biography.com/people/sigmund-freud-9302400.
2 The curious reader may review explicit examples of this comparison on his pages xi, 3–4, 24, 40, 47–48, 109, 110, 112, 130, 164–71, 182, and 207. On Freud's estimation of *Totem and* Taboo, see Jones (1953) 1961: 287.

Chapter 5. An Architecture of Solidarity and Conflict

1 There are also disputed inferences that Freud later had an affair with his wife's sister, Minna Bernays.
2 Cited at http://en.wikipedia.org/wiki/Anal_sex; accessed June 6, 2017.
3 It should be noted that, while Freud regarded male homosexuality as neurotic, he was considerably harsher in his judgment of lesbianism.
4 *Life and Work of Sigmund Freud*, vol. 1, 152, cited in www.nathanielturner.com/freudsnegro.htm. See also Kramer (1996: 22, 42–43n1) for an extensive further listing of Freud's aggressive remarks about "negroes," in one of which he expressly compared himself to the lion and derogatorily analogized his patients and Americans

generally to "negroes." Indeed, apparently in a moment of frustration, he compared psychotherapy, in its difficulty or tenuousness, to "the white-washing of a negro."

5 I am grateful to my dear friend Doris Sommer and to another kind member of the audience at a lecture I delivered at Harvard University on March 6, 2017, for urging me to consider the possibility that Freud identified with the "negro" in the "no negro at noon" joke. Doris in particular enlightened me with her close reading of two of Freud's major publications on humor.

Chapter 6. The Castrator and the Castrated

1 See http://www.freud.org.uk/about/collections/detail/10158; also Jones [1953] 1961: 391.

2 See the items at http://www.freud.org.uk/about/collections.

3 "Musée d'Ethnographie du Trocadéro," *Wikipedia*, en.wikipedia.org/wiki/muse% 27Ethnographie_du_trocadero.

4 Perhaps influenced somewhat by Freud, Fernando Ortiz ([1947] 1995) also memorably reflects on the brownness, masculinity, and symbolic Africanness of tobacco in contrast to the whiteness, femininity, and symbolic Europeanness of sugar.

5 See, e.g., http://quoteinvestigator.com/2011/08/12/just-a-cigar/.

Chapter 7. The Contrary Ontologies of Two Revolutions

1 In response to my comment that "people make the gods but the gods make us, too," the psychoanalyst, initiate of the Ewe Gorovodu priesthood, and anthropologist Judy Rosenthal added, "Fo Teté [one of her priestly mentors] told me this years ago" (personal communication, December 21, 2015).

Chapter 8. Commodities and Gods

1 I employ the masculine pronoun advisedly. While some Ọ̀yọ́ monarchs have likely been female, the vast majority have been male.

2 According to Marx, the difference between capitalism and previous modes of production is that money multiplies. That is, as the capitalists skim off more and more of the surplus value of the goods that the workers produce, the number of tokens representing that value multiplies. For Marx, such multiplication of money is a form of fetishism, creating the sense that the value came from somewhere other than the workers' labor. Twentieth-century deficit spending in the US and the invention in Brazil of the currency known as the *real* (meaning "real") suggest that the multiplication of money, in the absence of rampant inflation, is really an indication of the confidence of buyers and sellers in the productivity of the other buyers and sellers and their confidence that other people will always want to continue participating in that network of exchange.

3 Some Haitian Vodou priests speak similarly, describing the *lwa* gods as powerful "winds" (*van*).

4 Note that the name of this river differs from the name of the god of war and iron, Ògún.

5 Some priests in Brazil describe such impounded sacred things as "imprisoned," high-lighting their character as people (http://jornalggn.com.br/noticia/no-rio-movimento-quer-liberacao-de-objetos-religiosos-em-posse-da-policia-civil).

6 Note that the letter *k* is unusual in Spanish orthography, this sound normally being rendered as "c" or "qu," depending on the context. The use of the letter k in writings about Afro-Cuban religion suggests a "correction" toward a supposedly original African norm that not all Cuban practitioners of these religions prefer. In fact, the writing of Efik, Ibibio, and Yorùbá in Roman script by English-speaking missionaries is more recent than the arrival of most Afro-Cubans' African ancestors and of their religions on that island. In many cases, the ancestral languages of Black Cuba were written in Spanish orthography in Cuba before they were written in the current English-based orthographies of Efik, Ibibio, and Yorùbá. Yet authoritative books about these African traditions and in some of these African languages began arriving in Cuba in the late nineteenth century. Hence, the use of the letter *k* in Cuban writings represents more of a symbolic than a real restoration of the "original" African forms of Afro-Cuban religions. Therefore, my rather inconsistent use of the letter *k* in the spelling of Abakuá terms is not an effort to re-Africanize these religions; it simply reflects the inconsistencies in the Cuban literature: there are certain Abakuá terms that I have never seen written without a *k*, so I leave them as I found them.

7 In processions, the normal order is Encrícamo, Ecueñón, Empegó, and Eribó.

Chapter 9. The Madeness of Gods and Other People

1 Regarding Mandarin, Ralph Litzinger and Minhui Yang, personal communication, November 25, 2015.

2 The similar expressions in Ewe for "making a god" are wɔ *vodu* and wɔ *trɔ* (Judy Rosenthal, personal communication, December 21, 2015)

3 To see a virtual guided tour about this theme, see http://sacredart.caaar.duke.edu/fireinthesky.

4 As in the Yorùbá-Atlantic traditions so in Haitian Vodou, pots (*govi*) containing consecrated stones are another dwelling place of the gods, who are said to speak (*pale*) to the initiated through these vessels.

5 Practitioners of the Afro-Surinamese Winti religion dwelling in Amsterdam expressed perhaps the most extreme Protestant- and Jewish-sounding iconoclasm that I have heard in the Afro-Atlantic world. Both the iconography and the ethics of this religion have been influenced by Jewish slave owners and Protestant missionaries. For example, Riedwyn Import and Export, the largest supplier of Winti religious goods in Holland, sells menorahs for use by Winti priests who wish to commemorate their Jewish ancestors. And the shop attendants tell me both that the Winti spirits predated humans in God's creation of the world and that "seating" them in physical things is invariably associated with spiritual malfeasance—that is, with the use of spirits called *adumakama* ("I-came-to-do") because they will do anything that the possessor of the thing asks. "Anything!" In the view of my Winti mentors, the

only legitimate ritual practice involves prayer and bathing in mixtures of the old-fashioned European brews, distilled spirits, soft drinks, and perfumes preferred by each Winti spirit, which serve to harmonize the worshipper and his or her body with the spirits of earth, water, forest, and sky. However, these Surinamese-Dutch critics of animated things fully acknowledge the existence of coreligionists who consider animated things legitimate and who value their efficacy.

Conclusion to Part III

1 These cases remind me of the thousands of cases in which African American men who stepped out of their assigned place in the social hierarchy of the US South and were then lynched based on an allegation that they had raped, touched, sassed, or looked at a white woman. To deny the truth of the accusation was to deny the sacredness and irresistibility of the fetish—be it a holy book or a white woman. Hence, all other standards of plausibility and skepticism about the motives of the accuser were suspended. Just as a book has been fetishized and pedestalized to justify a killing that undoubtedly had some other, more comprehensibly strategic purpose, so white women were fetishized and pedestalized as the post–Civil War linchpin of rich white men's effort to keep control over poor white men, as well as white women and Black people in general.

Conclusion

1 Two of the sacred objects carried by Òṣun priestesses during a religious procession in Òṣogbo (and documented by Verger [1981: 80, plate 148] during his visits to that city in 1948 or later) look remarkably like curtain rods with rings on them. The rings are clearly too large for a finger, but the form of this sacred object is quite unlike that of the thousands of Yorùbá sacred objects that I have studied over the years. The possibility that artist Susanne Wenger introduced this form into the priesthood that she joined, just as she introduced a radically new form of shrine architecture, is worth investigating. What would not be unusual about such an introduction is that, if it happened, it sacralized important social relationships by canonizing objects that commemorate the history of those relationships.

REFERENCES

Akìwọwọ, Akínṣọlá A., and David Font-Navarrete. 2015. "Awo Àyàn: Metaphysical Dimensions of the Òrìṣà of Drumming." In *Wood That Talks: Transatlantic Perspectives on the Oriṣa of Drumming*, edited by Amanda Villepastour, 35–50. Jackson: University Press of Mississippi.

Althusser, Louis. 1969. "Freud and Lacan." Translated by Ben Brewster. *New Left Review* 55 (May–June): 51–65.

Amavilah, Voxi Heinrich. 2010. "References to Africa in Adam Smith's *Wealth of Nations* and Some Key Propositions Surrounding Them." Munich Personal RePEc Archive, May 26. https://mpra.ub.uni-muenchen.de/22923/1/MPRA_paper_22923.pdf.

Anderson, Benedict. (1983) 1991. *Imagined Communities*. Rev. ed. London: Verso.

Apter, Andrew. (1991) 2004. "Herskovits's Heritage: Rethinking Syncretism in the African Diaspora." In *Syncretism in Religion*, edited by Anita M. Leopold and Jeppe S. Jensen, 160–84. London: Equinox.

Apter, Emily. 1993. Introduction to *Fetishism as Cultural Discourse*, edited by Emily Apter and William Pietz, 1–9. Ithaca, NY: Cornell University Press.

Arendt, Hannah. 1944. *The Jew as Pariah: Jewish Identity and Politics in the Modern Age*. Edited and with an introduction by Ron H. Feldman. New York: Grove.

Babalọla, Babatunde Abidemi. 2017. "Ancient History of Technology in West Africa: The Indigenous Glass/Glass Bead Industry and the Society of Early Ile-Ife, Southwest Nigeria." *Journal of Black Studies* 48 (5): 501–27.

Babalọla, Babatunde Abidemi, Susan Keech McIntosh, Laure Dussubieux, and Thilo Rehren. 2017. "Ile-Ife and Igbo Olokun in the History of Glass in West Africa." *Antiquity* 91 (357): 732–50.

Bahia, Joana. 2013. "As Religiões Afro-Brasileiras em Terras Alemãs e Suíças." ICS Working Papers. Lisbon: Instituto de Ciências Sociais da Universidade de Lisboa—Laboratório Associado.

Bahia, Joana. 2012. "'De Miguel Couto a Berlin': A Presença do Candomblé em Terras Alemãs." In *Migração e globalização: Um olhar interdisciplinar*, edited by Glória Maria Santiago Pereira and José de Ribamar Sousa Pereira, 223–41. Curitiba, Brazil: Editora CRV.

Ball, Edward. (1998) 2014. *Slaves in the Family*. New York: Farrar, Straus and Giroux.

Baptist, Edward E. 2014. *The Half Has Never Been Told: Slavery and the Making of American Capitalism*. New York: Basic Books.

Barber, Karin. 1981. "How Man Makes God in West Africa: Yoruba Attitudes toward the Oriṣa." *Africa* 51 (3): 724–45.

Barley, Nigel. 1994. *Smashing Pots: Works of Clay from Africa*. Washington, DC: Smithsonian Institution Press.

Barnes, Sandra T., ed. 1989. *Africa's Ogun: Old World and New*. Bloomington: Indiana University Press.

Bayart, Jean-François. 1989. "Africa in the World: A History of Extraversion." *African Affairs* 99: 217–67.

Beier, Ulli. 1982. *Yoruba Beaded Crowns: Sacred Regalia of the Olukuku of Okuku*. London: Ethnographica Ltd./National Museum, Lagos.

Beliso-De Jesús, Aisha. 2015. *Electric Santería: Racial and Sexual Assemblages of Transnational Religion*. New York: Columbia University Press.

Belting, Hans. 1994. *Likeness and Presence: A History of the Image before the Era of Art*. Chicago: University of Chicago Press.

Benjamin, Walter. (1936) 2002. "The Work of Art in the Age of Its Technological Reproducibility." Translated by Edmund Jephcott and Harry Zohn. In *Walter Benjamin: Selected Writings*, vol. 3, *1935–1938*, edited by Howard Eiland and Michael W. Jennings, 101–33. Cambridge, MA: Belknap/Harvard University Press.

Berman, Sheri. 2013. "The Promise of the Arab Spring: In Political Development, No Gain No Pain." *Foreign Affairs* (January/February): 64–74.

Berman, Sheri. 2007. "How Democracies Emerge: Lessons from Europe." *Journal of Democracy* 18 (1): 28–41.

Blackmon, Douglas A. 2008. *Slavery by Another Name: The Re-Enslavement of Black Americans from the Civil War to World War II*. New York: Doubleday.

Böhme, Hartmut. (2006) 2014. *Fetishism and Culture: A Different Theory of Modernity*. Translated by Anna Galt. Reinbeck bei Hamburg: Walter de Gruyter GmbH.

Bourdieu, Pierre. (1984) 1988. *Homo Academicus*. Translated by Peter Collier. Stanford, CA: Stanford University Press.

Bourdieu, Pierre. (1979) 1984. *Outline of a Theory of Practice*. Translated by Richard Nice. Cambridge: Cambridge University Press.

Brame, Gloria G., William D. Brame, and Jon Jacobs (1993). *Different Loving: The World of Sexual Dominance and Submission*. New York: Villard.

Brooks, David. 2010. "The Underlying Tragedy." *New York Times*, January 15, A27.

Brown, Karen McCarthy. 1987. "Alourdes: A Case Study of Moral Leadership in Haitian Vodou." In *Saints and Virtues*, edited by John S. Hawley, 144–67. Berkeley: University of California Press.

Buck-Morss, Susan. 2000. "Hegel and Haiti." *Critical Inquiry* 26: 821–65.

Carney, Judith Ann. 2001. *Black Rice: The African Origins of Rice Cultivation in the Americas*. Cambridge, MA: Harvard University Press.

Chakrabarty, Dipesh. 2000. *Provincializing Europe*. Princeton, NJ: Princeton University Press.

Chernoff, John Miller. 1979. *African Rhythm, African Sensibility: Aesthetics and Social Action in African Musical Idioms*. Chicago: University of Chicago Press.

Clapperton, Hugh. 1829. *Journal of a Second Expedition into the Interior of Africa, from the Bight of Benin to Soccatoo*. London: John Murray.

Conrad, Alfred H., and John R. Meyer. 1958. "The Economics of Slavery in the Ante Bellum South." *Journal of Political Economy* 66 (2): 95–130.

Cosentino, Donald J., ed. 1995. *Sacred Arts of Haitian Vodou.* Los Angeles: Fowler Museum of Cultural History.

David, Nic, Judy Sterner, and Kodzo Gavua. 1988. "Why Pots Are Decorated." *Current Anthropology* 29 (1): 365–89.

Dew, Charles B. 2016. *The Making of a Racist: A Southerner Reflects on Family, History, and the Slave Trade.* Charlottesville: University of Virginia Press.

Dikötter, Frank. 1997. *The Construction of Racial Identities in China and Japan.* Honolulu: University of Hawai'i Press.

Drewal, Henry John. 2008. *Mami Wata: Arts for Water Spirits in Africa and Its Diasporas.* Los Angeles: UCLA Fowler Museum of Cultural History.

Drewal, Henry John, and John Mason. 1998. *Beads, Body, and Soul: Art and Light in the Yorùbá Universe.* Los Angeles: UCLA Fowler Museum of Cultural History.

Drewal, Henry John. 1989. *Yoruba: Nine Centuries of African Art and Thought.* New York: Harry N. Abrams.

Du Bois, W. E. B. (1903) 2007. *The Souls of Black Folk.* Oxford: Oxford University Press.

Durkheim, Émile. (1915) 1965. *Elementary Forms of the Religious Life.* Translated by Joseph Ward Swain. New York: Free Press.

Durkheim, Émile. (1893) 1947. *The Division of Labor in Society.* Translated by George Simpson. New York: Free Press.

Economist. 2013. "Did Slavery Make Economic Sense?" September 27. http://www .economist.com/blogs/freeexchange/2013/09/economic-history-2.

Engels, Friedrich. (1884) 1978. Selections from "The Origin of Family, Private Property, and the State." In *The Marx-Engels Reader,* 2nd ed., edited by Robert C. Tucker, 734–59. New York: W. W. Norton.

Fabian, Johannes. 1983. *Time and the Other: How Anthropology Makes Its Object.* New York: Columbia University Press.

Fanon, Frantz. (1952) 2008. *Black Skin, White Masks.* New York: Grove Press.

Fanon, Frantz. (1963) 1971. *The Wretched of the Earth.* Translated by Constance Farrington. New York: Grove Press.

Fernandez, James W. 1986. *Persuasions and Performances: The Play of Tropes in Culture.* Bloomington: Indiana University Press.

Fogel, Robert William, and Stanley Engerman. (1974) 1995. *Time on the Cross: The Economics of American Negro Slavery.* New York: W. W. Norton.

Foucault, Michel. 1980. *Power/Knowledge: Selected Interviews and Other Writings, 1972–1977.* New York: Pantheon.

Francis, Peter, Jr. 1999. *Beads of the World.* 2nd rev. ed. Atglen, PA: Schiffer.

Frankenberg, Ruth. 1993. *White Women, Race Matters: The Social Construction of Whiteness.* Minneapolis: University of Minnesota Press.

Freedberg, David. 1989. *The Power of Images: Studies in the History and Theory of Response.* Chicago: University of Chicago Press.

Freud, Sigmund. (1899/1900) 1965. *The Interpretation of Dreams.* Translated by James Strachey. New York: Avon Books.

Freud, Sigmund. (1930) 1961. *Civilization and Its Discontents*. New York: W. W. Norton.

Freud, Sigmund. (1927) 1961. *The Future of an Illusion*. New York: W. W. Norton.

Freud, Sigmund. (1926) 1959. *The Question of Lay Analysis (1926)*. In *The Standard Edition of the Complete Psychological Works of Sigmund Freud, Volume XX (1925–1926)*, translated and edited by James Strachey, 170–270. London: Hogarth.

Freud, Sigmund. (1913) 1946. *Totem and Taboo: Resemblances between the Psychic Lives of Savages and Neurotics*. Translated by A. A. Brill. New York: Random House.

Freud, Sigmund. 1928. "Humour." *International Journal of Psycho-Analysis* 9: 1–6.

Freud, Sigmund. 1927. "Fetishism (1927)." In *The Standard Edition of the Complete Psychological Works of Sigmund Freud, Volume XXI (1927–1931)*, translated and edited by James Strachey. 147–57. London: Hogarth.

Freud, Sigmund. 1915. "Thoughts for the Times on War and Death: The Disillusionment of War." In *The Standard Edition of the Complete Psychological Works of Sigmund Freud, translated and edited by James Strachey, Volume XIV (1914–16)*, 273–300. London: Hogarth Institute and the Institute of Psycho-Analysis.

Freud, Sigmund. [1905a] 1910. *Three Contributions to the Theory of Sexuality*, translated by A. A. Brill, MD. New York: The Journal of Nervous and Mental Disease Publishing Company. https://www.stmarys-ca.edu/sites/default/files/attachments/files/Three_Contributions.pdf.

Freud, Sigmund. [1905b] 1960. *Jokes and Their Relation to the Unconscious (1905)*. In *The Standard Edition of the Complete Psychological Works of Sigmund Freud, translated and edited by James Strachey, Volume VIII ([1905] 1960)*, 1–247. London: Hogarth Institute and the Institute of Psycho-Analysis.

Fromont, Cécile. 2014. *The Art of Conversion: Christian Visual Culture in the Kingdom of Kongo*. Chapel Hill: University of North Carolina Press.

Gates, Henry Louis, Jr. 1988. *The Signifying Monkey: A Theory of Afro-American Literary Criticism*. New York: Oxford University Press.

Geertz, Clifford. 1973. "Religion as a Cultural System." In *The Interpretation of Cultures*, 87–125. New York: Basic Books.

Gell, Alfred. 1998. *Art and Agency: An Anthropological Theory*. Oxford: Clarendon.

Genovese, Eugene. 1974. *Roll, Jordan, Roll: The World the Slaves Made*. New York: Pantheon.

Geschiere, Peter. 2013. *Witchcraft, Intimacy, and Trust: Africa in Comparison*. Chicago: University of Chicago Press.

Gilder Lehrman Institute of American History. 2014. "Was Slavery the Engine of American Economic Growth?" https://www.gilderlehrman.org/history-by-era/slavery-and-anti-slavery/resources/was-slavery-engine-american-economic-growth.

Gilman, Sander L. 1993. *Freud, Race, and Gender*. Princeton, NJ: Princeton University Press.

Gilman, Sander L. 1992. "Freud, Race and Gender." *American Imago* 49 (2): 155–83.

Gilman, Sander L. 1986. *Jewish Self-Hatred and the Hidden Language of the Jews*. Baltimore: Johns Hopkins University Press.

Goffman, Erving. 1963. *Stigma: Notes on the Management of Spoiled Identity.* Englewood Cliffs, NJ: Prentice-Hall.

Graeber, David. 2001. *Toward an Anthropological Theory of Value: The False Coin of Our Own Dreams.* New York: Palgrave.

Hall, Jacqueline Dowd. 1983. "'The Mind That Burns in Each Body': Women, Rape, and Racial Violence." In *Powers of Desire: The Politics of Sexuality*, edited by Ann Snitow, Christine Stansell, and Sharon Thompson, 328–49. New York: Monthly Review Press.

Hall, Stuart. (1996) 2001. "Gramsci's Relevance to the Study of Race and Ethnicity." In *Critical Dialogues in Cultural Studies*, edited by Stuart Hall, 411–40. London: Routledge.

Harvey, David. 1982. *The Limits to Capital.* Chicago: University of Chicago Press.

Hegel, Georg Wilhelm Friedrich. (1805–6) 1977. *Phenomenology of Spirit.* Oxford: Clarendon.

Hegel, Georg Wilhelm Friedrich. (1822) 1956. *The Philosophy of History.* Translated by J. Sibree. New York: Dover.

Herder, Johann Gottfried von. (1784–91) 1968. *Reflections on the Philosophy of the History of Mankind.* Translated by T. O. Churchill, abridged and edited by Frank E. Manuel. Chicago: University of Chicago Press.

Herskovits, Melville J. (1941) 1958. *The Myth of the Negro Past.* Boston: Beacon.

Herzfeld, Michael. 1987. *Anthropology through the Looking Glass: Critical Anthropology in the Margins of Europe.* Cambridge: Cambridge University Press.

Higginbotham, A. Leon. 1978. *In the Matter of Color: Race and the American Legal Process: The Colonial Period.* New York: Oxford University Press.

Hitler, Adolph. (1925–26) 1941. *Mein Kampf.* New York: Reynal & Hitchcock.

Hodder, Ian. 2012. *Entangled: An Archaeology of the Relationships between Humans and Things.* Malden, MA: John Wiley.

Johnson, Paul C. 2014. *Spirited Things: The Work of "Possession" in the Afro-Atlantic Religions.* Chicago: University of Chicago Press.

Jones, Ernest. (1953) 1961. *The Life and Work of Sigmund Freud.* Edited and abridged by Lionel Trilling and Steven Marcus. New York: Basic Books.

Jones, Ernest. 1953. *The Life and Work of Sigmund Freud.* 3 vols. New York: Basic Books.

Jones, Rachel Elizabeth. 2017. "Art Review: 'Spirited Things: Sacred Arts of the Black Atlantic,' Fleming Museum." *Seven Days.* October 4. https://www.sevendaysvt.com /vermont/art-review-spirited-things-sacred-arts-of-the-black-atlantic-fleming -museum/Content?oid=8727752.

Kaldera, Raven ed. 2014. *Paradigms of Power: Styles of Master/Slave Relationships.* Hubbardston, MA: Alfred Press.

Karatani, Kojin. 2003. *Transcritique: On Kant and Marx.* Translated by Sabu Kohso. Cambridge, MA: MIT Press.

Kennedy, Randall. 1993. "Introduction: Blacks and the Race Question at Harvard." In *Blacks at Harvard: A Documentary History of African-American Experience at Harvard and Radcliffe*, edited by Werner Sollors, Caldwell Titcomb, and Thomas Underwood, xvii–xxxiv. New York: New York University Press.

Klein, Christopher. 2013. "The Kentucky Derby's Forgotten Black Jockeys." *History in the Headlines*, May 3. http://www.history.com/news/the-kentucky-derbys -forgotten-black-jockeys.

Kramer, Robert. 1996. "Insight and Blindness: Visions of Rank." Editor's introduction to *A Psychology of Difference: The American Lectures*, edited by Robert Kramer, 3–47. Princeton, NJ: Princeton University Press.

Kroeber, A. L., and Clyde Kluckhohn. 1952. *Culture: A Critical Review of Concepts and Definitions*. Papers of the Peabody Museum of American Archaeology and Ethnology, Harvard University, Vol. 47, No. 1. Cambridge, MA: Peabody Museum/Harvard University Printing Office.

Kuhn, Thomas S. 1962. *The Structure of Scientific Revolutions*. Chicago: University of Chicago Press.

Lakoff, George, and Mark Johnson. 1980. *Metaphors We Live By*. Chicago: University of Chicago Press.

Lander, Richard, and John Lander. (1832) 1839. *Journal of an Expedition to Explore the Course and Termination of the Niger*. 2 vols. New York: Harper & Bros.

Larose, Serge. 1977. "The Meaning of Africa in Haitian Vodu." In *Symbols and Sentiments*, edited by Ioan Lewis, 85–116. London: Academic Press.

Latour, Bruno. 2010. *On the Modern Cult of the Factish Gods*. Durham, NC: Duke University Press.

Latour, Bruno. 2005. *Reassembling the Social: An Introduction to Actor-Network-Theory*. Oxford: Oxford University Press.

Latour, Bruno. 1993. *We Were Never Modern*. Cambridge, MA: Harvard University Press.

Latour, Bruno, and Steve Woolgar. (1979) 1986. *Laboratory Life: The Social Construction of Facts*. Princeton, NJ: Princeton University Press.

Levine, Norman. 2008. "*Das Kapital*: A Critique of the Labor Theory of Value." *Critique* 36 (1): 91–106.

Lévy-Bruhl, Lucien. (1910) 1985. *How Natives Think*. Princeton, NJ: Princeton University Press.

Lieberman, Jeffrey. 2015. *Shrinks: The Untold Story of Psychiatry*. New York: Little, Brown.

Lienhardt, Godfrey. 1961. *Divinity and Experience: The Religion of the Dinka*. Oxford: Oxford University Press.

MacGaffey, Wyatt. 1993. "The Eyes of Understanding: Kongo Minkisi." In *Astonishment and Power: The Eyes of Understanding: Kongo Minkisi / The Art of Renée Stout*, edited by Wyatt MacGaffey et al., 21–103. Washington, DC: National Museum of African Art/Smithsonian Institution.

Maggie, Yvonne. 1992. *Medo do Feitiço: Relações entre magia e poder no Brasil*. Rio de Janeiro: Arquivo Nacional.

Malinowski, Bronislaw. (1922) 1984. *Argonauts of the Western Pacific: An Account of Native Enterprise and Adventure in the Archipelagoes of Melanesian New Guinea*. Prospect Heights, IL: Waveland Press.

Marcuzzi, Michael. 2013. "Ring-around-the-Rosie Atlantic: Transatlantic Uses of Rings among Batá Drummers, Caravan Guards, and Muslim Insurgents." *Journal of Religion in Africa* 43 (1): 29–52.

Marx, Karl. (1867) 1990. *Capital: A Critique of Political Economy, Volume 1.* Translated by Ben Fowkes. London: Penguin Books/New Left Review.

Marx, Karl. (1853) 1978. "On Imperialism in India." In *The Marx-Engels Reader,* 2nd ed., edited by Robert C. Tucker, 653–64. New York: W. W. Norton.

Marx, Karl. (1843) 1978. "On the Jewish Question." In *The Marx-Engels Reader,* 2nd ed., edited by Robert C. Tucker, 26–52. New York: W. W. Norton.

Marx, Karl. (1844) 1976. "A Contribution to the Critique of Hegel's *Philosophy of Right*: Introduction," translated by T. B. Bottomore. In *The Marx-Engels* Reader, 2nd ed., edited by Robert C. Tucker. New York: W. W. Norton.

Marx, Karl. (1852) 1963. *The Eighteenth Brumaire of Louis Bonaparte.* New York: International Publishers.

Matory, J. Lorand. In preparation. *Zombies and Black Leather: Haitian and White American Connection and Alienation in Haiti and White America.*

Matory, J. Lorand. 2016. "Collecting and Exhibiting at the Crossroads: In Honor of Eshu." *Material Religion* 12 (3): 378–80.

Matory, J. Lorand, exec. producer. 2015a. "Lucumí Music: Singing, Dancing, and Drumming Black Divinity." Film. Durham, NC: Center for African and African American Research, Duke University. http://sacredart.caaar.duke.edu/content /lucum%C3%AD-music-singing-dancing-and-drumming-black-divinity-0.

Matory, J. Lorand. 2015b. *Stigma and Culture: Last-Place Anxiety in Black America.* Lewis Henry Morgan Lecture Series. Chicago: University of Chicago Press.

Matory, J. Lorand. 2015c. "Stureplan People: Racial Fantasy and Human Reality in Today's Sweden." *Transition* 118: 47–60.

Matory, J. Lorand, creative and exec. producer. 2015d. *Zombies Are Real: The Haitian and American Realities behind the Myth.* Film. Durham, NC: Center for African and African American Research, Duke University. http://sacredart.caaar.duke.edu /content/zombies-are-real-haitian-and-american-realities-behind-myth.

Matory, J. Lorand, exec. producer. 2012. *Human Traffic: Past and Present.* Film. Durham, NC: Center for African and African American Research, Duke University. https:// vimeo.com/46554135.

Matory, J. Lorand. 2009. "The Many Who Dance in Me: Afro-Atlantic Ontology and the Problem with 'Transnationalism.'" In *Transnational Transcendence*, edited by Thomas Csordas, 231–62. Berkeley: University of California Press.

Matory, J. Lorand. 2008. "The Illusion of Isolation: The Gullah/Geechees and the Political Economy of African Culture in the Americas." *Comparative Studies in Society and History* 50 (4): 949–80.

Matory, J. Lorand. 2007. "Free to Be a Slave: Slavery as a Metaphor in the Afro-Atlantic Religions." *Journal of Religion in Africa* 37 (3): 398–425.

Matory, J. Lorand. 2005. *Black Atlantic Religion: Tradition, Transnationalism, and Matriarchy in the Afro-Brazilian Candomblé.* Princeton, NJ: Princeton University Press.

Matory, J. Lorand. (1994) 2005. *Sex and the Empire That Is No More: Gender and the Politics of Metaphor in Ọyọ Yoruba Religion.* 2nd ed. New York: Berghahn Books.

Matory, J. Lorand. 2003. "Gendered Agendas: The Secrets Scholars Keep about Yoruba-Atlantic Religion." *Gender and History* 15: 408–38.

Matory, J. Lorand. 1994. "Rival Empires: Islam and the Religions of Spirit Possession among the Ọ̀yọ́-Yorùbá." *American Ethnologist* 21 (3): 495–515.

Matory, J. Lorand. 1986. "Vessels of Power: The Dialectical Symbolism of Power in Yoruba Religion and Polity." Master's thesis, University of Chicago.

Mauss, Marcel. (1923–24) 2000. *The Gift: The Form and Reason for Exchange in Archaic Societies.* Translated by W. D. Halls. New York: W. W. Norton.

Mbembe, Achille. 2001. *On the Postcolony.* Berkeley: University of California Press.

Miller, Ivor. 2009. *Voice of the Leopard: African Secret Societies and Cuba.* Jackson: University Press of Mississippi.

Morgan, David. 2005. *The Sacred Gaze: Religious Visual Culture in Theory and Practice.* Berkeley: University of California Press.

Noyes, John K. 1997. *The Mastery of Submission: Inventions of Masochism.* Ithaca, NY: Cornell University Press.

Nye, Robert A. 1993. "The Medical Origins of Sexual Fetishism." In *Fetishism as Cultural Discourse,* edited by Emily Apter and William Pietz, 13–30. Ithaca, NY: Cornell University Press.

Olupọna, Jacob K. 2011. *City of 201 Gods: Ilé-Ifẹ̀ in Time, Space, and the Imagination.* Berkeley: University of California Press.

Ortiz, Fernando. (1947) 1995. *Cuban Counterpoint: Tobacco and Sugar.* Durham, NC: Duke University Press.

Patterson, Orlando. 1982. *Slavery and Social Death: A Comparative Study.* Cambridge, MA: Harvard University Press.

Phillips, Ulrich Bonnell. 1918. *American Negro Slavery.* New York: Appleton & Co.

Pietz, William. 1988. "The Problem of the Fetish, IIIa." *Res: Anthropology and Aesthetics* 16: 105–24.

Pietz, William. 1987. "The Problem of the Fetish, II: The Origin of the Fetish." *Res: Anthropology and Aesthetics* 13: 23–45.

Pietz, William. 1985. "The Problem of the Fetish, I." *Res: Anthropology and Aesthetics* 9: 5–17.

Postone, Moishe. 1993. *Time, Labor, and Social Domination: A Reinterpretation of Marx's Critical Theory.* Cambridge: Cambridge University Press.

Puner, Helen Walker. 1947. *Freud: His Life and His Mind.* New York: Grosset & Dunlap.

Richman, Karen E. 2005. *Migration and Vodou.* Gainesville: University Press of Florida.

Ricoeur, Paul. 1973. "The Model of the Text: Meaningful Action Considered as a Text." *New Literary History* 5 (1): 91–117.

Risen, Clay. 2016. "Jack Daniel's Embraces a Hidden Ingredient: Help from a Slave." *New York Times,* June 25, 1, 4.

Roach, Joseph. 1996. *Cities of the Dead: Circum-Atlantic Performance.* New York: Columbia University Press.

Rosenthal, Judy. 1998. *Possession, Ecstacy, and Law in Ewe Voodoo.* Charlottesville: University of Virginia Press.

Sahlins, Marshall. 1996. "The Sadness of Sweetness: Native Anthropology of Western Cosmology." *Current Anthropology* 37 (3): 395–428.

Said, Edward. (1978) 2003. *Orientalism.* London: Penguin.

Saussure, Ferdinand de. (1912) 1983. *Course in General Linguistics*. Translated by Roy Harris. London: Gerald Duckworth.

Schermerhorn, Calvin. 2015. *The Business of Slavery and the Rise of American Capitalism, 1815–1860*. New Haven, CT: Yale University Press.

Scott, James C. 1990. *Domination and the Arts of Resistance: Hidden Transcripts*. New Haven, CT: Yale University Press.

Smith, Adam. (1776) 2003. *The Wealth of Nations*. Edited by Edwin Cannan. New York: Bantam Classics/Random House.

Sperber, Jonathan. 2013. *Karl Marx: A Nineteenth-Century Life*. New York: Liveright.

Stallybrass, Peter. 1998. "Marx's Coat." In *Border Fetishisms: Material Objects in Unstable Spaces*, edited by Patricia Spyer, 183–207. London: Routledge.

Stampp, Kenneth M. 1956. *The Peculiar Institution: Slavery in the Ante-Bellum South*. New York: Alfred A. Knopf.

Stepan, Peter. 2006. *Picasso's Collection of African and Oceanic Art: Masters of Metamorphosis*. Translated by Paul Aston et al. Berlin: Prestel Verlag.

Stewart, Charles, and Rosalind Shaw, eds. 1994. *Syncretism/Anti-Syncretism: The Politics of Religious Synthesis*. London: Routledge.

Strathern, Marilyn. 1988. *The Gender of the Gift: Problems with Women and Problems with Society in Melanesia*. Berkeley: University of California Press.

Tate, Claudia. 1998. *Psychoanalysis and Black Novels: Desire and the Protocols of Race*. New York: Oxford University Press.

Tate, Claudia. 1996. "Freud and His 'Negro': Psychoanalysis as Ally and Enemy of African Americans." *Journal for the Psychoanalysis of Culture and Society* 1 (1): 53–62.

Taylor, Alan. 2016. *American Revolutions: A Continental History, 1750–1804*. Boston: W. W. Norton.

Thompson, Robert Farris. 1983. *The Flash of the Spirit: African and Afro-American Art and Philosophy*. New York: Random House.

Thornton, John. 1992. *Africa and Africans in the Making of the Atlantic World, 1400–1680*. Cambridge: Cambridge University Press.

Turner, Victor W. 1967. "Symbols in Ndembu Religion." In *The Forest of Symbols: Aspects of Ndembu Ritual*, 19–47. Ithaca, NY: Cornell University Press.

Vega, Marta Moreno. 2000. *The Altar of My Soul: The Living Traditions of Santería*. New York: One World.

Venice-Murano: The Glass Museum. 2015. Museum guide. Venice: Fondazione dei Musei Civici di Venezia and Marsilio Editori/Milan: Skira Editore.

Verger, Pierre Fatumbi. 1981. *Orixás: Deuses Iorubás na África e no Novo Mundo*. Salvador, Brazil: Editora Corrupio Comércio/São Paulo: Círculo do Livro S.A.

Viveiros de Castro, Eduardo. 2004. "Exchanging Perspectives." *Common Knowledge* 10 (3): 463–84.

Vlach, John Michael. (1978) 1990. *The Afro-American Tradition in Decorative Arts*. Athens: Brown Thrasher Books/University of Georgia Press.

Warnier, Jean-Pierre. 2007. *The Pot-King: The Body and Technologies of Power*. Leiden: Brill.

REFERENCES

Weber, Max. (1904–5) 1958. *The Protestant Ethic and the Spirit of Capitalism*. Translated by Talcott Parsons. New York: Charles Scribner's Sons.

Weber, Max. (1922–23) 1946. "The Social Psychology of the World Religions." In *From Max Weber*, edited by H. H. Gerth and C. Wright Mills, 267–301. New York: Oxford University Press.

Weiss, Margot. 2011. *Techniques of Pleasure: BDSM and the Circuits of Sexuality*. Durham, NC: Duke University Press.

Williams, Eric E. (1944) 1980. *Capitalism and Slavery*. New York: G. P. Putnam.

Wolf, Eric R. (1982) 2010. *Europe and the People without History*. Berkeley: University of California Press.

INDEX

Locators in italics refer to illustrations.